PASSING
on the
FAITH

The Story of a Mennonite School

Marlin

thanks for all your
great help + support in giving
leadership to LMH.

Donald B Kraybill

12-4-91

PASSING
on the
FAITH

The Story of a Mennonite School

Donald B. Kraybill

Joanne Hess Siegrist, Photography Editor

Good Books®

Intercourse, PA 17534

For Omar Eby,
stimulating Mill Stream teacher
who stirred my interest in writing.

Photo Credits
Grateful acknowledgements to Jonathan Charles and Elton G. Moshier, as well as numerous
others, who contributed photographs. Page 226 top: Lancaster *Intelligencer Journal* photo.

Design by Dawn J. Ranck

Passing on the Faith: The Story of a Mennonite School
© 1991 by Good Books, Intercourse, Pennsylvania, 17534
International Standard Book Number: 1-56148-051-7
Library of Congress Catalog Card Number: 91-74054

**Library of Congress Catalog-in-Publication Data is available from the publisher upon
request.**

Table of Contents

Table of Figures

Introduction

North American education has prospered in the twentieth century. The rising demand for technical and scientific skills in modern life has spawned enormous educational efforts. But education is more than the acquisition of technical expertise; it is also an immersion into cultural values.

Educational efforts in North America flow primarily through two streams. Public schools bring students from diverse cultural backgrounds into a common pool of cultural values. Public education accentuates the common cultural heritage, provides a gateway to assimilation and achievement in national life and cultivates the habits of citizenship. Private schools, the second stream, divide into two tributaries—havens for the elite and enclaves for the religious. Religious schools are typically established to preserve a distinctive heritage—to pass it on to younger generations. Thus, unlike public schools that blend diverse students into the cultural mainstream of modern life, religious schools not only resist the mainstream currents but seek to preserve distinctive heritages in the face of them.

This story of a Mennonite school is more than the story of a school. It is the story of a rural people seeking to pass on their religious faith while in the throes of becoming modern. It is the story of a people struggling with the relentless forces of industrialization in the middle of the twentieth century. Should they send their youth to public high schools or create their own educational enterprise? How can they best pass on their religious convictions? Was high school even necessary?

The following pages explain why and how the Mennonites of Lancaster County opened a high school in 1942. The book also traces the multitude of changes and the controversies surrounding them that the people and their school experienced since the early '40s. Primarily the saga of a school, this light social history also chronicles the clash between deeply held religious convictions and modern ways.

Storytelling is an especially delicate task when many of the main characters live on to hear the story told. I have tried to be fair to the living and the dead, but I have also sought to be honest. Each storyteller spins a different yarn of the same event. This story of Lancaster Mennonite High School is shaped by my sociological interests as well as my personal experiences. I have surely overlooked episodes that others may consider significant, and I undoubtedly accented issues some may consider trivial. But such is the craft of storytelling.

This effort was truly a community endeavor. Dozens of persons generously contributed time and ideas. A list of formal interviews appears in the appendix. Besides these lengthy interviews many other persons answered questions by telephone, and others shared stories, files and photographs, all of which enriched the detail and human interest of the history. Several persons deserve special thanks for their help in facilitating the research. Past and present school officials, Noah G. Good, J. Lester Brubaker and J. Richard Thomas graciously assisted in all phases of the research, provided easy access to files and contributed helpful suggestions. Without their interest and cooperation the project would have been impossible. Photography coordinator, Joanne Hess Siegrist, contributed hundreds of hours gathering and copying photographs from sundry files and attics. Her persistence, enthusiasm and skill in tracking long forgotten snapshots has enhanced the detail and beauty of the text. Photographer Jonathan Charles accommodated continual pleas for more photographs. Mary Lou Houser provided a sketch of the original campus buildings for the book. The staff of the Lancaster Mennonite Historical Society gave generous support and assistance in all phases of the research. The staff of Lancaster Mennonite High School aided my many requests for help in a pleasant and prompt fashion. To all of these folks and dozens unnamed, I am deeply grateful for their support, interest and abundant help.

Others aided in the research activities and preparation of the manuscript. Student assistants—Stephanie Hackenburg, Joy Kraybill, Sheila Kraybill, Diane Tregaskis, Anne E. Weidner—kindly provided clerical help and tabulated data. Reviewers of a working draft of the manuscript included J. Lester Brubaker, Fern Clemmer, Myron Dietz, Janet Gehman, Noah Good, Ernest Hess, John R. Kraybill, Charles Longenecker, John Rutt, Joanne Hess Siegrist, David N. Thomas, J. Richard Thomas, Carolyn Charles Wenger, Edna Wenger, Grace Wenger and Orville Yoder. Readers of partial segments of the manuscript included Ivan Glick, Clyde Hollinger, and Arnold Moshier. I appreciate the helpful suggestions offered by the reviewers for improving the accuracy of the text. Anne E. Weidner prepared the index. Brenda Troutman supervised and performed many waves of word processing in her typically cheerful manner. Jeanette S. Martin served as an able editorial assistant. Phyllis Pellman Good at Good Books provided superb editorial support. The trail of debts runs deep and wide. To all who so ably contributed to this community effort—thank you.

—Donald B. Kraybill

CHAPTER ONE

Charting a Different Course

Pre-1940

"Would you let the state clothe your children?"
—John Lehman

A Declaration of War

Local headlines on June 3, 1942, announced an all-night electrical blackout. Lancaster was staging an air raid. On Thursday, June 4, the United States Senate declared war on Bulgaria, Hungary and Romania. Germany, Italy and, of course, Japan were already on the at-war list. Six months after Pearl Harbor the war had disrupted everything. Gas, sugar and steel were tightly rationed. The draft had yanked thousands into active duty. Bombs were exploding in Europe, ships were sinking in the Atlantic and Lancaster boys were dying. Mennonite conscientious objectors, "conchies," were headed for Civilian Public Service camps. By the end of 1942 over 100 Lancaster Mennonites would be scattered across the country in alternate service projects.

Spurred on by U.S. involvement in the spreading war, Lancaster Mennonites in the early 1940s grew more committed to opening their own high school.

Mennonite volunteers clear debris from the old Yeates campus in June 1941.

On June 3 and 4, 1942, some 200 Mennonites gathered five miles east of Lancaster to declare war on briars and bramble. With shovels, picks and saws they attacked a jungle of brush covering the old Yeates School, abandoned for 18 years. A crop of tall weeds had invaded parts of the 85-acre property. At home in the desolation, wasps and squirrels occupied offices and classrooms. Potatoes and mud covered the basement of an old classroom building and tobacco laths littered its attic. Traces of Latin remained on old blackboards. Some buildings were accessible only by crawling through tangled vines in basement windows.

Eighty-year-old contractor Jacob Hershey supervised the work frolic. Bishops dressed in bib overalls chopped down trees while youth on tractors pulled out stumps. Despite wartime shortages, Lancaster Mennonites were forging ahead with plans for a four-year high school. Cleanup efforts continued throughout the summer. Some repair jobs had to await the end of wartime rations. But, ready or not, the school welcomed its first students on September 14, 1942.[1]

Why were Pennsylvania Mennonites opening their first high school in the worst of times—with restricted travel, scarce supplies and limited labor? Lancaster County already had 38 public high schools scattered across its fertile farmland. Hearing of the proposed Mennonite high school, a newspaper editorial bluntly asked, "What's wrong with our public schools?"[2] Who were these folks? And why were they starting a high school in 1942?

Mennonite Roots

Mennonite roots reach back to Reformation times in Europe. Dismayed by the pace of the Protestant Reformation, a small group in Zurich, Switzerland, baptized each other as adults in 1525. Already baptized as infants in the Roman Catholic church, they were dubbed "Anabaptists," or rebaptizers, by their opponents. Adult baptism was a daring step—a capital offense punishable by death. The young radicals argued that the Bible, not civil authority, was their supreme authority. Taking the words of Jesus literally, they believed that following him in daily life meant living peaceably with others—even enemies. Turning the other cheek, going the second mile, loving enemies—these were the benchmarks of love in the kingdom of God embodied by the new movement.[3]

Civil and church authorities mounted a campaign to exterminate the illegal baptizers who threatened civil and religious order. Hundreds of Anabaptists soon faced the dire choice of recanting or dying. Anabaptist hunters stalked the countryside. Embracing their nonresistant faith, thousands burned at the stake, starved in prison and drowned in lakes and rivers. Others were driven into rural hideaways in Switzerland and southern Germany. The harsh persecution fueled the movement as it spread throughout Europe and etched a sharp line of separation between Anabaptists and the larger world. Eventually many Anabaptists became known as Mennonites—named after a Dutch Anabaptist leader, Menno Simons.

Although many of the early Anabaptists were university trained, they blamed much of the corruption in the Catholic church on the "higher" learning of priests and pastors. In the Anabaptist view, these medieval shepherds had led their innocent flocks away from the practical teachings of Jesus. Disdaining formal theology and emphasizing simple biblical authority, Anabaptist congregations ordained pastors from the ranks of their own members. Such leaders served the community without training or pay. This distrust of formal theological education, the experience of stinging persecution by educated authorities, and living in rural areas for decades fostered a suspicion among Mennonites toward advanced education.

Early Schools

Searching for religious freedom, South German and Swiss Mennonites began arriving in Lancaster County by 1710. They tilled the soil, established churches and over the years found their place alongside other "plain" groups with similar origins. Mennonites, like many other immigrants, embraced practical education in colonial times. In fact, Mennonites established some of the first, if not the very first, schools in Lancaster County.[4] Like those of other religious groups, Mennonite meetinghouses often served as schools. In other cases, schoolhouses stood adjacent to meetinghouses. One historian claims that every Mennonite meetinghouse was either used as a school or affiliated with one.[5] Church and school blended together as Mennonites taught their own children and others from the neighborhood.

By 1834 some 4,000 private schools, organized by a variety of religious groups, dotted Pennsylvania's countryside. Built by volunteer contributions, these one-room operations were often crude, cold and dismal by today's standards. They were, however, noble efforts to educate the young without the benefit of state direction or public taxes.[6] Mennonites, as well as others, operated these small village schools for youth from various religious backgrounds. Looking back to the early 1800s, Mennonite minister Henry Garber nostalgically described these educational efforts. "The church and school house stood side by side, Christianity and education went hand in hand. The pastor often was the teacher and the Bible was one of the textbooks."[7]

The educational climate soon began to change. Amid swirling opposition, the "Free School Law" of 1834 established Pennsylvania's first public schools. Many German sectarians opposed the establishment of public schools. They feared higher taxes, the breakup of their church schools and the loss of the

Mennonite men frequently served as public school directors at the turn of the century. Several Mennonites pose here with other directors at their Manheim Township public school in 1908.

German language.[8] Nevertheless, school districts were gradually formed throughout the state. Property taxes were levied. School directors, elected for each township, had the authority to build schools, hire teachers and provide a free education for *all*. Although mandated by the state, these free, or common, schools were under the thumb of local residents. In an effort to appease the Germans—Lutherans, Reformed, Mennonites and others—the state allowed the language of instruction to be determined by local school boards. However, in many cases these common schools accelerated the shift from German to English.

Lancaster County Mennonites soon relinquished their private schools and joined the new "free school" effort. Their buildings often became public schools. Mennonites were elected school directors and frequently taught in these small rural schools. Sorting through public records, Noah Good discovered that nearly 200 Lancaster Mennonites served as teachers, and at least 250 were elected as school directors in the 1800s and early 1900s.[9] Mennonites, for the most part, felt at home in these small public schools where hymns and moral virtues were taught alongside spelling and subtraction. John Kraybill, teaching in a public school in the early 1930s, taught his pupils to sing "Love Lifted Me" in their morning devotionals.

Although the public schools were free, many farm children attended sporadically. A statewide code in 1895 required attendance for 70 percent of the school term until pupils were 16 years of age. School directors also received new powers to enforce attendance laws. School boards purchased textbooks, required vaccinations and imposed quarantines when necessary. And, for the first time, local districts were authorized to establish high schools. Flags were soon required in classrooms or on school grounds.

Most Mennonites cooperated with the efforts to fortify the common schools. However, some Amish parents in several districts of eastern Lancaster County ignored the compulsory attendance laws. Mennonite school directors in these districts were required to sue, if necessary, to enforce the law. Filing suits was forbidden by the Mennonite church, for such legal force contradicted Jesus' words to "turn the other cheek." Caught between the law and the teachings of their church, Mennonite directors found it awkward to prosecute the Amish, their Anabaptist cousins. In the fall of 1899, the Lancaster Conference of the Mennonite church asked members serving as school directors to resign to eliminate the conflict. An outcry from lay members across the county caused the church to reverse the decision in the spring of 1900.[10]

The school code of 1895 included a "garb law" which prohibited teachers from wearing distinctive religious clothing while teaching. This created difficulties for Mennonite women who wore a white prayer veiling. In an unusual move, Lancaster Conference leaders wrote a resolution of protest to their state representatives.[11] Many school directors, sympathetic to the Mennonite practice, looked the other way. In some districts Mennonite women wore a black veiling to appease school directors. In other townships teachers were dismissed. Several Mennonite school directors were charged in a legal suit by the Commonwealth for permitting Mennonite teachers to wear the traditional veiling. Despite these skirmishes, Mennonites supported public schools as teachers, directors and pupils in virtually every township of the county in the first third of the twentieth century.

Second Thoughts about Public Schools

As the Great Depression eased in the mid '30s, Mennonites began to question their embrace of public education. In Delaware a 1925 state law required pupils in public schools to salute the flag. The pledge of allegiance was viewed by some Mennonite parents as a willingness to bear arms in defense of the country, and thus some Mennonite children refused to salute. This controversy sparked churchwide attention and triggered the formation of a Mennonite elementary school in Delaware in 1928.[12] In 1927 the Lancaster Mennonite bishops declared that "the faith of nonresistance does not sanction the saluting of the flag . . . however the flag must be respected . . . and must not be harmed or mutilated."[13] Local authorities were sensitive to Mennonite sensibilities and the flag salute never became a provocative issue in the Lancaster area.

In 1930, *Gospel Herald*, the official Mennonite church paper, carried an article by A. D. Wenger asking, "Who should educate our children?" The old question was "shall we educate or not?" Now, Wenger argued, Mennonites must ask a new question: "Shall we let the state with fairy tales, entertainments, militarism and evolution, crush out the simple faith implanted by loving fathers and mothers?"[14]

Other Mennonites in the 1930s also began advocating church schools. Henry Garber, former public school teacher, farmer and president of the Eastern Mennonite Board of Missions and Charities, contended that loyal church schools would bring a blessing to the Mennonite church. Moral standards in our public schools, he said, are "alarmingly low. . . . Such education will only make a thief more clever." Church schools, believed Garber, "will train Christian young people for service."[15] Daniel Glick, enthusiastic leader of a sprouting Christian school movement, said the Mennonite church "went with the big crowd" as the public school system was established. "We went the way

Students attending the short-term Bible school held in the Ephrata Mennonite Meetinghouse in January 1940. They boarded in local homes during their six weeks of study.

of the world," Glick reasoned, "and started to feed our children at the public intellectual crib."[16]

Discontent with public schools in Lancaster County came to a head in the spring of 1937. In East Lampeter Township, local citizens—mostly Amish—clashed with school authorities who planned to replace 10 one-room schools with a consolidated one. In a surprising legal move the Amish blocked construction for two months. The widely publicized dispute subsided as the consolidated school opened in the fall of 1937.[17] The Amish, however, soon charted a different course. They opened their first parochial school in the fall of 1938, nearly the same day the township sold its one-room schoolhouses.

One of the schools on the auction block was bought by nine men who dreamed of starting a Mennonite elementary school. The men had been meeting since 1935 to discuss private schooling for their children. In the fall of 1939 they opened the Locust Grove Mennonite School. Privately organized, the school received the blessing of the Mennonite bishops and became Pennsylvania's first Mennonite school in the twentieth century.[18] Although the bishops permitted the parochial schools, they did not actively promote them.

A Mushrooming Movement

Other Mennonite elementary schools soon appeared in Lancaster County, as well as in other Mennonite communities. In fact, 39 Mennonite elementary schools sprang up in several states from 1940 to 1949. Annual meetings to promote Christian schools were established. Teacher-training conferences were convened on a regular basis. Articles and pamphlets heralded the values of church schools. In the decade of 1942-1952, nearly 100 articles on Christian schools appeared in the *Gospel Herald*.[19] The Christian day school movement flourished from the late '30s to the mid '50s, but its adherents always remained a minority within the Mennonite church. Enthusiasm fluctuated over the years, but by 1990 more than 70 Mennonite elementary schools were scattered across the nation, 30 of them in Pennsylvania and a dozen in the Lancaster area.[20]

The elementary school movement stirred new interest in church-related high schools. Mennonites had earlier established high school-level academies in Elkhart, Indiana (1894), Hesston, Kansas (1909) and Harrisonburg, Virginia (1917).[21] Each school eventually evolved into a college—offering both high school and college level courses. Eastern Mennonite School in Harrisonburg, Virginia, provided both a high school and a college curriculum in the 1930s and '40s.[22] Thus, in 1940, the only Mennonite high schools across the country were those affiliated with a college.[23]

Many Lancaster Mennonites remained skeptical of high school. The majority were farmers, satisfied with a practical elementary education. Turn-of-the-century bishop and patriarch Jacob Brubacher was a pioneer of Sunday schools and an ardent supporter of public elementary schools. But, to his thinking, advanced education was unnecessary and occasionally he preached against it.[24] Eight years in the basics were enough to make a good farmer. Nevertheless, more and more Mennonites were attending high school.

Several Mennonites proposed a college-level school in the Lancaster area in the first two decades of the twentieth century, but the idea died.[25] Even after Eastern Mennonite School opened in Virginia in 1917 the Lancaster bishops refused to appoint representatives to its board of trustees. Meanwhile, some Lancaster youth who wanted advanced biblical studies and a Mennonite high school experience were driving south to the Shenandoah Valley of Virginia. Finally, in 1933, the Lancaster bishops agreed that young people who desired an education could attend Eastern Mennonite School, if their parents approved.[26]

In the spring of 1938 the bishops endorsed plans for a six-week Bible School at the Ephrata Mennonite Meetinghouse in northern Lancaster County. The new venture opened in January of 1939 with Bible classes offered on a daily basis. Young bishop J. Paul Graybill, recent mission worker in Philadelphia, served as principal. The courses promised to bring victorious Christian living, promote loyalty to Christ and the church, arouse convictions for missions, indoctrinate against false teaching and offset the harm of worldliness. Seventy-seven students registered for the first year. This positive educational experience softened bishop resistance to church-sponsored education.

An Urgent Plea

Lancaster Mennonites, numbering 13,000 in the late 1930s, were organized into 11 bishop districts—regional clusters of local congregations. A bishop supervised the ministers and deacons in his district, administered baptisms, communions and weddings, enforced discipline and handled confessions and excommunication. Meeting together periodically, the dozen or so bishops governed the Lancaster Mennonite Conference.[27] Major changes in church policy, however, were brought to the semi-annual meetings of the Conference, a body of some 140 ordained leaders—deacons, ministers and bishops.[28]

The idea of a Mennonite high school in Lancaster began brewing in the late '30s. In a July, 1939, letter, J. Paul Graybill proposed a feasibility study to fellow bishop Amos Horst. "Since the board of bishops might not be ready to proceed with a high school," Graybill said, "perhaps they would at least authorize the Bible School Board to study the need for one." The study was never done.

The initiative came instead from another direction. Soft-spoken Henry Garber, esteemed Mission Board President, prodded the bishops with a petition to begin a high school. Garber had a growing conviction for Christian schools where young people could be taught the faith and mobilized for mission work. A dance at the Mount Joy High School in 1933 displeased Garber and he reported his concerns to the public school principal. Garber was a minister in the Mount Joy congregation where he shared leadership with bishop Henry Lutz, secretary of Lancaster Conference.[29] Garber likely received a nod from Lutz that the bishops would consider a petition for a high school.

In the spring of 1940 Henry Garber collected 15 signatures for a petition which he likely wrote.[30] It asked the bishops to establish a Mennonite high school for five urgent reasons: (1) children must remain in school until they are 17 years of age, (2) the moral conditions of modern high schools are disturbing, (3) evolution is taught in the public high schools, (4) public school extracurricular activities do not harmonize with the teachings of Scripture or the practice of the church, and (5) in a Mennonite school, "our own brethren can instruct and guide our youth to safeguard them from an apostate and pleasure loving world."

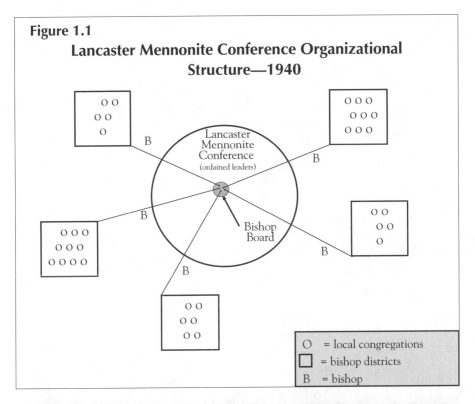

Figure 1.1
Lancaster Mennonite Conference Organizational Structure—1940

O = local congregations
☐ = bishop districts
B = bishop

The 1938 senior class of Mount Joy's public high school. This class introduced the first junior-senior prom. The two Mennonite seniors on the far left, third row, chose not to attend.

In the spring of 1940 fifteen Mennonite leaders signed a petition to open a Mennonite high school.

The Threat of Public Schools

"The public high schools," argued many, "are leading Mennonite youth away from the church rather than to it." Some youth were finding spouses in the public high schools and leaving the church. In a widely circulated broadside of 1942, Mennonite minister John Gochnauer answered the newspaper editorial of 1940 that asked, "What's wrong with our public schools?"[31] He listed a host of objections: (1) there is a grave danger to compromise with worldly tendencies, (2) teachers question the deity of Christ and the inspiration of the Scriptures, (3) students in biology are taught the "facts" of fanciful and unproven theories instead of the simple voice of revelation, (4) ancient history loses its charm with the neglect of the great men and women of the Bible, (5) recreational and social activities stimulate a desire for the lure and appeal of the dance and movie rather than the ornament of a meek and quiet spirit, (6) competitive games seriously interfere with classroom work, (7) Christian girls in physical exercise classes are required to don slacks or even shorts to the detriment of the sense of modesty that is so vital to the charms of Christian youth, (8) repulsive behavior pervades washrooms, and (9) a growing political tendency makes students unduly "state minded" by insisting on the flag salute, urging the purchase of war stamps and bonds, stimulating political convictions and fostering a fascination for military activities and training.[32]   But even Gochnauer, who would eventually become vice-chairman of the new Mennonite high school, conceded that not all public schools were objectionable.

Minister Amos Weaver compared the Mennonite response to public high schools with the Hebrew slavery in Egypt. "For a number of years Mennonite fathers and mothers of the Lancaster Conference were groaning under the driving lash of the taskmasters of public education, especially in many of the high schools. They were much burdened because of the school plays, operettas,

*The front page of the **Intelligencer Journal** reports the sale of 10 one-room schools in East Lampeter Township in November 1938.*

pageants, minstrel shows, etc., with their worldly, unchristian, vain, and foolish emphases. Then the moving picture came into the schoolroom, at first fairly clean and seemingly harmless, but gradually dragging along with it some of the vulgarity and filth in which it thrives. . . . Next the fad of undress for 'gym' exercises in 'gym' suits that just 'suited' the evil one, became the common thing. In some places dancing was introduced into the school, and the modern dance became the right-hand maiden of the scarlet sin. Then parents 'cried mightily unto God,' and God heard their crying and groaning, and sent deliverance."[33]

The litany of concerns with public schools included evolution, the flag salute, physical education, drama, competitive sports, dancing, musical instruments, bands, orchestras, ultra-patriotism and worries that military training might be tied to schools. Noah Good noted that because public schools reflect the expectations of their communities they sink into paganism, modernism and almost any other "ism" when the supporting parents allow it.[34]

Others argued that public schools would improve if Christian teachers exerted their influence in the classroom. Indeed, in 1940 some 85 Mennonites were teaching in public high schools in the Lancaster area. By comparison, 81 Mennonites were involved in other professional jobs including 55 nurses and four physicians.[35]

The Transformation of Public Schools

The articles and speeches bubbling out of the emerging Christian school movement shared a common fear of "state controlled schools" and the "state system." "Would you let the state clothe your children?" asked Mennonite John Lehman. "Yet we let the state mold the minds of our children according to their standards."[36] In a common refrain, church-school advocates heralded a return to colonial days when the Mennonite church operated its own schools. Deep in the Mennonite soul lingered a suspicion of the state, nurtured by long years of European persecution. Fear of the state was rising once again. Why were Mennonites suddenly turning their backs on the common public schools they had supported for nearly a century?

Public education was radically transformed in the first half of the twentieth century. Schools rode the tidal wave of industrialization as the nation's workers moved from farm to factory. This massive societal shift revolutionized education in nearly every way.[37] The Pennsylvania Department of Education enlarged its staff in the summer of '38 to handle plans for building 1,000 consolidated schools under a $75 million federal program. Little red schoolhouses were abandoned by the hundreds. More than 130 one-room public schools folded in Lancaster County between 1911 and 1940—nearly five per year. The 257 that remained in 1940 had vanished by 1960. Consolidation triumphed in the 1950s as the county's 62 school districts shrank to 17, each sporting a large modern high school.

An industrialized nation needed workers with more than an eighth grade education. And so the twentieth century became the century of the public high school. The school code of 1911 specified new standards for salaries, teacher certification, length of school term and curriculum. Pennsylvania's superintendent of public instruction said, "The public school furnishes a ladder stretching from the gutter into the university . . . on which youth can enter the portals of professional life." [38] American youth were beginning to climb the ladder. In 1905 nine percent of the country's population were high school graduates; in 1930 the number had climbed to 45 percent.

In 1930 Lancaster County had 38 high schools, but only 13 of them were four-year schools. Aggressive state leaders promoted consolidated schools. The state even paid local districts $200 apiece for closing one-room schools. Educators sneered at the "antiquated and outworn" one-teacher schools and vigorously promoted the virtues of consolidation. The magic of the factory— specialization, professionalization, standardization, centralization and efficiency—the magic that produced Model T cars and vacuum cleaners galore, was shaping the character of public education. Large, efficient schools with a specialized and professionalized staff would, the experts said, produce a better educational "product." Better roads and faster school buses in the '30s made it possible to transport pupils to the faraway and newly consolidated schools. Prospective teachers were prepared in four-year colleges. The statewide goal of 1934, "trained teachers in every classroom," became "four-year college educated teachers" by 1940. The number of Lancaster County teachers educated in four-year colleges soared dramatically from a skimpy three percent in 1920 to 51 percent by 1940.

The desires of the state guided this massive revolution. Aggressive state dictates rested on the deep conviction that a free, quality education was the cornerstone of a successful democracy. Public schools would homogenize immigrant youth from diverse ethnic, racial and religious backgrounds and prepare them for responsible citizenship. Part of the transformation was a shift of power from local to state hands. Statewide policies regulated the educational enterprise. The mandates of the Commonwealth increased the school term, hiked the age for attendance, specified building codes, regulated the curriculum, certified teachers, set minimum salaries and much more. These fundamental changes within public education in the first half of the twentieth century prodded the Christian day school movement.

Mennonites and neighboring farmers celebrate a good harvest.

The Deeper Threat

Beneath the consolidation efforts, deeper trends tormented the Mennonite soul. Factory work and professional jobs were beginning to transform family life. Growing specialization pulled many time-honored functions away from the family. Schools were fast becoming not only a place to learn math, science and spelling, but the center of social life as well. Drama, sports, dances, physical education and many other activities drew students away from home. To hardworking Mennonite farmers, physical education classes were a meaningless spectacle. In the eyes of families interested in a basic education, all of these activities were not only frivolous, they also enticed youth off fields and out of barns. Moreover, they exposed youth to worldly amusements outside the scrutiny of their family. The new public schools threatened to unravel the heart of the Mennonite family.

Emphasizing science and rational thinking, modern education aimed to produce independent thinkers—citizens who could carry the banner of democracy. This passion for self-achievement and individual rights troubled Mennonite leaders. Although they wanted clear-thinking, level-headed youth, they also desired young people with meek and mild spirits. Youth trained in the public schools might become arrogant and find it difficult to comply with the standards of the church.

To American educators in the first half of the twentieth century, public schools were vehicles to "improve, strengthen and unify American life."[39] The schools would blend youth from diverse ethnic backgrounds in a common American pot. There, the young would learn the virtues of citizenship in a free democracy—one that could no longer be taken for granted with the dark clouds of war raging over Europe. But for a people who hoped to remain separate from the world, who believed that faith in Jesus Christ led them away from the mainstream rather than into it, the transformation of public education was as threatening as the war clouds in Europe. And that is why the Mennonites declared war on briars and bramble by the old Mill Stream in the summer of 1942.[40] They hoped to preserve their faith by passing it on within the walls of their own school.

CHAPTER TWO

Staking Out
a Middle Ground

1940-1942

"Hothouse plants will wilt in the scorching sun."
—Mennonite school opponents

Caught in the Cross Fire

A variety of social currents churning in the early '40s spawned Lancaster Mennonite School. The changing character of state-controlled public schools—consolidation, curriculum innovation and compulsory attendance—fed a major stream of Mennonite concern. In addition, the schools' encroaching influence on family life through extracurricular activities, physical education classes and the possibility of military training made Mennonite parents uneasy. The fires of patriotism, ignited by the Nazi attack on Poland in September of 1939, and now burning in the public schools, alarmed other parents.

With educational expectations rising around them, more and more Mennonite youth were attending high school. Some were trekking south to the Mennonite school in Virginia. The rising tide of the Christian day school movement—spreading across the Mennonite church in the '30s—also brought new ideas and enthusiasm. Recent missionary endeavors at home and abroad required a new corps of trained Mennonite workers. All of these converging forces generated the human and spiritual resources necessary to launch a new school.

The dream for the new school almost died, however, in a cross fire of opposition within the Mennonite community. Proponents of the new venture were hit from two directions. On the one side were traditional Mennonite farmers who simply thought high school was superfluous. They wanted their children back on the farm after eighth grade. Old-fashioned, down-to-earth, vocational education had served them well over the generations. Why change now? This separatist stream of Mennonites rejected higher education along with many other American values.[1]

At the other end of the spectrum, progressive Mennonites served on public school boards. Comfortable in the cultural mainstream and cheering the changes in public education, they wanted their children to taste "real life" in public schools. Parochial schools, they feared, would make Mennonites even more separatist, exclusive and clannish. They wanted no part of an "anti-school school." Parochial school graduates, like "hothouse plants" growing in a sheltered greenhouse, they argued, would wilt in the scorching sun of adult life.

From both sides of the fence came the charge that a school would simply cost too much. Parents already shouldering the rising cost of public schools would have to pay a double tax.

As criticism of the new venture flared, J. Paul Graybill, emergent spokesman for the proposed school, took the objectors head-on. One by one he refuted some 25 objections to Mennonite schools in a widely circulated manual.[2]

Parochial school supporters were caught in this cross fire of opinion. Although opponents stalled the high school movement, supporters were able to rally a middle ground of support and press forward. Advocates of the school were progressives in some ways. They favored high school education. But they also shared the conservatives' fear of "state-controlled" schools. Thus, a church-controlled high school struck a reasonable middle ground in the eyes of the advocates.

Along the spectrum of plain religious groups in Lancaster County, a Mennonite high school was a middle road of another sort. The Old Order Amish who had parted ways with the Mennonites in Europe drew firm lines of separation around their community. They rejected automobiles, electricity and tractors. But until the late '30s the Amish had supported local one-room public schools. The consolidation of schools and the stricter attendance laws, however, frightened them. A high school education, to their thinking, was not only unnecessary for farming, it would cultivate an independent spirit that would surely destroy the traditional order of their community. After a series of legal disputes, the Amish began operating their own elementary schools in the late 1930s. A U.S. Supreme Court decision endorsed their separate educational system in 1972. Throughout the twentieth century they have continued to forbid high school attendance.

At the other end of the plain spectrum in Lancaster County stood the Church of the Brethren. With roots reaching back to Germany in the early 1700s, the Brethren shared many Anabaptist beliefs and practices with the Amish and Mennonites.[3] Flowing with the rising educational tide, a group of Brethren began a college at Elizabethtown on the western fringe of Lancaster County in 1899. Elizabethtown College eventually affiliated with the church and served many Brethren. Numerous Brethren graduates became teachers and

A. Grace Wenger, a Mennonite from Bareville, delivered the oration at Elizabethtown College in 1940. She taught literature at Lancaster Mennonite School in 1956-66.

administrators in the public schools of Lancaster County. Already at home in the public schools they often governed, the Brethren had little interest in the Christian day school movement arising in the late '30s and '40s. Indeed, the Brethren never opened any elementary or high schools in the county.

Thus on the one side of the plain spectrum stood the Brethren, sporting a college but unenthused about lower levels of parochial schooling. At the other end stood the Amish. They shunned both high school and college but eventually opened dozens of one-room elementary schools. The Mennonites, with elementary schools and soon a high school, but lacking a college, staked out a middle ground among Lancaster County's plain groups.

Driving in the Stakes

The formal process of opening a school began in the spring of 1940. The second season of the successful Ephrata Bible School had finished in February. The Mennonite bishops met at the Rohrerstown Meetinghouse on Monday, March 11. Among other actions they "vigorously protested against the use and distribution of tobacco in any form" and rejoiced in the "growing conviction among our brethren against raising tobacco." They "vigorously protested" reading the Sunday paper, especially its "funny page" of comics, which in bishops' eyes were "very detrimental to the spiritual welfare of God's people." In a historic move, they "favorably considered" Henry Garber's petition to start a high school.[4]

Warming up now to the idea of a high school, the bishops agreed to bring Garber's petition to the full Conference body on Thursday, March 14, 1940. Gathered in their semi-annual meetings, ordained leaders were told to give the petition "prayerful consideration and study" until their October conference. The next day the *Intelligencer Journal's* front page pictured A. Grace Wenger, a Mennonite, with the headline, "Bareville Girl to Deliver E-town College Oration."[5] Following in the footsteps of her older sister Edna, Grace Wenger was slated to graduate from Elizabethtown College. Mennonite leaders had much to pray about until October. Not only were their youth driving to Virginia for high school, they were also graduating from the Brethren college in western Lancaster County. The powerful forces of education were knocking on several doors of their sectarian home.

The war in Europe intensified throughout the summer of 1940. Some 500 Nazi war planes bombed England in an August blitzkrieg. By the end of the month the United States planned a military draft that would eventually tap millions. Schools opened in September with a flurry of patriotic exercises. Photographs of children saluting the flag appeared in local papers. Lancaster's

The Mellinger's Mennonite Meetinghouse. Lancaster Mennonite Conference leaders met here in 1940 when they voted, by a slim margin, to open a high school.

McCaskey High School made the flag salute a daily exercise in every home-room. Seven dozen small flags, designed for teachers' desks, were hurriedly ordered. Dr. Smith, superintendent of city schools, presented teachers with an eight-step program to teach students the value of democracy and make them better patriots.[6] Geneva Simpkins, elementary teacher in Rohrerstown, re-signed when the public school board told her to "salute or quit." A Jehovah's Witness, she had refused to lead her pupils in the flag salute.[7] On Saturday, September 7, 1940, Lancaster's evening newspaper offered a five-photo spread on the "proper ways to salute the flag of the United States."[8] The flag rippled anew with the passions of patriotism.

By mid-September, plans to draft some 16 million men ages 21 to 35 were finalized. October 16, 1940, was declared draft registration day. On Thursday, October 3, county superintendent of schools Arthur Mylin announced that public schools would close for the draft registration. Teachers would assist election boards to register men at public schools. On Friday, October 4, presidential candidate Wendell L. Willkie spoke to a cheering crowd of 7,000 at Lancaster's railroad station, while Mennonite leaders struggled with the fate of their high school.

A Slim Majority

Gathered in their fall conference at Mellinger's Meetinghouse on October 4, 1940, Mennonite leaders voted on the proposed high school. A two-thirds vote was required for passage. Loud voices of opposition made the outcome uncertain. In a three-page statement, bishop Amos Horst, assistant secretary of the Conference, introduced the petition. "Rampant forces today," he noted, "make the problem of acquiring a secular education more acute than a generation ago. The direct teaching of the Word of God is woefully neglected and rampant iniquity makes the influence of the school a critical period in the life of the child. . . . We believe that the child should be saved from the influences of wicked men and women in this world and that we should teach them very early the true way. . . . In the state controlled schools . . . the children are with others who follow the order dictated by the state organization which in many cases has been good . . . but in other instances reveals the vanity and iniquity of this age."

Horst went on to say that a church-directed school would "promote Christian ideals and standards of Christian living . . . provide wholesome instruction and activities that are conducive to Christian living . . . lead to the true way of life . . . and avoid the unholy and intemperate activities that are so prevalent in the state controlled school." He argued that a church school's educational standards should be excellent and creditable, but when "state standards for credits infringe on our testimony, then we should follow the course of true devotion to God and his word."[9]

After presenting the petition to the Conference body, Horst concluded, "The influence of this meeting and its action on this question will affect the future of the church and our young people in this part of the Lord's Vineyard." A plea to table the resolution for six months because of the "varied minds" in the conference body was apparently overturned. The resolution to begin a high school passed, but only by the slimmest of margins. The school advocates had gained enough middle turf to carry the day. Perhaps the surrounding fires of patriotism and the pending draft registration, at public schools, announced the day before had made the difference.[10]

The close vote stalled the bishops' plan for the next steps. How should they proceed? Six months later they inched forward. In the spring of '41 three bishops—Noah Risser, Stoner Krady and Simon Bucher—were elected to "study the high school question" and report their findings.[11] At the same meeting the bishops announced that "brethren who voluntarily go into military service or training will forfeit their church membership." Testing the educational waters, bishop Horst circulated a questionnaire to the families of his district asking if they "were satisfied with the state-controlled high school system."[12]

On June 19, 1941, the bishops called a special meeting at the East Chestnut

Street Meetinghouse to discuss the high school. After a morning of discussion, the secretary noted "considerable sentiment *against* taking up the work." The middle ground was shrinking. Sometime in the afternoon the tables turned, and "it was *finally* decided" to prepare a constitution, develop a plan to elect trustees and submit both to the fall conference for ratification.[13] Ordained leaders gathered at Mellinger's Meetinghouse on October 3, 1941. Bishop Noah Risser opened the meeting with a call to faithfulness "in the midst of an evil world." Among other business the body approved the proposed constitution and the high school was finally underway.[14]

The Search for a Place

In three special meetings between October 14 and November 19, 1941, the bishops spurred the project forward. Three bishops—Noah Risser, Amos Horst, Henry Lutz—were appointed to a Religious Welfare Committee, charged with keeping a watchful eye on the school. The bishops nominated prospective school trustees. In a mail election, the ordained men of the Conference chose 12 trustees who then organized themselves by secret ballot.[15] Ten of the trustees were ordained ministers or deacons. Many were retired farmers without a high school education. Two had some college training. Five of the trustees had signed the petition to begin the school. Parke Book, an ordained minister, was elected chairman. Book and secretary of the board, John Kraybill, had each lost an arm in farming accidents.

The bishops and newly elected trustees met in a joint meeting on November 19, 1941, chaired by bishop Noah Mack. After the group sang "Saviour Teach Me Day by Day," Mack appealed to the trustees to "work along conservative lines." He urged bishops and trustees to work "as one body . . . to unify and gain the confidence of the constituency." The trustees stood, signifying their willingness to abide by the constitution. Bishop Mack solemnly charged them "to provide school privileges for our youth that will bring glory to God."[16] Now the ball was in the trustees' court. They would gather some 23 times over the next nine months—often kneeling in prayer as they began their meetings. Charged with an awesome task, they sought the Lord's guidance and direction.

The trustees debated the pros and cons of a centrally located single school versus several regional ones. Eventually they agreed on a "central, four year, accredited high school," and laid plans to explore sites and costs. The second trustee meeting was held December 9, 1941, two days after the Pearl Harbor attack. As the United States plunged into war, the trustees began exploring more than half a dozen sites. Undecided if they should build a new facility or purchase an existing one, the board agreed that they wanted "a central location, accessible by highway in all seasons, equipped to care for future needs and imposing the least financial burden on the church." From December 1941 through April 1942 the trustees spent endless hours inspecting sites and gathering estimates for their new project.

Mennonite attorney Samuel Wenger drove daily along U.S. Route 30 from his home in Paradise to his Lancaster office. One day he noticed a for-sale sign on the old Yeates School in Greenland, five miles east of Lancaster city. After several times of informally inspecting the run-down 85 acres with its meandering Mill Stream, Wenger was convinced of its potential. Over the next months he made it a "matter of daily prayer" and quietly took church leaders to see the site. His secret dream was that someday it would become a Mennonite college.

Meanwhile the board investigated other sites: (1) a two-acre plot east of Mountville with a 10-room house; (2) Weber-in-the-Woods, a four-acre plot with a 10-room house north of Roots Auction on Route 72; (3) a vacant property on South Ann Street in Lancaster; (4) a large mansion along the Fruitville Pike north of Lancaster city; (5) Crandal Health Institute west of the Susquehanna River; (6) the Grubb Estate along Route 72 north of Manheim; and (7) a 20-acre plot of land adjacent to and owned by the Mennonite Home at Orrville, west of Lancaster city. Additional sites were also discussed but eventually dropped for a variety of reasons.[17]

The trustees decided to pursue the old Yeates School at Greenland, despite its drawbacks: high flood waters in the past and the cost of cleanup and repair. Many remembered the destructive flood of '36 when the farmer living in the small cottage on the south side of the Mill Stream was rescued from the roof of his porch by rowboat. The buildings had lain vacant for 18 years. Nevertheless, on February 4, 1942, the trustees decided to make an offer of $17,750 on the Yeates property, advertised for $40,000. Frugal as they were, they agreed to go as high as $20,000 if necessary. The owner rejected their bid, saying, "It was much too low!" But he offered subparcels for as low as $18,500. Considering the price for the whole property too high and rejecting the idea of parcels, the trustees decided "to drop Yeates and consider other sites."[18]

The trustees met with the board of the Mennonite Home for an all-day meeting to explore the land near that institution. Although building supplies were restricted by the war, Mennonite contractors thought they could obtain materials to construct a school building. Could they build on the 20-acre plot owned by the Mennonite Home, west of the present-day Park City mall? The land had been donated to the Home and required a court order to free the deed. The trustees discussed the legal complications with attorney Wenger. He strongly urged them not to build expensive new facilities. Moreover, he was sure that the Yeates property, even with repairs and improvements, could be financed for $50,000.

By March 11 the trustees learned from contractor Jacob Hershey that a new school building near the Mennonite Home would cost $135,000, plus the land at $231 an acre. The board was stunned by the figures. The Mennonite Home site was doomed. In the meantime, several bishops led by bishop Mack had visited the Yeates property again. They urged the trustees to "make another effort to secure it."

Striking a Deal

Sugar sales in Lancaster were frozen the last week of April 1942 until rationing books could be distributed. In the midst of these and many other wartime restrictions the trustees announced plans to open a school in four months. But they still lacked a campus. On Monday, April 27, 1942, school trustees, under extreme pressure, met all day at Weaver's Book Store in Lancaster. Bishop J. Paul Graybill, newly elected principal of the school, argued for waiting a year. The scarcity of tires and supplies made both traveling and building difficult. Moreover, public sentiment in the church frowned on spending money in the tight wartime economy. Others, however, believed that God had provided the Yeates site just at the time when Mennonites were finally willing to support a church high school. It was "too good a bargain, too good an opportunity to miss and we'd better take it even if we aren't totally ready," some supporters argued.

After a lengthy discussion at Weaver's Book Store, the trustees instructed their finance committee to "use their judgment and buy the Yeates property." While the rest of the board remained in session, the finance committee and chairman Book walked from Weaver's Book Store to attorney Wenger's office to meet the realtor and the owner. The realtor, eager to sell, shaved his commission to clinch the deal. Within a few minutes the trustees had a property. Returning later to the board meeting, the finance committee re-ported the terms: 85 acres for $36,000; 10 percent down and immediate possession. "Ridiculously high," fumed opponents of the school. But by 1991, on the edge of suburban sprawl, the land's value had soared into the millions.

Reactions to the purchase of the campus were mixed. Ira Hartz, a civic-minded Mennonite farmer, told Morgantown public school principal Noah Good, "I'm not in favor of the new school." When Elizabethtown College dean and chemistry professor A.C. Baugher learned that one of his students, Clyde Stoner, was the newly appointed business manager of the Mennonite school, he laid aside his chemistry notes and lectured for an entire class period on the

The campus, about 1942, as sketched by Mary Lou Houser.

(top) Students on the bridge watch rescuers search for Alvin Yost who drowned in the Mill Stream in 1952. The farm cottage and barn, south of the stream, stand in the background.

(bottom) A skating party on the pond by the boys' dormitory in 1953.

A near tag at home plate during the 1957 junior/senior outing.

(top) Faculty members making doughnuts during a snowstorm in 1958. From left: Mary Ethel Heatwole, Rosa Moshier, James Bomberger, Doris Bomberger.

(bottom) A class outing by the Mill Stream in the 1950s.

(top) Students walk between classes in the mid-1950s. The dormitory, built in 1949, appears in the background.

(bottom) Students prepare for 1960 commencement ceremonies held in a large tent erected on campus. An annual World Wide Missionary Conference was held in the tent several days after graduation.

(top) A student social on the site of the present classroom building, May 1961.

(bottom) An annual tug of war in the fall of 1961. The chapel and dormitory stand in the background.

(top) A brief time out on the skating pond in December 1962. From left: Seniors Donald B. Kraybill, Nelson W. Martin, Glenn E. Metzler.

(bottom) Students applaud their classmates at a social in 1962 near the site of the present gym.

(top) A faculty and student volleyball game, October 1963, in front of the auditorium/gym, near the site of the present gym.

(bottom) Trapping muskrats was permitted in early years as a diversion from academic studies but eventually it was prohibited. This early 1960s view shows the administration building, the auditorium/gym, and the chapel from the south side of the Mill Stream.

merits and problems of church-related schools.

Plans for the old Yeates School prompted an editorial in the *Intelligencer Journal*. The newspaper noted that "the greatness of Lancaster has been accomplished in a large measure by the plain sects sticking to the land. . . . The Mennonites have followed their true bent by purchasing 85 acres of land." The paper went on to say, "It would be a fine thing, if out of this new move would . . . arise a real agricultural school in Lancaster County . . . which doesn't take away the love for the land" from Mennonite youth.[19] The "fine thing" which the editorial envisioned never emerged. The Mennonites who studied by the Mill Stream were more enthused about Bible studies and missions than farming. Those who wanted to farm had already learned the art quite well by the time they arrived in high school.

The Leadership Troika

Men of hope, the trustees had been busy gathering personnel despite not having a site. In January of 1942 they reviewed a dozen prospects for dean of the school. After paring them down to Noah Good and Chester Lehman, they elected Good by secret ballot.[20] Good, an ordained minister in Reading, was a 15-year veteran of public schools and currently principal of the Morgantown High School. Reflecting on his public school days Good said, "I became involved in the promotion of sports and plays and some of those things a little more than a lot of our people thought Mennonite ministers should. I always thought the idea of public schools was good, but in church schools we could do some things that we couldn't in public schools."

In January 1942 the bishops elected J. Paul Graybill, former mission worker and newly-ordained bishop in the Weaverland District, principal of the school. Clyde Stoner was elected secretary-treasurer. Within a week he agreed to serve and, although not ordained, reluctantly promised to wear a frock-tail plain suit—the standard for ordained leaders. The troika of Graybill, Good and Stoner formed the Supervising Committee, which directed the school in its first decade. Graybill, responsible to maintain ties with the bishops and the larger church, directed religious life on campus as well. Good organized the academic program, while Stoner balanced the books and wrote the minutes. The Supervising Committee met for the first time on February 16, 1942, at bishop Graybill's home. After a time of prayer and consecration, they read the school constitution, then began charting the academic program and recruiting faculty.

Early in May, principal Graybill sent a questionnaire to Lancaster Conference leaders as well as to Mennonite leaders elsewhere. He asked their guidance on academic offerings, student regulations, music, athletics and dormitory life. Should the dress standards of the school be higher than those in the local congregation? What safeguards should the school, as a true servant of the church, endorse to avoid liberal tendencies? Most respondents counseled him to be wary of competitive games, special music groups and plays.[21] "Avoid narrow-minded teachers that ride a hobby and drive pupils into liberalism," counseled one leader. Said another, "Keep bodies fully clothed." "Draw up plain, simple, sensible and scriptural rules for dress," urged still another. For the most part, respondents wanted school standards *above* those in local congregations—sweet music to Graybill's ears.

In a preliminary bulletin the Supervising Committee said, "Every effort will be made to make the four-year high school, 'equal to the best.'" The teachers, it promised, "will be fully certified and experienced." The founders of the school, reflected Noah Good, "wanted religious education, a very plain school and a very Mennonite school."

The Old Yeates School

What did the trustees buy at Greenland? Farm buildings—a barn, corn barn, henhouse, milk house and a small cottage—bordered the south side of the Mill Stream. On the north side of the stream stood five buildings, including a mill,

The old Eshelman's Mill, used as a dormitory for Yeates boys (1907-1923), provided classroom space and dormitory rooms for the new Mennonite school.

The farmer's cottage, south of the Mill Stream, served as a girls' dormitory in the early years of LMS. Fannie Frankhouser, 1940s student, stands on the 1890 bridge that spans the Mill Stream.

used by the Yeates School. The waters of the Mill Stream powered milling operations since the mid-1700s. For three decades in the early 1800s the water turned the wheel of a cloth mill. The original structure burned in 1850. Rebuilt by Benjamin Eshelman and used to grind grain, it became "Eshelman's Mill." In addition to the miller's stone house, a stone barn and a Georgian-style farmhouse stood west of the mill. A tobacco shed had been erected northwest of the stone barn.[22]

Site of frequent floods, the property was sold in 1907 to the Yeates School, "the Oldest Church Boarding School for Boys in the United States." Operated by the Episcopal Church, it began in 1857 in Lancaster city. Catherine Yeates endowed the school in honor of her father Jasper Yeates—a well-known Lancaster judge on the Supreme Court of Pennsylvania. The Yeates School, like many other academies in the 1800s, offered the equivalent of a high school education before public high schools appeared. The boarding school appealed to those able to afford a private education, and it cherished a reputation for "developing brilliant scholars." Students from Lancaster and afar learned not only academics, but also refined manners for upper class success. The institution's bulletin for 1919-1920 touted the qualities of a small school. "Large numbers prevent close watch of the refinement of manners. Gentle breeding is apt to be lost in the rough and tumble of a crowd. We restrict the number

(top) Students and faculty of the Yeates School which occupied the campus from 1907 to 1923.

(bottom) Mennonite students gather on the steps of the old mill in the early 1940s.

of boys to preserve the home character. . . . Refinement of manners and neatness in person, dress and room are looked upon as essential."[23] With the rise of public high schools, Yeates closed its doors in 1923.

The Yeates School had renovated many of the buildings in 1907. The old mill was converted into a classroom/dormitory called Jasper Hall. The nearby miller's house, used for classrooms and manual arts, became Locust Cottage.

Gardiner Hall, on the left, provided office space for both Yeates and Mennonite adminis-trators. The old barn, on the right, was used for a variety of functions by both schools.

A new facility housing a kitchen was dubbed Catherine Hall. The old stone barn was remodeled into Alumni Hall. A swimming pool graced its ground floor and the old haymows were converted into a second floor auditorium. The spacious brick farmhouse, Gardiner Hall, held a library, game room and a large common area. The headmaster, Dr. Gardiner, lived on the second floor. A disastrous fire on Easter morning of 1914 destroyed the historic house and many school records.[24] A new Gardiner Hall, built promptly on the same site, was flooded twice within a month of construction. The fire and floods discouraged Headmaster Gardiner so badly that he resigned. This brick structure is the only Yeates building standing in the 1990s.

Mennonite Daniel Weaver, Sr. served as caretaker and farmer for the Yeates School for many years. After the school closed in 1923 the property was eventually sold to Fred Wiker and William Coventry in 1930. The buildings, used for sundry farming operations over the next 10 years, fell into disrepair. Gardiner Hall became a summer home where the owners entertained guests. The tobacco shed west of the stone barn was torn down and used to build a new barn on the south side of the stream. Tobacco, stored in the damp cellar of Locust Cottage, was stripped in the nearby mess hall. As the buildings dete-riorated, weeds, vines and bramble flourished. When their parents snoozed on Sunday afternoons, neighborhood boys, including Mennonite Ralph Weaver,

(top) Locust Cottage was the miller's home before 1907. A classroom building for the Yeates School, it provided storage for crops until Noah Good's family arrived in 1942.

(bottom) The Yeates School had its own trolley station along the Lincoln Highway. Standing beside it in about 1920 is Daniel B. Weaver, caretaker for the school. The building was later moved next to the mill for maintenance storage.

(top) *Catherine Hall, a mess hall in the Yeates days, became the commercial building for the new Mennonite school.*

(bottom) *Ivy covers the old barn before cleanup crews cleared the walls in the summer of 1942 and turned it into the auditorium/gym.*

explored the spooky vacant classrooms.   South of the Mill Stream, a meager farm operation continued. The wooded area hosted a game refuge for the Mill Stream Sportsmen Association. Pheasants proliferated. In fact, they became so numerous that Ralph Weaver remembers them sitting on the porch railings of the Weaver home.

(top) Yeates boys swim in the heated pool in the basement of the old barn about 1920.
(bottom) Mennonites converted the Yeates swimming pool into a dining area in 1942 and later into a library in the 1960s.

A Mennonite Conversion

As the Mennonites tackled the bramble in the summer of 1942, they renovated the buildings and retrieved the loveliness of the old campus. It sparkled with the beauty of earlier days but never quite regained the prestigious charm of the Yeates era. The unpretentious, down-to-earth mentality of the new occupants tempered the conversion of buildings. Jasper Hall (the mill) was renamed the classroom building. Catherine Hall became the commercial building. Locust Cottage, dubbed Brother Good's residence, was home for the new dean of the school. Gardiner Hall was converted into the administration building with a girls' dormitory on the second and third floors. Alumni Hall, the old stone barn stripped of its ivy, became simply, the auditorium. The swimming pool on the ground level was covered with wood flooring to provide a storage area beneath and a dining room above. The second floor, used by the Yeates School for dances and plays, became an auditorium/gym. The practical, utilitarian names set the tone for the serious, no-nonsense values that were shaping the new venture.

A massive cleanup effort renovated the desolate campus throughout the summer of 1942. Hundreds of Mennonites gave thousands of hours and a multitude of material donations to pave the way for a September school opening. Some of the debris was dumped on an old Yeates race track south of the Mill Stream. The dump site was selected because, as one Mennonite volunteer said, "Mennonites will never have foot races here!"

The old Yeates flagpole, a few yards east of Gardiner Hall, nagged the volunteers as they cleaned up the rubble in the summer of '42. "We didn't know what to do with the pole," remembers John Kraybill. "We were afraid to take it down because of the war." A nonresistant church with its ultimate allegiance pledged to the kingdom of God could hardly hoist a flag—not even in wartime.

A Mennonite cleanup crew works around the tall flagpole at the front of Gardiner Hall, later the administration building, in June 1942.

Figure 2.1

Key Dates in the School's Formation

East Lampeter Controversy	Spring 1937
Locust Grove School Opens	Fall 1939
Ephrata Short-Term Bible School Opens	Winter 1939
High School Petition Presented to Bishops	March 14, 1940
Lancaster Conference Approves High School	October 4, 1940
Lancaster Conference Approves Constitution	October 3, 1941
First Trustee Meeting	November 19, 1941
Old Yeates School Purchased	April 27, 1942
Lancaster Mennonite School Opens	September 14, 1942

And yet a bare, 40-foot flagpole might strike visitors whose sons were dying as an unpatriotic, almost ugly, gesture. On the other hand, it was a good, sturdy wooden pole—one that might prove useful some day, reasoned these practical people.

After worrying about finances, the trustees rejoiced that contributions over $31,000 and loans from church members enabled them to bypass the bank. Property and repair costs totalled $51,836. In August of '42 the trustees' ledger dipped to $19.72, but tuition funds soon replenished it. Near the end of the first school year, the trustees solicited funds across the church to erase a debt of $26,000 and begin new renovations.

As the Mennonites staked out new drains and plumbing lines on the campus they were indeed claiming a kind of middle ground. Within the Mennonite church they were paving a middle road between the conservatives who feared high school and the progressives already entrenched in the public schools. The founders wanted a high school, but only if it could be safeguarded by the church. Between the Amish to the east and the Brethren to the west they were carving out another middle niche. Unlike the Amish, they welcomed education beyond eighth grade. But unlike the Church of the Brethren, they were not comfortable having a college—even a church-operated one—in their own backyard. The founders pressed for a four-year accredited high school, but that was enough. Finally, they were also charting middle ground between their farms and the social charm of the Yeates era. Yes, their youth could leave their plows for education—if it served the church and prepared them for missions. But the founders had little interest in matching the prestige of the Yeates institution. That, in Mennonite eyes, would surely lead to pride.

CHAPTER THREE

Safeguarding the Church

1942-1943

"Self-denial and obedience belong to a well-rounded education."
—J. Paul Graybill

Stemming the Drift

From the Civil War onward, Americans left their plows for factories where they joined throngs of recent immigrants. The vibrations of industrialization that shook the nation from 1870 to 1930 began to touch the Mennonite community as well. With farming deeply rooted in their souls, Mennonites, for the most part, were still tending crops and milking cows. In 1940 over 60 percent of Lancaster Conference Mennonites were farming, compared to only 15 percent of the county work force. Less than one-half of one percent of Mennonites in the Lancaster area were employed as professionals.[1]

The first decades of the twentieth century brought a host of inventions to the doorsteps of America—electricity, telephones, cars, tractors, sweepers,

Lancaster County Mennonites aboard the S. S. Deutschland in a New York harbor on February 22, 1934. They gathered to bid farewell to their first overseas missionaries who were sailing for Africa.

airplanes, radios, refrigerators and mass-produced clothing. Unlike their Amish cousins who banned cars, tractors and electricity, Mennonites welcomed many of the innovations in stride. They drove cars and enjoyed the fruits of industrial progress along with their neighbors. Yet the Machine Age tormented them in some ways. To buffer outside influences, radios were declared off limits for ministers. When television arrived it was forbidden for laity and ordained alike.

Although they embraced most technological advances, Lancaster Mennonites were troubled by some of the changes awash around them. Increasing mobility, encroaching urbanization, a rising emphasis on public education, the growing influence of national media and greater access to mass-produced goods all threatened to unravel the close-knit bonds of their community. They coped with the social turbulence of the industrial era in two ways. First, they "witnessed" to the larger "unsaved" world. With a burst of enthusiasm they organized a variety of outward evangelistic ventures—overseas missions, urban evangelism, short-term Bible schools in other states, Gospel tract distribution and a multitude of service and relief projects. In 1934 the first wave of overseas missionaries was commissioned to Africa. These outward initiatives, especially missions, thrust Mennonites beyond the parochial fences of Lancaster County.

Second, Mennonites fortified their defenses against the tentacles of urban culture. Fearful of being swallowed up by the larger society, they drew increasingly sharp lines between their community and the outside world. The German language, an important line of defense, was dropped in the last decades of the 1800s. Now the forces of industrialization, like a gigantic broom, threatened to sweep Mennonites into the main street of modern life. To protect their identity, church leaders emphasized distinctive practices—especially dress—in order to "stem the drift" into the whirlpool of modern culture. "Worldliness" in the Mennonite mind represented the vices and questionable values of the larger society.

The twin doctrines of nonconformity and nonresistance marked the major boundaries of the Mennonite world. Distinctive garb and taboos on social behaviors staked off the borders between church and world. Plain dress symbolized obedience to the Scriptures, loyalty to the Mennonite church and nonconformity to the world. The doctrine of nonresistance—nonparticipation in the military and non-use of lawsuits—continued as a test of church membership. The American flag, symbol of a patriotism that would kill enemies rather than love them as Jesus taught, did not reflect the humble stance of nonresistance.

Church membership standards tightened in the 1920s and '30s to stem the growing tide of worldliness. Neckties and jewelry were off limits. Women were required to wear the traditional head covering and plain bonnet as well as a two-piece cape dress for modesty. The distinctive plain suit, required for male

Short-term Bible school students meet in the early 1940s in front of Noah Good's home on the new campus.

leaders, was strongly urged for other men as well. Solos, special music by quartets and instrumental music were taboo in worship services. Supported by many Scriptures, the guidelines were written in the *Rules and Discipline* of the Lancaster Mennonite Conference.

Underlying the growing restrictions was a deep concern to preserve the biblical faith passed down from Anabaptist martyrs. Such preservation, reasoned the leaders, required taming the assertive individualism that soared along with industrialization. To keep the body of Christ pure—to maintain the boundaries of separation—required teamwork. Members needed to yield to the wisdom of the church. Based on many biblical passages, leaders taught that the Christian way was a narrow one of self-denial, meekness and humility. It entailed obedience to God and the church. Members were taught to not love the world or its things. Wearing jewelry, donning flashy clothing and singing solos were all considered self-exalting—an abomination in the eyes of God. The church, called out from the world, must ever guard against the seduction of worldliness, which in time would corrode the purity of the redeemed community. During Lancaster Mennonite School's first year, the bishops drafted a new version of the *Rules and Discipline*, etching clear lines of separation between church and world.[2]

Lancaster Mennonite School, soon known as LMS, embodied these Mennonite responses to the Machine Age. It worked to secure the Mennonite community by preserving Mennonite distinctives, while at the same time cultivating missionary impulses among its students. Many of the school's sponsors championed a passionate commitment to missionary work, hoping that LMS would thrust hundreds of Mennonite youth into missions around the world. The visionaries also prayed that the school would indelibly imprint the lines of separation into the minds of their youth, so they wouldn't lose their moorings as they sailed off to African mission fields. The school was not only poised to safeguard youth from "rampant iniquities" in public schools, it also hoped to prepare them for service in a world being revolutionized by change.

Safeguarding the School

The bishops saw part of their task as safeguarding the school itself. Some feared that in time it might turn on them and "liberalize the church." A school out of control might actually speed the drift of the church toward worldliness. They remembered all too well the disaster at the Mennonite college in Goshen, Indiana. It became so liberal that it had to be closed for the 1923-24 school year. Lancaster bishops had spoken against the worldliness of Goshen College for many years.[3] As they hammered out the constitution, the bishops took no chances.

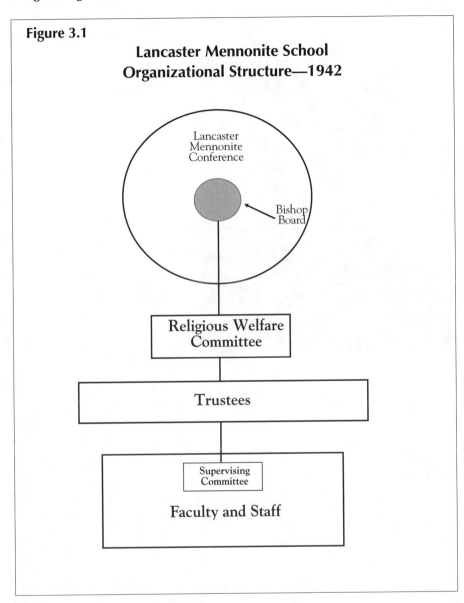

Figure 3.1

Lancaster Mennonite School
Organizational Structure—1942

Lancaster
Mennonite
Conference

Bishop
Board

Religious Welfare
Committee

Trustees

Supervising
Committee

Faculty and Staff

The document declared that the bishops "shall have full control and supervision of the organization and all its activities."[4] The bishops appointed three of their own to a Religious Welfare Committee to "act on their behalf . . . in controlling and supervising the organization." The Religious Welfare Committee screened teachers to assure that they "upheld the doctrine and discipline of the church." The bishops on the Religious Welfare Committee scrutinized school policies on music, athletics, drama, dress, books and many other matters.

Bishop J. Paul Graybill was appointed the first principal of the school.

The trustees of the school, elected by ordained leaders, were nominated by the bishops. Without question, this was the bishops' school!

The bishops also appointed the principal, religious patriarch of the school. They aspired to have a fellow bishop in that all-important role, although it was not dictated by the constitution. Upon the shoulders of the principal fell the awesome burden of protecting both the youth and the institution. Not trusting its destiny to one person, the bishops placed the operation of the school in the lap of a three-person Supervising Committee—principal, dean and business manager. Trustees and teachers, said the constitution, were to be "in full harmony with the Doctrine and Discipline of the Lancaster Mennonite Conference." Moreover, the constitution specified "Ten Safeguards." The first one declared, "All instruction . . . shall be in harmony with the Word of God and the *Rules and Discipline* of the Lancaster Mennonite Conference." Other safeguards prohibited tobacco, profanity, radios, musical instruments and obscene literature, as well as public games and contests. The Supervising Committee was responsible to design dress regulations that harmonized with the Conference's *Rules and Discipline*. Finally, these constitutional fortifications could only change with the consent of Lancaster Mennonite Conference. With these precautions, the bishops hoped that both the school and their youth would be secure for the future.

A Safe, Sane Vision

The trustees, said vice-chairman John Gochnauer, hoped to "provide safe, sane and satisfactory training under wholesome Christian influences entirely free from . . . wrong emphases in public schools—teaching biology (evolution), the great system of competitive athletics, the absorbing social and entertainment program and the possible introduction of compulsory military training."[5] The bishops turned to J. Paul Graybill to safeguard their safe, sane place.

Appointed principal at the age of 42, Graybill became the school's philosophical architect. After a year and a half of college studies at Millersville Normal School, he taught three years in a public school.[6] Ordained a minister at age 20, Graybill served 16 years as superintendent of the Philadelphia Mennonite Mission with firsthand exposure to the vices of urban life. He was ordained bishop in the Weaverland District in 1939. An innovator and visionary, he spearheaded weekday summer Bible schools throughout the Conference, served as principal of the six-week Ephrata Bible School and launched a quarterly periodical, *The Pastoral Messenger*. "J. Paul," as he was called by colleagues, shaped the school's ideological dream in its first decade. What was his vision?

Conscientious to the core, Graybill was strongly committed to biblical authority. He hoped the new school would immerse youth in biblical studies and energize them for missions. Propelled by deeply held principles, Graybill argued that church schools would not only keep "thousands of young people in the church," they would also produce belief in a missionary vision. "Bible convictions produced by teachers day after day will do much to meet the unbelief, skepticism and materialism of the day."[7] These convictions, argued Graybill, would thrust youth directly into missionary service or at least make them supportive of the missionary movement.

His vision flew in the face of the soaring spirit of individualism saturating modern education. In his words, "Mennonites from the Bible teach self-denial; world educators often teach self-assertion. . . . The Bible trains people to be submissive and obedient; the world educates and trains people to demand their rights to rule."[8] Self-denial, yieldedness, submission, obedience and humility were common words on his lips. They were the virtues of Christian character and the building blocks of Christian community. J. Paul himself carried a sterling reputation for yielding to the "mind of the church" even when he personally disagreed.

Noah Good, dean of the school, shared J. Paul's convictions. Two weeks after the school opened, Good preached a sermon on the "Yielded Life" at the Mellinger's Mennonite Meetinghouse.[9] "The world accents force, strength, and the exaltation of the self," said Good. But the Christian life "is a continuous life of yielding." After the Christian has "renounced self and accepted Christ into his life as the ruling power . . . he still needs to yield himself." Applying these insights to dress regulations and separation from the world, Good counseled listeners to obey church leaders. Guided by these understandings, Graybill and Good crafted student regulations to cultivate a life of self-denial and humility.

In his heart of hearts, Graybill believed that a school could do what individual congregations couldn't. Sprawling factories, rapid travel and mass fashions were eroding Mennonite distinctives. Congregations were losing control of their members. Individualism was stalking the Mennonite camp. Throughout his prolific writings Graybill contended that a Mennonite school should have *higher* standards than the church at large. School regulations, he believed, should match the high ideals of the Conference even when they exceeded congregational practice. In a persuasive article Graybill offered eight reasons for lofty standards.[10] A school, he argued, has the power to enforce regulations "if it is willing to take a stand." Schools mold the ideals of youth, the next generation of church leaders. Furthermore, he added, "self-denial and obedience belong to a *well-rounded* education." And, he noted, enrollment is voluntary. Those not willing to accept the regulations don't need to attend. Graybill emphasized that a school should lead the congregations, set the standards, stem the tide, not drift thoughtlessly into worldliness. Graybill's vision of a "well-rounded" education would, however, severely irritate some parents and students over the years.

Contending for biblical authority, nonconformity, nonresistance, church loyalty and missions, Graybill's ideas blazed the trail for the new school. Although his views felt harsh to some, he was not a thoughtless autocrat. His convictions were carefully reasoned. Some of the faculty joked that he should have been a Jesuit priest, given his finely honed mind. Yielding to higher authorities and cultivating self-denial weren't designed to batter the self-esteem of youth. They were, in Graybill's mind, biblical principles with a noble goal. In his words, "I believe we need to give our boys and girls a sense of belonging to something. . . . We belong to a school, and through that we belong to the church. We belong to a church that dares to teach God's word and give it to the world."[11] Losing themselves in obedience, youth would discover an emotional niche in a faith community. According to the Bible, Graybill argued, youth must be "guarded by restrictions . . . that require obedience and submission. . . . After maturity . . . the individual will be more able to make choices of his own. Restrictions are not intended to take away liberties . . . but to serve as a pattern of life through which *proper habits* of thought and life may be formed."[12] What were these proper habits that Mennonite students were expected to acquire in their "well-rounded" education?

Cultivating Proper Habits

The Yeates boys had learned refined practices for upper class life. But the collective habits of the new school were crafted to cultivate loyalty to the Mennonite church. A few days before the school opened, the Supervising Committee drafted the practices.[13] Hats, caps and bonnets—of modest color and design—would be worn while traveling to and from campus. Two-piece cape dresses, full to the neck with long sleeves, and skirts "consistent with modesty" were the order of the day. Prints or designs on dresses were to be small and inconspicuous. Transparent fabric was forbidden. Girls were required to wear a prayer veiling "large enough to fully serve its purpose." The veilings, or "coverings," were expected to have ribbons, or "strings," which were rarely tied. Both boys and girls wore black, "well-supported" stockings. The plain coat was recommended, but not required, for boys. Shirt collars and sleeves were to be buttoned.

The taboo list included long neckties, gaudy hats, sporty-colored socks and shoes, large, gaily colored bow ties, vividly colored sweaters and sport shirts. Students were to dress modestly at all times, "not exposing parts of the body or calling attention to them by the clothes worn." This garb of humility and simplicity was to clarify the lines between church and world. Proper dress, students learned, would signify biblical obedience and serve as a badge of group identity. Dress would not be used as a tool of self-glorification and attention-seeking. Faculty members were to "maintain order and . . . exercise this authority in kindness." Noah Good observed that although the Religious Welfare Committee "in loving concern tried to help both faculty and students see the value of regulations . . . the school from the very beginning had to struggle with student restlessness and resistance."[14]

Pupils were expected "to obey without question or show of resentment." Some students learned the discipline of submission and gained a niche in the community of faith. Others were tempted to test the boundaries of authority. For some others the rigid rules seared a bitterness into their souls that still lingers. The lines of separation, defined by the habits of dress, would become the theatre for testing the limits of freedom and authority in the school over the years.

Other guidelines also shaped the tone of the institution. Students were not to bring magazines, or books of fiction and fashion, on campus. The Religious

Students and faculty sometimes fished for carp in the Mill Stream in the first years of the school. U.S. Route 30 crosses the bridge in the upper end of the meadow.

Welfare Committee screened books and magazines for the school library. Radios, phonographs and recorders were absent from dorm rooms. Talking via windows, pipes and stairways was taboo. Students learned that after the last bedtime bell, "no voices shall be heard at all." And because food attracted mice and flies it could not be stored in dormitory rooms. A variety of other regulations, "for the good of the individual and the good of the entire school," regulated the flow of behavior.

Students found each other attractive despite their "fully clothed" bodies. Friendships thrived, but "systematic courtship" was only permitted for 18-year-olds. "Intense courtships" were to be "dropped." "Steady friends" traveling as couples to and from campus had to receive permission and arrange for "chaperonage." Holding hands was forbidden. Dancing was unthinkable.

Beyond the school, four-part a cappella singing marked Mennonite worship in the '40s. Lancaster Conference banned musical instruments, solos, duets and quartets for fear they would dilute the quality of congregational singing. Special music would cultivate pride by calling attention to particular persons. Performers might show off, and thus not only harm their souls, but erode congregational singing as well. Supporting these concerns, the school endorsed the habits of the church—even rejecting sheet music. LMS emphasized group singing from Mennonite hymn books. Several courses in music were offered, as well as a chorus for all. Public music programs, however, were off limits.

For similar reasons dramas and plays were forbidden. Acting violated integrity when actors appeared to be someone else. Drama was artificial—not a genuine expression of life. Moreover, public schools sponsored questionable plays and dramas. For all of these reasons drama belonged offstage in a Mennonite school.

Competitive sports, soaring in popularity in the public schools, were much discussed, but unwelcome. Intramural games—basketball, ping-pong, baseball, quoits and checkers—flourished. Competitive interscholastic sports with winners and losers, all-stars and score cards were ill-fitted for a life of modesty and simplicity. Moreover, the "all absorbing" demands of such sports hindered academic excellence and spiritual growth. Talking to students in the first year, Noah Good argued for balance. "Go into your athletic periods with zest and vigor . . . and bring out a good sweat . . . You'll become flabby and lazy without exercise." But, he added, the school has "no interest in having the best teams in various sports, undefeated for the greatest number of times. We are interested in the health of pupils, pleasant times . . . high standards . . . usefulness, and loyalty to the church and to God."[15]

The Big Day

The fall of 1942 was the worst of times to open a school. Strict tire quotas and scarce gasoline supplies disrupted travel. Patriotic fervor ran high. Three days before the school opened, the front page of the *Intelligencer Journal* carried a large hunting license. It entitled Marines to "hunt or trap yellow, Japanese slant-eyed rats—no bag limit."[16] Victory gardens flourished. Victory stickers on windshields identified patriotic drivers who saved fuel by sharing rides with others. On September 3, the first daylight air raid vacated Penn Square in Lancaster city in minutes. A newspaper editorial proposed that the "thorny objector problem" could be solved by forcing "objectors" to serve as noncombatants in the armed forces.[17] The war effort brought labor shortages. School districts raided each other for teachers. Twenty-five one-room schools begged for teachers a week before classes.

The war gave the Mennonites a surprising break. Struggling against the odds to ready their campus, they discovered that public schools planned to delay their opening two weeks to finish the harvest. Because of dire labor shortages, an army of 13,000 county children picked tomatoes, dug potatoes and cut tobacco before opening their books. LMS opened its registration lines on Monday, September 14, 1942.[18] With only 60 registered ahead of time, officials were "tired and perplexed" but extremely pleased to welcome 151 new students. The flood of students forced a revision of schedules and teaching assignments.

More beds were quickly ordered for the 60 dormitory students. The Harvey Weaver family lived adjacent to the campus. They learned after registration day that instead of four "dorm girls," eight would fill their third floor rooms. Tuition for the year was $135 for commuters and $245 for five-day dorm students. Twelve of the students transferred from Eastern Mennonite School in Virginia. Although many young Mennonites were still in public schools, officials were pleased with the turnout.[19]

Generous goodwill bolstered the school's early days. Congregations canned some 1200 quarts of vegetables, fruit and chow chow. They also donated large quantities of fresh apples and pears. Sewing circles in many congregations made tea towels, draperies, washcloths, sheets and comforters galore. Attorney Wenger donated a ping-pong table. Others gave stoves, typewriters, furniture and eating utensils. Hundreds of parents and friends volunteered thousands of hours scraping walls, hanging paper, scrubbing floors, washing windows and wiring buildings.

The Staff

Staff members had been hurriedly hired in the early days of September. Head cook Hettie Musser, earning $13 a week plus room and board, was assisted by

In the early years school cooks served students a variety of foods canned by local Mennonites.

Dean Noah Good (foreground) and business manager Clyde Stoner work in their administrative suite on the first floor of the former Gardiner Hall in 1942.

Bessie Good. Sister Leah Kauffman served as matron for the girls and Brother Kenneth Fisher, an older student himself, supervised the dormitory boys. Kauffman and Fisher were charged to be "constantly alert to guard and guide the moral and spiritual lives" of the students. The trustees hired Sam Ressler for $95 a month as campus caretaker. Students were paid 30 cents an hour for kitchen work and other chores.

Three state-certified teachers were employed with annual salaries between $1,000 and $1,200. John Wenger, brother to the attorney, taught mathematics and Introduction to Bible. Lois Garber, daughter of mission leader Henry Garber, taught English, Old Testament Studies and, of course, Missions. "She was simply a marvelous teacher," said Ivan Glick nearly 50 years later. Teaching Latin and New Testament was "wonderful and sensitive" Edna Wenger of Bareville. The women were surprised, but pleased, to learn that they would teach Bible classes. But, within two years, all Bible courses were shuttled into the safety of male hands. The women "just naturally" told their classes to call them "Miss Wenger and Miss Garber." But by the second week of school they learned that all teachers and staff would be addressed as "Brother" or "Sister," a habit that continued until 1970. This trio of teachers jokingly called

The girls' gym class under the instruction of teacher Lois Garber in 1942-43.

themselves the "subsupervising committee."

Meanwhile, the official Supervising Committee was also laboring in the trenches of instruction. Clyde Stoner lectured on history and demonstrated the art of song leading to the boys. "J. P." Graybill, as he was called by students, taught a variety of Bible courses and woodworking. German and science courses were in Good's bailiwick. By this time Good had sold his home in Morgantown and moved his family into the miller's stone house on campus. He paid the trustees $17 a month for rent. Conveniently close to his work, the location was tempting for pranksters and sometimes awkward for Sister Good, who had to hang out the family wash in the face of student giggles.

The school began with a consecration service on Tuesday morning, September 15, 1942, in the second floor auditorium of the old barn. Nine of the 12 Lancaster bishops, a full contingent of trustees, as well as parents and friends gathered for the service. On the floor that once held hay and later the feet of dancing boys, students and faculty knelt to pray. Aging bishop Noah Mack opened by saying he "carried a burden for a school like this for over thirty years." Mack charged Principal Graybill with "exercising prayerful vigilance" in guarding "the doctrine and order of the church." The entire student body rose when Mack asked, "Would they submit graciously to the authority of the school and consecrate their lives to God?" After kneeling together for prayer, J. Paul gave a "stirring challenge" on the objectives of a Christian education.[20]

(left) Basketball in the upper floor of the auditorium/gym about 1943. Teacher John Wenger referees the game.

(right) Students Miriam Ebersole and Rhoda Krady, standing on the Mill Stream bridge, are clad in the typical dress of the early 1940s.

The Program

"From the beginning," said Noah Good, "we wanted to combine high academic standards with a definite church relatedness and Bible centeredness. We wanted to omit some so-called frills . . . we wanted our students to have science courses as good or better than they'd receive in public school." The small faculty of six offered some 30 different courses across four grade levels in the first year. Four courses each were taught in English, science, history/social studies and mathematics. Eight were given in Bible, two in German and three in Latin. In addition to two music courses, many students joined a "mixed chorus." Students took at least one Bible course per year. A one-year sequence of full-time biblical study was also offered. Physical education classes, required by the state, were also on the roster. Extracurricular offerings included nature study, typing, shop, homemaking, bird study, mission projects and oral expression. Agriculture, however, was missing.[21]

A devotional "watch" welcomed the day in the dormitories. Twenty-minute chapel services, directed by J. Paul, prefaced the daily routine. Tuesday mornings featured a special hour-long chapel. A student program provided levity for the last class session each Friday. Divided into six 50-minute periods,

Students walk between classes on the new campus.

classes ended at 3:50 p.m. Evening prayer circles and devotional talks inspired dormitory students. For senior student Paul Kraybill, the refurbished old campus, after sleeping for 20 years, offered "a Rip Van Winkle experience" as students, like the Yeates boys of earlier years, hopped over puddles on cinder pathways.

Some 600 visitors swarmed over the campus for an open house following the school's dedication on November 27, 1942.[22] Visiting bishop John Lapp preached the dedication sermon. Homemade signs in the girls' dorm welcomed guests to the "Dew Drop Inn" and "The Bettie-Mae Shoppe." Throughout the year, church leaders, eager to inspect the new venture, came from as far away as Canada and Virginia. Daniel Kauffman, editor of the churchwide periodical *Gospel Herald*, whose *Doctrines of the Bible* would be used in "Bible Doc" classes into the '70s, also stopped by. And surprise of surprises, Ernest Miller, president of liberal Goshen College, spoke in chapel. Bishops and ministers frequented the campus, eager to check the pulse of the new undertaking. School closed for the fall meeting of Lancaster Conference, high point on the local Mennonite calendar. Milton Brackbill conducted week-long revival meetings in March 1943. Speaking in an extended chapel, bishop Stoner Krady taught the students a new chorus:

Thank you Lord for saving my soul;
Thank you Lord for making me whole;
Thank you Lord for giving to me,
Thy great salvation, so rich and free.

In the winter of 1943 the special Ephrata Bible school relocated along the Mill Stream. Forty-eight short-term students moved into campus dormitories for six weeks. Parallel with the high school program, the Bible school offered daytime, evening and weekend courses to over 200 students. On a stormy night in the midst of the special Bible school the electrical transformer blew out. Students blundered around with candles and flashlights. Others pushed cars out of muddy, yet-unpaved driveways. The spirit of adventure continued as later in the term several competitive basketball games erupted between dormitory and special term students.

Creative Diversions

With the rushed fall opening, faculty worries focused on the new academic program, not on recreation. With few facilities, no competitive games and a heavy academic program, students sought relief from the press of their studies. Paul Glick, sent to LMS by his parents, was particularly restless. Occasionally sporting a long tie and black derby, he drove several girls to school each day in his 1929 Model A Ford. Always eager for fun, he welcomed a dare to drive his old jalopy up the steps of the Classroom Building. Popping the clutch, to the cheers of his peers, he bounced the old flivver, step by step, up to the porch. Bored with academic duties and with a keen knack for annoying authorities,

A study session on the steps of the Administration Building in the early 1940s.

A martin birdhouse was placed atop the lower half of the old flagpole. Noah Good's home is in the background.

Glick also brought a flag to school in mid-November. Declaring it a patriotic wartime duty, he tied the national emblem to the rope on the old Yeates flagpole standing in the center of campus. With three girls, including a bishop's daughter, singing "The Star Spangled Banner," Old Glory rose to prominence. "J. P." was not amused—not with dedication services and open house a few days away. As classes ended that day, teacher John Wenger asked Glick to bring Old Glory down. "Oh, no," said Glick. "In wartime the flag flies around the clock." And fly it did for three historic days until janitor Sam Ressler pulled it down.

Meanwhile, the Supervising Committee, frightened by the incident, discussed it with the Religious Welfare Committee. In a joint meeting they searched for a solution.[23] Because "many people are flag-conscious," they hoped "to avoid outside pressure." Some committee members thought they should fly a "moderate size" flag rather than "have a patriotic order place one here and publicize the fact in the newspapers." They finally decided to leave the matter rest, "as quietly as possible and not place a flag on the pole at present."

Pondering the matter on his way home, Religious Welfare Committee member bishop Amos Horst—a carpenter by trade—found a happy solution. A few days later he told the trustees, "I already did it, so I hope you approve it!" Horst had brought a large purple martin birdhouse to campus. He instructed Sam Ressler to saw off the top half of the pole and mount the birdhouse. And so from the pole where Old Glory had flown, martins now would fly. It was a more fitting, a more comfortable centerpiece for a nonresistant school.

Birds, however, could be troublesome in other ways. On his way to school one day Paul Glick caught an old black starling in the fog. Pleased with his catch, he sold it to another student who concealed it in a paper bag and dared sophomore class president Eli Miller to release it in chapel. Miller opened the bag while "J. P. was praying around the world." The harsh shriek of the terrified bird flapping at a window in those solemn moments brought prompt expulsion to Glick, who, authorities soon learned, had caught the starling. Free now to follow his heart Glick entered basic training two months later to prepare for a stint in military intelligence. Eli Miller received a demerit and lost his class office for opening the bag. It was also Miller, who on another occasion drank a bottle of ink on a 58-cent dare, after checking with Noah Good to make sure that ink wasn't poisonous. In Miller's words, "It took a whole box of cough drops to take the awful taste out of my mouth."

The Religious Welfare Committee and the Supervising Committee agreed that students must have "some sort of diversion from secular subjects." They considered games, tournaments and, yes, even "carefully supervised contests." They agreed for one diversion to permit boys to trap muskrats along the Mill Stream. There were other diversions as well. Carloads of dorm boys drove to nearby farms where they picked corn and trenched celery after school in the fall months. Missionary adventures and nature stories dominated the talks and dreams of students. This campus is a "happy, hurry-scurry place," observed student Rhoda Krady, as students scampered here and there on cinder paths.

Early morning hikes and sunrise splashes in the Mill Stream provided other diversions. There were debates and poetry readings, as well as nursery rhyme recitations in Latin. The famous orations of Brutus and Antony were given in

The first edition of the student paper, **The Millstream,** *was published in January 1943. The format changed in 1959-60.*

one of the Friday student programs. The physics class broke the academic monotony with a field trip to the Franklin Museum in Philadelphia. Teaching German in the science room annex of the old barn one day, Brother Good left the guinea pigs out of their cage on the lab table for an afternoon snack. One of the pigs nearly upset an acid bottle to Good's horror and the students' delight.

There were other diversions as well. Candy consumption in the school store soared to such heights by February that the Supervising Committee asked Brother Stoner to devise a plan to limit its use. By mid-year the library had 371 books, partially keeping an October promise to provide an "abundance of reading matter." A student journal, the *Millstream*, made its debut in January of 1943, under the guidance of Edna Wenger.[24] J. Paul Graybill felt the journal's name was too pretentious and doubted it would survive. However, by year's end he told the trustees that it was already paying its own way without advertisements. Wenger advised student editors until 1956.

A system of merits and demerits reinforced desirable habits. Driving off campus without permission yielded two demerits. Making a ruckus in chapel brought one demerit and loss of class office. Sneaking out dormitory windows at night was worth a warning. Other deviant acts brought a ban on outdoor

The Millstream staff, 1942-43. Paul N. Kraybill, editor, is on the front left.

athletics or ping-pong for a week.

Two couples who "confessed to seriously violating dormitory regulations on a Sunday evening" were expelled for their misconduct—holding hands and kissing. Disturbed by what they considered "an outrageous overreaction," the dormitory boys signed a petition protesting the dismissal. Although "J. P." believed in yielding, he was not about to yield to student opinion. The boys who signed the petition were asked to "submit a written apology for the same." The ringleader of the petition, refusing to apologize, was expelled from the dorm and finished the school year living at home.

The discovery of a letter filled with "immoral suggestions" written by a dorm girl to a male student brought a full search of her room. A cache of 14 more letters was "sufficient evidence" for dismissal. The surprised girl was taken by "J. P." in his car to her startled father, tending his produce market in Lancaster. Seven years later she wrote to Graybill, apologizing. "I'm sorry for all that happened. God has forgiven me and I'm sure you will too."[25]

A Monument to God's Grace

Commencement on June 1, 1943, celebrated a graduating class of 16. Student numbers had dwindled slightly. Some left for ill health or farm work,

The first graduating class, June 1943.

others lost interest and six were expelled. Shortly after graduation, sophomore pranksters were sobered to learn that a bull had gored to death classmate Harold Kennel on his father's farm.

The senior class song, "Onward and Upward With Christ," was sung to the tune of "The Son of God Goes Forth to War." The last lines of the senior class poem read,

We'll clasp our hands with the King of Kings
And march on to victory!

The winds of war had penetrated the school's vocabulary even in its first year! But there were many spiritual victories and glorious testimonies of personal growth.

"Our hearts were touched," J. Paul told the trustees, "by the large body of students who have grown in loyalty to the church and the Lord." Jotting in his diary after week-long revival services, he noted, "Fifty stayed for afternoon meeting, lives changed—wrongs confessed." Surely the ambitious effort was paying off. Student testimonies concurred. Graduating senior Paul Kraybill, looking back nearly 50 years later, said, "The teachers had a tremendous impact on me. The year really brought alive a new sense of Christian calling and world mission. It exposed me to a whole new world." Another student, later serving in overseas missions, said, "I wouldn't be a missionary if I hadn't gone to LMS."

It was no small feat for rural folks to put a four-year, accredited high school on the map amidst the adversity of war. Some neighboring public high schools offered only two- and three-year programs of high school study. Moreover, the new school held the distinction of being the first freestanding Mennonite high school in the nation. Other Mennonite high schools, following on the heels of LMS, numbered 22 by 1991.[26]

Principal Graybill summed up the first year with a vision for the next 50. "May Lancaster Mennonite School ever remain a monument to the Grace of God, a place for the enrichment of lives, a training school for workers, a bulwark of whole Gospel truth, and an example of a church that honors the Lord by obedience to his Word, a life of self-denial and a life not conformed to this world."[27]

Drawing the Lines of Faithfulness

1943-1953

"We had a good time."

—*student Charles Longenecker*

Teach Me Thy Way, O Lord

The J. Paul Graybill era spanned 11 years (1942-53). The school carved out an identity, stabilized its academic program and established corporate habits that shaped its life into the '70s. A base of support jelled around the school. The biblical words, "Teach me thy way, O Lord," became the official motto, merging religious and educational missions. Enrollment doubled to 306 by the fall of 1952, with 70 graduates per year. By the spring of 1953 some 530 students

Faculty and administrators, 1943-44. Front row: Leah Kauffman, Edna Wenger, Lois Garber, Myra Hess. Back row: Mahlon Hess, John Wenger, J. Paul Graybill, Clyde Stoner, Noah Good.

had received diplomas. The professional staff of six swelled to 18 by the end of Graybill's tenure, with a total of 35 faculty laboring over the years.

Mahlon Hess, editor of the *Missionary Messenger*, arrived as boys' dorm manager and Bible teacher in 1943. He was a "stickler for details," remembers one student, "the sort of fellow that made you memorize the toes of kings in the Old Testament." In two years, Hess, off to African mission fields, was replaced by J. Lester Brubaker. Always a gentleman, courteous and polite, Brubaker taught two four-year stints with a one-year leave for study. Chaperone of the boys' dorm, he taught Old Testament, Oral Expression, English and music. Alumnus Charles Longenecker still feels the sting of the D he received in Brubaker's music class. Recalls another student, "He had an interesting laugh, but I can only remember good things about him."

In the school's fourth year Clyde Stoner headed into Civilian Public Service, so Martha Moseman arrived to teach the growing number of commercial courses. In the same year, 45-year-old Amos Weaver, a weaver by trade and name, joined the faculty. An ordained minister, Weaver taught Bible and served on the Supervising Committee in Stoner's absence. Teaching algebra and plane geometry was Clayton Keener, former varsity basketball player and public school principal. Keener arrived driving a '46 Hudson with a mattress and board for a back seat. His favorite adage, "Consistency, thou art a jewel," was proclaimed in plane geometry classes and elsewhere.

Dorm students enjoyed tapping messages to their friends on the water pipes stretching into John Wenger's classroom below their dorm rooms. After teaching five years, Wenger left to practice math in a family quarry business. Harvey Bauman, teaching science and Problems of Democracy, arrived in the fall of 1947. In the same year Amos Weaver added the student pastor role to his portfolio. Nature lover Lois Garber helped student speakers control their stage fright by reminding them that "an audience is just a bunch of cabbage heads." In the fall of 1950 students learned that she, along with Clayton Keener and his family, were sailing to the mission fields of Africa.

Avid bird watcher Donald Jacobs joined the faculty in the fall of '49. He taught music, physical education, shop, Bible, personal evangelism and, later, American History. With a keen intellect and a flare for fun, Jacobs taught his personal evangelism students the order of truth: "Facts, faith and then feeling." Sitting cross-legged on his desk, Jacobs engaged his students with stimulating lectures. Sometimes he would wave his arms and dash wildly to the window to glimpse a passing bird. He was also remembered for demonstrating cartwheels for his physical education classes on the school's front lawn.

With a flourishing program, students met new teachers each year. J. Irvin Leaman, considered for the assistant principal role, pastored students and taught Bible. Elton Moshier came from New York state along with India missionary Lloy Kniss. In fact, many teachers served as short-term missionaries in "home mission projects" in other states during summer months. Others left LMS for overseas mission assignments, and "returned" missionaries were often hired to teach. Stories of their work seasoned classroom discussions. (Over the years, several faculty—Mahlon Hess, J. Lester Brubaker, Paul Kraybill and later James Bomberger and Omar Eby—edited the conference periodical, *Missionary Messenger*, on a part-time basis.) By 1953, Edna Wenger was the lone survivor of the original full-time teachers. J. Paul Graybill became part-time principal in '52-'53, the last year of his tenure. Assistant principal Amos Weaver carried day-to-day operations.

No Snap Courses

Noah Good orchestrated the academic program. Called "Brother Good" in person and sometimes "Goody" behind his back, he often stood when teachers entered his office. "It was the kind of courtesy," said teacher Myra Hess, "that Mennonites needed to learn." "Goody," remembers one teacher, "was the throttle and J. P. held the brake on the school in those early years." In Good's own words, "I had an agreeable and very good relationship with Brother Graybill. He recognized lines of responsibility and thought I should lead the school academically. We didn't always see exactly alike, but it wasn't hard to get along." Having supervised plays and operettas in public school, Good admitted a bit of difficulty adjusting to LMS. "I wasn't sure a debating club was all that bad . . . but I tried to be loyal and cooperative and carry things out the way the Bishop Board and Conference wanted." He was a "bright academic light" recalled one student. "He was very patient," said another. "When he got upset, he got upset, but he waited a long time to do it." Early on he demonstrated another skill—catching flies barehanded without losing a beat in his lecture.

Commercial courses and a two-year Bible sequence were added in the school's second year under Good's leadership. The academic program, approved by the Pennsylvania Department of Public Instruction, split into three tracks: General, Commercial and two-year Bible. Most students took the General Course. The program required a Bible class each year, as well as music and electives. The Commercial track, oriented toward business education, included at least four courses in bookkeeping, typing and shorthand. When introducing a "Personal Use Typing" course, Good insisted, "It will be rigorous, not a snap course." Few students enrolled in the two-year Bible course. For the most part, they pursued the four-year diploma. The course titles in 1949-50, shown in Figure 4.1, profile the shape of the curriculum.[1] For transfer student Omar Eby, coming from the conservative Mennonite backwaters of Hagerstown, Maryland, the academic expectations felt stiff. The easy A's and B's of Hagerstown High became C's at LMS. But nonetheless, it was a "marvelous, wonderful" entry into a bigger world for Eby.

In addition to typical high school fare, the school promoted Bible classes,

Figure 4.1

Academic Course Distribution, 1949-1950

Academic Courses	Number
Agriculture	1
Bible	12
Business Education	10
English and Literature	4
Foreign Languages	6
Mathematics	6
Music	5
Science	4
Shop	1
Social Studies	5

Student being criticized *Sara Miller*

Criticism Blank

In the following groups I have checked your weak points and your strong points as I seem them. In certain groups I have not checked anything as you seem about average on these points. Several places I explain what I mean in the margin.

___ Irreverent
___ Cool and indifferent toward
     spiritual things
✓ Inspiring and enthusiastic
     Christian

___ Too fickle and light-hearted
✓ Pleasant and cheerful
___ Too serious

___ Stubborn and self-willed
✓ Unselfish

___ Lazy
___ Idles time away
✓ Industrious

___ Too easily irritated
✓ Emotionally well balanced

___ Rude and impolite
✓ Friendly
___ Courteous and thoughtful

___ Lack of respect for superiors
___ Merely tolerates authority
✓ Cooperative with superiors

___ Careless about clothes
___ Careless about cleanliness
✓ Neat in appearance and dress
___ Too much attention on clothes
     and style

___ Shirks responsibility
___ Dependable

___ Follows crowd too easily
✓ Courageous for the right

___ "One track" mind
✓ Variety of interests

___ Too self-conscious
___ Braggart
✓ Poised and at ease in society

___ Too talkative
___ Good conversationalist
✓ Too quiet *sometimes*

___ Poor English
___ Too much slang or loose talk
✓ Good command of proper English

___ Speaks too slowly
___ Speaks too fast
___ Poor enunciation
✓ Good speaker

___ Wasteful and careless with personal
     property
___ Poor respect for property of others
✓ Takes good care of property

___ Too much interest in the boys
___ Too much interest in the girls
✓ Well balanced in social interests

"Crit slips," used by students to evaluate their peers, reveal the esteemed values of the school's culture.

business and music. The Future Mennonite Farmers, formed in 1944, held club activities, field trips and demonstrations. In the eighth year, '49-'50, shop and agriculture were offered for credit. And while some students begged for a "full agricultural program," they would wait until 1973 for a certified "ag teacher" to arrive. Indeed, in the first decade the trustees frequently talked of the "farm problem." They struggled to integrate the fledgling farm operation—with its several hogs, hens and steers across the Mill Stream—into the school program. Student John Metzler argued that farming held a "missionary challenge." Even farmers, he said, could be missionaries at home and abroad. The lack of bloom in the agriculture program likely resulted from lukewarm administrative support and a feeling that farming skills could be learned at home.

By 1949 an elaborate "point system" tracked a student's "whole life."[12] Points—accumulated from grades, conduct, attendance and student activi-

Remington typewriters fill Clyde Stoner's classroom in the commercial building in the 1940s.

ties—paved the way for promotion each year. First and second honor rolls rested on surpassing 100 and 80 points respectively. Minor misconduct erased points. Major infractions yielded demerits—student horrors that cancelled *all* points in a quarter. The points had comprehensive tentacles. For instance: a grade of A equaled four points, the chorister of a student religious program received one point, the *Millstream* editor earned ten points and so forth. Moreover, points tracked social conduct, campus work and attendance. Athletics were conspicuously missing in the merit system. Physical fitness was encouraged but points were not awarded for winning games.

There were peer points to gain and lose as well. Each spring students could send "crit slips" with good or bad news to peers. The slips carried pleasant words, praise for smiles or personality traits, as well as stinging suggestions for improving dress, demeanor or etiquette. One student might receive several dozen slips and another just a few. Some students, 45 years later, remember messages and authors—especially negative ones.

Practical Beauty

"LMS is like a boy with outgrown clothes," said Amos Weaver in 1946.[3] The commencement audience that year packed the auditorium in the old barn. The overflow scattered into nearby classrooms. Several hundred sat in the dining room and others listened by way of a loud-speaker in the faraway classroom building. The expanding program stretched the seams of the old Yeates School. Already in the second year the cottage across the stream housed some eight dormitory girls and Sisters Garber and Hess. Several girls dormed in the second floor of Brother Good's home. They sometimes crocheted by candlelight far into the night under a table draped by blankets. In this way they avoided detection by Brother Good. With others living in neighboring homes, nearly half of the noncommuting girls lodged outside the dorm. The old Yeates mess hall had turned into a commercial building filled with Remington typewriters to bolster business education. An annex to the science room and dining hall was added to expand the auditorium/barn.

Frustrated by large crowds and packed dormitories, the trustees announced building plans in January of 1946. They envisioned a large 1200-seat auditorium surrounded by classrooms and dormitory rooms. Supporting the expansion, Moses Gehman told the trustees that "thinking Mennonites are thinking much more favorably about high school than they were five years ago."[4] The proposed building would accommodate an enrollment of 400 and the auditorium would host large church gatherings.[5] The 156-by-140 foot building was staked out in 1946 on high ground above the Mill Stream flood plain. Despite a kitty of $93,000, postwar building restrictions stalled the project until 1949.

In the fall of '47 chapel services shifted from the classroom building to the auditorium/barn.[6] The chapel transfer pushed physical education classes and athletics outdoors for several years. Outdoor courts for tennis, basketball and volleyball were quickly constructed. A year later a skating pond was carved out for winter fun near the classroom building. Happy memories of predawn and late-night skating encircle the pond. Hand-holding was taboo, however, while skating. In extremely cold weather students sometimes skated on the

The new girls' dormitory, the first facility built by Lancaster Mennonite School, opened in the fall of 1949.

Mill Stream to Bonholtzer's Dam two miles downstream. On these occasions, school officials grudgingly permitted boys and girls to hold hands provided, of course, that one of the pair wore gloves.

In the fall of '47 the bishops urged the trustees to press forward with the new building, "since our people are in an unprecedented period of prosperity."[7] Finally in January of 1949 the trustees approved plans for a sharply trimmed building that offered living space for 100 girls, as well as limited indoor recreation. The proposed auditorium would need to await the construction of a chapel nine years later. Built by Mennonite contractor Abram Horst, the $142,000 dormitory welcomed girls in the fall of 1949. Describing the "good taste" of the austere brick building, Noah Good said, "A strong, safe and durable building without ornamental or decorative work fits our Mennonite concept of practical beauty."[8]

As the girls moved into their new quarters, the trustees were shocked by another development. A drive-in theatre was planned east of their property.[9] Curious girls might sneak a look from their second floor windows and courageous boys might sneak over fences. Consulting Attorney Wenger, the board hoped to lodge a protest, only to learn that it was "too late to do anything." Later, however, the trustees rejected a request to place utility poles on the school property to service the drive-in theatre.

A Good Time

The campus ethos, strict and orderly in the late '40s and '50s, "was lubricated with lots of independent students," remembers Charles Longenecker. "We had a good time." Students cherish warm memories of leisurely lunch times. They played ball, strolled the campus, ran races and socialized at will. Strolling, however, could not cross gender lines. Although free to "mingle," private conversations between boys and girls were off limits. The dining hall served as a mixer. Boys and girls selected random numbers for weekly seat assignments around family-style tables. A secluded spot behind the book rack in the library provided private space to meet and whisper romantic words beyond the scrutiny of Sister Edna Wenger's eyes. Seven-day dorm students could obtain "courtship privileges" once a week if they were 18 years of age. Dorm girls speculated weeks in advance about which boy might invite them to pull candy at the winter taffy pulls. A whisper, a smile, a note, a nod or subtle wave was the language of romance. Hettie Musser, "King of the Cookstove," was once accused of putting castor oil in the apple crisp to curb the "boy craziness" of girls. Confronted with the rumor, she blushed and vehemently denied it.

Students explored their interests and the world in "secular" clubs and

Dormitory students in the dining hall on the ground floor of the auditorium/gym in 1948. Food was served family-style.

*The cover of the first **Laurel Wreath,** printed in 1946, was designed by senior Naomi Kennel.*

The 1952 senior class trip to Washington, D. C.

extracurricular activities. The student yearbook, the *Laurel Wreath*, made its debut in 1946 with the first graduating four-year class. Club activities included needle craft, art appreciation, first aid, stylus, oral expression, campus improvement, nature study, agriculture and homemaking. Classes and clubs took excursions to the Franklin Institute in Philadelphia, museums in Washington D.C., the Hershey Chocolate factory, the Ephrata Cloister, the state Capitol in Harrisburg and many other sites. Several boys, in the fall of '52, excused themselves to hear Presidential candidate "Ike" speak at a whistle-stop at the Lancaster train station.

Annual spring outings often featured a rope-pulling tug of war, a picnic in the meadow across the stream and a story around a campfire. All-night chess games, played in tiny closets, added spice to student life.

Off campus social life flourished as well. Popular activities included straw rides on farm wagons—disapproved by the Supervising Committee—and social gatherings at the homes of friends. Some hosts of overnight parties remember packing six girls into one bed. The class of '46 had a "great big feast" at Kenny Lehman's home. A good singer, Lehman entertained the crowd by singing and playing "Old Man River" for the crowd on his family's baby grand piano. A few months after graduation, walking near his home, Lehman was struck and killed by an auto. Classmates returned and sang together at his funeral.

Tragedy also struck the campus itself. On the impulse of a dare to swim across the flooding Mill Stream, sophomore Alvin Yost plunged into the swirling waters in the spring of 1952. Cheering students on the Mill Stream bridge suddenly fell silent as powerful undercurrents pulled Yost beneath the water. Emergency lights flooded the Bonholtzer Dam throughout the night as teachers and students searched in vain for the body. Rescue workers recovered his body two days later above the dam. Reflecting on the pain, students bowed "in humble submission" to God's will. The *Millstream* concluded that "the Lord's ways are right and good."[10] The Supervising Committee decided that the tragedy itself was ample punishment for those who made the dare.

Evangelize or Fossilize

A religious rhythm regulated campus life. A "morning watch" for private devotions opened the dormitory day. Daily chapel services prefaced classes for dorm students and commuters alike. The Student Religious Program, an extended chapel on Tuesdays, was led by students. "Prayer circles" proliferated. A half-hour girls' circle, as well as one for the boys, assembled each evening. On Thursday evening, dormitory students mingled in a conjoint prayer circle. A day student circle welcomed commuters once a week. In addition, the entire class of one particular year gathered in monthly prayer meetings. A sense of

A group of underclassmen socialize between classes in the early '50s.

missionary excitement also pervaded the air. Souls were dying without Christ in mission fields from Africa to Alabama. Teachers reminded students that Jesus might actually return this year. It was an exciting time to serve the Lord.

Spiritual sensitivities peaked each semester in the two-week revival services held in chapel by visiting evangelists. One student remembers the typical theme was "repent for the kingdom of God is at hand." Indeed, the school had accepted the gift of a large sign which they placed beside the Lincoln Highway. It proclaimed, "Repent and believe the Gospel, now is the day of salvation." Students in the revivals were called to a personal, saving relationship with Jesus Christ. Many of the rebellious and the cocky were born again. Those already committed confessed sin and recommitted their lives to God's will. Evangelists pled for students to "lay their all on the altar" and "fully surrender themselves wholly unto the Lord."

The mysterious moving of the Spirit in these emotionally charged moments sometimes led to extended sessions that nibbled into the academic schedule. Souls were saved, sins confessed and hundreds of students vowed to more fully commit their lives to Christ. One student, in a typical testimony, said, "I never felt so happy in all my life." God sometimes moved in mysterious ways to bring repentance. A group of highway cowboys, including Paul Landis and Herbert Minnich, commuted to and from school. Speeding to school one morning near the present State Police Headquarters, the cowboys slid sideways onto a lawn to miss a car that swerved in front of them. Later that morning, as the revivalist gave the altar call, all four went forward to make scared, but sincere commitments that became "real turning points" in their lives.

The faculty sometimes met with the visiting evangelist for prayer after school. In some cases faculty feared that student testimonies weren't sincere. The Supervising Committee debated whether or not publicly confessed sins merited a demerit. Evangelists sometimes pressed hard for confession of hidden sins—sins which some students thought could only be masturbation. Indeed, a boys' hall manager noted that after revivals foul language and hitting each other in "private parts" declined. For the most part, the revivals united the campus, transformed lives and energized students for missions.

The distribution of gospel tracts was a major mission activity across the church in this era. Visiting evangelist Ralph Palmer, who personally handed out 325,000 tracts in 1950, told glowing testimonies of the way God used gospel tracts to convert the wayward to salvation. *Forty-Eight Hours in Hell*—one of many tracts floating around the campus—described the journey of a person who claimed to have experienced the torment of eternal damnation. The Sunshine Sowers, a tract band, provided students many opportunities "to witness for the

The Tract Club gathers to float bottles stuffed with Gospel tracts down the Mill Stream.

Lord." *The Way*, a small weekly gospel tract, was folded and distributed to homes in Lancaster city. One year the club randomly selected 250 names from the New York city telephone directory and mailed them *The Way*. Another time the tract band stuffed copies of *The Way* into bottles and floated them down the Mill Stream, hoping unsaved souls would experience the joys of salvation.

J. Paul Graybill told students the church must either evangelize or fossilize. Motivated by the great commission, students eagerly "witnessed for the Lord" in ways that led others "to a saving knowledge of Jesus Christ." Evangelistic activities animated the campus. Letters from missionaries describing the remarkable moving of the Holy Spirit in African revivals were eagerly read and discussed. A variety of religious clubs offered outlets for the spiritual energy stirred by revivals. A Christian service club took students to minister to "shut-ins." One year an "itinerant evangelism" trailer, headed for Mennonite missions in the southern states, stopped on campus for several days. Students contributed $197 toward its journey. Although the school cloistered students from "rampant evils" in the public schools, it also stretched their vision and thrust them outward to "mission fields" in other states and foreign lands.

Drawing Sacred Lines

In clubs, classes and religious programs, students in the late '40s and early '50s debated the issues of their elders. Should Mennonites raise tobacco? Is it "consistent" to own life insurance? What are the dangers of radio? What is the world? What does nonconformity to the world mean? How does one discover

Merrill Derstine, Allen Beiler and Kenton Brubaker sport the styles of 1949-50 outside the dining hall.

God's will? And while students debated the theoretical lines between right and wrong, the elders of the school drew real ones. With many social changes afoot in the postwar prosperity, firm lines were etched into campus life to teach the Lord's way. The lines of understanding offered space for change, yet curtailed the drift toward worldliness.

Skating on the pond was taboo on Sunday. Students could attend the Pennsylvania Farm Show, but only if accompanied by parents. A scarf could replace a bonnet for girls with chronic health problems, but not a worldly bandanna. Boys were permitted to remove their sweaters and jackets in warm weather, but they were not allowed to roll up their sleeves and unbutton their shirt collars. "Incidental" basketball games with outside teams were permissible, but not organized ones. Boys could watch girls play basketball on the outdoor courts, but not in the auditorium/gym. "LMS Pennants" were inappropriate for a plain school. Quartets and duos were off limits, but larger octets and sextets which masked individual display were acceptable in the '50s. By 1952 "graded" sheet music was permissible in classrooms.

A wire recorder, used to record public sermons, could not be used, said the trustees, in the boys' prayer circle. Clerical classes, however, sometimes practiced their shorthand skills by listening to sermons on the wire recorder. The trustees contended that a portable phonograph for classroom use was not fitting. By a secret ballot of ten to six, the trustees in 1948 allowed Lois Garber to show "missionary slides" from a recent trip.[11] A year later, however, the bishops ruled that showing slides of nature scenes at LMS was not advisable "because the dangers involved in such a step" might lead to Hollywood movies.[12]

The class of 1950 proposed an arch over the main entrance to the school as their class gift. Although the trustees welcomed gifts, they concluded that this one "was not justifiable since it served no useful purpose. A more useful gift would be more consistent." That more useful and consistent gift came in the form of two sandstone pillars by the entrance way.[13] No, J. Lester Brubaker was told, his Oral Expression class could not practice the formalities of a tea "since this is not consistent with the practices of our rural people." A program on dining room etiquette, said the Supervising Committee, would be more "appropriate."[14] The trustees agreed to post "No Hunting" signs around the meadows if they could secure ones "without a legal clause threatening the prosecution of violators."

Working closely with the county superintendent of schools, the school was careful to meet educational requirements for state approval. But when invited to join the Mennonite Council on Secondary Education, the trustees decided

Officers of the class of 1946 on graduation day. Left to right: Ruth Shue, Ivan Charles, Daniel Krady, Katherine Hertzler.

Mabel Weaver, Jean Kraybill and Dorothy Reifsnyder rolling the campus lawn in 1949. The old mill (boys' dorm and classroom building) is in the background.

"to stay out of it."[15] Lancaster Mennonite Conference was not formally affiliated with the Mennonite church at large and since the Council was headquartered in the progressive Midwest, it was best, the trustees reasoned, to stay aloof. Thus, school officials struggled to draw the lines of faithfulness, charting the path between right and wrong, rightly dividing the word of truth.

Irregularities

Despite an abundance of carefully drawn lines, Supervising Committee minutes note frequent "irregularities" of conduct—pranks and mischief. As in any school, students and sometimes teachers tested the boundaries—sometimes in fun, other times innocently and even at times maliciously. Irregularities even appeared in the midst of the holy of holies itself—the Supervising Committee. After the first year Clyde Stoner quietly laid aside his frock-tail coat for a regular plain coat. One day Stoner noticed that even Noah Good was wearing dark blue socks instead of the prescribed black ones. Moreover, a "fantastic report" spread across campus of teachers playing checkers during chapel and even betting on the games! The Supervising Committee promptly called the faculty to a special meeting which J. Paul opened with prayer. After thrashing the matter out, the Committee concluded the reports were only "exaggerated rumors."[16] Later the trustees were shocked to learn that in the spring of '49 a faculty member had encouraged boys to travel to Philadelphia to see big league baseball games. The board expressed "grief that such conditions existed in the school" and asked the Religious Welfare Committee to thoroughly investigate.[17]

The rules and regulations, argued Clayton Keener, should be carefully enforced or else changed. "I'm not morally opposed to chewing gum," he said but the regulation against chewing gum which is "flagrantly violated" should be dropped if it's not enforced.[18] Schoolish irregularities of graffiti, foul language and tripped fire alarms marred the purity of an otherwise placid campus. Noah Good reported that some boys used wild, worldly and unchristian names for their ball teams.[19] And he told the trustees in 1950 that young Mennos were driving fast and recklessly through the campus on Sunday evenings.[20]

Even girls were driving recklessly. The Shirk twins, Mary and Betty, took an impulsive drive around the softball field in the midst of a game as they headed home. A base runner was startled as she slid into their car and injured her ankle. The twins were aghast. They were merely on a joyride. Such irregularities deserved a demerit, said the Supervising Committee. Father Shirk, who believed in matching school penalties with home punishment, extended mercy after concluding the twins had suffered enough.

Girls who weren't showing off their driving skills were showing their speed with pink strings on their coverings. And one year an unthinkable report circulated of senior girls smoking. Teacher Harvey Bauman was particularly perturbed by some junior girls in '52 who "periodically erupted with formal cheers" at an after-school ball game. The cheers were written out, he said, " in rhyme—the nonsense, ridiculing type used in public school."[21]

A rash of infractions hit the campus in the spring of '52.[22] A dozen fellows, some progeny of ministers and bishops, were openly rebellious. They were charged with smoking, telling filthy stories, loitering in cars, playing pinball machines while traveling to school, and even betting. After a class outing, some met dates off campus and headed to New Holland to play miniature golf, where Parke Miller's "taxi" was reportedly seen. Some confessed their sins in chapel and others remained rebellious. In a campus-wide crackdown, the Discipline Committee awarded demerits to many and withheld diplomas from others. Such were the irregularities in those days that tantalized students and sometimes broke the hearts of caring administrators.

The Husk of Separation

Throughout the Graybill era the school struggled to maintain dress regulations. Edna Wenger remembers J. Paul comparing plain dress to the husk on an ear of corn. "The husk isn't worth very much, it's only husk. But you never saw a good ear of corn that didn't have husk on it. You need the husk to protect the corn. The husk isn't important, yet, it is important." Boys were "encouraged" to wear hats to and from school in warm weather and were continually reminded that hats were "required" from late November to April. Sleeves could not be rolled and shirt collars had to remain buttoned.

Distressed with a growing number of brown shoes and sporty stockings on boys, J.Paul urged them to stick with black. "I know this may be a small thing to you, yet it symbolizes the Christian modesty and meekness which becomes the lowly followers of the Lord."[23] Black female students from Philadelphia rather liked the black stockings, remembers Omar Eby, in contrast to others who openly pined for flesh-colored hose. Girls had to be reminded year after year to wear their bonnets to and from school. Indeed, said J. Paul, to appear in public wearing a covering without a bonnet reflects "a boldness that does

Students leave the front door of the Administration Building about 1945.

not characterize modesty and womanly reserve." Loud colors, gaudy prints and fancy collars on dresses appeared virtually each year and students were rebuked again and again.

Speaking to the girls about skirts, Mahlon Hess was startled to hear chortles of laughter when he mistakenly said skirts should hang midway between thigh and knee. The preferred line, midway between knee and ankle, became a perpetual but ambiguous battleground. Certain that hemlines were rising and angered that students were neglecting counsel, administrators issued an edict declaring that dresses must meet the midway line on the very next day. Distressed that their hems could not be lowered enough, a cluster of girls sewed ruffles on their skirts overnight. Cackles of laughter from boys the next day brought embarrassed blushes. Insulted, the girls boycotted classes for a day and won the support of sympathetic teachers who argued on their behalf. Embarrassed by long dresses hanging beneath their coats, girls riding the public bus from Paradise to LMS sought relief. To avoid public jeers, they lifted their hems by tying cords around their waists and then removed the ropes at school. Still other girls wore fashionable shoes while riding the bus and exchanged them for black ones upon arriving on campus.

Those were the days, remarked an ex-Mennonite, when some preachers made you feel like you were going straight to hell if you wore a necktie. Looking back, Edna Wenger mused, "I'm surprised we could get the girls to dress that way, with ribbons on their coverings and hair parted in the middle. We were making them dress like their grandmothers, even more conservative than their mothers." The Mennonite church in the Lancaster area shuddered with shifting crosscurrents in the late '40s and early '50s. Pockets of disgruntled members, distressed by rigid dress rules, the ban on radios and the taboo on quartets in worship, among other things, spun off and formed new congregations unaffiliated with the Conference.[24] The *Rules and Discipline* of the Conference were tightened in the fall of '43, the school's second year. Eleven years later in September of 1954 The *Rules and Discipline* were revised again. This version, in some aspects, was even more strict than the one of 1943.[25] The '40s and '50s were two of the more stringent decades of the twentieth century as the Mennonite church coped with the social changes spurred by industrialization.

J. Paul Graybill, conscientious bishop that he was, struggled to keep the school in line with Conference standards. He was a spiritual watchman, not about to float downstream with the drifting tide of the times. But the burden was growing heavy. In a chapel message on November 16, 1951, he poured out his heart.[26] "A week ago today I was in bed and had a good bit of misery. I spent time crying over the school . . . don't think I am hard, this is not an upstart of today. . . . Some of these convictions are 25 years old, long before the school began. You cannot charge me with flying off the handle. I may have been firm, but I was always kind. . . . I hear it talked about me, that it is just me. Personally, I'll forgive anyone, but I am set for the defense of the regulations no matter how much talk." He went on to explain that back in the '20s a large church school (Goshen College) closed down because of liberalism. "I don't want that ever to happen to LMS."

Then he drew a line. Those who do not wish to comply with the regulations, "we ask you to stay away from school. We are not going to chase after each one." Graybill then reminded students of the written regulations. Parting the hair in the middle for girls, high neck lines, no lace on collars, no frills on capes, no short sleeves and so on. He pled for them to obey. "Obey even though you don't fully understand. Obedience is a characteristic of the child of God. . . . In other churches people who say they are spiritual wear finger rings and favor going to the army." He closed by reminding them that it was a heart matter. "Surrender on these points . . . and you will have a flood of God's grace come into your heart. Yield entirely and see what the Lord will do for you."[27]

It was a turning point for Graybill. Six weeks later, two days after Christmas in 1951, he resigned. The school he had argued for and prayed for was, he believed, like many congregations, drifting downstream. It was too painful for him to bear.

The End of an Era

Early in 1952 the bishops appointed Amos Weaver assistant principal after convincing Graybill to continue as a nominal principal for another year. Unfortunately, Graybill's health "failed rather completely during the Christmas holidays" of '52. He was on campus very little in the spring of '53, the last semester of his tenure.[28]

Graybill, recalls a teacher, would sometimes spank students emotionally, projecting his guilt on them in chapel talks. Carrying a keen sense of accountability to God and to the church for the welfare of the school, he became defensive near the end of his tenure. Hearing complaints in the faculty room, a young teacher approached Graybill privately, only to be confronted with the retort, "So you think I'm not running the school right?" Caught in a social vise, Graybill was pressured from multiple sides.

Many in his home bishop district of Weaverland opposed high school education, including church high schools. Having argued persistently the importance of high school, he had to persuade the conservatives, even prove to them, that a church controlled high school would not lead to pride and worldliness. With the bishops, who had entrusted him with this dangerous venture, he had to demonstrate that the school by the Mill Stream would not go the way of worldly Goshen College. Personally, he was fully persuaded that a school with high religious standards could help the church pass on the faith and resist the wayward drift toward worldliness. With a keen sense of anointing, he carried an awesome accountability to God for his stewardship of the school. No one doubted that, despite his gloomy appearance, J. Paul cared deeply about LMS. Now, some 50 years later, even the ringleader of the boys' petition in the first year hopes that Graybill's enormous contribution to the school will be honored in the memories of students.

With a sense of sadness, J. Paul told Amos Weaver, " I hope you will be more successful than I was," as he handed over the gavel.[29] He found some satisfaction in knowing that "Amos Weaver thinks pretty much like I do." There were, of course, many reasons for praise. Five hundred and thirty-three graduates had joined the ranks of the Alumni Association, begun in 1943-'44. In his final report spanning the 11 years of his tenure, Graybill noted that three graduates had already been ordained to the ministry. A "goodly number," noted Graybill, were in mission work. More than 130 served as Sunday school teachers, 61 as church and Sunday school officers, and 62 were leading church youth groups. Hundreds of others labored in service occupations, and dozens had entered college. "A few left the church," Graybill said, "but, in a world of relative things, we can expect that."[30] Dozens of testimonials in the pages of the *Millstream* and hundreds of alumni hearts affirmed the words of '50 graduate, Jean Kraybill Shenk, "LMS was a great place. I thank God for the privilege of attending all four years and appreciate my parents' willingness to sacrifice so I could go."

CHAPTER FIVE

Expanding the Vision

1953-1967

"Thinking is a noble and divine occupation."
—*Amos Weaver*

Sputnik Days

The school grew steadily in the 14-year period from 1954 to 1967. By the twenty-fifth anniversary in 1967 three new buildings stood on campus and the student body had swelled to 560. Amos Weaver served a ten-year stint as principal from the fall of '53 through the spring of '63. Returning from missionary work in Africa, bishop Clayton Keener took the helm from '63 to '67. With principals coming through the turnstiles, internal operations revolved more and more around the dean's office. "He was the main figure," said one teacher. "Everyone thought of it as Noah Good's school."

During this period the country enjoyed pleasant postwar prosperity with Eisenhower in the White House. Technological progress brought automatic

Hundreds of Mennonites attended the Brunk Tent Crusades in the 1950s. This one is located at the old Lancaster Airport along the Manheim Pike, June 1951.

transmissions, electric typewriters, televisions, dishwashers and power mowers to American homes. International developments were less pleasant in those years. American-Soviet relations were freezing. Amos Weaver, taking office in 1953, said, "The world's on fire with communistic atheism." The fear of invading communist troops disturbed the otherwise pleasant dreams of Mennonite children. To clarify God's endorsement of the United States the phrase "One nation under God" slipped into the pledge of allegiance. The Soviets startled the world by launching Sputnik into a space orbit in 1957. LMS students, frightened by the Cuban missile crisis of November of 1962, listened to transistor radios as they walked between classes, worried the world might explode.

As rising numbers of Lancaster Mennonites entered nonfarm occupations the debate shifted from the merits of a high school education to the pros and cons of college. Church members were becoming increasingly entwined with the larger culture and enjoying the prosperity spreading across the land. Thus Mennonite leaders in the '50s wrestled with a variety of issues threatening to blur the church's separation from the world.

Among other questions, they asked if the use of special music groups—trios, quartets and choruses—in worship services would erode four-part congregational singing? Were cape dresses and plain suits really biblical essentials? Would televisions and radios funnel secular ideas into Mennonite homes and dilute spiritual commitment? Might showing slides and motion pictures in church auditoriums lead members to Hollywood movies? If individual cups replaced the common cup in communion services, would congregational unity wither? Did the Bible really require men and women to sit apart in worship services? Would less kneeling for prayer signal a decline in humility? Did the Revised Standard Version of the Bible threaten biblical inspiration? Were women disobeying biblical teaching when they cut their hair?

Church leaders struggled to follow biblical injunctions and respect historic Mennonite ways in the midst of rapid changes. To deter the drift toward mainstream culture, elders organized "Nonconformity Conferences" to undergird biblical principals of separation from the world.[1] But as one sage noted, by the time study conferences were organized the water was already over the dam. The '50s were also times of spiritual renewal. Tent meetings, conducted several weeks each summer by the Brunk brothers and later by Myron Augsburger, stirred hundreds of confessions and renewed Mennonite commitments. Convicted by the powerful revivalists, some farmers publicly promised to stop raising tobacco.

Tethered to the board of bishops in its first 25 years, LMS was steered by conservative, but not ultra-conservative, sentiments in the church. School trustees from '53 to '67 all wore plain suits even though many men across the conference never wore or had shed their regulation coats. Of some 500 students in 1966, 23 percent were children of ordained leaders, signaling the school's conservative tilt. The policies established by J. Paul Graybill continued to shape the ethos of the school throughout the Weaver/Keener years.

A Breath of Fresh Air

Although in many ways Amos Weaver was a caretaker of earlier policies, he was, in the words of one teacher, "really a breath of fresh air . . . the difference between low and high morale." "He was a short spunky chap," said Noah Good, "quite impressive because of his self-taught education." Open to dialogue, he was a fair man of deep convictions who enabled people to work together. "He was a counseling type of person. Students felt they could disagree with him and he left them say pretty much what they felt," remembers Edna Wenger. "He had a certain fairness that made people respect him. It amazed me that people respected him as much as they did because he wasn't a college man or anything." Noah Good remembers that Weaver "didn't take a strong hand in the educational life of the school because he recognized he didn't have

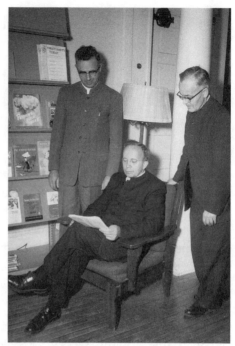

(left) Amos Weaver in 1972 with the bicycle he received from the faculty upon his retirement.

(right) The Supervising Committee in 1959. Left to right: Clyde Stoner, Noah Good and Amos Weaver.

much experience for it."

Indeed, his ninth grade education was scattered across eight different schools, due to his father's untimely death.[2] Baptized at the age of 16, he gave up his habit of smoking during a bout with the flu at the age of 20. Ordained a minister in the Paradise congregation at age 40, he conducted over 30 two-week revival meetings throughout the Conference. A remarkable vocabulary, coupled with able writing and speaking skills, attested to Weaver's self-education. Students and faculty alike perked up for his provocative chapel talks. In the third year of his principalship, he developed vocal cord problems which made speaking difficult for him. He offered to resign but the bishops reappointed him without teaching responsibilities. Although his hoarse voice never healed, he continued to speak in chapel.

The bishops relaxed their grip on the school when they gave its leadership to the 53-year-old nonbishop. But they had good reasons to trust Weaver. An original member of the board, he had eight years of experience at LMS, including a year on the Supervising Committee. And in Weaver's own words,

J. Paul Graybill "likely picked me." Although Weaver was open to dialogue, he also shared the bishops' vision for the school. Over a two-week span of chapels in 1954, he taught students to apply nonconformity to all areas of life. On another occasion he compared the church and the world to an old fable about a fly that was deceived by a spider in a fatal friendship. "The world," Weaver said, "is the enemy of God. Through the process of assimilation the fly became part of the spider. . . . May God preserve us from the insidious venom of flattery, conceit, and the glittering babble of friendship with the world which only conceals the snare of death."[3]

Weaver argued for strict lines of separation from the world, yet, he was flexible. In 1954 the revised *Rules and Discipline* of Lancaster Conference no longer required ties on devotional coverings. In the next chapel Weaver announced that covering strings could be dropped at school as well. Conservative leaders criticized him "pretty hard for that" and one sent a very critical letter. There were limits, however, to his flexibility. When Weaver discovered that some women faculty had "banded together to stop wearing covering strings," he reminded them that they should be examples for students. With a mirror sitting on his office shelf, Weaver could survey the size of coverings on the heads of female students during conversations with them.

"My inclinations," said Weaver, "were with the conservative element of our church. . . . But I also had to sense what young people were doing and thinking. . . . There came a time when on my own I suggested that girls wear skirts and blouses for athletics so they didn't have to wear cape dresses while playing ball. The trustees supported me, but that was a pretty big step." Weaver had the gift of perspective. "When I think about plain clothes, I amuse myself by asking what Jesus would look like in a plain hat." Weaver also had a knack for acting courageously. One day he surprised two boys exchanging punches. He asked them to stop. Oblivious to his plea, they continued. Weaver quickly stepped between them. Startled, they stopped.

Weaver's flexibility ebbed when students began imitating the mophead haircuts of the Beatles, the British singing group. He confronted students in chapel on November 12, 1965. "Every Beatle type mophead you see is a living testimony to the widespread power and sway of the devil in our midst. . . . Followers of these avowed anti-christ Beatles have dethroned Christ from their hearts and are unquestionably the dwelling place of demons." Many delinquent parents, he contended, "are raising a generation of demon-possessed hoodlums dancing to the Devil's tune, who, like the pied piper, is leading them all down the slimy slum road to eternal hell."[4] Some faculty members chided Weaver for what they thought was an overreaction by a 65-year-old elder.

Reflecting on the early years, Weaver said, "We hoped to have a school that would conserve our way of life, which we thought was pretty much right, the way Christians ought to live. We hoped our school wouldn't drift like others. But my philosophy was we're serving our generation. What those do after this, is their responsibility. We do what we can; we're living for today. We serve the Lord today and the church today."

The shift was subtle, yet significant. Compared with Graybill, Weaver was less burdened about the future, more willing to respond to present realities. More important, Weaver brought a new twist to church-school ties—one that would loom prominent in the future. "I was a *servant* of the church and so was the school," said Weaver.[5] The idea that the school could enforce higher standards than congregations was waning. The highest compliment to Weaver's efforts echo across the years in the words of the 1963 yearbook dedication. "You always saw our side of the story," the students said, "and then gave advice that made us strive to be our best." That was, indeed, a breath of fresh air.

Conserving Soils and Souls

The mushrooming student body cramped the facilities of the old Yeates School throughout the '50s.[6] Meals were served in relays in the crowded dining

The school's all-male Board of Trustees (1953-54) was largely composed of ordained leaders who were also farmers and businessmen.

A 1963 view of a study hall in the library located on the ground floor of the auditorium/gym. This area was a swimming pool in the Yeates era.

room, toilet facilities were inadequate and classroom space was tight. Principal Weaver called the pressing needs "acute." Classrooms "strain the teachers," said trustee Landis Brubaker, because they are "long, dark and narrow." Even the Supervising Committee in May of 1957 considered "screening students and restricting registration" because of the crunch. What should receive priority for expansion?

Home economics received the first nod. In the summer of 1954 Noah Good moved off campus to a modest brick home a half-mile south of the school. The old stone cottage soon housed classrooms for two year-long courses in home economics.

Attention then focused on the fledgling agricultural program.[7] As church members slipped into nonfarm occupations, headed for college and trained for missions, rural life advocates spoke out. Bible teacher J. Irvin Lehman discussed the tie between faith and land in an article titled "Conservation of Soils and Souls." In his words, "The ultimate aim of toiling in the soil is the conservation of souls. . . . We do not want to suggest that living on a farm will directly result in the salvation of the soul. We do believe, however, that there are factors inherent in rural life that are favorable to Christian living which are not found in other vocations."[8] Chairman of the trustees James Hess, himself a farmer, agreed. Arguing for an enlarged agricultural program, Hess said, "We can best

(top) The Agricultural Building, constructed in 1956.

(bottom) Teacher J. Clarence Garber instructs a shop class in the Agricultural Building in 1959.

serve God as an agricultural people. . . . We desire to have the majority of our young people prepare themselves to serve God on the farm."[9] But those enthused about missions and professions doubted that the church's future rested on farming. Amos Weaver, rooted in the soil himself, argued that "we stand in danger of losing both our farming skills and our religion. . . . Do we want to train our youth as producers of material wealth, or as evangels of the faith, as purveyors of garden produce or of Gospel truth?" Weaver contended that Mennonites living in the Garden Spot of the World should "export the commodity" of the simple gospel around the world rather than agricultural products.[10]

The debate over soil plagued the school's agricultural program for several decades. Eventually the school launched a program to bolster agriculture. In 1955 the trustees agreed to build the "oft proposed" agriculture/shop building and hired farmer/teacher Clarence Garber to teach agriculture. With a square, but "plain, neat and economical" brick building in place, two year-long courses in agriculture were offered in '56-'57. But the farm initiative never thrived. Rural sentiments throbbed in the hearts of trustees—many of whom were farmers. Administrators, however, were more animated by academics as well as by missions and service. Besides, the Future Farmers of America refused to support local chapters in parochial schools, thus eliminating that possibility at LMS. Furthermore, by the late '50s newly consolidated public schools were touting large state-of-the-art shops and agricultural programs. These paled the meager efforts by the Mill Stream and attracted a fair share of Mennonite boys to public schools.

The school's next phase of expansion focused on souls. Chapel services in the auditorium/gym became increasingly crowded and moved for several years to the basement of the girls' dorm. Commencement activities were often held in a large tent erected on campus for the annual Worldwide Missionary Conference sponsored by the Lancaster Conference Mission Board. Should the school curtail enrollment because of limited facilities or should it build an auditorium large enough to seat thousands for Conference-wide gatherings?

In a special meeting in January of 1957 the trustees struck a middle road. They lifted the lid off enrollments and planned a 700-seat chapel/auditorium with kitchen and dining facilities in the basement. With $80,000 of a needed $125,000 in hand, ground was broken on October 9, 1957. The building was "going up with a bang" by December. By the fall of '58 the chapel opened for morning services. For their gift, the class of 1960 proposed painting biblical symbols and the school motto on the front of the chapel/auditorium. The trustees opted for "just the plain motto." Thus thousands of students were

(top) The first buildings constructed by Lancaster Mennonite School: the girls' dormitory in 1949 (lower right), the Agricultural Building in 1956 (lower left), the Chapel in 1958 (upper right) and the Classroom Building in 1965 (upper left).

(bottom) The 1965 senior class sings their class song at graduation ceremonies in a large outdoor tent. Reflecting the sputnik era, their class motto proclaimed, "Launching with a Living Christ."

(top) Teacher Myron Dietz jump-starts his car on a cold day in January 1963.
(bottom) Teacher Elizabeth Nolt teaches table etiquette to a group of students in 1963.

Members of the class of 1964, on their Washington D. C. trip, leaving the Supreme Court building. Girls were required to wear black bonnets and fellows dress suits.

(top) Senior chorus presents a public program in the chapel on December 17, 1964.
(bottom) Students cheer a home run at a 1965 intramural softball game.

(top) Donald Clymer at bat in an intramural game in October 1965.

(bottom) Passing peanuts while holding hands at the 1965 senior social.   From left: Irene Shelly, Phyllis Pellman, Martin Lehman, Barbara Shellenberger.

(top) A student panel discusses "urban renewal" in January 1965. Sweaters were often worn by girls to cover the required cape dresses.

(bottom) At the 1965 senior social, students attempt to outtalk each other about an animal. From left: John D. Landis, James Hostetter, John Eby and Clair Zimmerman.

(top) An intramural volleyball game in 1967.
(bottom) Lena Smoker, Sheryl Summers and Thelma Zink enjoy a joke at the end of classes
in the spring of 1968.

A scrimmage game of basketball in 1971. The LMH team is wearing cutoffs.

(top) Dormitory "cheerleaders" sparked the dormitory football team to a 14-0 victory over commuter students in October 1969.

(bottom) Making homemade ice cream at a social gathering in March 1971.

Students in Noah Good's German class in 1959.

greeted year after year with the mural "Teach Me Thy Way, O Lord." Individual students faced the prayer painted on the cinder block front wall some 700 times over the course of their four years.

Although the existence of the chapel allowed athletic activities to return to the old auditorium/gym, the new building did not provide adequate space for mass meetings. A Tabernacle Study Committee, formed in 1963 under the Mission Board, explored the possibility of building a large, open-air pavilion for mass meetings.[11] The project never jelled. The construction of a new auditorium/gym on the school campus in 1975 partly met the need for mass meetings, but the 1946 dream of a comfortable auditorium had to await the construction of an auditorium/fine arts center in 1991.

With the completion of the chapel in 1958 growth in the 1960s was driven by academic interests. Classes were scattered around campus—the old classroom building, the new girls' dorm, the old auditorium and the ag building—forcing students and faculty alike to plod through foul weather. What should be done? In the summer of '62 the trustees discussed building a two-year junior college as well as spinning off satellite high schools and junior high schools in other sections of Lancaster County.[12] At a special meeting in January of 1963, trustees and administrators debated some 15 wide-ranging issues concerning the school's future. Sentiment eventually drifted toward constructing a new classroom building on the LMS campus that would allow for modest enrollment growth.

Led by principal Clayton Keener on a windy Monday in February of 1964, the school community gathered around a shovel at the site of a new classroom building. In true Mennonite fashion the community sang together before breaking ground. As the skeleton of the building emerged, the trustees were distressed that the carpentry crew had shed their shirts in the heat of early summer. It was a "poor testimony to students," said the trustees and they sent their protests to the foreman.[13] The building was finished in late 1964. Over Christmas vacation, faculty moved into the building as the painters left by the rear door. "It was a big and abrupt moving day in the middle of the year," remembers Noah Good. Dedicated on the morning of January 4, 1965, the building was in use by noon.

The new space for classrooms and offices spurred a campus-wide shuffle. The old administrative building eventually was remodelled into staff apartments. First floor classrooms in the old mill were converted into bedrooms, making a three-story boys' dorm. The old auditorium/gym became once and for all a

A senior class meeting in 1959 on the second floor of the old auditorium/gym.

"Physical Education Building." Commercial classes vacated the old Yeates mess hall and pastoral counseling moved to the agricultural building. The spacious new classroom building was the crowning event of the Weaver/Keener years.

Several minor property decisions had long-term ripples. Responding to a request from the Lancaster Mennonite Historical Society, school trustees donated land in the fall of 1960 for a historical library east of the Mill Stream.[14] Learning of the trustee action, the Historical Committee "expressed appreciation for the gift." Word of the trustees' generosity spread and soon a Mission Board committee requested 25 acres of land on the southwestern edge of the campus for a retirement complex. And yes, they would pay for it. But the trustees, with regret, said no. "In the best interests of the future of LMS," they couldn't parcel off more land.[15] And so it came to be that the daughters and sons of Menno could prepare for their future and read of their past, but not retire, by the Mill Stream.

Gathering Golden Eggs

Staffing the growing school with qualified teachers was a yearly struggle. Noah Good described the annual scramble as "desperate," "difficult" and "urgent." Turnover was high and new teachers were hard to secure for several reasons. First, with few Mennonites attending college, the pool of prospective teachers was small. Second, LMS preferred certified teachers, and certification required teaching in public school. Mennonites teaching in public schools often wanted to stay there for family, financial and friendship reasons. Third, LMS salaries were meager and fringe benefits virtually nil. The school's operating budget balanced on tuition revenues. The trustees wanted to pay fair salaries. But they hesitated to raise tuition for fear of losing students. Thus, many teachers gave untold years of sacrificial service at meager salaries. Responding to salary complaints from married men in 1960, the trustees increased the allowance "for a wife from $100 to $200"—hardly an incentive for marriage.[16]

Still another obstacle to hiring faculty was the growing number of Mennonite agencies competing for the small pool of Mennonite professionals. Moreover, rigid expectations for faculty dress and behavior presented a fifth barricade. Some faculty had sparse convictions for plain dress but agreed to comply while on school premises. Noah Good summarized the recruitment dilemma succinctly, "To retain this form of simplicity some were hired without the proper academic or personality qualifications."[17] Others were well qualified, superb teachers. Singing the praises of his team, Amos Weaver said, "The Lord

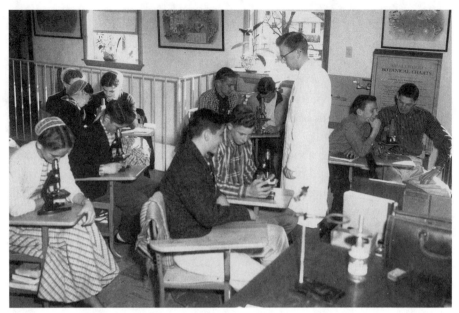

Charles Longenecker conducts a biology lab in 1958-59.

has been especially gracious in giving us a spiritual, capable and cooperative faculty."[18]

Trying to recruit graduate student Charles Longenecker for the fall of 1958, acting dean Harvey Bauman wrote, "We are not as liberal as many would like ... but we are open-minded and fair." He then reminded Longenecker to wear a plain suit and not to stir up student opinion on special singing, radio broadcasting or the use of modern versions of the Scripture.[19] Expectations for faculty behavior were actually rather stiff in the '57-'58 Teacher's Handbook. Following the Conference-wide *Rules and Discipline* of 1954, the school expected "sisters" to wear black hose and shoes, cape dresses with long sleeves, dresses at least one-third of the way from knee to ankle, and a devotional covering larger than the minimum for students. "Ties" on coverings "shall not be omitted." Expectations for the "brothers" included a plain coat, black shoes, plain-colored hose and no necktie. Faculty were not to advocate radio broadcasting nor to use slides in their classes. Moreover, magazines such as *Life* or *Look*, although "not trashy," were not to be brought on campus since they violated Christian standards. Although expectations for wearing covering strings, black shoes and black hosiery gradually relaxed, the other faculty guidelines remained intact throughout the '60s.

Prospective teachers completed a three-page questionnaire designed by the Religious Welfare Committee which asked, among other things, their views on

the inspiration of the Bible, regeneration, nonconformity to the world, nonresistance, life insurance, radio, television, special singing and the seven Mennonite ordinances. After candidates had their initial contacts with the dean,
the Supervising Committee reviewed the prospective employees and forwarded
their names to the trustees. Upon receiving the blessing of the trustees,
candidates were then interviewed by the Religious Welfare Committee. Those
passing the hurdles were then appointed to the faculty by the trustees. Continuing faculty were asked yearly to reaffirm the school's standards and policies.

LMS found itself in a quandary. By upholding the stiff standards of Lancaster
Conference, it aligned itself with the conservative sector of the church. The
conservative stance was unattractive to a growing number of young intellectuals—the very ones the school needed for faculty. College-educated Mennos
imbibing in the larger culture often scoffed at the separatist stance of the school.
Shucking off their plain garb, they had little enthusiasm for indoctrinating
teens in the conservative ways of the past. There were, however, bright
intellectuals willing to wear plain coats and cape dresses in order to pursue
loftier goals. Deeply committed to the church and persuaded of the importance
of Christian education, they believed that in the long run they could make a
significant difference at LMS—and they did.

Charles Longenecker joined the "open-minded and fair" group in the fall of
'58 to teach biology. Despite a starting salary of $2350, Longenecker had an
opportunity "to teach completely in my field and I was given a high degree of
autonomy. I was given freedom to develop the program and I liked it." In 1959
Arnold Moshier, exuding enthusiasm for music, joined his brother Elton, a
faculty member for several years. Eager to mobilize the musical talents of
students, Arnold championed special music groups, to the dismay of some
trustees. Omar Eby, back from an African mission stint in 1960, wanted
college-bound students to read some Faulkner and Hemingway along with the
Martyrs Mirror and the writings of Menno Simons. Irked that *Black Like Me*
and *The Old Man and the Sea* were banned from the school library because of
their salty language, Eby lent the paperbacks out of the bottom drawer of his
desk. When his classroom rocked with laughter at the spicy retorts of Eliza
Doolittle in Shaw's *Pygmalion*, Eby prayed that Principal Weaver was far from
his next door office.

Bishop Leroy Stoltzfus, stout chairman of the Religious Welfare Committee,
confronted Eby one day about his brown shoes. Eby informed the stocky bishop
that black shoes didn't match his brown plain suit. And why, Eby questioned,
did the bishop serve communion in his congregations to girls out of line with
LMS dress standards? Startled by the retort, the conservative bishop dropped

the matter and Eby continued walking the campus in his brown cordovans. Such independent-minded young faculty were enough to frighten administrators and make old trustees wonder how such folks had managed to slip through the Religious Welfare Committee. Trying to restrain the new generation of Mennonites, Amos Weaver told Eby, "Our Conference and school has laid some golden eggs and you are one of them. Now don't kill the goose that laid the golden egg."

Searching for bright teachers who would dress plainly, the trustees found a golden egg in a non-Mennonite basket. Stanley Kreider, math teacher since 1956, urged Noah Good to contact Myron Dietz, whom Kreider had met at Millersville College. Dietz was a member of the Old Order River Brethren, an Anabaptist group that dressed even more plainly than the Mennonites. The River Brethren baptized by immersion whereas the Mennonite mode was pouring. Bishops Leroy Stoltzfus and David Thomas were dispatched to Mill-

Young faculty in the early 1960s. Left to right: Omar Eby, Myron Dietz and Stanley Kreider.

ersville College to inspect Dietz. They found a "guy with a great big black hat, a big beard and a twinkle in his eye." Bishop Thomas worried that such a conservative fellow might feel out of place in the school. Indeed, two conservative-minded teachers had recently left, charging the school was too liberal. Bishop Stoltzfus, however, was charmed by the twinkle in Dietz's eye. So returning to the trustees the two bishops reported, "We like him, he's committed and he wants to come."

The trustees feared, however, that Dietz might persuade Mennonite youth of the merits of immersion baptism. So Bishop Thomas returned to Dietz to discuss immersion. "Will you promise," asked Thomas, "not to make students uncomfortable who aren't immersed?" Dietz winked and said, "I'll try." "And I just loved it," said Thomas, "the way he winked and said 'I'll try.'" And so with the Religious Welfare Committee's blessing, Dietz with his flowing beard, effervescent wink and charming manner became the school's first non-Mennonite teacher. "He has become the soul of the school," said Charles Longenecker. "Here is a guy who dresses like an Amishman, thinks like a liberal and yet is solidly Anabaptist. He's forthright, well respected and knows what he's talking about." In the words of Stanley Kreider, Dietz "has charisma, convictions and a loving way of letting it all out . . . he just says what's on his heart."

Reflecting on his bearded golden egg, Bishop Thomas said, "He was honest. He didn't put on a front. He was able to get along with all sorts of students and it was important that they learned that you could be different and still get along." Thus in the mid '50s and early '60s a cluster of new faculty jelled—the Moshier brothers, Kreider and Longenecker, Dietz and Larry Wenger—a stable core that shaped the heart of the school for the next two decades as others moved through the revolving door.

The heavy burden of church regulations in the Weaver/Keener years was often lifted by the levity and love of three ordained churchmen—Noah Hershey, H. Raymond Charles and David Thomas. Without the aid of college degrees, their self-taught wisdom warmed the hearts of Mennonite teens. Basing their Bible classes on patriarch Daniel Kauffman's *Doctrines of the Bible* and counseling hundreds of students, these elders embodied a loving, caring presence. Their graceful ways spanned the gap between the rigid expectations of the *Rules and Discipline* and rambunctious youthful impulses. Their wisdom, wit and love wooed many young hearts churchward. H. Raymond Charles, president of the Mission Board, compared teaching with his other work. "Those days at LMS were *most* rewarding. . . . At a recent banquet oodles of people came up to me and talked about their memories from Bible Doctrine class. Now that's rewarding, that's fulfilling. I enjoyed those years."[20]

Bishop Thomas, moderator of the bishops, also taught for eight years. Master diplomat and skilled storyteller, he personified the loving care of the church in the classroom. Thomas conducted his classes "without ever giving a demerit"— a fact that astonished a colleague who levied some four demerits a week on rowdy students. In an early morning prayer meeting, perplexed teachers discussed ways to handle classroom disruptions caused by a nearby construction crew blasting away at stubborn rock. Asked how he coped, Thomas said, "When the warning siren goes off we all run over to the window and watch the blast and then in three minutes we're back in our seats. It's sort of fun and it breaks the routine." For those chafing at the rules and regulations, Hershey, Charles and Thomas offered a warm, humane encounter with the church.

Exploring Life Individually

The rising tide of individualism in the larger society touched the school in many ways. The uniform standards of earlier days, designed to hold group loyalties above personal aspirations, were slowly eroding. While the bishops debated the debilitating effects of individual communion cups on congregational unity, students were tasting the delights of individual expression. The 1964 *Laurel Wreath*, dedicated to Myron Dietz for sharing his "individual exploration of life in Christ," touted the theme "Exploring Life Individually." The subtle, but growing, focus on individual expression replaced earlier pleas for self-denial, obedience and submission. Budding individualization opened the door to what a *Millstream* editor in 1955 called "the terrible filth of pride, self-centeredness, boastfulness, and a host of other horrors."[21] The changes, small and nearly undetected, were nonetheless persistent.

An expansion of pastoral counseling, personal interviews, guidance counseling, as well as attempts to deal with deviants "privately," cast the spotlight increasingly on the individual. Private confessions of sin to the student pastor replaced public confessions in revival meetings. Kneeling for prayer, the posture of a humble and yielded spirit, gave way to standing and seated prayers in worship. Even the trustees cooperated in '59 by permitting the *Laurel Wreath* to print the academic degrees attained by individual faculty members. Although individual photos of seniors had appeared in the yearbook from the beginning, underclass members finally were pictured singly in 1960. With the blessing of the Religious Welfare Committee, the trustees even agreed to offer "individual voice culture lessons" in 1965, paving the way for solos, feared in the past as mere expressions of egotism.[22]

Laurel Wreath dedications also marked the surging individuation. Although some dedications to individuals graced early yearbooks, many were collective: "to our parents," "to our faculty," or "to our pastors." After 1962 all the dedications honored an individual. Prior to 1968 individual dedications were to "Brother Weaver" or "Sister Wenger." Beginning in '68 the person's full name was used without a prefix.[23] The theme of the '68 yearbook pivoted on the phrase, "The building block of any group is the individual." By 1972 student editors proclaimed, "We fought for our individuality." But that is getting ahead of our story. Nevertheless, the concept of the individual, missing from early school documents, was clearly on the rise.

Between 1953 and 1967 many early dress regulations persisted while others relaxed, permitting more and more individual expression. Required habits for boys which endured through 1967 were: shirts with collars, elbow-length sleeves, bow ties, long trousers for athletic events and a taboo on "extreme haircuts." When daylight saving time arrived, top buttons could be opened and sleeves rolled up two cuff lengths. The list for women, as usual, ran longer: cape dresses, sleeves to the elbow, dresses covering the "whole knee at all times"

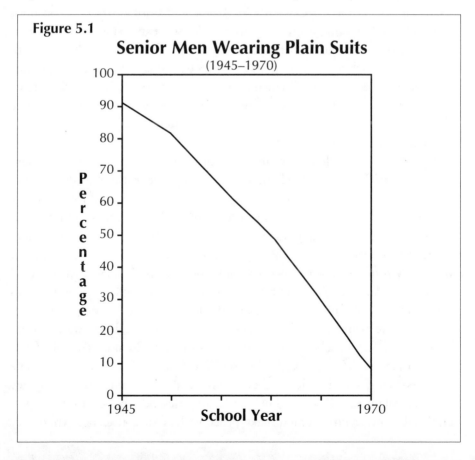

Figure 5.1

Senior Men Wearing Plain Suits
(1945–1970)

and a devotional covering with a one-and-a-half-inch front piece. Following the biblical injunction in I Corinthians 11, hair was to be worn long, uncut and arranged up under the covering. For both men and women, shoes of a "dark shade" were prescribed and "decorative articles of ornamentation"—all forms of jewelry—were taboo.

Porous openings in the dress code permitted some individual expression to sprout. Boys wore T-shirts for athletics and opened collar buttons and tossed off the hats required in earlier years when traveling to and from campus. The proportion of senior boys wearing plain suits in formal yearbook photos in 1967 plummeted to 15 percent from an earlier high of 90 percent.

Changes abounded for women as well. Covering strings were dropped in 1954 and, at the same time, the practice of parting hair in the center declined. Skirts and blouses in the late '50s and culottes in 1966 were permitted for physical education classes. Hemlines were also rising. Skirt lengths in the early '60s—one-third of the way between knees and ankles for upperclass women and three inches below the knee for underclass women—rose to merely "covering the whole knee" by 1967. Color and print restrictions on dress material faded, offering even more avenues for self-expression. By 1964 bonnets were only "encouraged" for off-campus trips. Throughout the '60s both students and teachers wore sweaters to bypass the dress code. Sweaters permitted greater expression of individuality but, more importantly for girls, offered an acceptable substitute for capes which were increasingly despised. Male teachers with little conviction for plain dress often shed their plain suits for sweaters in the classroom.

Year after year battle lines were etched anew as the school strove to remain separate from the world of fad and fashion while its constituency drifted ever closer to it. The school's rules and regulations, noted Principal Keener in his 1965 annual report, "are a thorn in the flesh" for both students and patrons. Despite relaxing some requirements, LMS continued to curb the call of fashion. Some years the thorns were "flat top, duck tail and crew cut" haircuts. Other years they took the form of pegged pants, blue jeans with rivets, trinkets of adornment and pins. At other times pullover sweaters, fancy trim and lace, as well as bright and vivid colors became the focus. Teachers complained that students were being trained in hypocrisy since many had two wardrobes: a conservative one for school and a fashionable one for off-campus social affairs.

Strict faculty dress standards also forced a struggle of conscience for some teachers. How could male teachers maintain personal integrity when they donned a plain suit at school but wore a long tie and lapel coat off campus? How did some faculty women make peace with their conscience when they wore smaller coverings, shorter, non-cape dresses and spike heels away from school? Despite the pressures for change from within and without, the school remained remarkably plain as it celebrated its twenty-fifth anniversary in 1967.

The Zest of Student Life

Many continuities threaded their way through the 14-year period from 1953 to 1967—weekly student religious programs in chapel, annual Mill Stream outings, class days, parent visitation days, prayer circles, revivals, taffy pulls,"crit slips" and skating. Student life, said a *Millstream* writer, was "filled with zest." Indeed, students were flexing their political muscles. *Millstream* articles on tuberculosis in the early '50s were gradually replaced with essays on "Christian Civic Responsibility." As students began thinking more about their place in the larger society, they debated "my duty to my country" and "my duty as a Christian citizen." The rising political consciousness turned inward as well. For the first time in the history of the school, students organized a Student Forum in 1954 with elected representatives from each class—a form of student power that would have frightened J. Paul Graybill.

The Student Forum in these early years elected prayer circle leaders, gave pep talks on chapel reverence and suggested changes in library hours. But their innocence soon waned. In the spring of '62 they brought Old Glory back. The Supervising Committee, unsure how to field the student request for a flag, took it to the trustees. In an eight to five vote the trustees agreed to allow "an American flag of appropriate size" to be displayed in the library.[24] Assistant

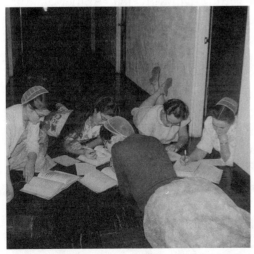 

(left) Group study in a hallway of the girls' dormitory in 1959.
(right) Dormitory girls Lois Wert and Virginia Hart in 1955-56.

Principal Keener, reportedly sympathetic to the students' request, had gained a new appreciation for the stars and stripes while living overseas.

Pressing their political fortunes even further, six members of the Student Forum appeared before the trustees in the spring of '65 asking if girls could wear culottes for athletic classes. The board agreed, provided "they cover the knees," only to be rebuffed by the Religious Welfare Committee. A year later, however, the Religious Welfare Committee changed its mind on culottes.[25] The Student Forum pushed onward for a piano in the music room and for musical instruments in the dormitories, but these were firmly denied.[26] Looking beyond their own needs, the Forum organized a sacrificial effort to raise funds for international hunger and relief work. Skipping occasional meals, bypassing a milk shake and making do with old clothes, students scraped together a total of $6,707 in 1967.

Spiritual zest was stirred anew each year in the two-week fall revivals. "The devil is the world's greatest trapper," said evangelist Roy Geigley in the fall of '53. "He's out setting traps and snares to lure Christians into evil." The two-week spring revivals were replaced with a one-week youth Bible conference in the spring of '55. Alumnus John Ruth preached messages that year on sin, salvation, sanctification and service. "He hit many of us hard," said one student, "as he brought this right down to our experiences and reminded us that we were put into this world for the purpose of serving our Saviour." The revival "embers were glowing again" in the fall of '56, in the words of a *Millstream* editor. At the close of the last message, over one-fourth of the student body responded. "We had an unforgettable time singing, giving testimonies and praying, while those who had gone downstairs were getting right with God. As they came up they too began to give their testimonies and make confessions. Chapel lasted till dinner-time that day."[27]

"The biggest thing in school this year," said Amos Weaver in the fall of 1960, "was the stirring messages that Noah Hershey brought from the book of Joshua." Students responded each morning and more than 75 made commitments on the final day. As soon as the invitation was given it was like "opening a flood gate." For the next two hours scores of students testified until more than 200 had given testimonies, "urging others to yield themselves fully to Him and find the same joy and peace they had found." Amos Weaver noted that veteran Christians had never seen anything like it and he remembered none that "exceeded this one nor have I seen its equal anywhere else."[28]

In the fall of '61 students gave "glowing testimonies and made new commitments" under the preaching of alumnus Paul Landis. But the devil was also busy trapping. The trustees learned that a rash of discipline problems in

(top) Faculty Athletic Committee, 1959-60. Left to right: Stanley Kreider, Miriam Wenger, Alta Hoover, Arnold Moshier, Bill Leakey.

(bottom) A coed volleyball game in 1959 near the site of the present gymnasium.

classrooms were "caused by pupils who didn't respond to the revival appeal." The spring and fall renewals were sustained by daily chapels conducted by ordained leaders, as well as ten weekly, voluntary prayer circles. Each class, as well as the dormitory students, had a male and female prayer circle. "Finding

God's will" was the paramount student quest. The revivals—high points of spiritual ecstasy—helped to clarify that quest for many.

Beyond revivals there was enthusiasm aplenty for sports. In fact, throughout this era administrators frequently complained of "growing pressures for more sports." The old standbys remained in place—skating, softball, tennis, shuffle-board, ping-pong, tennis, basketball and volleyball. New additions over these years included track, flag football, soccer, weight lifting and hockey. While intramural competition flourished, interscholastic competition remained nil. Wider use of television in these years spurred the rise of professional sports across the nation. The bishops in the fall of '62 lamented that sports were "finding their way into the lives of our people, including the organization of congregational teams." The bishops urged members to follow the *Rules and Discipline* of the Conference and not "indulge in regularly organized contesting ball teams."[29]

A growing array of social events also added spark to student life. "Socials" welcomed new students and sometimes celebrated Halloween and Thanksgiving. "Senior warm-ups," "junior-senior outings," "Mill Stream outings," class parties, deep-sea fishing trips and taffy pulls offered welcome diversions from academic routines. In the late '50s dorm students gathered after supper on the lawn along the Mill Stream and played prisoners' base, zip-zap-zir and flying dutchman. The Spanish class under the tutelage of Paul Landis held an annual pig roast at the home of a student. As restrictions on dating relaxed over the years many of these events offered a chance for couples to pair off.

Men's prayer circle led by Paul Reed in 1959.

Shuffleboard was a favorite indoor game in the 1950s and '60s.

Clubs waxed and waned with student and faculty interest. Needle craft, nature, Sunday school teaching, art, stylus, campus improvement and tract clubs fizzled. Bird study and first aid, however, continued over the years. New groups made their debut—Camera Club, Nurses Club, Ham Radio Club, Boys' Chef Club, and a Christian Youth Writer's Stimulus. In '62-'63 dormitory students organized two literary societies—the Herculeans and the Socratarians. The trustees, recognizing "certain dangers in the use of dramatics, discouraged drama in public programs."[30] Restricted to informal "skits" for fellow students, the literary societies presented "productions" of "The Open Window" and "Cinderella" in '64.

The Sounds of Change

Despite relative stability, some changes were afoot. The academic abilities of new students were screened for the first time in the fall of 1954. Designed to detect weak students transferring from Christian day schools, the annual entrance exam stirred controversy over the years as some students were rejected after failing the test twice. In another change, advanced courses in biology and economics joined the curriculum. A course in sociology was added, but none in psychology. Driver Education classes began in the fall of '62 with bishop Clayton Keener behind the wheel. As some students began driving lessons

Students play "Guard your Partner" at the junior/senior outing in May 1963.

others began riding to school in a bus. In the fall of '66 a group of parents began operating a bus—a pattern that grew over the years. In the '65-'66 school year the faculty were divided into academic departments and department heads were named.

Controversy swirled around the music program in the Weaver/Keener years. Restricted from participating in interscholastic sports, students pressed for public music programs. The clamor, according to one faculty member, "raised a lot of stink." Four-part a cappella singing had become a distinctive mark of Mennonite worship in the twentieth century. Special music groups—quartets, trios, solos and special choruses—troubled conservative leaders for two reasons. First they feared that staged performances by special groups would stifle the participation of all members and erode congregational singing. Music, rehearsed and presented *to* an audience, was quite different from singing that flowed spontaneously from the hearts of *all* members. Second, special performances focused attention on the abilities of a select few, cultivated pride and disturbed equality in congregational life. Although many Mennonites had musical instruments in their homes, organs and pianos were missing in church buildings. Leaders feared that musical instruments would not only clutter the simple beauty of unadorned worship, but also drown out congregational singing and herald its death.

Choral groups existed from the school's beginning, but their purpose was music education, *not* performance. Classes in "chorister training" to prepare congregational song leaders were a mainstay of the school's program. The bishops monitored the music program closely—a signal of its significance for the church. The bishops sensed they were losing the battle for plain clothing. Now, they worried that congregational singing, a key mark of Mennonite identity, was also endangered. But the bishops would not yield without a struggle. The battle lines were drawn more tightly in 1954 when the newly revised Lancaster Conference *Rules and Discipline* explicitly banned special music from worship services. The *Rules and Discipline* of 1943 did not mention music. Congregational singing was simply taken for granted. The revision of '54 explicitly stated, "Conference *requires* that only congregational singing shall be engaged in, in all public worship services."[31] Music groups were permitted in private gatherings as well as in evangelistic street meetings, jails, hospitals and retirement homes. The bishops carefully scrutinized the school's music program—the training ground for the next generation of congregational leaders.

In the late '40s student quartets sang at informal school events and by the mid '50s they sang occasionally at the Mennonite Retirement Home. Informal photos of quartets had appeared in the *Laurel Wreath*, but in the spring of 1955 a full page photo of a mixed quartet appeared in the yearbook—a symbolic if not direct response to the bishops' stricter music policy enacted in the fall of '54. The senior chorus sang for parents during an Open House program in the spring of 1950 but a formal public program was still nine years away. Were choral presentations acceptable in a "music program," if it was not a formal "worship service?" The trustees favored a student music program in the large tent during the 1955 commencement. The bishops, however, said no.

Pleas for public music programs rose both within and without the school. Five student choral groups—Mens' Chorus, Ladies' Chorus, Junior Chorus, Senior Chorus and Chorale Singers—became popular within the school, but they had no audience for their music. In the spring of 1956 Chorale Singers, a select chorus, gave a program at the Philhaven Hospital. Feeling the rising pressure, Noah Good argued for more "approved forms of expression" in public music programs.[32] But the Supervising Committee could do little more than wage a new campaign to teach chorister training and congregational singing. In the spring of '57 Elton Moshier took the Mens' Chorus on two weekend tours to northern Pennsylvania. The trustees, without consulting the bishops, allowed a school chorus to sing at the Alumni Fellowship meeting that same year. By this time formal photographs of quartets were common in the *Laurel Wreath* and classes often had their own quartet, although choral groups could not sing in chapel.

The music curriculum received a boost in 1959 when Arnold Moshier became the first full-time music instructor. Worried about his contagious enthusiasm for music, school officials insisted that he not promote special music programs. Thus, he was quite surprised when Noah Good in 1959 asked if the Senior Chorus could present a program of music in an afternoon activity event near Thanksgiving. Moshier was even more astonished a few days later when Good asked, "How would you feel if we invited parents of the Senior Chorus to come to a special Christmas program?" With a flurry of practices Moshier's chorus plunged into Christmas music and prepared the school's first public program for the Yuletide season of '59. Word of the upcoming evening spread and many friends attended. The chapel filled a half hour before the starting time. For Moshier it was "the most exciting moment of my life!" The joy of the occasion was soured a bit by several trustees on the back bench whose stony faces betrayed their displeasure. One even refused to shake hands with the new music director.

The Christmas programs, soon popular in Mennonite circles, were often given twice a season with limited tickets per student. Enjoying the music themselves, the trustees soon agreed to produce and sell recordings of school choruses. In several months nearly 900 records had sold. With the advent of public programs and Moshier's enthusiasm, the Senior Chorus spiraled to over 200 students. In the words of the 1967 yearbook, LMS and Senior Chorus were "almost inseparable."

Apart from expeditions to prisons, hospitals and "old people's" homes, music groups were not permitted to sing in churches. This barrier also began to crumble. Near Easter in 1960 Arnold Moshier took 24 members of the Senior Chorus to the federal penitentiary in Lewisburg, PA. Under his guidance the same students sang on a weekend tour of Mennonite churches in upper New York state. Encouraged by student interest and thwarted by the school's ban on programs in churches, Arnold and Maietta Moshier organized the Chora-leers outside the purvey of the school. Selected by Moshier from the student body and recent alumni, the Choraleers became a highly accomplished and popular touring chorus in churches. Unsanctioned by the school, they were free from its dress code and other restrictions. Still active in 1991 but, in Moshier's words, "less intense since 1987," the Choraleers had a far-flung music ministry. Their tours in the United States and overseas, as well as their tapes and records, touched the lives of thousands. Moreover, Choraleers provided a significant growth experience for hundreds of students passing through LMS.

Throughout the '60s and early '70s a cappella music became *the* mode of student expression. Students vied for entrance into the more prestigious choral groups—Select Chorus and Campus Chorale. A one-semester music course was required for graduation. Indeed, music had become the heartbeat of the campus. In 1966 the trustees gave their blessing to student groups singing in churches. Special music was in vogue and became widely accepted in the worship services of Mennonite congregations. These were years of "blood, sweat and tears" for Moshier as he struggled against the "cut and dried" rules that he found in 1959. But the new opportunities expanding in the '60s and '70s offered hundreds of students significant involvements in a unique Mennonite art form—a cappella singing.

The ban on musical instruments, however, generated even more sweat and tears. With the acceptance of special singing groups, the debate tilted toward instrumental music. The school constitution barred musical instruments and radios from the premises. The bishops argued that the use of instrumental music would, in time, bring instruments into worship services and erode congregational singing.

By 1955 faculty were requesting phonographs for music appreciation and English classes. Upon a request from the trustees, the bishops in the spring of '56 finally agreed to "countenance the use of recordings in dormitories and classrooms," subject, of course, to the oversight of the Supervising Committee and the Religious Welfare Committee.[33] In the fall of '56 new Hi Fi phonographs appeared in dorms and classrooms, but students could not play their own records.

In his first year Moshier taught students musical intervals by using a pitch pipe. Soon, however, the school provided a two-octave keyboard for teaching intervals but balked at the idea of a piano. A permanent music room in the new classroom building offered a suitable home for a piano in 1965. Students badgered the trustees for a piano and for musical instruments in the dorm, but their request was denied in '65 and again in '66.

With mounting pressure for instrumental music, the Religious Welfare Committee appointed a committee of four in July of 1965 to evaluate the goals of the music program. The major goal, concluded the committee, was to enable every student to "participate in four-part, a cappella, congregational singing."[34] Instrumental music, surprisingly, did not even appear in the report! A piano would need to await a 1970 change in the school's constitution. In the spring of '68 the Supervising Committee allowed musical instruments in the Campus Cove for an outdoor Song Fest. They made it abundantly clear, however, that musical instruments remained banned from dormitories and other school programs. Although the role of instruments stirred debate into the '80s, the school enjoyed warm support for its public choral programs. Enriching students and inspiring audiences, the events enhanced the school's public image as well.

Hollywood Vices

As the use of radios, television and photography grew after World War II, Mennonite leaders feared an embrace of mass media would harm the church. Owning a television soon became cause for excommunication in Lancaster Conference.[35] Technology that funneled harmful values into the lives of members was discouraged. Popular entertainment, television and motion pictures purveyed "Hollywood" vices which church leaders believed would corrode and corrupt the hearts of youth. They worried that the use of slides and filmstrips might lead to members acquiring television and attending movies in public cinemas.

The use of audiovisuals also sparked campus debate. It was milder, however, than the music controversy. When the bishops approved phonographs in 1956 they did not bless audiovisuals or filmstrips. For the most part, however, the school tapped new technologies as they became available. In 1954, for exam-

Sir Lawnfal, Sam Miller, gives a cup of water and stale bread to a leper, Blair Seitz, in a "skit" presented by the Herculean Literary Society in 1963.

ple, they bought a new Underwood Electric Typewriter, which turned out letters "like a printing press." The only technical devices banned by the 1942 constitution were musical instruments and radios. Although radios were off limits for ordained leaders, Noah Good, with his scientific bent, had tinkered with them in his campus home since the mid '40s.

Noah Good, writing to the trustees for the Supervising Committee in December of 1955, argued that a wide selection of slides and filmstrips could be used effectively by teachers.[36] He proposed that visual aids be restricted to educational purposes and not used for entertainment. The bishops in October of 1956 considered allowing the use of slides at LMS, but the motion failed.[37] Slides of missionary ventures were shown occasionally with trustee approval. Teachers Charles Longenecker and Luke Shank wrote to the trustees in March of 1960, arguing that students were unfairly limited by the prohibition on audiovisuals. In fact, they noted, good educational films are available for the cost of postage.[38] On July 4, 1960, after several months of discussion, the Religious Welfare Committee allowed the use of filmstrips and slides with two qualifiers: they could be used in classrooms but not chapel, and the Supervising Committee needed to approve each usage. "Sound and motion pictures," however, remained taboo.[39]

The chapel, similar in function to a church auditorium, was considered a sacred space, preserved for worship without musical instruments. After moving into the new chapel, a special action of the bishops was required to desacralize the old edifice. In 1962 H. Raymond Charles received special Bishop Board permission to show slides of a recent mission trip in the "old auditorium."[40] A change in the school's constitution that same year permitted the use of radios, tape recorders and record players under the thumb of both the Supervising Committee and the Religious Welfare Committee.

Pleas for motion pictures, however, continued to mount. Finally in the summer of '65 the Religious Welfare Committee approved the use of motion films for classroom instruction provided they were screened by the Supervising Committee. Perhaps the Religious Welfare Committee found it easier to accept films without the conservative voice of its chairman, bishop Leroy Stoltzfus, whom the bishops had declared inactive a few weeks earlier. In any event, the reels on the school's new film projector were spinning in the fall of '65. In these transition years, Principal Keener previewed each prospective film to determine its fate. Television, of course, remained off campus.

The Twenty-Fifth Anniversary

Singing "Lamps lit with thy love," the graduates of 1967 celebrated a quarter

The literary staff of the 1960 **Laurel Wreath.**

century of Mill Stream education. An era was fading. Of more than 130 faculty over the years, Edna Wenger remained the only charter member. Some 23 teachers had served in overseas "mission fields," before or after teaching. Good and Stoner had logged 25 years as administrators/teachers. Landis Brubaker, lone charter trustee, also spanned the 25 years. The first board chair, Parke Book, had passed away 10 years earlier. Second generation students now walked in the footsteps of their parents. Graduates of early years were beginning to hold the reins of churchwide leadership. In all of these ways the torch, sometimes flickering, was about to pass to a new generation.

Although college beckoned more and more graduates, nearly 75 percent of the class of '67 completed the General curriculum, while 19 and seven percent followed the College Preparatory and Commercial tracks respectively. Only one senior received an agricultural diploma and none majored in domestic science or Bible. Nearly 93 percent of the student body resided in Pennsylvania. The greatest number of out-of-staters (29) hailed from Delaware and Maryland. About 2 percent (12) of the students were non-Mennonite. Reflecting a pattern of these years, slightly over one-third (37%) of the graduating class attended LMS all four years. In fact, 30 percent came for their last two years and 17 percent for their senior year only.

In two-and-a-half decades the student body had grown from 150 to 560;

nearly 2300 graduates had carried off sheepskins. The original faculty of six had swelled to nearly 40, and now included three bishops and six ordained ministers. With such growth the intimate family spirit of earlier years waned. In his annual report of 1967, Noah Good confessed that he no longer knew all the students personally and had to "look up some of them by index cards"—a confession unheard of in earlier years. He also lamented that family-like ties among the faculty had vanished. Typical of institutional growth, the public and private lives of faculty gradually split into separate spheres. The burgeoning school received welcome support from a wider constituency, but it also nurtured a bureaucratic climate with growing rolls of red tape. Sensing the detriments of size, Noah Good warned that "the size of the school may well become self-defeating."[41]

In its first two-and-a-half decades the Mill Stream venture remained remarkably faithful to its founding vision. Over these years the bishops retained rather firm control of the school. It had remained a safe, sane place for Mennonite youth and in many ways had helped to stem the tide of worldliness so feared by the founding fathers. Even as late as 1967 it was able to claim dress standards stiffer than those in many congregations, while still attracting a growing enrollment. The school had carved out its niche, at least within the Mennonite community, if not in the larger world.

Student editors of the 1967 *Laurel Wreath* asked, "What is LMS?" Their answers splattered in bold print across the twenty-fifth anniversary edition profile the lines of identity.

"LMS is...

Brother Good's smile and Brother Dietz's laugh

Bow ties for boys and capes for girls

Singing in Senior Chorus

The annual Scrooge play at Christmas

A yearbook without advertisements

Meeting God in a new way during revivals

Chewing an eraser to shreds during a POD test

Calling teachers "Brother" and "Sister"

Honor points, tardy slips and conduct grades

Spontaneous singing before chapel

Exchanging deepest problems with closest friends

Undying love for a school we are proud to attend."

Despite the continuities across the years, change was in the air. In their commencement dedication, the graduates of '67 pondered how they might "Radiate God's Love in Urbanization." Seven student speakers discussed evangelism in urban areas. Topics included "I Will Lift Mine Eyes unto the Skyscrapers" and "The Challenge of the Ghettos." The city, especially New York, was vying with Africa as an exciting, new mission field. On campus, life was astir as well. Six teachers citing urgent concerns for the future of the school wrote a two-page statement to the trustees. A faculty/administrative committee trying to envision the next 25 years had proposed using outside evaluators to assess the school's goals. By the commencement of 1967 the outside evaluators were busily examining the school's future direction.

The bishops were also busy, revising once again the *Rules and Discipline* of Lancaster Conference. They were searching for a virtually impossible compromise: how to placate progressives clamoring for more freedom and, at the same time, muffle a growing chorus of conservative voices threatening to leave the conference?

Twenty-five years of consolidation, growth and expansion had created an image of success. Below the surface, however, all was not well. Faculty unrest, the scrutiny of outside evaluators and changes churning in the church marked turbulent undercurrents that threatened the school's well-being.

Setting a New Direction

1967-1972

"The school is at a fork in the road, perhaps already past it."
—Howard Witmer

Running Out of Steam

The late '60s were turbulent times in American society. Martin Luther King and Robert Kennedy fell to assassins' bullets. The war in Vietnam spawned a counterculture with student demonstrations, communes, experimental drugs and hippies of all sorts "doing their own thing." These were also turbulent times for the Mennonites of Lancaster and their Mill Stream school. Prodded by rapid social changes, Lancaster Mennonite Conference issued its newly revised *Rules and Discipline* in 1968. Unhappy with new trends spreading across the church, a cluster of bishops and ministers withdrew from the Conference in the fall of '68. Within a five-year period ('67-'72), the school experienced sweeping changes—a new constitution, a new philosophy, a new name, a new adminis-

The old mill that had served as a boys' dorm and classroom building was dismantled in 1973. The administration building, the former Gardiner Hall, in the background, is the only Yeates building remaining in the 1990s.

trative structure, a new principal and, of course, a new logo. What triggered such massive changes so quickly?

The celebration of the school's twenty-fifth birthday opened the doors for evaluation and reflection. The founding generation had faded into retirement or had passed away. Children of alumni were now attending the school. A new generation was slipping into the seats of power. Some alumni were even sitting on the board of bishops. Questions were rising both within and without the school. Where was it headed? Did it fit the vision of the changing Mennonite community or merely reflect the dream of an earlier generation? Others wondered if there was any vision at all. The voices calling for change in these years were often loud and sometimes harsh. The impetus for change flowed from teachers, parents, alumni and outside evaluators; rarely from trustees or administrators. Said one observer at the time, "The locomotive simply ran out of steam."

The making of a new school began in early 1967 with a small evaluation committee composed of two teachers and the dean. After meeting twice they proposed asking outside evaluators to review the school's mission and program. In March of 1967 six faculty members sent a statement of urgent concerns to the trustees. Decrying lagging morale among teachers, disgraceful acts of vandalism and an abundance of rules without reason, the faculty proposed among other things a single administrative head, a full-time certified guidance counselor and a formal philosophy for the school. If these proposals are tossed aside, they warned, "We should not be shocked if the school declines in quality . . . and present teachers lose heart and go elsewhere."[1]

With this urgent prod the trustees appointed a committee of outside evaluators. They asked the venerable J. Paul Graybill to chair the group in what must have been a bittersweet honor. Other members included alumni Paul Kraybill, class of '43, secretary for overseas missions at the Eastern Mennonite Board of Missions, and former LMS teacher J. Lester Brubaker, professor of education at Eastern Mennonite College.[2] The evaluators began their work in May of 1967 and by late June they delivered a 15-page report with some 30 recommendations. The report called for a 25 to 33 percent increase in salaries, fringe benefits for employees, a written contract for teachers, hiring a guidance counselor, writing an educational philosophy and instituting regular faculty meetings and a curriculum review.

More importantly, however, the evaluators found administrative atrophy. Job descriptions were nonexistent. The principal, appointed by the bishops, had not met with the trustees during the entire school year. Teachers frequently complained that the Supervising Committee "passed the buck," "acted indecisively" and "let things fall between the cracks." The evaluators asked for a continuing review of administrative roles to establish a "clear line of author-ity" and a "single administrative officer to head the school." The administrative architecture, in short, needed a major overhaul. By October of 1967 the bishops agreed to have a full-time principal be the sole administrative head. The bishops also appointed a committee to write an educational philosophy.[3]

Since the departure of J. Paul Graybill in 1953, the school had lacked a leader with a persuasive and compelling vision. The absence of a philosophical architect between 1953 and 1970 levied a heavy toll. Principals typically served part-time while tending to other church duties. Moreover, they served out of a sense of obligation—because no one else was available. Even Noah Good, the thread of continuity over the years, confessed that the classroom was his first love.[4] Clayton Keener, principal from '63 to '67, had to be persuaded anew each year to serve. He repeatedly asked the bishops to search for younger leadership. In early 1967 the bishops announced that chairman of the trustees, James Hess, would become principal. But in a quick about-face they appointed bishop Howard Witmer a month later. Witmer served for two years, '67-'69, and received high marks for his conciliatory style. However, filling the joint role of church figurehead and chief disciplinarian of the school made Witmer uncomfortable.

Noah Good assumed the dual role of dean and principal in a transition year, '69-'70, until permanent leadership was found. In these years trustees often noted that the "march of time" required younger leaders, yet they seemed sluggish, afraid to act decisively. Conservative leaders across the Conference, threatening to secede in the mid and late '60s, also held the school hostage to the status quo. Changes in the school provided ample proof to the conserva-tives that indeed Lancaster Conference was going astray—yielding to the pressures of worldliness.

In the Face of a Crisis

In the summer of 1968 a group of teachers, dismayed by weak discipline and inept administration, discussed their concerns with trustees. Two weeks before school opened the chairman of the trustees told the Religious Welfare Com-mittee that "something should be done."[5] Trustee officers themselves lacked the resolve to intervene. The fall of 1968 kindled a real crisis. The steady growth enjoyed by the school had peaked in '67-'68 with an enrollment of 563—a mere increase of three from the previous year. Suddenly enrollment tumbled. A loss of 70 students in the fall of 1968 threw the school into a tailspin.

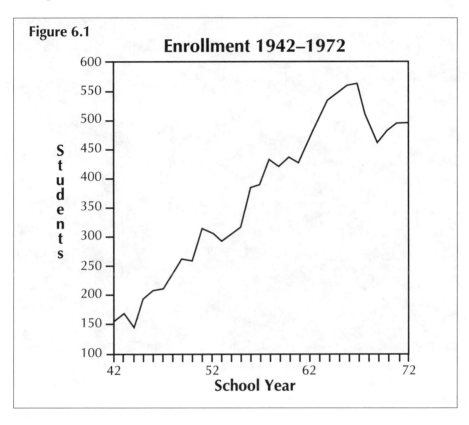

Figure 6.1

A budget deficit already loomed over the operation. Tied to tuition for its income, the school found itself in a serious financial crisis, triggered by the plummeting enrollment. Barebone salaries irritated teachers, forced many into part-time jobs and encouraged still others to teach elsewhere for higher wages. The school's feeble commitment that it "may" pay up to $500 of an employee's medical expenses frustrated one faculty member. In the fall of 1968 he wrote, "Medical bills are not merely the straw that breaks the camel's back—they can become the economic noose that hangs the teacher. . . . Surely, surely there must be some responsible person, somewhere, who will not only agree but act."[6] Thrown into a fiscal crisis and lacking decisive leadership, the school faced one of its dimmer moments in the fall of '68.

There were, however, three glimmers of light. First, the revised and more tolerant *Rules and Discipline* passed the Lancaster Conference in the summer of 1968. Second, on September 19, 1968, Lancaster Conference in a 281/32 vote released a conservative flank of 47 leaders and their followers.[7] In a rather amiable separation, the withdrawing group eventually formed the Eastern Pennsylvania Mennonite Church. The exit of these conservative voices—

The old barn was dismantled in 1975. Over the years the ground floor hosted a stable, a swimming pool, dining room, library and locker room. The second floor served as hay mow, dance floor, auditorium, chapel, classroom and gymnasium.

about three percent of the Conference membership—freed the school to change more rapidly. Third, in December of 1968, James Hess, on behalf of the trustees, asked J. Lester Brubaker if he would consider an administrative assignment at LMS.

Despite these positive omens, the trustees faltered throughout the winter of '68-'69. Indeed the chairman, noting that many other trustees shared his feelings, said, "I confess my inability, inadequacy, lack of insight and experience" in the face of this crisis. He reminded fellow trustees of the dangers of having "all school men" run the school.[8] Then he briefly summarized the school's implicit philosophy. "Our prime goal," said Hess, "is to operate the school so that students will want to conform to scriptural standards." They wanted "a deeply spiritual atmosphere, a truly biblical approach to life, a born again, dedicated, self-sacrificing faculty, every classroom experience Bible related, and a faculty zealous for the things of God—faithful and able."

The trustees in the spring of '69 found themselves badgered from all sides by teachers, alumni and businessmen with suggestions for change. Twenty-nine faculty members met with the board in February. Using the metaphors of their time, they charged that "the fuel which launched the school in its early years has been exhausted." They wanted to ignite the second stage, but said "we seem unsure *why* or *how* to do it."[9] The school, contended the faculty, needs a new sense of mission and stronger leadership for the '70s and '80s. They proposed developing a five-year plan, securing financial subsidy and, among other suggestions, conducting a survey of the constituency. The idea of sounding out the school's constituency was a subtle but significant turn. Rather than taking its cues from the bishops, the school was now looking elsewhere for direction.[10] Survey questions offered telltale evidence of the frustrations flying about: high tuition costs, weak academic image, limited course offerings, inadequate facilities, rigid dress standards, lack of instrumental music and a minuscule sports program. These were some of the many culprits often blamed for the shrinking enrollment.

The docile Alumni Association, formed in 1943-44, now moved into action with a flurry of suggestions. They began by offering to pay the salary of a full-time guidance counselor "for the coming school year!" They hoped to assist in other projects as well—a piano, a film library, salary subsidies and a gymnasium. A gym? Indeed, the Alumni Association proposed "handling the construction of a gym facility."[11] Intended as a friendly suggestion, such an offer surely sounded to trustee ears like a threat to hijack the entire enterprise.

An advisory committee of businessmen met and brainstormed: stop the rumblings and complaints, "sell the school better," give the teachers "more say" in operating the school, raise tuition, ask alumni to solicit funds, "talk up LMS" and much more.[12] Another group proposed leasing land for a major motel east of the Mill Stream.[13] Still another proposition called for renting dormitory rooms to tourists over the summer.[14] How to solve the financial crisis?

The school had always fed on tuition revenues. If tuition rose to balance the growing budget many trustees feared that the school would be priced beyond what many families could afford to pay. To bridle tuition while also raising salaries and improving facilities would require substantial gifts. Trustees and faculty discussed these issues on April 24.[15] Tiring of the suggestions and complaints, the chair of the trustees concluded the meeting by warning, "Without spiritual improvement on the part of all concerned, the school will not be able to surmount the present crisis." In May of 1969 teachers lacked contracts for the fall and some were "weighing carefully" whether or not they would return.[16]

Another outside advisory committee, once more including Paul Kraybill and J. Lester Brubaker, nudged the trustees out of the stalemate.[17] The advisors proposed two significant changes for '69-'70, which the trustees adopted on

June 2, 1969. First, Noah Good would head the school, holding dual titles of principal and dean. Three assistant principals would report to him: Howard Witmer for Religious Life Activities, Clyde Stoner for Business Management and Myron Dietz for Student Relations. Second, the venerable Supervising Committee would slip into an *advisory* role. It was a significant turn of events—the death knell for the Supervising Committee and the birth of a single administrative head. By June 23, 1969, the bishops placed their blessing on the proposal and appointed Noah Good as principal/dean.

The crisis, however, persisted. Enrollment fell an additional 34 students in the fall of '69—the lowest in six years. "Is LMS Dying?" asked an editorial in the *Millstream*.[18] The slipping enrollment spurred three more initiatives: a revised constitution, a new philosophy and a new principal.[19]

Charting a New Organization

The revised constitution, approved by both the bishops and Lancaster Conference, became effective in July of 1970. Apart from minor revisions in 1966, the original constitution had endured for 28 years. Now a younger generation wanted change. The new constitution embodied sweeping revisions and marked a major shift from the early charter. The new manifesto conferred a new name—Lancaster Mennonite High School—spelled out a new organizational chart and positioned the school for a new decade. In brief, the bishops handed the controls of the school over to the trustees—particularly the trustee executive committee.

New language set a fresh tone. The word "safeguard," so prominent in the old constitution, vanished in the new one. Ten "safeguards" listed at the end of the old, now became "standards." Discretion to use radios, record players, musical instruments and audiovisuals fell into the hands of administrators and trustees. The 10 references to the board of bishops in the old document dipped to four in the new. "Indoctrinating" youth was replaced by "teaching."

The new tone was milder. Early teachers had pledged "their loyalty to the Doctrine and Discipline of the Lancaster Mennonite Conference" and agreed to "teach in *full* harmony with and *nothing* contrary thereto." Now faculty were simply expected to be "in harmony with" the *Rules and Discipline* of the Conference. References to plain attire and separation from the world vanished. The solemn declaration in the first sentence of the old document—"We the Board of Bishops" shifted now to cold legal language—"Pursuant to action." Gone was the authoritarian tone of bishop superiority as well as the sectarian view of a school sheltering youth from an evil world. Under the new constitution the school hoped to "provide educational opportunities under Christian influence." Reflecting the demise of the old, cautious stance, the new charter shrank from 14 to 10 articles, and from 15 to 12 pages.

The constitutional revision was more than a cultural face-lift. Changes rippled through the power structure as well. Instead of the bishops nominating trustees, each bishop district now appointed a trustee. This opened the door for appointing more lay persons with special expertise in education. Moreover, the trustees themselves could appoint an alumnus, two persons with special expertise and a representative from another Mennonite conference. With bishop districts appointing trustees, the board was enlarged from 12 to 22 members.

The Religious Welfare Committee, which in the past acted on behalf of the bishops to "control and supervise" the school, now merely "advised" trustees and administrators and "reviewed" prospective faculty. The enlarged board elected an executive committee of seven to meet monthly, to act on its behalf. The full board now met only quarterly. The new trustees were loosely tethered to the Religious Welfare Committee and the Bishop Board. Although "directly and fully responsible to the Lancaster Conference," the coupling was looser than the former pattern of direct accountability to the Religious Welfare Committee and Bishop Board.

The new constitution bore the marks of negotiation. The authors of the new document could tell conservative critics that indeed the school remained fully responsible to and fully under the church. But the progressives knew that without clear lines of authority to the bishops, the trustees could act rather independently. Now they rarely needed to ask for bishop approval, thus reducing bishop control. In other significant changes the office of principal and dean merged into a single administrative head—principal.[20] The Supervising Committee, the old locus of power, was superseded by a Principal's Coordinating Committee, chosen by the principal for "counsel and coordination."

The bishops had largely divested themselves of the school with two exceptions: the appointment of the principal and the Religious Welfare Committee.[21] The power which formerly rested with the bishops, the Religious Welfare Committee and the Supervising Committee now trickled over to the Trustee Executive Committee and the principal. A variety of trustee committees, some with faculty and administrative members, shaped policies and practices formerly set by the Religious Welfare Committee. On the one hand, the changes democratized the organizational chart, allowing freer participation by a variety of lay members, but, on the other hand, the shift centralized authority in the office of the principal. Internal lines of accountability, at least, were clarified.

Architects of the new design were surprised that changes came so swiftly and painlessly, given the stiff resistance of a few years earlier. Many of the changes, however, had been maturing in the Mennonite womb for at least a decade. For the younger generation, it was a time to celebrate. They had retrieved the school on their own terms. They would pass on the faith in new ways to their children. But for the old sages sitting on the sidelines, things had gone awry. Original board member Landis Brubaker watching the transformation said, "It looks as if the school wants to run itself." The school, to use Brubaker's words, began running itself in July of 1970 as newly elected trustees and a new principal assumed responsibilities under the new game plan. James Hess continued to chair the trustees for a year until John Harnish took the helm.

A Philosophical Conversion

The restructuring reflected a philosophical ground swell. Critics charged that the early vision had withered and the school was drifting aimlessly by the mid '60s. A Philosophy Study Committee worked in tandem with the Constitutional Revision Committee throughout the '69-'70 term. Lacking a clearly stated philosophy, the school had been shaped around a variety of early documents which outlined an implicit philosophy of education. J. Paul Graybill's writings, the constitution and numerous school publications set forth a distinctive understanding of Mennonite education.

A comparison of the 1970 philosophy statement with earlier documents reveals a striking shift in world view. To be sure, a solid thread of continuity—the centrality of the inspired Word of God—linked the two eras. In the words of the new philosophy, the Bible is "the ultimate guide and highest authority for the Christian." Apart from this theme linking the generations, the language of the new statement was rife with modern vocabulary. It highlighted the development, rights and choices of the individual. The word individual was entirely missing in the early statements. The vocabulary of humility, obedience, self-denial and simplicity—all emphasizing the subordination of the individual to the community—had vanished by 1970.

In a bold statement that echoed modern views, the new philosophy asserted that the goal of education is "the development of the *individual* toward the highest achievement of Christian character and maturity. It helps *each* person understand *himself* and acquire the knowledge *he needs* to make wise *choices* as an *individual* with a *free* will."[22] The short two-page document mentioned *individual* or *each person* a dozen times!

Education is described as the *right* of each person to make *choices*—a word that appears three times. The terms "individual" and "student" replaced the condescending language of "pupils," "our children" and "young people" that peppered earlier documents. Discipleship and service appeared as new code words. Respect for the Mennonite church and loyalty to the Anabaptist *heritage* superseded loyalty to church *standards* and obedience to authority. The authoritarian stance of earlier days, that expected pupils "to obey without question or show of resentment," mellowed to assisting, enabling and helping individuals make responsible choices. Obedience appeared once in the new statement, calling students now to "a life of obedience to Christ," not to church and school regulations. Individuation and choice are key marks of the modern world—a world which the school was quickly joining.[23]

Despite the new philosophy, arrogant individualism was not running rampant. Anthropologist Gertrude Huntington who visited the school in 1972 after the philosophical update found the single most prevalent theme in chapel services "was the need to be submissive." Students were frequently told "you can't run your own life, you need a master, you can't do it by yourself, turn over the steering wheel of your life to God."[24] The submission to church regulations of earlier years had been transformed to spiritual submission—yielding one's life to God's will.

The school's tie to the church and to the world were also revised in the new philosophy. The strong emphasis on separation from an evil world and, hence, the need to safeguard youth, disappeared in the 1970 statement. Although the school had tried to stem the tide of worldliness, the church itself had drifted ever closer to the world over the years. More and more Mennonites entering the professions were working hand in hand with non-Mennonites and dressing like them as well.

The "world," however, remained an important category in Mennonite thinking. The new philosophy allotted a special section on "Relation to the World," but spelled it out in new terms. Gone was the imagery of withdrawal and separation. The school became "the focal point for learning about . . . and understanding the world." The school, rather than stemming the tide of worldliness, now encouraged a "commitment to service in the world . . . and prepared students for meaningful contributions to society." No longer erecting barriers and standing aloof from the world, the school was now poised to send servants into it, to make it a better place.

The school's marriage with the church was also transformed. Now the school *related* to the church with *understanding* and sensitivity, seeking to *respect* varying traditions. The Graybill vision that the school could enforce uniform standards for church life was buried without ceremony. Updating its tie to the church, the school now "instills in *each* student the ability to make responsible

choices and achieve *voluntary* convictions. . . ."[25] Community, the fad word of
the age, appears seven times on one page of the new philosophy statement.
Used in vague ways to refer to both the non-christian as well as the school and
the Christian community, the word articulates a more egalitarian, democratic
vision of the church than the hierarchical one reigning in 1942.

The impetus for change was as significant as the content itself. Although a
trustee-appointed committee steered the study, it was the faculty themselves
who wrestled with the school's philosophy in the spring of 1970. The new
charter bore the imprint of professional educators, not the hopes of ordained
leaders. Clearly, the power had slipped from the laps of church elders into the
hands of professional faculty and administrators. They were the ones now
guiding the new school by the Mill Stream. Captives of their own times, the
authors of the new philosophy celebrated their release from the tyranny of
former years. Although Graybill's vision was buried, he was not. Nor did he
praise the new changes. Reviewing the proposed philosophy, he lamented the
lack of scriptural principles—"obedience, submission and honor"—which high
school age youth should be taught. Moreover, he found "entirely missing . . .
the subjects of non-conformity, separation, and simplicity."[26] But his voice
echoed the sentiments of another generation—one whose time had passed.

A New Head of Steam

A new organizational chart and a new philosophy called for a new leader.
Since 1957, former LMS teacher J. Lester Brubaker had taught education at
Eastern Mennonite College in Virginia. But he had not forgotten the school
by the Mill Stream, nor had it forgotten him. Noah Good occasionally wrote
asking if he would consider teaching English. Charles Longenecker on sabbatical at Eastern Mennonite College in the mid '60s lived in Brubaker's house.
Hungry for new leadership, Longenecker told Brubaker, "we really need a guy
like you at LMS to head up our administration." After completing a masters
degree in secondary school administration and a doctorate in curriculum,
Brubaker felt a "call to administration" and held a "warm spot" in his heart for
LMS. But he had shed his plain coat in the mid '60s and soon exchanged his
bow tie for a long one. And thus he assumed he could "never come back to
Lancaster."

With the departure of its more conservative voices in the fall of '68,
Lancaster Conference was poised for change. The first minister ordained
without a plain suit began preaching in the Lancaster area in December of 1968.
About this time, Brubaker received a letter of inquiry from the trustees. Would
he consider an administrative assignment?[27] A flurry of correspondence be-

tween Brubaker and the trustees ensued until the bishops appointed him principal almost a year later. Brubaker told the trustees he couldn't consider "serving at LMS" if they were "satisfied with the status quo." Moreover, he could only come if one person was directly responsible to the trustees for the entire school operation. He also noted that he "would not be happy at LMS" if the school was seen as a means of "whipping students into line on dress standards."[28]

Paralyzed by the crisis of '68-'69, the board waffled. Finally, in October of 1969, Brubaker pressed for clarification—did they intend to invite him or not? "Some people seem to be assuming that I am coming to LMS next year," he wrote, but there "are no commitments on either side." In short order, the Bishop Board appointed him principal in November of 1969 with one condition—the blessing of the Religious Welfare Committee.[29] Wearing his lapel suit and long tie so the three bishops would see "me at my worst," Brubaker met the Religious Welfare Committee. It was a pleasant interview. The long tie issue didn't come up until Brubaker raised it himself. In an amiable fashion they struck a deal. He would shed his tie and lapel coat and wear a plain suit at school and whenever he represented the school out in the churches.

The agreement was nearly breached on March 2, 1970. A news release from Eastern Mennonite College appeared in the Lancaster newspapers announcing Brubaker's appointment. A photo of the new principal wearing a long tie appeared over the inscription "Dr. J. L. Brubaker." When he learned of the

J. Lester Brubaker became principal in 1970-71.

innocent turn of events, Brubaker fired a letter to Chairman Hess and Conference Moderator, bishop David Thomas. He apologized for "any embarrassment" and hoped the "continuing usefulness of LMS in the Lancaster area had not been marred."[30] In any event, the publicity spread a fresh image of a new school across the Lancaster community.

In appointing Brubaker, the bishops and trustees took a bold step. They placed their trust, and the welfare of their school, in the lap of an unordained "school man" for the first time. Brubaker brought impeccable credentials. He had taught at high school and college levels in both Mennonite and public settings. Carrying advanced degrees in administration and curriculum as well as consultancy experience in public schools, he was conversant with educational reform in the public domain. But he also knew the story of Mennonite education. He served as a staff member of the Mennonite Elementary Schools Association and wrote a doctoral dissertation on the rise of Mennonite elementary schools.[31]

Holding to "conservative inclinations," he nevertheless became the catalyst for sweeping changes at LMH—changes which had been repressed for at least a decade. In Brubaker's words, "The place was ripe for change." Continuing commitments tied him to Eastern Mennonite College. Thus, the new principal drove up to Lancaster weekly during the 1970-1971 term, spending Mondays and Tuesdays at the high school. He became full-time principal in the summer of '71. From the outset of his appointment, however, he began guiding the currents of change floating down the Mill Stream.

The Dean of Continuity

Noah Good described the new principal as " alert, aggressive, creative and diligent." In fact, Good noted that good relations with the incoming principal "made the 'lame duck' problem less acute." The long-time dean turned his responsibilities over to Brubaker "with real satisfaction." "I enjoyed administration," said Good, "but it was never my first choice.[32] It was nice to return to the classroom, where you really, so to speak, could have fun," he said.

Return to the classroom? Good had been there for 28 years while he also served as dean. Now at age 66 he relinquished administrative duties to teach German and French for another seven years. In a remarkable fashion he had shouldered the administrative burden of the academic program while teaching a diversity of courses. A renaissance man of sorts, he taught all the science courses in the early years—general science, physics, chemistry and biology, as well as French, German and Spanish, not to mention Latin, Problems of Democracy, Public Speaking and, on occasion, First Aid.

Some teachers had complained that the heavy teaching detracted from his administrative chores and they asked the trustees for full-time administrators. But Good's efficient mix of teaching and administration had bolstered an often tight budget. The heavy work load meant he rarely ate lunch with faculty, if at all, and often communicated with them by formal memos—a stiffness despised by some. There was no debate, however, about one issue: his sacrificial service and diligent work provided the continuity and austerity that kept the school afloat over the years.

Good's skill as a crafty fly catcher and his reputation for neglecting overcoats in the coldest of weather were known by many. His enduring contribution, however, was administrative stability. Submitting his evalution on Good's performance, J. Paul Graybill called him a scholar and a strong administrator. "The good educational standing that LMS enjoyed was largely due to Brother Good's deanship."[33] At the end of his twenty-fifth year as dean, students hailed his efforts in a yearbook dedication. They gave him high marks for steering "a fledgling infant into a well-established institution of high academic and spiritual reputation."[34]

And while his tireless efforts served the school well, his era was slipping by. The Noah Good who had promoted plays as a public school teacher before coming to LMS was not pleased with the growing interest in drama in the late '60s. In a memo to Myron Dietz about the prospects of students dramatizing "another" Anabaptist play, Good wrote, "Many of us who feel deeply about the whole Anabaptist Vision are horrified to think that anybody would write those deeply spiritual experiences into a play to be acted before a public audience for entertainment and call it education. It still makes me sick to think of last year's events. . . . I wanted to carry that ugly stuffed image . . . out and burn it. It seemed to me like heathen imagery. . . ."[35] A younger generation was clamoring for drama, interscholastic sports and instrumental music; the time for new leadership had arrived.

A fellowship meal marked Good's retirement from the deanship in May of 1970. He noted that former administrators sometimes meddle when things don't go right, making everyone unhappy. Two years after the transition, Good said, "I've been trying to keep out of their wool, to let them administer now that they're the administrators, and I enjoy doing it this way." The new principal commended Good for making the transition to teaching remarkably well—he never came back to the office nor obstructed pending changes. Brubaker, now setting a new agenda for a new generation, was overturning policies of earlier years with the former dean sitting in the faculty meetings. Early in the transition, Brubaker brought a proposal to the faculty that veered sharply from former ways. After a brief discussion, Noah Good made the motion to approve the new direction—a symbol of his true character and nobility.

The Rise of Sports

While church leaders tinkered with organization, a host of other changes were also afoot. Students were clamoring for more sports in louder voices. As music captured front stage in the late '50s and early '60s, so sports carried the torch in the late '60s and early '70s. With Mennonite farms dwindling, Mennonite youth had more time for leisure. Mass media and growing athletic programs in the public schools gave sports greater visibility and attracted some youth to other schools. Indeed, sports was one of many reasons cited for the slumping enrollment. Frowning on athletics from the beginning, the school made a turnabout in this period. The word "sports" appeared for the first time in the 1967 yearbook when it replaced the well-worn "athletics." The six pages devoted to sports in the '67 yearbook jumped to 18 by 1972. Although rapid, the shift was not painless.

Feeling the heat for more sports, the trustees appointed a study committee of five ordained leaders. Should LMS permit scrimmage games with other schools, join interschool leagues and participate in the annual Mennonite Basketball Classic with other Mennonite high schools? The faculty were split down the center on the issue of intramural competition as well as with scrimmage games with other schools. One teacher argued that interaction with other schools would help overcome "Mennonite isolationism." He warned that contacts with the "world involved risks, and we just shouldn't plunge into it without careful thought."[36] In January of 1969 the study committee proposed limiting competitive games to intramural athletics and staying out of the Mennonite Basketball Classic. Recognizing that scrimmage games with other schools have "already been arranged by teachers and parents," the committee *discouraged* these as much as possible and urged school officials not to sponsor them. The wording, however, did not *prohibit* scrimmage games! The trustees approved the report.

Several weeks later students won permission for an athletic award program for intramural sports, "hoping to convince others that a well-rounded sports program is a vital part of a Christian school."[37] The Alumni Association joined the students in pressing for better facilities. Larry Newswanger, Alumni president, told the trustees in February of 1969 that "the Alumni have considerable interest" in a new gym facility and asked the board to act on this issue.[38]

In '69-'70, Good's last year in administration, the pressure for scrimmage games with other schools increased. Prior to this time, when LMS teams played other schools it was done, in the words of Ernest Hess, on a "hush, hush kind of basis—totally unofficial." In the fall of '69 Lowell Stoltzfus, physical education instructor, asked Good for permission to organize a basketball team to scrimmage with other schools. It would not, of course, be an official team. Simply called the "Lancaster" team, it would not be publicized in the *Millstream*. Stoltzfus noted that sports had provided him with a "whole new area of witness." Worried about the trend, Good fired back a memo the same day saying the trustees would need to decide. He feared this would "just be the first step to organized, planned, and publicly announced interscholastic games."[39]

Writing to the trustees a few days later, Good said, "We are now faced with a rather conspicuous program of scrimmage games which will certainly whet the appetite for official participation. . . . We need to decide what is scrimmage and how much of it we want."[40] Sensing their defense was sagging, the trustees in December of 1969 reaffirmed their objection to interscholastic sports but approved "scrimmage games with other schools." For the first time in the history of the school, the 1970 *Laurel Wreath* heralded photos of a soccer team as well as basketball teams for men and women.

The sports offensive continued throughout '69-'70. The barn from the bygone Yeates era still served as a gym. Distressed when the trustees declared the old gym floor safe even though it "vibrated considerably," a faculty committee urged them to visit the building during a class and see the "absolute necessity" of a new gym.[41] Indeed, by January of 1970 a Building Committee was reviewing options for a new gym. The students pressed the attack forward with great enthusiasm. Over Easter vacation a student work day netted some $18,000 toward a new athletic field for track, hockey and soccer. Hundreds of students worked for friends, washed cars and sold baked goods in a vigorous effort that one school official called "the best thing that ever happened for public relations."[42] A student editorial called the fund drive the "last kicks of a dying school, or the beginning of a new spurt of health."[43] It was, indeed, a new burst of health.

On May 1, 1970, chapel services were held across the Mill Stream on the muddy site of a new athletic field. In a ground breaking ceremony, students and faculty alike pulled a plow through the field. Teacher Wilbur Lentz gave a talk entitled "Life is like a football game." It was a new day for the high school. Moreover, school officials agreed to use excess funds from the work day for a new gym.

As the Brubaker administration eased into place in the summer of 1970, sports continued their upward swing. In October the trustees agreed for the first time to offer a limited program of varsity sports and interscholastic athletics to "exercise special skills and develop qualities of Christian sportsmanship." Varsity competition in men's and women's basketball, soccer, field hockey and track was slated for "Christian and acceptable non-public schools."[44] Playing without official uniforms, the boys wore Bermuda-length shorts for the first time in LMS history. The girls, of course, were clad in culottes, but many of them, in another first, played without coverings and with hair tied in ponytails. By the fall of '71 LMS teams were decked out in official uniforms. It was a new day by the Mill Stream. In the fall of '72 the school hosted the "Big Three Eastern Mennonite Soccer Tournament."

Although interscholastic league competition would stall for several years, the school had taken an irrevocable turn. Students rejoiced that "the sleeping Mennonite Giant—the largest Mennonite High School in the world—has finally come alive athletically."[45] Many adults openly cheered the new turn of events. Others cheered under their breaths, and still others, including some trustees, despaired at the school's departure from its 28-year ban on interscholastic sports.[46]

The press for the new gym continued onward. Under the slogan "Gimme a Gymmie," students organized yet another fund drive for the new facility. Raising over $21,000 in two work days in the spring of '71, they received kudos on the editorial page of local newspapers and congratulations from President Nixon.[47] The records of 1971-72 document a growing consensus for a new gym. Only the matter of size and location remained open. Bishop David Thomas, mustering up his best diplomatic skills, suggested calling the new facility an auditorium/gym in deference to the school's bygone founders.

Dress, Drama and Instrumental Music

Changes in dress, drama and instrumental music also shaped the five-year period from '67 to '72. In the last year of the Good administration, '69-'70, boys were permitted to don long ties of a "dark solid color" and girls shed their capes. The dress code became an "appearance code." Assistant principal Myron Dietz urged faculty to "nip the long hair boys immediately," at the beginning of the '69-'70 term. He also advised faculty to "nip any short skirts in the bud." In the last months of his administration, Noah Good lamented "the perennial struggle with dress" and expressed "pity" for the girls who one week wore extremely short skirts and the next week wore maxi skirts down to their toes. They were not, Good said, "defiant or looking for sex appeal," but were merely "attention getters." Some of the girls wore "a little tuft of hair in front of the ear," a fad that Good found particularly irksome. One girl, he noted, had a curl about seven inches long and an inch-and-a-half in diameter.[48] By

The Junior Ladies Sextet of 1973 carried on the musical tradition of a cappella singing.

1971-72 school policy permitted the tufts of hair to expand into two large ponytails. Although flowing hair was taboo, ponytails signaled a new step in permissible hairstyles.

As the Brubaker administration found its stride in the fall of 1970, the faculty dress code vanished. Men began wearing long ties with lapel coats and some faculty women laid aside their capes. Some men began touting flashy ties and bold sport coats in the classroom. To curb the faculty flamboyance, the trustees enacted a faculty appearance code in the spring of '72. Teachers were asked to conform to the student code and refrain from wearing wedding bands and mustaches. Wedding bands were considered a form of jewelry prohibited by New Testament teaching. In 1971-72 a faculty member wearing a beard and a mustache was asked to remove them. A beard in the early '70s was the flag of the hippy counterculture. Beards were acceptable when, as in the case of Dietz, they reflected a denominational practice. Off campus, faculty women were encouraged to wear their veilings and not arrange their hair in a flowing fashion.

Musical instruments became acceptable with the new constitution of 1970. By June of that year the trustees had agreed to place a piano in the music room with two conditions. Funds would have to be raised privately, and the piano could only be used for teaching purposes—not for accompaniment or public

Teacher Daniel Wenger directs one of the first instrumental groups in 1973.

programs. Wooing sympathetic businessmen, Arnold Moshier and the Campus Chorale raised the funds and the piano arrived in the fall. A year later the trustees permitted a piano in the dining hall beneath the chapel for weddings and other special occasions. It remained banned, however, from chapel services upstairs.[49] In the spring of 1971 an instrumental string quintet of four violinists and a cellist under the direction of teacher Dan Wenger began practicing. The *Faculty and Staff Bulletin* of March '71 said instrumental music was being introduced at a faster rate than expected and asked teachers "to cool it, please . . . keep it at a minimum."

By the fall of '71 the trustees approved a music ensemble of "orchestra type" instruments, provided it did not perform rock and roll, jazz or other forms of pop music. Under Dan Wenger's leadership the group performed at a Thanksgiving banquet in 1971. The '72 *Laurel Wreath* opens with a full page, color photo of an unveiled student strumming her guitar. Faculty dorm advisors were also plucking guitars. For the moment, chapel services were preserved from the encroaching instruments. But one thing was certain: the 1970 constitution had welcomed new and unusual sounds to the Mill Stream.

Drama was also on the rise. Over the years the acceptable language for dramatic presentations evolved from "skits" to "plays" to "drama." The junior class presentation of Dickens' *Christmas Carol* in 1968 included a full array, albeit amateur, of costumes, props and actors. The Christmas "skit" was given a two-page spread in the *Laurel Wreath*. The Student Forum in 1968 begged for a dramatics club. Finally, the trustees in the fall of 1971 permitted the school to "move cautiously" into drama with six guidelines. The productions were to be small and simple—not planned for the general public. The plays should "raise intellectual and moral values and result in radical changes of life style for all involved." Furthermore, they should not make evil look attractive nor be merely entertainment.[50]

With all the changes awash, had all the boundaries crumbled? In the spring of 1971 the trustees banned television from classrooms and a year later they scuttled "regular playing cards" from campus.[51] All had not been tossed aside.

Under New Management

The Brubaker administration ushered in a host of changes that Charles Longenecker described as a "whole new era—almost a new institution." The first two years of that era (1970-72) witnessed changes in image, management, faculty, curriculum, constituency relations, professional associations and student life. Professionalization, the word of the day, drove the transformation in all of these areas.

Organizations seeking a new identity often opt for a new name. The name Lancaster Mennonite School sometimes confused outsiders. Was it a Bible school, an elementary school or a high school? Moreover, its image had become tainted among some Mennonites as a relic of the past. The newly named Lancaster Mennonite High School became LMH. The initials, LMH, accompanied by a creative logo, shaped a new image. Other identity changes were in the offing as well. The Student Forum became Student Council and drafted a new constitution. Campus Chorale replaced the Select Chorus. Revival meetings were soon replaced with Commitment Week in the fall and Christian Growth Week in the spring. "Brother" and "sister," fraternal terms of spiritual community, fell in favor of Mr., Mrs., and Miss. Intended to set a fraternal tone of Christian equality, the "brother and sister" titles, in actuality, signified one-way authority. Students had used them to address teachers, who, in turn, called students by their first names. Although the shift in titles did not change the one-way pattern of authority, it did reflect the new professional tone of the school.

The publicity streaming in greater volumes from the campus projected a new image of quality and excellence. A promotional brochure touted the headline, "Training Youth in Academic Excellence," a decade before excellence became a national fad. The first panel inside the brochure proclaimed "high standards," an obvious attempt to correct dubious perceptions. The message of the new image was clear: LMH is a professional school with high academic standards.

With administrative authority consolidated in the principal's office, a more assertive management style emerged. Long-range planning for facilities and new programs rose to the fore. The school developed a five-year plan and hired an architectural firm to develop a campus master plan. The possibility of developing a junior high school program for seventh and eighth graders moved into the spotlight. Internal management was cleaner, crisper and more prompt with leadership responsibilities now lodged in one office. Although the faculty for the most part cheered the new changes, they also knew whom to criticize for unpopular decisions. The withdrawal of building keys from faculty hands irked some of them. As J. Lester Brubaker harvested a situation ripe for change, he also delegated authority. He encouraged faculty and departments to take the lead in changing curriculum and urged committees—both faculty and trustee—to take greater initiatives.

The professionalization of the faculty proceeded abreast with other changes. With relaxed dress standards, greater attention focused on academic qualifications. A formal written contract spelled out the expectations and legal conditions of employment.[52] Regular faculty meetings were held, with some devoted to professional development. Special funds were set aside for professional improvement and faculty were soon expected to take advanced courses on a regular basis. Salaries rose, and hospitalization benefits improved. A retirement program for school employees swung into place. Principal Brubaker developed a faculty handbook in a loose leaf binder, which, according to one faculty member, "became Lester's legacy to the school." It systematized policies, made them readily available and provided for easy updating.

And while the husk on the ears of corn was changing, dress did continue to matter. The new principal expected teachers to dress as professionals—not teach with open collars or wear casual sportswear to class. He "was a stickler on dress," remembered a faculty member. "If you didn't wear a plain suit, then he expected you to wear a tie. I think it was a symbol of professionalism for him."

A relaxed, spontaneous mood accompanied the professionalization. Reflecting the new tone, the faculty gave a humorous program in a special assembly. With guitar, trombone and tambourine, they entertained students with a host of humorous skits and ditties, poking fun at their own idiosyncracies. Singing of Elton G. Moshier, nicknamed "Eggum" for E.G.M., they harmonized to the tune of "Home on the Range":

"An expert with cam-ra and film this teach
There's a picture wherever he's been
He loves to tap sap from those stately hard trees

And make sugar by boiling it thick.
Oh yes Egg-um's our man
There's not much he doesn't do
Just mention a song, and request it of him
And he'll probably sing it for you."

At the first faculty conference under the new administration, J. Lester Brubaker discussed "Meeting Student Needs through Relevance and Individualization." Exercising more ownership of the curriculum, faculty were divided into instructional areas with leaders for each cluster. With the demise of the Supervising Committee, a Principal's Coordinating Committee—administrators and instructional area leaders—met monthly to steer the academic program. Instructional areas were encouraged to review their curriculum. A flurry of revision took place. Ten new English courses appeared by 1971-72, along with a host of new history, Bible and science courses. Using a jagged edge strategy, instructional areas proceeded at different rates in their curriculum revision. So numerous were the curriculum changes, students complained they "couldn't begin to count them!"

The new school launched a spirited program of public relations. No longer

Teacher Elton Moshier directs traffic at the end of the school day as students enter Rt. 30.

tagging along at the bid of the Bishop Board, the school asserted itself and cultivated new constituencies. The trustees and the administration each established a Public Relations Committee. A monthly *Report* was mailed to parents updating them on school activities. Parents were surveyed about their attitudes toward dress requirements and other school policies.

Everett Newswanger directed the public relations activities on a part-time basis. Brochures flashing the new logo were prepared for prospective students and potential donors. Fund raiser Robert Messner joined the team as officials sought contributions to curb the rising tuition. Now the school, which only years earlier frowned on slides, skits and radios, was promoting itself with all three of these media.

Ties to the larger educational world were also fortified. School choruses began participating in the annual Music Festival of the Mennonite high schools. Growing numbers of students enrolled in the Lancaster County Vocational-Technical program on a half-day basis. The new principal selected four students as Outstanding Teenagers of America in a national program recognizing student leaders. The faculty began attending the Mennonite teacher conventions sponsored by the Mennonite Secondary Education Council. The school affiliated with the Mid-Atlantic Christian Schools Association and faculty attended its annual convention.

A part-time guidance counselor and plans for a full-time one signalled the school's growing commitment to help individuals make choices in a complicated world. The entrance exam for prospective students fell by the wayside. Parents were asked to participate in an intake interview along with their child prior to admission. Citizenship grades replaced the old conduct and effort grades. Honor points rewarded academic work. A chapter of the National Honor Society, formed in the last years of the Good administration, flourished. Instead of devoting a special day to Student Religious Programs in chapel, students participated in a wide variety of chapel programs—a marked departure from the past when only ordained leaders led chapel services. The "pupils" and "young people" of the past had indeed become "students" and "individuals." Although they clearly weren't running the school, they had a new voice and a greater hand in shaping its affairs. Charged by some with "listening to the students too much," J. Lester Brubaker summed up the new stance. "We sought to express an attitude of caring and respect without being soft."[53]

The changes swirling through the school between 1969 and 1972 were unprecedented. Even though many of the shifts had been ripening for a decade, it was surprising that the school and its constituencies could absorb so much change so quickly. The school and the Mennonite church, said J. Lester

Students head for the parking lot at the end of classes in the late 1960s.

Brubaker, are "caught up in the cultural changes of the larger society. The world, as traditionally referred to, is no longer 'they' but 'us.' With the loss of certain taboos, we find that youth and frequently their parents want to get rid of all taboos. They lack a sense of history and heritage and want the changes they want, now—not tomorrow—and, regardless. The role of the school in relation to cultural change is always difficult to define, and doubly so when the school is church-related and seeks to promote religious values."[54]

In many ways the transformation by the Mill Stream mirrored the social features emerging in the modern industrial world—bureaucratization, specialization, professionalization and individualization. The school was becoming an institution in its own right, shaping its own destiny—no longer the hand-maiden of the bishops. But the journey toward greater institutionalization carried ironies as well. On the one hand there was greater clarity of roles—job descriptions proliferated—yet the clarity provided both faculty and adminis-trators more freedom and autonomy. Formal memos, documents, five-year plans and minutes of sundry committees cluttered the bulging filing cabinets of school personnel and testified to the growing formality. And yet with clapping in chapel and humorous faculty skits there was a new ethos of spontaneity. Authority and responsibility for the entire operation clearly rested in the principal's office. But at the same time, parents, teachers and students alike were contributing ideas on many fronts.

Surely the school was charting its own course more visibly than ever before. Nevertheless, constituency opinions were taken quite seriously—patron surveys, rare rituals in the past, were on the rise. The changes marked a growing functional separation between church and school. Professional educators guided the school while the bishops tended to "churchly" matters of biblical interpretation, ordinances and congregational life. Lay church members, however, were indirectly "running the school" more than ever, via survey feedback, committee membership and financial contributions. So although the bishops had let their school out to pasture, it was still grazing in a pasture fenced in by the church.

CHAPTER SEVEN

Professionalizing the Program

1972-1983

"God blesses work that is bathed in prayer."
—J. Lester Brubaker

"A Big State of Flux"

J. Lester Brubaker remained principal until the summer of 1983. Under his leadership the academic program expanded and the faculty became more professionalized. The '70s brought new changes in facilities, sports, music, drama and, of course, the appearance code. The changes rippling through the school in these years reflected the transformation afoot in the church. Describing the Mennonite landscape in 1973, assistant principal Ernest Hess said, "Lancaster Conference is in a big state of flux. Many people are wondering if we are going to give up all the things that make us unique."

Mennonites were rapidly leaving their plows for professions. A survey of LMH students in 1974 showed a striking decline in farming over three genera-

A bulldozer demolishes the old mill building in 1973.

tions. Although 80 percent of grandfathers farmed, the number dropped to 40 percent for fathers and shrank in half again to 20 percent for student aspirations. Moreover, 47 percent of the students aspired to professional jobs—40 percent above their parents. This rate equaled the hopes of non-Mennonite students in public high schools.[1] The occupational turnabout, compressed into three generations, boosted Mennonites into the mainstream of society and sprawled them in many directions.

Noah Good, speaking in 1974, described the exodus from the farm. "We've entered an entirely different category of society. Earlier we were a peasant, dirt-farming, wrench-wielding group. Now we have a lot of white collar office people administering large businesses. . . . This is an entirely different bracket of society than we were in when the school opened in 1942." Faculty debated whether the school should follow tradition and close for the Pennsylvania Farm Show or vacate on Memorial Day—the preference of suburban parents. As Mennonites participated in new sectors of society, the distinguishing practices of separation were being dropped across the Conference. Discussing noncon-formity in 1973, some bishops said, "Apparently the cape dress and plain suit are lost. The matter of jewelry can still be helped. Modesty must be empha-sized."[2]

The bishops themselves were changing. Speaking in 1972, bishop David Thomas, moderator of Lancaster Conference, said, "I haven't worn a hat now for months. There was a time when I wouldn't have gone to a funeral in the summer without a hat. I went to two funerals last week without a hat. Ten years ago I wouldn't have served without a hat. I just wouldn't have. There was a time when wearing a hat was a pretty important thing." By the end of the '70s some bishops had not only taken off their hats, but were laying aside their plain suits as well.

The diversity of life styles spreading across Lancaster Conference weakened centralized authority and increased congregational autonomy. By the mid '70s the bishops found it difficult, if not impossible, to enforce the *Rules and Discipline* revised in 1968. They concluded that "the written discipline is no longer the unifying factor it once was." More and more decisions were being made on the district and congregational levels.[3] Between 1975 and 1981 the bishops earnestly grappled with the growing gap between the *Rules and Discipline* of 1968 and the actual practice of many members. The issue came to a watershed vote in the spring conference of 1981. In a historic 365 to 20 vote, ordained leaders agreed to give congregations a choice. They could follow the *Rules and Discipline*, or affirm the more general 1963 Mennonite Confession of Faith and develop their own guidelines for membership requirements.[4] This historic decision opened the door to even greater diversity and ended the century-long reign of a written discipline.

Without the compass of a Conference-wide discipline, LMH had to chart a delicate course across the treacherous waters of diversity in the '70s. If the school changed too quickly, conservatives would drop their support. So would progressive parents, if the school merely upheld the status quo. During the '70s LMH moved into the mainstream of the Conference. In fact, the growing sports program tilted it toward the more progressive congregations by the early '80s. By that time two smaller Mennonite high schools had opened their doors to more conservative constituents.[5]

In these years the LMH appearance code was viewed more and more as a *school* code rather than a handbook of *church* regulations. The school, of course, could not enforce regulations that had withered in the Conference itself. Nevertheless the school functioned amid a wide array of religious convictions. Trustees sometimes found themselves trying to enforce regulations no longer practiced in the congregations of many students. A bishop on the Religious Welfare Committee said, "J. Lester Brubaker would plead and ask how can you expect me to carry out what you bishops can't in your own congregations?" Brubaker spelled out the dilemma this way. "How does the school remain both stable and flexible in a church with varied and rapidly changing practices?" [6]

The Mennonite Legacy

The erosion of traditional symbols of identity—plain suit, cape dress and prayer veiling—left a vacuum in the Mennonite soul. Theological winds from four different directions blew across the community during the '70s. Some folks clenched *traditional* symbols tightly—arguing that their demise signaled the end of Mennonite faithfulness. Others claimed to retrieve the essence of Mennonite identity in historic *Anabaptist* themes—discipleship, community, service and peacemaking—which translated into practice in a variety of ways. Their identity no longer rooted in uniform practice, these Anabaptist enthusiasts advocated abstract, historical and international themes.

Charismatic winds fanned the hearts of other Mennonites. These breezes brought freedom of expression, emotional spontaneity and biblical simplicity to some who had strained under the strict regulations of earlier years. The winds of religious *Fundamentalism* also buffeted the Mennonite community. Offering theological certainty when many time-honored doctrines were under assault, the firm beliefs of Fundamentalism appealed to many. All four theological currents claimed the authority of Scripture. These theological winds tossed the school about as it sought a sensible course across the Mennonite waters of the '70s.

Historian John Ruth talked to students about "The Mennonite Monkey" on their back in the spring of 1973. Speaking on the meaning of Mennonite identity, he urged them not to reject their Anabaptist heritage. The Mennonite Church, contended Ruth, offers the kind of society and brotherhood that people are looking for today.[7] Stories of Anabaptist persecution abounded as the Mennonite Church celebrated its 450th anniversary in 1975. As part of the celebration, students re-enacted the 1527 drowning of Anabaptist martyr Felix Manz in the Mill Stream. The 1975 *Laurel Wreath* reminded students that "we sprouted from years of persecution." Mennonite History, taught by Myron Dietz, offered many students a stable anchor in the midst of change. With external symbols fading, hymn 606 in the *Mennonite Hymnal*, "Praise God from Whom All Blessings Flow," became a sort of Mennonite national anthem. Several senior classes sang it for some monks on their Washington D.C. trip when they visited a Franciscan monastery.[8]

The new gymnasium was completed in 1975.

Holy Spirit conferences, Jesus Rallies and new charismatic congregations all reflected the spiritual flavor of the times. A Jesus '75 Rally near Morgantown, Pennsylvania, attracted some 30,000 attendees, including many Mennonite youth. A charismatic club appeared at LMH in 1973. The rising charismatic movement kindled spirited discussions in Bible classes on spiritual gifts and the "work of the Holy Spirit." Prayer and share groups spread across the campus.

Theological differences within the school surfaced over several issues. The Vietnam War spurred new debate on the meaning of patriotism and the place of Old Glory. The Student Forum had received permission to place a flag in the library in 1962. Sometime thereafter Old Glory disappeared. In the fall of 1968, the Student Forum, nudged by the national wave of patriotism, asked the Supervising Committee to purchase a flag for the library and another one for the balcony inside the front lobby. The Supervising Committee approved the request.[9] For five years Old Glory greeted guests in the lobby and stood in a quiet corner of the library.

In the fall of '73 some faculty members questioned if an American flag belonged in a Mennonite high school. They argued that the Vietnam War had turned the flag into a symbol of "loyalty to the law and order elements of society . . . who support the American war efforts and all the militarism connected with it." Patriotism could better be expressed, they proposed, by displaying the towel and basin—Mennonite symbols of service. Teacher Jane

Short said, "We don't want to get caught up in a Christianity that mixes up allegiance to God and Country. . . . Our first allegiance is to God's nation and God's nation is beyond nationalism. . . ."[10]

A faculty committee recommended removing the flags "to affirm that Jesus is Lord and to express our allegiance to God's kingdom." The committee proposed creating a display of flags from each country where alumni serve. The faculty approved the request and passed it to the trustees who suggested a compromise: place a small American flag in the library and exhibit flags of alumni countries. The alumni display, "One People in Many Nations," would hold 30 small flags of the countries where alumni lived. And so the flag retreated from the lobby to the library, where once again in the '80s it was mislaid, not to return again.[11]

The flag issue typically heated up in times of war—World War II, the Cuban missile crisis, the Vietnam and Persian Gulf wars. The school's ambivalence over the years about the flag reflected a deep paradox within the Mennonite soul. Governments, Mennonites believed, were established by God to maintain order. Members were taught to pray for and respect national leaders. Yet the Bible also taught that allegiance to God's international kingdom superseded national loyalties. Thus, over the years the flag often received a cool welcome at LMH.

The school's involvement with Christian school associations also kindled faculty debate. By 1974 LMH was affiliated with four professional associations: the Pennsylvania Association of Christian Schools, the Mid-Atlantic Christian Schools Association, the Association of Christian Schools International and the Mennonite Secondary Educational Council.[12] Lancaster Mennonite Conference officially joined the larger Mennonite Church in a North American reorganization in 1971. Consequently LMH joined other schools in the Mennonite Secondary Educational Council in 1972-73. Ties with the Council flourished throughout the '70s and '80s.

LMH participated in the teachers' convention of the Mid-Atlantic Christian Schools Association and its fine arts festival. Some faculty members welcomed the interchange with other Christian teachers. But others deplored what they considered the Association's "God and Country" tone and Fundamentalist theology. At the teachers' convention in 1976, participants in an evening banquet sang "The Star Spangled Banner." Caught by surprise, some Mennonite teachers stood and sang, others stood quietly and still others remained seated. "It was the nationalism thing, the rah-rah American flag waving that bothered some of us," one teacher recalled.

J. Lester Brubaker encouraged participation in the Mid-Atlantic Christian

Schools Association. He felt such involvements were mutually beneficial and that membership outweighed the costs. Furthermore, Brubaker contended that the Christian school associations were evangelical organizations even though some Fundamentalist schools held memberships in them. In July of 1982 Brubaker took the issue to the LMH board, explaining that the faculty were divided on membership in the Mid-Atlantic Christian Schools Association with some stridently opposing it. Throughout the '80s students continued to participate in the arts festivals organized by the Association. Faculty, however, stopped attending the teacher conventions and the trustees dropped their membership in the Association of Christian Schools International after 1984.[13]

For some, the Mennonite legacy impeded full participation in American life and was a burden to toss off. For others it was a valuable compass that pointed the way for Anabaptist pilgrims. The controversies over the flag and the Christian school associations reflected Mennonite ambiguity toward the state as well as the struggle with competing theological views. The Mennonite legacy was alive and well, but also being transformed—from uniform practices to abstract themes, elastic enough to fit the growing diversity of the Mennonite community.

To God Be the Glory

Daily chapel services refurbished the spiritual life of students and defined the religious mood of the school. Speakers urged youth to commit their lives to Jesus Christ and his kingdom. Chapel services became more lively over the years. Those of the '70s reflected the informal, charismatic tone of the times. Speaking in 1972, David Thomas described the changes to a student, upset because she couldn't use a drum in chapel. Trying to convince her that chapel had indeed changed from earlier years, he explained, "The principal, a bishop, used to have all the chapels. Later, other ordained men led them occasionally. Then four years ago unordained faculty men could speak, and two years ago in 1970 women started having them. Last year Student Council began arranging and conducting some chapels. And sometimes when music groups came in from the outside we let them use guitars in chapel." The student, said Thomas, "thought we were so rigid because she couldn't have a drum, but I tried to show her that we really had changed a lot."

The changes continued throughout the '70s. Chapels were more relaxed and often student-led. Students sang spontaneously as they entered the chapel auditorium. Scripture choruses and praise songs were sung alongside hymns from the *Mennonite Hymnal*. The *Millstream* hailed "To God Be the Glory" as the most frequently sung hymn in 1975. Other favorites included, "I Sing the

By the late 1970s Campus Chorale was using instruments when giving programs in local congregations.

Mighty Power of God," "Take My Life and Let It Be" and "Blessed Assurance."[14] Although praise tunes flowing from Scripture were frequent favorites, a student charged that "nothing ruins four-part singing more than unison one-part ditties."[15] Applause in chapel—unthinkable before the '70s—soon accompanied the spirit of spontaneity. Edna Wenger speaking in 1972 said, "I never thought I'd hear clapping in an LMH chapel. It would make some early board members turn in their graves." Indeed, some of the living were squirming. "Clapping we just did not do—never, under any circumstances," said former principal Amos Weaver. "I learned to patty-cake when I was a baby and I put that away. I detest it." The clapping symbolized the spiritual mood of the times—spontaneous, informal, praiseful.

Spiritual high points continued—Commitment Week in the fall and Christian Growth Week in the spring. Although chapels were more relaxed, appeals for personal commitment were more restrained. Speakers encouraged public commitments, but they often asked students to write them on a card, tell a friend or raise their hand rather than walk forward. However, half of the students did carry commitment cards to the front of the chapel in response to Glendon Blosser's preaching in 1973. Dan Yutzy's instruction in 1981 brought "three first-time commitments." One student said, "I've been sitting in the boat too long. I felt it was time to pick up the oars and start rowing."[16] In what the *Laurel Wreath* called a historic first, H. Raymond Charles ended Commitment Week in the fall of 1981 with a special service. Students exchanged cracker-like wafers symbolizing peace and unity.[17]

Bible teacher Glen Sell coordinated chapel services throughout much of the '70s. Principal Brubaker spoke monthly. A slot each month was also slated for impromptu testimonies. Some faculty worried about the changes. Describing the situation in 1977, Janet Gehman said, "Perhaps we have come too far. For the sake of interesting students with variety, we may have sacrificed solid teaching."[18] A *Laurel Wreath* writer contended that the value of chapel was "up to the individual," and observed that some chapels "start the day off with a bang while others tempt students to rest in the Word."[19]

Bible classes also nurtured spiritual growth. From a dozen selections, students could choose to take at least four semester-long courses. Titles included

Students gather food for a Christmas can drive in the mid-1970s.

Creative Bible Study, Practical Christian Living, Mennonite Life and Thought, History of God's People, Life and Times of Christ and Tenets of Christian Faith. Beyond the classroom students participated in prayer and share groups, Gospel Teams and service projects. Glen Sell organized an extensive Gospel Team program. Small teams of students presented programs in churches and retirement homes. More than 100 students, backed by prayer partners, gave 25 to 30 programs a year.

Over the years LMH organized a variety of Christian service projects. Student Council often sponsored a canned food drive at Christmas—donating thousands of cans to needy families.[20] In 1974 some 384 students and 19 faculty members "missed a meal for Chad," and donated its value to Mennonite Central Committee's hunger relief efforts in the African country. Students gathered 434 pairs of eyeglasses for the Dominican Republic in 1975 and 605 pairs in 1977. Some 120 students gleaned corn from fields in the fall of '76 and asked the farmers to contribute the corn's value to overseas projects of the Mennonite Central Committee.

"I believe that God blesses work that is bathed in prayer," said J. Lester Brubaker.[21] The efforts of the school were awash in prayer. Early morning faculty prayer meetings invoked God's blessing on the day's events. Chapels, of course, included prayer. Some classes and most committee meetings were prefaced with prayer. Coaches sometimes prayed with their teams. Faculty counselors often prayed with students who also prayed for each other in small groups. In all of these moments students were taught and nurtured in the ways of faith.

There were also painful disappointments. Some students wandered from the paths of faith. They rebelled and mocked earnest efforts on their behalf. The number of rebels varied from year to year and their pranks ranged from harmless mischief to malicious vandalism. It was not unusual to have several expulsions and 20 to 30 in-school suspensions a year for cheating, lying, forging signatures, smoking, lighting smoke bombs, tossing firecrackers, flooding lavatories, vandalizing property and possessing marijuana. The '76-'77 school term was especially difficult. It was a time, in the words of the principal, when some students figuratively "spit in the faces of teachers by their thoughtless and disrespectful behavior."[22]

The Academic Program

The academic program expanded during the Brubaker years. Part-time teaching was discouraged. Faculty were expected to enroll in six hours of graduate credit for every five years of service. They also participated in a variety of professional training activities. Professional support staff burgeoned in the '70s—a certified guidance counselor, a part-time chaplain, an athletic director, a director of development, a full-time business manager and a trained librarian with a full-time secretary. Summarizing these additions in 1982, Brubaker asked the trustees, "Who blows the whistle to halt the proliferation?"[23] Despite the press for professionalization, faculty retained a strong sense of divine calling. Ninety-seven percent, in 1974, said they believed "it was God's will for them to come to LMH."[24]

One or more academic areas were reviewed and revised each year. Electives in virtually all the academic areas were added while others were dropped throughout the '70s. Latin vanished with Edna Wenger's retirement in 1974. She had chalked up 32 years by the Mill Stream. Home economics for boys appeared in 1975 and the first psychology course was offered in 1978-79. New programs blossomed in agriculture, art, industrial arts, photography and instrumental music. In 1978 Eastern Mennonite College, and later Goshen and

The Mill Stream provided a convenient laboratory for many science classes over the years.

Teacher Glen Sell, in the foreground, facilitates small group discussions.

Hesston colleges, began granting credit for advanced courses. The trustees, after several years of discussion, established a learning disability program in 1983.

Three-day mini-courses, introduced in the spring of 1975, spanned from horseback riding to planning a wedding, and from butchering to cake decorating. In later years the mini-courses included service and mission opportunities—mental health, voluntary service and the urban church. In the mid-'70s Cooperative Vocational Education (Co-op) enabled seniors to work in supervised settings in local businesses.[25] Others enrolled in courses at the Willow Street Vocational Technical School.

New forms of technology were also coming to LMH. In the summer of '73 the trustees approved the purchase of video equipment and a closed circuit television for instructional use, but *not* for live programs. The December 1972 *Millstream* reported "strange events" in room 206. A large crowd gathered around a small group huddled by a typewriter-like machine. A terminal had been linked by telephone to a computer at Franklin and Marshall College. The terminal had "constant use" before school and over lunch—even until 10:30

at night. Teacher Stanley Kreider reportedly "lost six pounds through the loss of lunches and efforts to control the crowds."[26] By the early 1980s eight microcomputers resided in the math department and the principal was asking "how many computers shall we buy?"

Surprisingly, the agricultural program bloomed as Mennonites left their farms. In the mid-'70s one-third of the students still lived on farms. The agri-industry was booming, offering new jobs in landscaping, horticulture, mechanics and animal science. J. Richard Thomas, farm boy from Manor Township west of Lancaster city, was hired in 1973 as the first certified agriculture teacher. He initiated agricultural courses which had lain dormant for several years. Within six months 50 students were enrolled. The program grew rapidly and, by the spring of '78, 195 students were studying cows and crops. The program, in Thomas' view, was "comparable to any of the public school programs."[27] J. Lester Brubaker and Thomas hoped to certify the Vo-ag program and establish a chapter of the Future Farmers of America. The state director of Vocational Education, however, denied the application because his approval powers supposedly were "limited to public schools."[28] Championing his own version of a Future Farmers chapter, Thomas formed a club of Future Agriculturalists of America (FAA) in 1974. By 1976 over 50 students, including some women, were judging cattle, listening to speakers and holding socials.

While some students found their roots in agriculture, others clamored for art. Course offerings, however, were sparse. In 1975 student Phil Lutz complained that having only two art courses stifled creativity and compared unfairly with the multitude of courses in music, athletics and English. Moreover, he argued, art is not a worldly invasion. Mennonites have been into art—quilting—for a long time.[29] Mary Lou Houser joined the faculty as an art instructor in the fall of 1977. She expanded offerings and encouraged students to exhibit their work in a variety of new ways.

The academic program interfaced in other ways with the larger world as well. State aid, funneled through Public Intermediate Unit 13, provided textbooks, instructional media and auxiliary services. A speech therapist was on duty part-time. Full-time remedial services were provided by the Intermediate Unit in a bus parked outside the school, satisfying the mandate to separate church and state.

Students began arriving at LMH on public school buses in the fall of 1973. State legislation required public schools to transport private school students living within their districts as far as 10 miles beyond district boundaries. Buses from some 10 different public schools soon brought students to LMH, confirming some 32 years later the wisdom of locating the school in the heart of

Public school buses transported many LMH students after 1973.

Lancaster County.

In 1980-81 faculty scheduled some 70 field trips, mostly to local sites. Small groups of student leaders exchanged short visits among the various Mennonite high schools. Sociology classes sometimes toured New York City guided by Myron Dietz and other faculty. The brush with urban poverty prompted one student to ask, "Why are some of us so privileged while others suffer?"[30] Faculty members hoped to push student horizons even beyond New York City. In the late '70s and early '80s the curriculum was "globalized." Courses were designed to emphasize awareness of and responsibility for the global community.[31] In the summer of 1973 six students accompanied teacher Dan Wenger to Europe in what would, in later years, become periodic overseas visits.

The crowning achievement of this era was accreditation by the Middle States Association of Colleges and Schools. Brubaker pressed for accreditation

(top) Students at a skating social, in February 1971, warm themselves at a bonfire.

(bottom) The view from the Mill Stream bridge as the old Eshelman Mill—used as a dormitory and classroom building—is demolished in February 1973.

Hoagies are packed for delivery at the 1974 hoagie sale.

(top) In 1974 an LMH class enjoys a lunch break while researching cemetery records on a field trip.

(bottom) A track meet in 1975.

(top) A chemistry lab in 1976. Girls often wore their hair in double ponytails in these years.

(bottom) Seniors following commencement in 1976, prior to the arrival of caps and gowns in 1984.

(top) Students on a field trip to New York city stand outside the Glad Tidings Mennonite Church with teacher Myron Dietz.

(bottom) A volleyball game on the second floor of the old gym.

Field hockey in 1980.

(top) Group discussions in a home economics classroom in the mid-1970s.

(bottom) Senior class advisors, Ernest Hess and Deb Van Pelt, perform as "California Raisins" in a senior masquerade social in the mid-1980s.

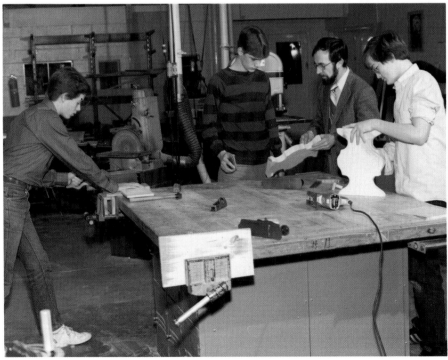

(top) Teacher Janet Banks conducts an English class in the 1980s.
(bottom) A shop class in 1985-86 under the supervision of teacher Wesley Newswanger.

because he felt LMH "was a good school and we were making it a better one. So why not have this stamp of approval so we could say to the community, this is a good school? We could be good academically, strongly Christian and Mennonite all at the same time." A faculty committee prepared a self-study throughout the '75-'76 school year. An 18-member Middle States evaluation team inspected the school in April of 1976. In December of the same year, school officials learned that LMH had earned the cherished stamp of approval.

The school's Statement of Philosophy, written in 1970, was translated into 18 educational objectives in 1975. The philosophy statement itself was revised in 1980.[32] The revised statement rested on the theological foundation of the 1963 Mennonite Confession of Faith. The primary purpose of the school, according to the revised statement, "is to provide a secondary education for persons of the Mennonite Church." A set of 14 educational objectives spelled out expectations for students: that they would "(1) grow in their under-standing of the Bible as God's authoritative word and commit themselves to be obedient to its teachings, and (2) learn the history and faith of the Mennonite Church and find direction for dealing with present-day issues."[33]

A Festival of Arts

What role should the fine arts play in a Mennonite school? That question loomed large in the 1970s. How much attention should drama, art, film and instrumental music receive? Traditional Mennonite thinking often considered artistic endeavors impractical and unnecessary. How did they advance the cause of Christ and deepen Christian commitment? Was drama more than frivolous entertainment? Moreover, it required actors to forfeit personal integrity by playing artificial roles—sometimes ones that dramatized evil. If a moral virtue was to be communicated, why not simply stand up and say it—without the expense of elaborate costuming and staging? Pressure from students, faculty and patrons pushed the school into new artistic expressions—new for Lancaster Mennonites.

The word "festival" signaled the mood of the times. It celebrated an about-face from the stern tone of the '40s and '50s that frowned on entertainment. In the early 1970s LMH choral groups began singing in the annual music festivals sponsored by the Mennonite Secondary Education Council. Students were participating in the Fine Arts Festival of the Mid-Atlantic Christian Schools Association. In the spring of 1973 students entered art work, sang solos and performed on the piano, violin and cello. During the '72-'73 term photography was "on the rampage," in the words of the *Millstream*, as shutterbugs in the Advanced Photography Club snapped away on campus.

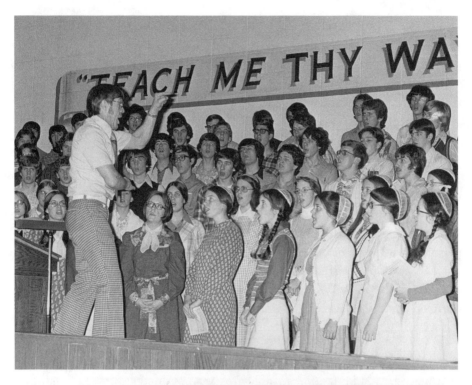

(top) Choruses under the direction of Arnold Moshier in the 1960s and 1970s were an integral part of the LMH experience for many students.

(bottom) LMH students often participated in music festivals involving other Mennonite high schools. This one in the mid-1970s was held in the new LMH gym.

In 1973 Merle Good began teaching a course on drama. The trustees reaffirmed their 1971 guidelines prohibiting dramatic productions for the general public.[34] Meanwhile, backstage, pressure for public performance was swelling. The junior class presented a play at their junior-senior outing and then again for their parents in the spring of 1973. An all-school talent night was held at the Harvest Drive Restaurant in the same year. The cooks sang and some 80 students entertained with solos, gospel rock, instrumental groups, a violin concerto and a small drama. "Midnight Sun" and other student bands performed. It was a first-time outburst of artistic talent.

In the '73-'74 term Merle Good organized a Film Club, advised a "song and drama" group and again taught drama. This time, however, his class prepared to stage "The Miracle Worker," a dramatization of Helen Keller's life. Interim director of development Charles Longenecker proposed a public performance. Proceeds would be split between a campus project and the Mennonite Central Committee. The trustees vetoed the idea.[35] A few weeks later the Student Affairs Committee again recommended public performances. Once again, the trustees balked. However, they invited Merle Good to discuss his "concerns about drama" with them.

Good told the trustees he hoped drama would not have to "slip into the Mennonite Church through the back door" like television. He wanted the school to give leadership and guidance to dramatic expression. On a practical level, he noted that stage lights were urgently needed to present "The Miracle Worker" in the upcoming school assembly. The trustees held their taboo on public performances but agreed to rent the lights. In short order, stage lights and a movie screen were installed in the chapel.[36] "The Miracle Worker," taking the honor of being the first all-school play, was presented in a morning assembly in May of 1974. In the same month "The Thread that Runs So True" was staged in the cafeteria for the annual junior-senior outing.

Other artistic developments transpired in 1974. Students were permitted to publish a short-lived literary magazine, *Wandering*. They could not, however, compete in district orchestra.[37] The trustees did agree to permit students to create their own audiovisual presentations.[38] And create they did! The Advanced Photography class crafted "Dirty Dan Strikes Again"—a super-eight-millimeter comedy movie for the second all-school talent night in April of 1974. Dirty Dan, the village villain, kidnapped Prudence Pureheart who was eventually rescued by Dudley Doright.

With the departure of Merle Good, dramatic activity declined in 1974-75. However, students continued to participate in the Mid-Atlantic Fine Arts Festival and began entering the regional Scholastic Art competition. The

An early full-fledged school play.

'75-'76 term brought new requests for artistic expression. In the spring of 1976 LMH held, for the first time, its own Fine Arts Festival featuring photography, art, music and speech.[39] Students in a drama workshop course were busily preparing to stage "Our Town" for the student body. Could they present an evening performance for family and friends? No, the trustees ruled. A public performance would violate the school's drama policy.[40]

Even in-house productions raised many questions. Were girls required to wear their coverings when they acted in plays? Could students chew tobacco in certain roles? Could she take her drama students to observe locally produced plays? asked teacher Rose Breneman. Uncertain what to do, trustees urged administrators to poll parental attitudes toward drama.[41] The results returned in the fall of '76.

About 30 percent of the parents "occasionally" permitted their own children to see motion pictures in theaters and 59 percent approved of their offspring attending public plays. Concerning LMH policies:

- •80 percent favored LMH drama classes attending a public play
- •73 percent favored LMH students giving a public play
- •84 percent favored their child acting in a school play
- •64 percent favored LMH showing movies for friends and alumni

Nearly 60 percent of the parents agreed that "drama is similar to other arts and communication media and can be used for good or evil. The Christian may participate in it as long as he does not need to compromise his call as a disciple of Christ." Although sentiment favored drama, one parent cautioned that "Mennonites shouldn't go hog wild with it." Another deplored "all these things creeping into our church and school. One standard after another is dropped. There is no stopping place." Said another, "Drama is a dangerous thing to fool with." On the question of movies a parent said, "If they were wrong years ago, why are they all right now—when there's more evil in them than ever?"

The trustees realized that, for the most part, the patrons of the school had sprinted ahead of them. In the spring of 1977 the trustees approved a new drama policy. It permitted public productions as long as they reinforced moral values and didn't make evil look attractive.[42] A year later in April of 1978, over 1,000 people attended the school's first public play, "The World of Sholom Aleichem," directed by Pat McFarlane. Meanwhile, in the spring of '77 other changes were in the offing. Seniors, the trustees said, could have the choice of attending a symphony or a dramatic performance on their Washington D. C. trip. And yes, the Student Council could show a two-hour motion picture, "A Man For All Seasons," as a public fund raiser. But no, they really should not use a Charlie Chaplin film to humor the audience at the outstart.

The spring of 1977 also brought instrumental sounds to chapel. A cappella singing, according to a new policy, would continue as the usual habit. But carry-in instruments—guitars, banjos and flutes—could now be used under special circumstances. In June the trustees gave students permission to begin competing in district orchestra and band for the first time.[43] Fred Longenecker went on to both district band and orchestra in the fall of 1977. The spring of 1977 had indeed been dramatic! The trustees were prodded by the parental poll. Artistic expression had found a new welcome by the Mill Stream.

The arts continued to flourish in the late '70s and early '80s. Propelled by the gift of a piano, music guidelines were revised in the spring of 1979. Pianos were now permissible in chapel services and public choral programs.[44] Shortly thereafter the parents of an alumnus who was killed in an auto accident donated a concert piano in memory of their son.[45] The gift piano, as well as instrumental courses, practice facilities and a public recital, signaled growing interest in instrumental music.[46] By 1982 LMH had, in the words of the *Laurel Wreath*, its first "full-fledged orchestra." Replacing a smaller instrumental ensemble, the orchestra performed in chapels and the annual Christmas concert. Craft work was added to the renamed and expanded Fine Arts and Crafts Festival. A wide range of entries were welcomed—home crafts, industrial arts, fine arts, photography and wood. Students also began to receive awards for art and literary submissions in the regional Scholastic Art competition. Kristine Yoder, in a new achievement, won a writing award from the National Council of Teachers of English in 1980. The *Millstream* and *Laurel Wreath* received first place ratings

PUBLIC COUNTRY AUCTION
APRIL 6, 1974
10:30 A.M.

Location: Lancaster Mennonite High School, 2176 Lincoln Highway East, Lancaster, Pa. 17602.

HAND-MADE QUILTS
Approximately 20-25 hand-made quilts of all designs and colors.

FURNITURE
Ten-piece dining room suite, hand-made cherry bench, cherry stand, occasional chairs, recliners, rocking chairs, desk, playpen, sofas, crib with mattress, bathroom cabinets, lawn chairs, love seat and table, lamps, end tables, chest of drawers, mattress, black walnut hand-crafted rocking chair, laundry and market baskets, new stereo.

CRAFTS
Afghans, pillow cases, comforts, decoupages, 3-D pictures, paintings, ceramics, crocheted items, stuffed toys, cushions, purses, aprons, hand-made candle holders, tablecloths, hand-made lace tablecloth, embroidery, hand-made dolls, crocheted rug, flower arrangements, crocheted poncho and shaw.

LIVESTOCK
Yearling heifer from good plus granddaughter of Ivanhoe from the herd of J. Eby Hershey and family, two 65 lb. feeder pigs, eight 40 lb. feeder pigs, holstein heifer, pet lamb (2 months old).

MACHINERY
Irrigation booster pump, Dutchman automatic poultry feeder (model B), 10 hole poultry nests, Bogg's potato grader, grass seeder, 12 h.p. Massey Ferguson garden tractor with mower, Egg-O-Matic egg grader, electric motor, electric paint remover, bicycles, chain saw, power saw, shop cleaner (vacuum), lawn mower, Black and Decker tools.

ANTIQUES
Crocks, iron kettles, hand-woven coverlet, glass insulator.

APPLIANCES
Toaster, double porcelain sink, refrigerator, electric fruit ripener, casserole, portable broiler, mixer, glassware, tupperware, sink faucets.

MISCELLANEOUS
Four-GR 78 x 14 and four-GR 78 x 15 new radial tires, auto harp with case, nursery stock trees and shrubbery, books, plants, ice skates, decorated cakes, milk cans, 8' x 12' wooden shed, two 55 gallon steel drums, building materials, 12 fishing tackle boxes, team autographed soccer ball of Philadelphia Atoms. There are also many other articles too numerous to mention.

OX ROAST 10:00 a.m. to 7:00 p.m. Tickets Available until Wed., April 3. Call 299-4849.

Donated Items: Accepted until sale time. Call 299-4849. Pickup provided.

PURPOSE: The auction is a part of the Fund Drive '74, an effort by students, at LMH to raise $40,000. With the cooperation of over 500 students we hope to raise $40,000 in two days which will give us the needed funds according to our latest estimate to start the construction of a new gymnasium.

Auctioneers: Abe Diffenbach
Abe Diffenbach, Jr.

Benefit auctions became favorite fund raisers in the mid-1970s.

in 1980 and 1981, respectively, in journalism competitions. Students began publishing their own creative arts magazine, *Silhouette*, in 1981-82. By the 1982-83 school year students were singing in the district chorus of the Pennsylvania Music Educators Association.[47] Ironically, as the old Mennonite art form of quilting began to enjoy a national renaissance, the daughters and sons of Menno were finding new ways to express their artistic bent.

Sports

The construction of a new gym in 1974-75 boosted school spirit. In the words of trustee James Hess, "the students picked up the ball. They just started raising money when the board wasn't even sure it was going to build a gym." Some board members worried that a new gym would turn LMH into a "sports capital." Principal Brubaker reminded trustees that the old gym in the Yeates barn was "really in bad shape." Such a building, said Brubaker, "doesn't honor the Lord." It's about time, he told the trustees, that like Joshua of old, we not only pray, but "get to work."[48] Urging the trustees to build, administrators contended that a new gym would not become a sports arena. An instructional facility, the "auditorium/gymnasium" would house the physical education program, provide facilities for intramural sports and seat some 1,800 people for churchwide meetings.

The bishops gave their blessing in the fall of 1972 and the trustees approved the million dollar project in the spring of 1974.[49] The trustees "drug their feet

A track meet on Blazer turf.

(top) Coach Susan Rohrer, upper left, and her team of Blazerettes.
(bottom) The new gym was used for a variety of sports.

pretty heavily," said Chairman Hess. While the trustees were dragging their feet, the students were running. In the spring of '73 the fourth student fund drive raised $30,000. An auction added flair to the usual bake sale, sub sale, chicken barbecue, car wash and work projects. Animated by the prospects of breaking ground, students chanted "40 grand turns the land" in the spring of '74. A donated heifer sold for $2,000 on the auction and a work-a-thon project raised a total of $51,700 to the glee of students. As the new gym neared completion in April of 1975, students chanted "a dream for 50 green" as they spearheaded still another fund raiser. Many were cheered on by grandmothers in traditional garb who held a campus quilting party to help the cause.

Meanwhile, the sports program was burgeoning. An invitational soccer tournament for other Mennonite high schools had become an annual fall tradition. Girls' softball began in 1973, in tandem with the first cross-country team. By 1974 junior varsity teams complemented the varsities. In the early '70s Virgil King, president of the Alumni Association, said, "We need a name for LMH teams to rally around. Perhaps it should be Blazers." Indeed the name stuck. Soon the Blazerettes joined the Blazers, only to be blown away in a few years by the winds of feminism when all teams were known simply as Blazers.

With 20 percent of the students in sports, Blazer spirit sometimes grew proud. Basking in a soccer win over Lancaster Country Day School, a *Millstream* headline proclaimed "LMH Farmers Plow Hippies." And after the game one team member exalted, "We farmers will clean up anyone."[50] But fewer and fewer Mennonite boys were actually plowing. The local farmer, renting the pasture across the Mill Stream, decided to quit because the "Phys. Ed. Department is taking over the meadow." Indeed, the barn, where school founders once sheltered animals and dreamed of an agricultural program, was soon swallowed by a multi-purpose athletic field.[51] A symbolic transformation, it marked massive changes underway in the heart of Mennonite life.

Interscholastic competition grew and stirred controversy throughout the '70s. Beyond competition with private schools, LMH began officially playing scrimmage games with public schools in 1974.[52] Pressure continued to mount for full-blown competition in the Lancaster-Lebanon League. Proponents of league membership voiced frustration over playing private schools. LMH teams traveled long distances, missed classes and lost family time. Bus travel was expensive and the small schools offered little challenge.

Despite these rumblings, J. Lester Brubaker warned that "a large group of school supporters would oppose a sports program out of sincere personal or inherited convictions."[53] From March of '76 to January of '79, Lancaster-Lebanon League membership was debated often and heatedly. In the fall of 1977 the faculty met with the trustees for a candid exchange.[54] "Are athletics wrong," the faculty asked, "or is it just the way they are played?" Some trustees worried about sports mania. Would LMH have cheerleaders? How would rowdy crowds be handled?

Student writer Dan Charles spoke for many conservative patrons in 1978. He acknowledged the benefits from sports—self-confidence and self-discipline. But he contended that sports are a national obsession that stirs glamour. In its hunger for sports, LMH should not "passively adopt the values of our society."[55] A poll found that 71 percent of the faculty favored league membership. Upon hearing the faculty sentiment, the trustees agreed in the summer of '78 to join the Lancaster-Lebanon League for outdoor sports.[56]

However, late in '78 administrators learned that League membership required full participation in all sports. For two weeks in January of 1979 the issue was debated. Myron Dietz, one of several faculty members opposed to the move, met with the Trustee Executive Committee. Acknowledging that he was a "sports nut" himself in his teens, Dietz feared that LMH was "buying into

Ice hockey on the skating pond in the mid-1970s.

a sports crazy American culture which would lead the school down hill." He
urged the trustees to "resist the popular demand and to at least follow their own
convictions." Unsure of their own convictions, the Executive Committee sent
the issue to the full board without a recommendation and asked for a poll of
patrons. Of the respondents, 61 percent favored league membership, 21 percent opposed it and 18 percent straddled the fence.[57] Meanwhile, proponents
of league membership scouted for support. Indeed, one observer said that the
coaches were furious with Dietz's opposition. The full board considered the
issue on January 22, 1979. Supporters rallied conservatively-inclined Glen Sell
to speak in favor of joining. Sell told the trustees that he enjoyed sports. "As
a boy I disliked school and wanted to quit. Sports held me together until I
began seeing the value of school. Some students find themselves through Bible
study and others through sports."[58] After Sell's presentation the trustees had
no questions. Weighing all the factors and fearing they might lose patrons
either way, they voted to join the Lancaster-Lebanon League. According to
one observer, 16 voted yes, four no and 11 abstained.[59] Students, of course, were
jubilant. It was a milestone in the school's history. Sports had come of age.
Preparations for membership were made in '79-'80 and LMH moved into league
competition in the fall of 1980. Reflecting the dramatic changes of the decade,

Spectators view a soccer game in the 1970s.

Principal Brubaker noted, "Now we find ourselves strong in sports but weak in music."[60]

As sports expanded, the school sought to maintain biblical principles of simplicity and modesty in athletic uniforms. After all, one of the reasons for founding the school was parental displeasure with immodest clothing in public school gym classes. Again and again throughout the '70s the trustees approved new and various uniforms for boys and especially for girls. In the eyes of students, some of the uniforms were despicable and ugly. As the girls' basketball and hockey teams prepared for league competition in 1980, the trustees requested that the proposed uniforms be modeled at a board meeting. Upon seeing them, the trustees concluded they were, indeed, "quite modest."[61]

Some Mennonite distinctives prevailed as LMH entered league competition. Parents and students cheered on the teams, not squads of immodest and glamourous girls. Games sometimes opened with a public prayer, rather than a pledge of allegiance. Sleeveless shirts were taboo for cross-country runners. In keeping with good Mennonite tradition, school officials promoted the sports program in a modest, low-key fashion.

LMH teams were soon making a name for themselves. In the second year of league competition, soccer and field hockey teams entered post-season play. Students were ecstatic. In the words of the 1982 *Laurel Wreath*, "Soccer Mania" had invaded LMH. Yearbook writers claimed that the biggest Lancaster County sporting events in the fall of 1981 were two soccer clashes pitting LMH against Hempfield High, defending Section II champ. The local television station sent a crew to film the Blazers in practice. LMH won both matches, 1-0. But after capturing the Section II title they were unable to clinch the League championship. Mennonite girls playing field hockey brought the first league championship home in 1982. School administrators noted that sports were building school spirit. Student attitudes turned more positive with the active sports program. "LMH is in the headlines," J. Lester Brubaker told the trustees, "a satisfaction to some and a regret to others. It likely attracts some students and turns others away."[62]

The grateful students paid their dues. They dedicated the 1982 yearbook to soccer coach Vernon Rice who had steered them to a Section II championship in two years of league play. Their tribute to Rice said in part:

> You guided us from a cow pasture to a rebuilt soccer field,
> Taught us first in a barn and then in a million dollar gym.
> Winning wasn't the only thing that mattered,
> It was how we played the game.[63]

Updating Modesty and Simplicity

Acknowledging in 1976 that trustees wearied of decisions about drama, sports and dress, J. Lester Brubaker reminded them that such matters needed continual updating. Along with drama and sports, the appearance code was changing as well. As diversity spread across Lancaster Conference in the '70s, LMH sought the safety of the middle road. Indeed, among students the dress code was "ridiculed, knocked down, kicked and stepped on," said student Fred Kniss. But he argued that the dress code was a valuable asset to help preserve an Anabaptist-Mennonite life style, in danger of melting into the American mainstream.[64] Students complained that the appearance code created a double standard—forcing them to uphold practices already dropped by their congregations. Jeff Hoover, president of the Student Council, told trustees "a double standard between school and church is devastating. It breeds cynicism and pseudo-spirituality . . . ."[65] He urged the board to keep the dress code in the center of the spectrum.

The appearance code continued to uphold modesty and simplicity as Christian ideals. Skirts were expected to reach the knees and be within three inches of the floor when the wearer knelt erectly. Low-cut neck lines, sleeveless shirts,

An outing in the LMH cove on the southeastern section of the campus in the mid-1970s.

Students enter the classroom building from the chapel in typical dress of the 1970s, including maxi skirts.

decorative jewelry and noticeable makeup were taboo. Girls were expected to wear skirts for all school activities except athletics. In 1975 the trustees approved girls wearing slacks on a backpacking mini-course if they also wore a "3/4 coat, tunic or skirt to cover their hips."[66] By the fall of 1977 slacks were permissible for extracurricular activities.[67] Although the guidelines on jewelry, T-shirts, open buttons and hemlines provided ample opportunities to test the boundaries of authority, the most contentious issues of the '70s were hair styles and the devotional covering.

Boys enjoyed engaging administrators in a cat-and-mouse game over hair. The appearance code required neatly trimmed hair that didn't hide the ear lobes or cover the collar of a dress shirt. Each year dozens of boys were sent to the office because of vanishing ear lobes. Administrators urged students to trim their hair and report back for an inspection. Tiring of the constant tit for tat, administrators began offering free haircuts in the office in the spring of '78. Boys were given two choices: be sheared by a secretary in the office or go directly to an off-campus barber and receive an unexcused absence.[68] A sign of independence and sometimes rebellion, long hair became a convenient way to irritate authorities.

Although long hair was taboo for fellows, it was the ideal for girls. Lancaster Conference had long urged women not to cut their hair in obedience to I Corinthians 11:6-15, a Scripture passage in which the Apostle Paul specifically prescribed long hair for women. Nevertheless, Principal Brubaker told trustees in 1973 that some girls were cutting their hair, and by 1976 he noted a large number had styled haircuts.[69] The traditional practice of arranging long hair in a bun under the devotional covering changed in 1971 when the appearance code permitted girls to wear flowing hair tied in one or two ponytails. The ties prevented girls from cutting their hair too short. But by the mid-'70s many girls balked at the ties. Some arrived at school with flowing hair. They quickly tied it with a rubber band before chapel and at day's end tossed the band aside as they dashed for the bus. Teacher David Thomas, rather than sending forgetful girls to the principal's office, kept an extra shoestring in his desk. When girls appeared in his class with flowing hair he offered them a string, but they usually found a better tie. Hair was permitted to flow freely in the fall of 1977. And as the sages predicted, hair was then cut even shorter and often styled. Young women were following the growing practice in many of their home congregations and effectively changing campus norms.

Faculty, for the most part, were expected to comply with the student

Students leave the southeast entrance of the classroom building in the early 1970s. The old auditorium/gym stands in the background.

The library in the classroom building.

appearance code. However, there were some differences. Beards were acceptable for members of religious groups that required them. For some Mennonites,
a beard brought emotional memories of rebellious hippies in the '60s. Several
young faculty, to the dismay of the trustees, wanted to sport beards. In March
of 1976 the trustees agreed that beards could be worn "for religious convictions
or as an expression of the simple life." Five faculty members soon developed
such convictions and began sprouting beards. Within two years references to
the beard vanished from the faculty appearance code.

The mustache, however, was another matter. An old symbol of European
military officers, forbidden by many Anabaptist groups, it was always taboo for
LMH faculty. Some teachers grew them over summer months and shaved them
off in September. A few maintenance men even wore them during the school
term. Several teachers pressed for permission to wear mustaches, noting that
students could wear them. Mustaches remained a point of contention for
several teachers until the taboo disappeared in 1979.[70]

The prohibition against wedding rings irritated other faculty. Long considered jewelry in Mennonite circles, wedding rings were slipping onto the fingers
of Mennonite couples in the '60s. After repeated pleas by some teachers the
trustees grudgingly lifted the restriction in 1978 by "strongly urging" that they

not be worn—meaning, of course, that they could be.[71] Thus, while wedding rings borrowed from the larger culture were entering the Mennonite world, the veiling, symbol of separation, was leaving.

The Demise of the Veiling

The women's devotional veiling became the most painful issue of the '70s. It had long served Mennonites as a symbol of nonconformity to the larger world. As older symbols of separation—plain suits, cape dresses and simple dress styles—faded, the veiling remained for many the final mark of separation. Mennonite women were easily recognized in public by the white veiling. But it was much more than a badge of group identity; it signaled biblical obedience. It reflected Mennonite willingness to follow the simple teachings of the Scripture in I Corinthians 11. Were Mennonites, the conservatives wondered, simply going to neglect clear biblical teaching? Wasn't it likely that tossing off the veiling would eventually erode biblical authority—the cornerstone of Mennonite heritage? Indeed, the veiling was one symbol that publicly demonstrated Mennonite willingness to take the Bible seriously and apply it to daily life.

The progressives, on the other hand, argued that the Apostle Paul's teaching in I Corinthians was intended for a particular cultural setting, not for all times. Where was the line between culture and gospel? Moreover, the veiling, according to biblical teaching, signaled a divine order of authority: God-

LMH cooks singing together in a devotional time in 1973.

Christ-Man-Woman. The currents of feminism stirring throughout the nation were also undermining the credibility of the veiling, to the dismay of conservatives. Would Mennonites, they wondered, join the fads of feminism and reverse long-held teaching on gender roles? For all of these reasons the demise of the veiling was emotionally laden and painful.

Even more excruciating were the sounds of a younger generation openly mocking a precious symbol of biblical authority. Students sometimes called the veiling a "lid, soup strainer, tea strainer, fly catcher and dandruff hat." Writing an essay on "What it means to be a Mennonite," one girl wrote, "I've heard it called many things—sin strainer, crash helmet, lid, cap, religious halo—I'm not sure I really know what it is."[72] Another student said, "I feel very confused about the covering and I don't know why I wear it and yet I feel that I should." Such remarks pained the hearts of parents and leaders who conscientiously advocated the veiling.

On their annual trip to Washington D.C. seniors wearied of all the questions from curious bystanders about their "little white caps." By the mid-'70s many students felt a crisis of conscience. In the words of one, "I do it without complaining, but I have no conviction for it." Another said, "When people ask me about the white thing on my head, I simply say it's a traditional practice of our religious sect but I don't believe in it."[73] Yet for many others the covering

Fellowship and study in dorm rooms in the mid-1970s.

Mr. and Mrs. J. Lester Brubaker mingle with students at a junior/senior banquet in the early 1970s.

continued to be a sincere expression of deep conviction.

Non-Mennonite students were not required to wear the veiling at LMH. A Mennonite student refused to comply in 1978 and threatened to bring her pastor to a board meeting to "defend her position."[74]   Another student wrote to the trustees comparing the veiling to circumcision in the Old Testament. She charged it was "no longer necessary for salvation and only a burden to the Gentiles." Requiring the veiling is hypocritical, she argued, because so many girls take it off as they run for the bus at 3:10. After reading her letter an old trustee, voicing the conservative view, noted, "This demonstrates a very arrogant, proud and unsubmissive spirit."[75]

Caught in the midst of rapid change laced with deep emotions, the trustees faced a quandary. If they lifted the veiling requirement, conservative patrons might boycott the school. Forcing students to wear it, on the other hand, not only lacked integrity and sparked ridicule, it was tantamount to hypocrisy. Moreover, progressive patrons would surely leave the school if the regulation continued. What to do when the meaning of a religious symbol evaporates?

The trustees themselves split along traditional and progressive lines in the late '70s. Half continued to wear the plain suit while the rest wore ties and lapel coats.[76] In the spring of 1979, as Lancaster County recovered from the nuclear accident at Three Mile Island, the trustees asked a committee to revise the appearance code. The pressing issue, of course, was the veiling. After vigorous discussion, the committee drafted a new code which the trustees approved in July of 1979.[77] Girls were *encouraged* to wear the veiling and asked to respect the different practices of others.

It was a delicate turning point in the school's saga. With it came tales of veilings being tossed into a parking lot bonfire to the delight of students who had worn them without conviction. The 1979-80 term marked the first time that women baptized in the Mennonite faith could walk through the school's doors without a veiling. By the end of the school year, only 22 percent of the girls wore a veiling for their senior yearbook picture.[78] Faculty women, however, were required to wear it until the fall of 1984.

The long story of headgear changes for women was coming to a close. The changes reflected new biblical interpretation and changing gender roles, and they marked the declining distance between Mennonites and the larger world. The dates in figure 7.1 chart the turning points.[79] The shifts occurred somewhat gradually due to the diversity of the student body.

Surprisingly the bishops said little about the multitude of changes touching the school in the '70s. They listened to periodic reports, but, following the spirit of the 1970 constitution, expected their brethren on the Religious Welfare Committee to speak for the church. Some bishops "raised a concern," however, when the trustees dropped the veiling requirement in 1979. They questioned the school's authority to make decisions on doctrinal matters. Moreover, they urged that future doctrinal changes be brought to the bishops before the trustees acted.[80] Future doctrinal issues? Did any remain? Surely the school had not intended to revise basic Mennonite doctrine.

Reflecting the social flux spreading across the Conference, the *Rules and Discipline* were largely forgotten. The school had witnessed sweeping changes between 1977 and 1979. J. Paul Graybill, who died in November 1975, was spared the pain of witnessing the dramatic shifts in dress and interscholastic sports.[81] Compressed into its 36th and 37th year, the changes came swiftly, as shown in Figure 7.2.

Caught in a caldron of diverse and deeply held convictions, trustees tried to be sensitive to patrons on all sides. Policy adjustments were often couched in vague phrases, designed to permit change while esteeming traditional practice. Thus, trustees could say they encouraged a customary practice, yet all the while permitting it to be modified. Vague terminology sometimes masked rapid change. The revised wedding ring policy "strongly urged that rings not be worn," meaning that they were acceptable. The 1979 appearance code "encour-

---

Figure 7.1
Headgear Changes Among Women, 1942-1985

1942-54	Hair worn in a bun under a veiling with tie strings
1954-55	Tie strings removed from veiling
1970-71	Veiling not required for athletics
1971-72	Hair worn down, but tied
1971-72	Bonnets not required for senior class trip
1977-78	Hair permitted to flow freely
1977-78	Cut and styled hair increases
1979-80	Veiling no longer required for students
1984-85	Veiling no longer required for faculty

Figure 7.2
Policy Changes, 1977-1979

1977
- Instrumental music permitted in chapel
- Slacks accepted for after-school activities
- Girls' hair worn flowing

1978
- Beards permitted for faculty for any reason
- Wedding rings permitted for faculty
- First public drama staged

1979
- Entrance into Lancaster-Lebanon Sports League
- Mustaches acceptable for faculty
- Piano acceptable in chapel
- Veiling not required for students

---

aged" students to wear the veiling, meaning, of course, it was no longer required. When the Religious Welfare Committee recommended "lifting the nonwearing of the mustache," it meant mustaches were acceptable. Urging faculty women to use "reasonable consistency" in hairstyles on and off campus signaled freedom to follow their hearts. Such is the language of social change, familiar to leaders everywhere who seek to gently finesse social change amidst diverse constituencies.

A Campus Face-Lift

Facility changes kept pace with the social flux. All the structures from the Yeates era fell in the '70s except Gardiner Hall, the old administration building. Administrative offices in the classroom building were added and enlarged in 1971 with Alumni Association funds. The striking addition, however, was the new gymnasium, completed in 1975. The fears of the founders materialized twice. Hurricane Agnes unleashed a devastating flood in the summer of 1972. Six years later, melting snow and heavy rains in January hoisted flood levels 18 inches above the Agnes record. The flood of January 1978 crested six feet above the floor of the Mill Stream bridge, filled the basement apartment of the old administration building and inundated the basement of the new gym. Water levels peaked to four feet in the newly enlarged Industrial Arts shop. The flood leveled the fence around the tennis court, swept a car downstream and lifted a house trailer off its foundation.[82]

South of the Mill Stream, athletic fields—soccer, hockey, track and baseball—sprouted and flourished in the late '70s and early '80s. East of the campus, the trustees sold land in 1973 for the sum of one dollar to the Mennonite Information Center to erect a replica of the Old Testament Tabernacle.[83] Two of the school's proposed building projects, however, never materialized. A five-year plan in 1972-73 projected a new boys' dormitory and a junior high building. With dormitory enrollments declining, the trustees decided to scrap the plans for the new dorm. In the fall of '73 a wing of the girls' dormitory became home for the boys.

A proposed million dollar junior high building was frequently debated between 1974 and 1978. After considerable research, two architectural designs and innumerable meetings, the project was abandoned. Declining enrollments in seventh grade, expansion of existing Mennonite schools and a variety of reservations from faculty, patrons and Mennonite elementary schools scuttled the idea.[84] The final construction project of this era enclosed a walkway between the chapel and classroom building in the summer of 1981.

For the most part the campus face-lift went well. There were, however, some hurdles. Hoping to obstruct teens driving "heat treated spiders," school officials placed 10 speed bumps on campus driveways over the Christmas holidays of 1972. The sizeable bumps irritated the entire community. They were promptly lowered and later replaced by five gentle hurdles in the fall of '73, to the relief of all.

The bishops added a minor obstruction of their own. The trustees considered naming buildings for individuals who had made a significant contribution to the life of the school. One faculty member, in jest, proposed calling the

Figure 7.3

Facility Changes, 1971-1981
Buildings Demolished

1973	Old mill (classroom/dormitory)
1974	Home economics building (Noah Good residence)
1974	Student center (commercial building/Yeates Mess Hall)
1975	Old gym/auditorium
1978	Small cottage south of Mill Stream
1979	Barn south of Mill Stream

New Construction, Expansion and Remodeling

1971	New and enlarged administrative offices
1973	Home economics suite in girls' dormitory
1973	Boys' dormitory incorporated into girls' dormitory
1975	New gym completed
1975	Old administration building remodeled into apartments
1977	Industrial arts and agricultural shop expanded
1978	Greenhouse built for educational use
1979	New office space provided in classroom building
1981	Chapel walkway enclosed and new music rooms

chapel/dining hall the "J. Paul Graybill Meetinghouse—Eating House." Uneasy about handing out such honors, the Religious Welfare Committee checked with the bishops. Deferring to the long-held values of humility and modesty, the bishops frowned on naming buildings after persons.[85] Building names should honor utilitarian purposes not individuals. Thus the Mennonite value system remained intact despite the vast campus face-lift.

The Brubaker Era

J. Lester Brubaker was the architect of the school's educational program for 13 years (1970-83). On sabbatical leave in 1978-1979 he returned to become superintendent, a position provided by the 1970 constitution.[86] Under this arrangement Ernest Hess served as principal while former agricultural teacher J. Richard Thomas filled the assistant principal slot. The administrative trio was reduced to two in 1982-'83 when Hess took a teaching sabbatical in Africa. In addition to teaching science, Hess served five years as assistant principal and four years as principal in the Brubaker administration. Thomas was assistant principal and athletic director for five years as well as teacher of Bible classes. A full-time business manager, Gerald Martin, replaced Clyde Stoner, who returned to full-time teaching in 1973. After Martin's departure in 1976, David Yoder began a long tenure as business manager.

Solicitation efforts intensified in the Brubaker years to increase tuition subsidies. Leaders hoped that gift income would curb tuition rates and keep LMH a "brotherhood school" rather than a haven for the elite. As student enthusiasm for fund drives waned, annual fund raising initiatives shifted to administrators. A phonathon to alumni began in 1981. Several development directors spearheaded fund raising efforts over the years.

Noah Good bid the classroom farewell in 1977 after logging 35 years with the school. The Moshier brothers departed in 1982 with some 53 years of service between them. In 1983 teacher Stanley Kreider, disturbed by the school's ever progressive stance, left to teach at the more conservative Faith Mennonite High School. Among the trustees there were changes as well. James Hess, signer of the original petition, retired in 1979 after 37 years of

Noah Good in the classroom in 1977, at the end of 35 years of service to the school.

sacrificial service on the board, 20 of those years as chairman. He spent an estimated year-and-a-half of his life sitting in school board meetings, not to mention thousands of hours of selfless service on related committees.[87] After both John Harnish and Lloyd Eby served brief stints in the chair, the trustees gave Jason Steffy their gavel in 1978 for a tenure that extended until 1991.

In 1978 Beulah Diffenbach, in a historical first, became the first female trustee. In 1972 Reba Smoker carried the honor of being the first female sports editor of the *Millstream*. In 1980 Shelby Landis became the first female to preside over the Student Council. The breezes of feminism were gently nudging the Mennonite community. But only gently—women were not in senior management positions, nor were they teaching Bible courses.

Rising enrollments peaked in 1977-78 with an all-time high of 579. But the good fortunes wavered as the number of students dropped in the last five years of the Brubaker era to a low of 470. Lagging enrollments, harsh inflation in the '70s, as well as recession in the early '80s squeezed financial operations. One-fourth of the faculty took voluntary salary reductions in 1981-82. Touched by their generosity, the trustees themselves responded with a goodwill offering of $4,000.

Efforts to unravel the enrollment decline were elusive. As Mennonites moved into professions, family size shrank. However, only about one-fourth of high school age Mennonites in the Lancaster area attended LMH. Other Christian schools and two more conservative Mennonite high schools were beckoning prospective students.[88] More culprits lurked beneath the dwindling enrollment: the strain of inflation and recession, the dress code—too progressive for some and too conservative for others—and the lack of interscholastic sports before 1980. In any event, the composition of those attending had shifted between 1972 and 1983. Lancaster Conference students dropped from 73 to 62 percent of the student body. The gap was filled by students from other Mennonite conferences—23 to 28 percent—and by non-Mennonite students, up from 4 to 10 percent. Despite these new students, the enrollment decline was worrisome.

Finishing his fourth year at the helm, J. Lester Brubaker called 1974 his best year yet. But his honeymoon was winding down. In November of 1975 he told the trustees that some younger faculty members "perceive the principal, otherwise known as, 'the administration,' as an authoritarian leader who does not convey to the board their true feelings and concerns." These faculty members, said Brubaker, want to talk directly with the trustees "about dress, drama and athletics. . . . They are not exactly angry, but they are frustrated, and prolonged frustration leads to anger."[89] On another occasion, when Brubaker proposed a

policy requiring teachers to remain longer on campus after classes for consul-
tation and committee meetings, some faculty members loudly objected.

All things considered, Brubaker received high marks as an administrator. In
a 1978 evaluation, faculty members rated him "patient, understanding, consid-
erate and courteous." Moreover, he "demonstrated a thorough knowledge and
understanding of school administration." In the words of Ernest Hess, "J. Lester
was the brains behind all the curriculum changes in the '70s." And yes, agreed
the faculty, his grooming and attire were "appropriate." The gentlemanly
demeanor from early Mill Stream days had not been lost. He was, said one
faculty member, "always a gentleman, a warm Christian brother."[90] Trying to
maintain personal ties in the midst of a bureaucracy, Brubaker took faculty
members out to lunch to celebrate their birthdays.

The faculty returned the goodwill in November of 1976 while Brubaker was
escorting the senior class to Washington D.C. Aware that Brubaker deplored
a large moose head recently donated to the school, they hung it in his office.
The faculty gathered for a photograph under the bull's horns and prepared a
scrapbook to celebrate the event. The songs and slogans included, "Don't
nobody dare hang no moose head on my wall," "Why doesn't my moose look

*LMH faculty gather in Principal J. Lester Brubaker's office in November 1976 to celebrate
the hanging of a moose head.*

as good as thy moose," "Between the horns of a dilemma," and the like. The faculty patiently awaited Brubaker's return on Monday morning only to discover that a janitor had removed the moose head over the weekend. Brubaker had the last laugh. Despite the snag, faculty gathered and sang their ditties and presented him the scrapbook. To the delight of all, Brubaker chided them for "moosing around too much" while he was gone.

Although enrollment was declining at the end of his watch, Brubaker had guided LMH through a tumultuous time of social change. His legacy left the school with a sterling academic imprint, a professionalized faculty and rising stature in the larger educational world. "He had an overall vision," noted a senior faculty member. "He was usually open to people and their input, but not easily pushed around. He was a leader. He had good interpersonal relationships and that made him approachable." The trustees and faculty roasted Brubaker lightly at a banquet in his honor in May of 1983. In the words of trustee Lloyd Hollinger,

> Now JLB could stand for jolly, live, and bald;
> and that would be true
> But better yet JLB means joyous, loving, brother;
> and that surely is you.
> God bless you, Lester.

The trustees presented JLB with a grandfather's clock, custom-made from a Mill Stream tree. Like the steady ripples of the stream, the clock marks the flow of pleasant memories in Brubaker's living room.

CHAPTER EIGHT

Partnering Together

1983-1991

"An LMH education involves learning disciplines for life."
—J. Richard Thomas

A Second-Stage Rocket

J. Richard Thomas became principal in the summer of 1983. "The first launching took place in 1970," said one faculty member, "and now with Thomas it was like a second-stage rocket cutting in and we took off with a new vision." Another staff member recalled, "Things really perked up around here when Dick came." Enrollment for the fall of 1983 had skidded to a 22-year low of 443 students. Executing a full-court press, the Thomas team bounced the student tally up nearly 90 students within a year and hit an all-time record of 588 by the fall of '85. Enrollment enjoyed a steady climb to nearly 700 by the '91-'92 term. In contrast to earlier days when many students transferred to

LMH for their final two years, most students now came for all four years. More non-Mennonites were attending also.

Born seven years after the school's start, Thomas took the helm as the youngest principal at the age of 34. A product of public schools, he held a degree in agricultural education and taught agriculture for two years in a public school. His career at LMH began as evening dormitory manager in 1972 while he was still teaching agriculture in a public school. A year later he began teaching agriculture and Bible at LMH on a full-time basis. In addition to teaching and dormitory supervision, he later served as athletic director and assistant principal.

The school flourished under Thomas' leadership. He crafted a mission statement based on the school's educational philosophy and, like a good statesman, repeated it everywhere: "LMH aims to provide an excellent education that challenges students to a life of Christlike mission, peacemaking and service in a global society." The school's founders would have been pleased. The mission statement articulated their early dreams in contemporary language. This banner of intent focused the vision and rallied support in the Thomas years.

Reflecting on the selection of the young, unordained principal, a faculty member in 1990 said, "It was the right choice, definitely the right choice. He was excellent with the kids. He could stand his ground and when he said something they knew he meant it. Yet he was always on their good side." The students showed their appreciation by dedicating the 1984 *Laurel Wreath* to Thomas. "You challenge us to remember our roots but also give us room to spread our wings and soar." A senior faculty member described the Thomas touch. "He's informal with a low-key style. He's very people oriented—interested in what they have to say. He's approachable. He has a way of getting up and talking to the kids that builds rapport—he knows the kind of stuff we're made of. Yet he comes through loud and clear on solid stuff—I feel he's really been a godsend."

Physical education teacher Miles Yoder served as assistant principal in the Thomas years. Yoder's primary task was student relations—working with student organizations and supervising school policies related to attendance and citizenship. In later years he also supervised faculty and maintenance operations. A second assistant principal, Marlin Groff, joined the team in 1988-'89. In addition to supervising faculty, Groff managed business operations and admissions. The Thomas-Yoder-Groff team met on a weekly basis reminiscent of the Supervising Committee of bygone days. Less visible and less rigid than the old committee, the new trio represented a swing away from the central-

The leadership team in the early 1990s. Left: Miles Yoder, J. Richard Thomas and Marlin Groff.

principal model of the '70s, which, of course, had earlier swung away from the Supervising Committee of old. So swings the pendulum of history.

Three other leadership clusters helped to guide the school as it moved into the '90s. A campus ministries team, headed by bishop Ernest Hess, coordinated chapels, spiritual life programs, guidance counseling and aptitude testing. A second team included Cindy Petersheim, the replacement for David Yoder who resigned as director of development in 1989. Petersheim, in concert with Thomas, Groff and Fern Clemmer, Director of Communications and Alumni Relations, formed a development team for public relations and fund raising. Third, the Principal's Coordinating Committee, formed in 1971 and composed of instructional leaders from various academic areas, continued to supervise the academic curriculum of the school. All in all, the leadership teams received high marks from parents. In a 1990 survey, 99 percent of the patrons rated communication with the school about their child's progress as "excellent or satisfactory."

Celebrating Diversity

The corporate culture that jelled in these years stressed partnership, diversity, affirmation, celebration, empowerment and, of course, shalom—the clos-

Ethiopian students display colorful skirts in the late 1980s.

ing wording of every Thomas letter. Administrators viewed the school as "partnering together" with family and church in the transmission of faith. A vision of mutual respect and accountability was articulated in that oft repeated phrase—"partnering together." With older forms of Mennonite identity badly frayed, the school emphasized the commonalities of Christian faith. The adhesive force of old externals—uniform dress, vocation and ethnicity—was replaced by appeals to a common faith, a unity grounded on theological beliefs, especially the affirmation of diversity. Personal talents and differences were celebrated as they enhanced the larger campus community as well as the church. The school promoted core values while also embracing the richness of variety. Education in these years was described as a conversation across the generations—a conversation essential for transmitting the heritage of faith. Like its founders, faculty and administrators were passing on the faith, but doing it with a flair for flexibility, diversity and celebration unknown in former years.

The student body grew more varied over the decades. From 155 students in 1942 the school expanded to nearly 700 by 1991-92 with 80 living in the dormitory. About 40 percent of Lancaster area Mennonite youth in the

Lancaster and Atlantic Coast conferences attended LMH. In central Lancaster County the rates exceeded 60 percent.[1] In the school's first year 87 percent of the students came from Lancaster Mennonite Conference. By 1990-91 that percentage had dropped to 53 percent. In another shift from early days, the percentage of Mennonite/Anabaptist students dropped from 99 to 76.[2] The non-Mennonite portion of students hailed from Protestant, Catholic and non-denominational churches. Students came from over 600 families and 100 congregations.

Non-white and international students were rarely found by the Mill Stream in the early years. By 1990-91 nine percent of the student body was non-white and four percent hailed from outside North America. By the late '80s and early '90s nearly two dozen Ethiopian students joined the student body each year.[3] In 1991-92 the 68 non-white students included 19 Ethiopians, 15 Hispanics, 15 African Americans and 16 of Asian parentage, as well as others. Since the early '70s LMH had welcomed High Aim students—a program offering finan- cial support to Mennonite minority students attending a Mennonite high school.

Reflecting the growing diversity, the class of '91 entered a wide array of occupations. Fifty-two percent pursued higher education after graduation. Of the males, four percent entered agriculture and 11 percent took on blue collar occupations.[4] A comparison of the 50-year trends appears in Figure 8.1.

Diversity had touched the trustees as well. The founding fathers were, for the most part, ordained farmers with few having high school diplomas. By 1991, 4 of the 26 trustees were female, 16 were college-educated and only 3

Figure 8.1

Enrollment Patterns, 1942-1992

	1942-43	1991-92
Total Students	155	693
Dormitory Students	59	80
Lancaster Conference Students (in percent)	87	51
Mennonite/Anabaptist Students (in percent)	99	75
Non-white (in percent)	0	10
International (in percent)	0	3

The Board of Trustees 1959-60 and 1990-91. The changes among the trustees reflected the new organizational structure of 1970 as well as the many changes afoot in the church in these years.

were driving tractors. Five were serving as pastors and half were alumni of the school. Present board members reflect the educational and occupational shifts afoot in the Mennonite community over the past 50 years. Among the faculty in 1990-91, 66 percent were members of Lancaster Mennonite Conference with a total of 92 percent holding membership in the Mennonite Church. Among the faculty, 30 percent were female and 44 percent claimed a master's degree. One thing was certain. Although the LMH of the '90s was a Menno-nite school, it hosted a new mix of students, staff and trustees..

Building for the Future

Diversity touched the architecture of the school as well. Three major construction projects were undertaken between 1983-91. "The stone pillars connect us to our past and the large modern windows symbolize the future twenty-first century," said J. Richard Thomas, describing the new archway entrance to the classroom building.[5] This southern addition to the classroom building, completed in the summer of '85, broke the brick tradition of campus construction. The stone archway did indeed reflect the past. It faced the Mill Stream and the vacant site of the old stone barn of Yeates' days. The addition provided a new main entrance, as well as consolidated offices, a media center and classroom space.

LMH students leave for a three-week German exchange program in the summer of 1989 from the main entrance, completed in 1985.

Several staff members lived in mobile homes on the southside of the Mill Stream for many years. The last home rolled out of the meadows in the fall of 1985, the same year that the school purchased the four-and-a-half-acre Weaver property west of the chapel. In 1987 a new baseball field was carved out on a high plateau on the southern end of the campus. And later a small tract of land west of the Weaver property and bordering Greenland Drive was acquired.

In a major initiative the school purchased the Pricebusters Mall in the spring of 1988. The two-story, 40,000-square-foot complex of about 12 stores had opened in 1984. The mall bordered the west flank of the campus entrance, a two-minute walk from the chapel. The building was up for sale in 1988. Worried about motels or even less desirable neighbors in their back yard, school officials decided to purchase the mall. It was not an idle concern. In October of 1985 an LMH student walking to a hockey game on campus was abducted and raped by an intruder.[6] Although the mall was not needed for classrooms, the trustees hoped to lease the property to church agencies and maintain a wholesome fringe around the campus.

The plan raised eyebrows and voices of dissent. Was the school straying from its educational mission? Would the mall become an embarrassing white elephant? One person charged the school with trying to "run the whole Mennonite show." Despite such worries the trustees voted unanimously to purchase Pricebusters in February of 1988 for $1.9 million. They voted in stride with the founding fathers of the school—hoping to keep the outside world at bay, at least a bit. But the vision for the mall was more than that. Home for a variety of church agencies, it would, in time, become the hub of the local Mennonite world.

Lancaster Mennonite Conference decided to move its offices to the complex from its long-time base in Salunga, west of Lancaster city. Within a year a condominium association had formed to manage the renovated mall. LMH retained a 54 percent ownership in the association. Eastern Mennonite College in Virginia soon opened a Lancaster Campus and several retail stores rented space in the building. The bishops moved their monthly meetings to the site—tagged 2160 Lincoln Highway East. Although far removed from daily operations of the school, the bishops ironically were for the first time within geographical reach. Many Lancaster Conference agencies now congregated near the Mill Stream. With the Lancaster Mennonite Historical Society and the Mennonite Information Center to the east, and now the new church center to the west, the high school sat in the center of a new complex of Mennonite institutions.

Responding to the purchase of the mall, a Lancaster newspaper editorial

(top) Jeff Lefever and Loretta Mellinger perform in the 1989 school play, "To Kill a Mockingbird."

(bottom) The 1991 play cast for "Our Town."

LMH trustees and alumni pull a plow to break ground for the auditorium/fine arts center on October 4, 1990.

commended the school for "bringing the same level of excellence to the planning of its campus as it always brought to the education of its students."[7] By 1990 with mall space occupied, rental income trickling in and conference offices conveniently clustered together, even dissenters were applauding the move. When the school's founders almost grudgingly bought the old Yeates property for $36,000, they had no idea that their purchase would someday circumscribe the heart of Lancaster's "official" Mennonite world.

The third major expansion of these years was a 1500-seat auditorium/fine arts center, fulfilling dreams—alive since 1946—for a large auditorium. The $3.5 million project took shape in the late '80s. Designed to accommodate daily chapel services, it would also host large public events and church meetings. Moreover, it provided facilities for an art department that had doubled course offerings in the '80s, classrooms for music, as well as facilities for drama. Circular seating surrounded a full-scale stage and orchestra pit. A ground breaking on October 4, 1990, marked 50 years to the date that Lancaster Conference leaders in a close vote had agreed to begin a high school.[8] The new facility opened in the fall of 1991. Future plans anticipated converting the first floor of the old chapel into a dining hall and its basement into classrooms. Although founding trustees would have winced at the thought of orchestra pits and dramatic productions, they would have cheered the strength and vitality expressed in campus renovations some 50 years later.

The Jubilee Campaign

In 1986 the school launched a Jubilee Campaign targeted at the 50-year anniversary. Building on the jubilee motif of the Old Testament, the effort hoped to end the era in a strong financial posture and provide a robust launch for the coming decades. The Jubilee Campaign, the boldest and most ambitious financial effort in the school's history, initially set a goal of $6 million. Plans for the auditorium/fine arts center, an auxiliary gym, a new kitchen and dining room, plus several classrooms, added $8 million of projected capital expenses.

The campaign was eventually divided into three phases. Phase I provided funds for the 1985 classroom addition, a new athletic field and several adjoining properties. Phase II focused on the $3.5 million auditorium/fine arts center, as well as several capital improvement projects. Phase III funds were designated for dormitory and old chapel renovations, as well as an auxiliary gym and new kitchen facilities to serve the growing school. By the spring of 1991 total contributions—cash, pledges and deferred giving—passed $8 million and the educational endowment topped $1.5 million. Each phase increased the educational endowment, thus enabling program improvements without hiking tuition to elitist levels. The campaign's ultimate target was a $7 million endowment for educational programs.

The school enjoyed financial support from innumerable alumni and friends

Dorm students gather at the front of the dormitory in 1991.

Quilts and Winross trucks often stirred brisk bidding at fund raising auctions.

as it approached the 50-year Jubilee. The 1990-'91 term marked the nineteenth consecutive year of balanced budgets. Over 200 volunteers assisted in a variety of school operations, some on a weekly basis. Dozens of alumni helped with the annual phonathon which raised $104,000 in 1991. Friends and alumni supported the annual fall auction with vigorous bidding, exceeding sales of $103,000 in the fall of 1990. Others constructed a benefit house on a donated building lot, yielding the school some $70,000. The Alumni Association sponsored annual travelogue nature films as well as an alumni dinner theatre. Numerous art projects, including an antique quilt exhibit, were organized to support the construction of the auditorium/fine arts center. The jars of chow chow, donated by parents in the '40s, were replaced in the '90s by art work from alumni and friends.

LMH was also aided by the state of Pennsylvania. In 1990-91 the academic program received some $30,000 in state aid for textbooks, educational media and equipment. An estimated 40 percent of the students rode to LMH on public school buses. A full-time reading specialist provided remedial services to students in a small trailer several feet from a campus building. U.S. Supreme

Court rulings required such literal separation to prevent "excessive entangle-
ment" of church and state. Part-time specialists funded by the state of Pennsylvania provided psychological and speech services to students. Uncle Sam's
lunch program helped to subsidize noon-time meals.

Endowment income and gifts paid 40 percent of the $3,025 required to
educate a student in 1990-91. Tuition income generated the remaining 60
percent of the $2 million annual budget. Beyond gifts to the operating fund,
the school received $.8 million toward capital projects and endowment in
'90-'91. Financial assistance in the amount of $122,000 was given to 150
students in 1990-91. Prudent management and economy of size, as well as hefty
gift income, enabled the school to hold tuition at modest levels in contrast to
other Mennonite and private high schools. Between 1984 and 1991 the
Consumer Price Index rose some 34 percent but tuition increased only 25
percent. In fact, tuition remained unchanged between 1984 and 1989. The
LMH price tag—$2,060 for 1991-92—dipped far below the tuition of most
private schools in the Mid-Atlantic region which often exceeded $4,000.[9]

Although modest, tuition costs over the 50 years had outpaced inflation.
Rising with inflation, the 1942 tuition of $135 would have equaled about $1100
for 1990-91 when the actual rate had risen to $1,860.[10] The fledgling Mill
Stream operation in 1942, however, hardly compared to the quality and scope
of the efforts 50 years later. The school had strayed from the founders'
commitment to balance the operating budget on the shoulders of tuition. But
it was a noble departure. Generous gifts by friends and alumni held school doors
open for students from diverse economic levels.

Governance Update

Throughout the '80s the trustees wrestled with the school's pattern of
governance. The board with some two dozen members met quarterly. An
Executive Committee of seven persons, meeting monthly, provided direct
oversight of the school's program. Policy decisions were often formulated by
subcommittees of trustees and staff. Proposals then moved to the Executive
Committee and eventually passed on to the full board for final approval. Lines
of responsibility between the Executive Committee and full board were somewhat hazy. Certain trustees worried that the larger board simply rubber-
stamped the work of the Executive Committee. If trustees were to be movers
and shakers of policy and not mere yea-sayers, how could they gain a grasp of
the issues in four quarterly meetings? Moreover, school officials panicked
when finely honed proposals, approved by subcommittees and the Executive
Committee, unraveled in the full board. Delicate personnel matters and

complicated decisions were also difficult to discuss in a large board.

After processing the issue for nearly a decade it was finally resolved in 1990-91.[11] With the consent of the bishops, the trustees adopted a new set of bylaws in January of 1991.[12] Under the new system a Quarterly Board of 20 to 35 members convened four times a year. Quarterly Board members were elected by church districts in the Atlantic Coast and Lancaster conferences. Additional, at-large members could be appointed to the Quarterly Board by the two conferences. The Quarterly Board served as a liaison with the churches, appointed the principal, approved an annual budget and building construction and also provided counsel to the Executive Board.[13] Most importantly, the Quarterly Board elected seven of its members to the Executive Board, vested with primary responsibility for operating the school. The Executive Board could craft policies and supervise the performance of school administrators without approval from the Quarterly Board. Thus, the seven members of the Executive Board held the major seats of power.

The new structure eased into place in July of 1991. The revision welcomed the Atlantic Coast Conference of the Mennonite Church as a full partner in the school in a more formal way. The Atlantic Coast Conference, nonexistent when the school began, had, over the years and especially in the '80s, participated more fully in the life of the school. The Lancaster Conference appointed two representatives and the Atlantic Coast Conference appointed one to the Religious Welfare Committee. These advisors met with the trustees and cast their votes with the school's personnel committee.[14] Either Conference could appoint additional persons to the Quarterly Board. Lancaster Conference, however, approved any changes in the bylaws and Articles of Incorporation.[15]

And what of the bishops now meeting monthly in the renovated mall beside the school? J. Lester Brubaker was the last principal whom they formally approved. Their waiver of this responsibility was officially clarified in the new 1991 bylaws. The school by the end of its 50th year was operated by the trustees on behalf of the church districts that had elected them.

The bylaws also formulated a new statement of purpose: "to provide secondary education for persons of the Mennonite Church in a setting where physical, social, emotional and spiritual development is valued." Furthermore, the school participates "with the home and church in preparing persons to follow the way of Christ by sharing faith, peacemaking, and serving in a global society."[16] The historic words—"Following in the way of Christ"—captured Anabaptist understandings of the gospel and focused the school's spiritual vision as it welcomed Jubilee.

Academic Rigors

Following an on-site visit, the Middle States Association of Colleges and Schools voted to reaccredit LMH in 1986 for another 10 years. The school's original visionaries would have reveled in the words of commendation from the outside evaluators. They applauded the school for its positive and wholesome climate, its orderly and well-disciplined student body and its total commitment to spiritual standards. The standards, based on Mennonite doctrines, included "an emphasis on the authority of the Bible, the necessity of a personal commitment to Jesus Christ and global awareness from a Christian perspective." The report concluded: "The philosophy of the school is *fully* integrated into the life of Lancaster Mennonite High School."[17] It was satisfying praise for faculty and staff who, in the judgment of the evaluators, had translated noble ideals into the fabric of daily life.

The burst of elective courses that burgeoned in the '70s paled in the '80s as the school began requiring more specific courses in many academic areas. Changing state standards increased the number of mathematics and science courses. Periodic curriculum reviews were conducted in the various instructional areas throughout the '80s. Major revisions of the English and the Bible curriculums were completed in 1987, bringing more required courses.

The school term was divided into two semesters, each with two quarters. A semester-long course typically generated .5 credits. As the school entered its 50th year in 1991-92 the 21 credits displayed in Figure 8.2 outlined graduation

---

Figure 8.2

Graduation Requirements, 1991-1992

Bible	2.0
Electives	3.7
English	4.0
Fine\Practical Arts	.5
Health	.5
Mathematics	3.0
Physical Education	.8
Science	3.0
Social Studies	3.5

requirements.[18]

To receive diplomas, students completed a semester-long Bible course each year: Creation and Promise, Jesus Story, Church and Anabaptist History, and Kingdom Living. Although titles and content had changed, the number of mandated Bible courses remained stable since 1942. Fine or practical arts requirements specified either two quarter courses or one semester course in art, home economics, music or technology education. This signaled a shift from early years when all students took at least one course in music. English requirements over the 50-year span remained the same. Social science requirements dropped by one course while science and mathematics requirements each rose by two. Social science requirements in 1991-92 included three global studies courses.

Certificates of achievement were offered in 1991-92 to students who completed course sequences in Secretarial Studies, Accounting and General Business. German, Spanish and French were offered in 1991-92. Beyond required courses, students enrolled in a variety of electives in different instructional areas. By 1991-92 some 140 selections were on the course roster. The offerings included such titles as Forest and Environment, Three-Dimensional Design, Office Technology, Shakespeare, Contemporary Clothing, Calculus, Guitar and Conflict Resolution.

Propelled by a belief that the kingdom of God transcended national bounda-

Figure 8.3

Course Distribution by Academic Area, 1991-1992

Academic Areas	No. of Courses
Agricultural Science and Technology	7
Art	8
Bible and Church History	7
Business Education	11
English	22
Foreign Languages	9
Health and Physical Education	5
Home Economics	7
Mathematics	11
Music	10
Science	10
Social Studies	13

ries, the academic program exuded a multi-cultural ethos in recent years. Nearly 10 percent of the student body represented racial minorities and an assortment of countries. Group exchange programs to a variety of nations immersed LMH students briefly in other cultures. Cross-cultural awareness also grew with 50 percent of the students studying a foreign language. Moreover,

In 1984 the Foods II class, taught by Edie Bontrager, won first place in a national con-test sponsored by Fleischmann's Yeast. (Lancaster Intelligencer Journal)

Students enrolled in a mini-course on biking prepare for departure.

all students were exposed to three global studies courses. Forty percent of the faculty members had lived overseas in service assignments. Janet Gehman, on leave from LMH, spent two years in China. Social studies teacher Dan Wenger was off to the Soviet Union in the fall of 1988.[19] The Student Council raised $7,000 to bring two South African students to campus for a year-long stint in '86-'87. Moreover, many LMH students entered new cultural settings in mission and service assignments in summer months, as well as in mini-courses offered by the school. In all of these ways the noble vision of global education was translated into practical learning.

Throughout the '80s the school developed several programs for students with special needs and gifts. A financial assistance plan helps students with monetary needs. In 1983 the Supplemental Program for students with learning disabilities began. That curriculum aids students in strengthening academic skills and developing positive self-esteem. Working in tandem, supplemental and classroom teachers develop an individualized educational plan for classroom courses. About 15 students participated in the Supplemental Program in 1990-91. A Resource Room Program, developed in 1985, assists mentally disabled students and others with special needs. About 35 students participated in the Resource Room Program in 1990-91. Mainstreamed into courses commensurate with their abilities, students receive educational plans tailored for each class.

Especially gifted students are enriched as well. By 1988 five courses qualified for credit at Mennonite colleges. A gifted program, begun in 1988, enables precocious students to substitute independent studies for certain required courses.[20] Faculty offer alternative assignments in mainstream courses to match the abilities of the gifted students. Although school officials support enriched activities for those who are especially able, they deliver them in a non-elitist way and often speak of "giftedness"—stressing that all persons have special gifts of one sort or another. "We're not a prep school," said Thomas. "We try hard not to be elite."

Glitches sometimes snagged the academic curriculum. In May of 1988 several parents wrote to the trustees, worried "that the theory of evolution is being taught as a possible way that God created man." A long-time faculty member noted this was the first time in the history of the school that parents had raised such concerns despite the unchanging stance of the science department. Responding to the parents, the trustees adopted a resolution that reaffirmed the words of the Mennonite Confession of Faith: "in the beginning God created all things by his Son." The resolution went on to affirm "teaching current theories of science with the understanding that such scientific theories continue to change because of continuing research."[21]

Such controversies hinged on deeply held values. A commitment to integrate Christian values throughout the curriculum permeated the mission of the school. Yet in a diverse community, beliefs differ. Nevertheless, throughout its history and especially in recent years, the school committed itself to transmitting core values. Mathematics teacher Aaron Martin talking about the uniqueness of LMH said, "Getting off the subject and onto things like values is part of the subject around here." In the words of a student, "Faculty constantly challenge us to think about values and priorities."[22]   "Our commitment to excellence at LMH," contended Thomas, "means more than learning the rigors of academia. It is that, of course. But it also involves partnering with home and church to pass on the faith."[23] One of several public school administrators enrolling their children at LMH said, "It's a school that cares about values without being elitist."

Achieving Success

One of the remarkable differences along the Mill Stream between the '40s and the '90s was student participation in a wide array of competitions—local, state and national. As the school entered the decade of the '90s, students vied

Erica Erb displays her work for the Fine Arts Exhibit.

Volanda Bender hurls for the Blazers in 1991.

for awards in nearly 50 annual contests ranging from tractor driving to fashion designing, from peace writing to dramatic acting. The school itself began an awards assembly in the early 1970s to recognize special achievements. This ceremony mirrored the national tide of individualism, surging since the late '60s. Competitive activities and celebrations of individual achievement flew in the face of J. Paul Graybill's contention that self-denial belonged to a well-rounded education. The school struggled with the issue. How could it recognize individual success without trampling long-held virtues of humility and modesty? How could individual accomplishments be celebrated without destroying the common fabric of community and neglecting the many students whose only award was a diploma?

Some students were receiving more than diplomas. In the four-year period from 1988 to 1991, 40 students were cited by the National Merit Scholarship competition as commended scholars, semi-finalists or finalists. Thirteen achieved the stellar distinction of finalist between 1980 and 1991. Throughout the '80s, average LMH Scholastic Aptitude Test scores ranked above public schools in Lancaster County, as well as above state and national averages. With 50 percent of the students typically taking the test, average LMH scores usually exceeded 1,000 points.[24] The strength of the academic program was confirmed by the warm welcome LMH graduates received in a variety of prestigious colleges and universities. Admission officers in many institutions of higher education saluted LMH for its sterling academic reputation.

Students in Dottie Nolt Weber's home economics courses began achieving distinction in the Fleischmann's Yeast contest in the early 1980s. Weber's students won third place in 1981 and second place in 1983 in the national competition. In 1984 Edie Bontrager's Foods II class won first place in the "Share the Health" contest sponsored by Fleischmann's Yeast. The class received a one-week, all-expense-paid trip to California as well as other prizes. Two years later Courtney Bender and Tina Sharp became the first LMHers to attend the Governor's School for the Arts, as Renny Magill claimed the first LMH gold medal in the National Scholastic Arts competition. Heidi Haselhorst received a writing award from the National Council of Teachers of English in 1987. LMHers received four gold keys in the 1989 Regional Scholastic Arts competition, the same year that Campus Chorale sang at the convention of the Pennsylvania Music Educators after a taped audition.[25] Three students qualified for the All-State Orchestra and one was off to Boston in an All-Eastern Orchestra Festival. The Laurel Wreath and Millstream continued to achieve state and national awards of distinction.

The Blazers also soared as they matured in league competition. Recognized

Hockey players cheer their team to victory.

as a county powerhouse throughout the '80s, the soccer team snatched seven sectional championships between 1981 and 1991, as well as three district titles. From 1981 to 1991, 46 LMHers achieved County All-Star distinction. Thirty-one of them came in soccer, with five statewide All-Stars. The field hockey team won the league championship in 1982 and placed third in statewide interscholastic competition in 1984. Sporting a school record of 23 wins, the Blazers claimed a district hockey title in 1988 as high-scoring Anne Lehman shot 21 goals for an All-American award.

The softball and baseball teams clinched sectional championships in 1985 and 1987 respectively. Basketball finally moved into the spotlight as men and women won Section III titles in 1991. That was the year Missy Hostetter topped a school record with 1,652 points. The boys captured the runner-up spot in the league championship. The girls finished second in the District III tournament and entered the state basketball play-offs. The sounds of celebration in the winter of 1991 were muffled, however, by tragic news—the murder of sophomore Kimberly Weaver and her parents. Students found themselves riding an emotional rollercoaster of basketball triumphs and devastating grief.

Missy Hostetter's speed and skill on the court set a school record of 1,652 points in 1991.

Two LMH firsts brought new joy a few months later. The softball team won the District III championship and entered state play-offs. And for her moves on the court and lightning speed at shortstop, Missy Hostetter was named Athlete of the Year by the *New Era* and *Intelligencer Journal*.

The annual awards assembly typically applauded some 50 students, many of them two or three times, for distinctive achievements. Students were, in the theme of the 1990 *Laurel Wreath*, "Making Our Mark." Some of the school's founders would have surely thought they were missing the mark by basking in the warm glow of public recognition. Such acclaim reflected a redefinition of the Mennonite self—a theological shift from self-denial to the celebration of individual gifts. School officials, however, reminded students that the glories of Lone Ranger individualism were hollow. One's talents, students were taught, should enhance the larger community and glorify God rather than self.

Preparing students for an awards assembly, Janet Gehman offered wisdom that other faculty echoed over the years. Paraphrasing the beatitudes, she told students that Jesus understood their need for recognition but also promised rewards for the quiet virtues of being—meekness, mercy and purity of heart. "Congratulations to those of you who will receive awards this morning," she said. "But congratulations also to all of you who have your eyes fixed on a higher prize—that of the high calling of God in Jesus Christ. The kingdom of heaven is yours."[26] Speaking of awards assemblies, J. Richard Thomas told the trustees, "We try to use such occasions to reward excellence and to call students to use their gifts for the kingdom of God rather than the kingdom of self."[27] Indeed, the celebration of achievement is restrained a bit. Awards are not given at commencement nor are the names of winners printed in the commencement program. Those with stellar grades do not sport special tassels with their caps and gowns.

Timeless Principles

Caps and gowns? Ironically, the students whose parents had bristled under dress regulations were now asking to wear caps and gowns at graduation. The class of 1984, by an 85 percent vote, asked to wear the special garb because, in the words of a student, it "brings a unity and simplicity"—words of music to J. Paul Graybill's ears.[28] Just four years after laying aside their coverings the girls were asking to wear caps. But J. Paul would have quickly recognized that these caps were a different sort of "husk." Caps and gowns were mainstream, upscale symbols, not the garb of a rural folk. They were ceremonial symbols—taken off and on as convenient—not the fabric of a separated life. The trustees approved the request and school officials noted that caps and gowns added a

(top) Graduation ceremonies by the Mill Stream in the early 1980s.

(bottom) Seniors Nedra King and Cindy Groff celebrate their graduation in 1989.
Caps and gowns were first worn in 1984.

special dignity to the ceremonies in 1984.[29]

Compared to earlier decades, dress issues consumed comparatively little energy in the '80s. Students, of course, grumbled about the lines of propriety, but the "big" dress battles of this era were jewelry, slacks and formal attire at the annual junior/senior banquet. Even discussions of gym uniforms faded into obscurity when the trustees in February of 1984 permitted students to select their own "bottoms, shorts and culottes, etc."[30] The school code of 1990-'91 prohibited jewelry and earrings. "Hats, distinctive military clothing, camouflage clothing and decorative jewelry are not allowed during the school day."[31] The jewelry policy was relaxed for the annual junior/senior banquet which in later years had moved to public restaurants. Spaghetti-strap, strapless and off-the-shoulder gowns remained off limits. The school discouraged renting formal attire and urged students to dress in ways that reflected the cherished values of simplicity and modesty.

For several years the Parent-Teacher Fellowship staged an all-night post-banquet activity in local recreation centers. On several occasions students organized post-banquet dances, to the dismay of trustees. In the early 1990s some students and parents were pressing the school to organize wholesome

Three cousins, Patrick Lehman, Sally Weaver and Chad Hurst, at the 1991 junior/senior banquet.

dances. Students jockeyed with school officials to open the junior/senior banquet to younger LMH students, as well as to friends from other schools. In a 1990 survey, two-thirds of the parents affirmed the policy of restricting this Mennonite version of a prom to LMH juniors and seniors.

For several years in the late '80s, some students and parents urged a revision of the appearance code to allow slacks. The skirt requirement forced many girls to buy a second set of clothing since they typically wore slacks at home. Although special wardrobes had existed since the black shoe days of 1942, such spending clashed with Christian concerns for simplicity and stewardship. Requiring skirts, in the eyes of some patrons, encouraged expensive, upscale wardrobes. The girls, said one bishop, "were dressed to kill." Moreover, many argued that slacks were not only more practical and warmer than skirts, they were more modest. Conservative Mennonites had long viewed slacks as violating biblical admonitions for distinctive male/female dress. One mother arguing against slacks said, "I believe that Deuteronomy 22:5 applies to women today."[32] The Student Council in the 1989-'90 term proposed accepting slacks. About two-thirds of the parents either supported the proposal or were neutral.[33] A revised appearance code permitting slacks was passed in May of 1990.[34] Observers estimated that 85 percent of the girls wore them at one time or another in the 1990-91 term.

And the fate of the veiling? Although the requirement for students had been lifted in 1979, teachers continued to wear it. A special committee studied the matter in 1984 and simply recommended that faculty women and staff be sensitive to the positions of their own congregations.[35] Since veil wearing was rapidly fading across Lancaster Conference in the mid-'80s, the issue was virtually moot. The trustees approved the recommendation, and by the fall of 1984 few faculty women wore the veiling. School officials suggested dropping the veiling statement from the appearance code in the spring of 1989. However, out of sensitivity to sincere convictions, the trustees enacted the following policy: "The school encourages Christian girls to practice their convictions regarding the veiling of I Corinthians 11:2-6."[36] About a dozen girls wore the veiling to school in the 1990-91 term.

Seeking to transmit the foundational values of 1942, the appearance code 50 years later "encouraged students to practice their convictions within school guidelines and to respect the beliefs and practices of others which differ from their own." Uniformity had given way to a diversity which required tolerance and respect in the face of pluralism. Acknowledging that clothing styles constantly change, the policy asked students "to follow the timeless principles of modesty, simplicity and the wise use of economic resources."[37]

Student Pep

The vigor of youthful enthusiasm flourished over the years. In October of 1986 Principal Thomas told the trustees that successful sports teams were raising school spirits and students were begging for pep rallies. Indeed, he confessed, the school already had one pep assembly and the faculty were trying to decide if others were in order. By the late '80s students were unleashing their energy in rallies in the fall and winter. Interscholastic sports, especially the victories of the '80s, gave students a new sense of pride in LMH. One long-time staff member noted that the old feelings of stigma—embarrassed feelings about being a Mennonite in the '40s and '50s—had vanished.

There was religious zeal as well. On one occasion several dorm students, exuding enthusiasm for their new-found faith, pressured other students to accept Christ as their savior. School officials had to counsel the zealous to be more sensitive. Chapel services continued to provide routine times to "celebrate, confirm, challenge and call students to commitment" in their Christian faith.[38] "It's common," said J. Richard Thomas, "to have students come to us before chapel and ask if we can pray about a particular need today. It creates an atmosphere of mutual support and care—a community that cares about the individual. Chapel reminds us that we are our sisters' and brothers' keepers and not just a lonely individual out to conquer the world."

Fall and spring spiritual growth weeks continued through the '80s plus a potpourri of share and prayer groups. Gospel teams and drama groups—Jubilee Unlimited, No Spare Parts and Some Assembly Required, among others—provided avenues for students to share their spiritual zeal with local congregations.

There were new sounds of musical vigor as well by the Mill Stream. The jazz band gave its first public concert in May of 1989. Participation in choral groups,

A 1990 artist's sketch of the projected auditorium/fine arts center.

Guest speaker Daniel Yutzy leads a chapel during a spiritual life week.

however, remained fairly stable in the '80s despite the school's growth. Instrumental groups, on the contrary, increased. By the early '90s students could join a concert band, jazz band and string orchestra, in addition to the full orchestra.

Students could also participate in some two dozen other clubs: choral, chess, radio, culinary, bird watching, earth keeping, as well as Junior Achievement and Amnesty International. Sub sales, dramatic productions, public music programs and art festivals continued strong. Taffy pulls melted into oblivion.

Old ways of restraining student zest with demerits fell by the historical wayside in the late '70s. Students in the '80s received citizenship grades on their quarterly report cards. Three after-school detentions or a major infraction typically triggered an unsatisfactory citizenship mark. During most quarters 98 percent or more of the students received satisfactory citizenship scores. Minor troublemakers were assigned a 45-minute detention on Tuesdays or Thursdays. Major deviants faced one to three days of solitary confinement with an in-school suspension.

Student energy expressed itself in humorous pranks which sometimes turned

Instrumental music groups flourished in the 1980s.

malicious and often flourished near graduation. In May of 1986 some 380 students from Mennonite high schools across the country gathered at LMH for the 24th annual Music Festival. The festivities were marred when officials learned that trays and silverware had mysteriously vanished from the cafeteria. The culprits refused to come forward. Lunches were served in paper bags in classrooms for two weeks until the pranksters reluctantly returned the missing tableware.

Like the students of earlier years, Mill Stream scholars in the '80s found each other attractive. The school handbook discouraged dating on campus and expected high standards in relationships between the sexes. But youthful romance was sometimes hard to bridle. In the spring of 1987 "physical contact" was on the rise. An announcement, read in all the homerooms, reminded students that high standards between the sexes put "kissing, holding hands and other kinds of indiscreet physical contact" off limits on campus.[39] On those rare occasions when pregnancies happened, the school worked carefully with students' local congregations to determine the appropriate response. "The school reserves the right to make the final decision in such a case," said Thomas, "but we will not make a decision without a recommendation from the congregation—the central unit of church life. The school and congregation working together need to provide the counseling, forgiveness, restoration and whatever needs to be done." Such was the nature of partnering between church and school in time of pain and need.

Poised for the Twenty-First Century

Copied from the factory model, the educational assembly line of many schools often adds to the fragmentation of modern life. Rich in specialization, large schools frequently dice the educational experience into slices of unrelated courses, diverse teachers and frayed days. Moving from class to unrelated class on the educational conveyor belt, students lose a sense of continuity and quickly become nameless statistics. Modern schools of massive size especially breed such fragmentation. The small size of LMH in its early years fostered a sense of community and integration, despite its being rather parochial and sectarian. Although it remained relatively small, LMH's growing size threatened to spoil its wholeness.

Cognizant of the 50-year benchmark and dreaming about the twentieth century, school officials asked, "How can we make a good thing better?" Encouraged by Orville Yoder of the Mennonite Board of Education, a task force began exploring models for developing a smaller unit within the larger one. Dubbing its project, "Schooling for the Twenty-First Century," the group projected a smaller grouping within the central campus facilities. Faculty members on the task force visited experimental models near Boston and Princeton, scoured relevant literature and brainstormed about new possibilities by the Mill Stream.

By the spring of 1991 the task force had drafted a working model for a smaller unit of 100 students within the larger school.[40] In the plan, a year-long course would shrink to six weeks, meeting each day for four hours. Students would focus on a single topic for six weeks with one teacher, thus enriching student/teacher ties, as well as building a stronger sense of camaraderie among students. Benefits for teachers include a single lesson plan and a reduction of students from 125 to 25. Every six weeks students would move to a new topic and a different teacher. Beyond traditional classroom activities, the daily, four-hour block of time offers possibilities for field trips, extensive laboratory experiments and expanded group projects. Philosophically, the model emphasized learning how to learn, with more responsibility falling on student shoulders.

Students in the smaller school would interact with other students during an hour-long lunch and study period. Twenty-First Century students would also link into the larger school for subjects like typing, physical education, art and instrumental music. And they would join other students in co-curricular clubs, athletics and all-school assemblies.

The project was slated to begin in the fall of 1992 as the school entered its 51st year. The model promised the delights of a small community while enjoying the rich resources of a larger system, minus the debilitating effects of bureaucracy. Rooted in the biblical notion of shalom, it nurtured hope for wholeness and integration—scarce qualities in modern life. As the school poised itself for the twenty-first century, the embryonic venture offered hope that the cherished virtues of community would pass on to future generations.

CHAPTER NINE

Celebrating Jubilee

"The mischievous students made some of the best church leaders."
—A. Grace Wenger

Will Our Children Have Faith?

"Will our children have faith?" Quoting Christian educators, J. Richard Thomas posed this question to the trustees in a meditation before one of their meetings. Surely they will, he suggested, but what sort of faith will they have?[1] Any community hoping to survive beyond one generation must engage in education. However, why do some religious communities turn their children over to public schools while others create their own to pass on the faith? The more peculiar the faith, the more likely a group will create its own schools to preserve a distinctive heritage. The quality of public education and its per-ceived threat to a community's values are also catalysts in the formation of religious schools.

At what moment in a group's history will it likely build a school? What mix of internal and external factors spur the development of a school? Once

Student Forum, 1958-59. Faculty advisor, J. Irvin Lehman, on the left. The Student Forum, later called Student Council, meets in 1989. Faculty advisor, Myron Dietz, on the left.

established, schools develop a momentum of their own to enhance their chances of survival. Had LMH not been established in 1942, would the faith of the 1990s be peculiar enough to merit its formation today? Or if it closed for a season, would patrons press to reopen its doors in this generation?

Circumstances 50 years later are certainly different than at the time of the school's founding. Lancaster County's population of 1940 has nearly doubled to 423,000.[2] Suburban developments sprawl across old pastures, and industrial plazas lie beside fertile farmland. Outlet stores and tourist sites by the hundreds, unheard of in the '40s, dot the countryside. The Mennonite Church has changed as well. Symbols of nonconformity have faded. Members participate in professional and business networks across the state and around the nation. Sons and daughters head off to college in unprecedented numbers. In short, diversity of all sorts—theological, cultural, occupational—encircles the Mennonite community of the '90s.

Some things remain the same. As the school approached its Jubilee the nation was once again at war. Old Glory was flying high. The flags of patriotism swirled with passion in support of American troops in the Persian Gulf. Some students brought small flags to school, reminiscent of 1942. Once again Mennonites struggled to sort out the competing claims of God and Caesar.

The transformation of LMH mirrored in many ways the social upheaval experienced by the Mennonite church. The school was, indeed, a microcosm of the controversies churning through the Mennonite community in these 50 years. As the church's formal agency for education, the school was charged with transmitting the ideals of faith—ideals that were ever shifting in the flux of social change. What is the role of a school in the life of a people? Should it mirror common sentiments or actively lead and steer the process of social change?

Schools are more than schools, more than academic institutions. They embody a community's values, the things it cares about. Over the years different things have mattered as the Mennonite church sought to find its way within the society surrounding it. As a servant of the church, LMH reflected the shifting conversations about the things that mattered. In these conversations spanning the decades, some practices and understandings fell by the wayside. Others were transformed. And still others persisted over the years.

Points of Divergence

Fifty years of education have passed alongside the Mill Stream. Has the school remained faithful to its vision? Or has it drifted into the mainstream of modern culture? Would the founding fathers rejoice at the sight of their Mill Stream enterprise today? Are the pep assemblies, jazz bands, pizza bashes, alumni dinner theatres, family movie nights and interscholastic sports in keeping with their founding vision? Such activities are hardly the marks of a "pretty plain operation," as superintendent of Lancaster County schools Harry F. Gerlach called the early Mill Stream operation.

Many features of campus life have diverged from the early days. With all the buildings from the Yeates era gone except one, the campus itself has been transformed. Still operated on behalf of Mennonite churches, the school has slipped away from direct control by Lancaster Conference. The bishops who once scrutinized it closely now watch from afar and entrust their concerns to representatives on the Religious Welfare Committee. Patron polls now supersede the dictates of the bishops. Professional educators have replaced the ordained churchmen who led the school in early days. Bible faculty in recent years are more likely to be professionally trained teachers than bishops straddling the fence between classroom and bishop district. No longer aloof from the Mennonite Secondary Education Council, LMH fully participates in the network of other Mennonite high schools. J. Richard Thomas, treasurer of the group for two years, was elected chair in 1990-91. A Bible curriculum, developed on the Lancaster campus in the late '80s, was adopted with minor revisions at many of the other Mennonite schools.

The vocabulary of the founding fathers diminished over the decades. Pleas for uniformity have given way to affirmations of diversity. The code words of the early documents—safeguard, self-denial, submission, loyalty, nonconformity and nonresistance—are missing in the texts of the '90s. The separatist stance that hoped to safeguard youth from the evils of the outside world has crumbled. Indeed, as J. Paul Graybill feared, the idea of school standards rising above the church's has largely been buried.[3] Has the school spoiled the church, as some founders fretted might happen? Or has the church spoiled the school? Perhaps both have been transformed by the tides of modernity.

A variety of trends mark changes in the student body near the end of the 50-year journey. The number of minority and non-Mennonite students is on the rise. These and teachers from beyond the Lancaster area enhance the school's diversity. More students are coming from both single parent homes and strained marriages where parents are divorced or separated. In many families both parents work outside the home and many students carry evening and weekend jobs. The number of students entering post secondary schools is also growing.

The outer husk of student life has certainly changed. Founders might

*The Senior Octet of 1960 and the literary staff of the 1991 **Silhouette** model the typical clothing of their day. Advisor Calvin Esh, second from left.*

(top) Many art related activities were used to raise funds for the auditorium/fine arts center.

(bottom) D. Brent Siegrist receives his diploma from Trustee chairman, Jason Steffy, on June 8, 1991.

Jessica Lapp teaches writing in a computer lab in 1989.

Mary Lou Houser instructs an art class in 1986.

Daily chapels were an integral part of the LMH experience. Student pastor John Landis leads a chapel in 1985-86.

(top) Students, clad in the garb of the early 1990s, enjoy a lighter moment.
(bottom) Coach Vernon Rice outlines the strategy for a new soccer play.

(top) Teachers Clyde Hollinger, Mary Lou Houser and Carl Shenk steady the plow at the ground breaking for the auditorium/fine arts center in October 1990.

(bottom) Students mix work and play at the annual senior hoagie sale in 1990.

The campus in 1991 with the completed Auditorium/Fine Arts Center. Route 30 appears in the background.

Arnold Moshier directs the Men's Chorus in 1960 without musical accompaniment. Instrumental music groups were on the upswing in the 1980s. The Jazz Band of 1990-91.

grimace at the sight of girls walking the hallways clad in slacks. Fellows sporting short sleeves and open collars would trouble others. The somber tone of early chapels has long vanished. The bishops of the '40s would surely be surprised to learn that kneeling for prayer has given way to applause in chapel services. Some would be startled to discover women leading worship behind the chapel pulpit. Their surprise would likely turn to sorrow at the thought of pianos, drums, skits and films within sacred chapel walls. But, do the sounds of jazz, cheers for varsity teams and applause for public drama mean the founding vision has withered? Has the heart of the vision drifted down the Mill Stream?

Strands of Continuity

Many strands of continuity weave the vision of the past into the tapestry of the present. The original Articles of Incorporation still grace the conference room of the school's administrative suite.[4] The 1942 articles spell out four objectives for the school. In the words of the first, the school hoped "to indoctrinate young people in the Word of God and to acquaint them with the teachings of the Mennonite Church." School personnel in the '90s shy away from the idea of indoctrination, but their intent remains remarkably similar to that of 1942. Current educational goals include helping students to appreciate the Bible as God's authoritative word and obey its teachings. Another aims to introduce students to the history and faith of the Mennonite Church.[5] These strands of continuity have not frayed over time.

The founders' second objective was to provide training, under a Christian influence and environment, for the development of Christian character. The enduring commitment to this purpose is evident in several ways today. In the words of the admission application, students and parents "covenant to consider the school community to be a group of persons led together by God. This realization affects the way we treat others and the way we open ourselves to learn from them." On behalf of the school, the application reads, "Our goal is to provide an excellent education in a context that promotes growth in your Christian faith and life." Stated as one of the educational objectives is the hope that students will make personal commitments to Jesus Christ and follow his example in servanthood and peacemaking.

The third objective of 1942 aimed to foster a lasting love for the church and prepare youth for future usefulness. Although the language has changed, the purpose remains firm. In the words of the present philosophy statement, the school participates with home and church to prepare persons for lives that contribute to Christ-like service and the general welfare of society. Moreover, it seeks to challenge students to lives of Christ-like mission, peacemaking and service in a global society.[6]

Fourth, the founders sought to guide youth in social relationships and to assist them in becoming "law-abiding and useful citizens." The current student handbook spells out "standards for guiding our life together," designed to develop qualities of good citizenship. In addition, the school, in the words of its philosophy statement, attempts to create a "setting where physical, social, emotional and spiritual development is valued." In all of these ways the founding vision is woven tightly into the fabric of the '90s.

Other continuities abound as well. The commitment to biblical literacy holds firm in the graduation requirement of four Bible courses. A student transferring to LMH from a public school in the early '90s was amazed how "everyone tries to find answers for everything in the Bible." Personal faith and spiritual growth are cultivated in daily chapels, prayer groups and personal conversations. Anabaptist understandings of faith are nurtured and passed on.

The commitment to high academic standards articulated in early years by Noah Good has persisted over the decades. The grading scale that requires a

---

Figure 9.1
Twenty-Year Faculty Veterans: 1942-1992

Faculty	Tenure	Years of Service
Clyde B. Stoner	1942-1984	42
Noah G. Good	1942-1977	35
Myron Dietz	1957-	35*
Charles Longenecker	1958-	34*
Edna K. Wenger	1942-1974	32
Elton Moshier	1952-1982	30
L. Larry Wenger	1962-	30*
Stanley Kreider	1956-1983	27
Janet Gehman	1965	27*
Daniel Wenger	1966-	26*
Arnold Moshier	1959-1982	22
Ernest M. Hess	1970-1991	22
Isaac L. Frederick	1972-	20*
Vernon R. Rice	1972-	20*

* Years of service includes 1991-92 school year.

The total years of service in some cases includes sabbatical and/or leave time. Several persons served in administrative and teaching roles.

94 for an A feels stiff to many students transferring from schools with other grading schemes. Teachers are pleased to hear college personnel say "we can trust an alumnus from LMH." Faculty continue to be hired not only for academic expertise, but for their faith commitment and character as role models. The school's original concern to permeate the curriculum with values "in harmony with the Word of God" continues today.

The transformation of the school sometimes wrapped old traditions in new packages. Fall and spring revivals have become Commitment Week and Christian Growth Week respectively. The older emphasis on nonresistance has shifted to peacemaking. Service of all sorts has replaced the pleas for nonconformity in the first two decades of the school. The linguistic shift from nonresistance and nonconformity to peacemaking and service reflects the church's changing stance toward the outside world—the turn from separation to engagement. Mission efforts to save dying souls in Africa have faded into calls to share faith and enter global service. Although couched in different language, the international focus of the school has held steady over the decades. The evangelistic spirit of early days remains alive in recent years as many students and graduates entered short-term mission stints with Youth Evangelism Service (YES) and Summer Training and Action Teams (STAT).

Despite many changes, the threads of continuity have not frayed. Core values have not floated down the Mill Stream; they are passing on to new generations in continuing conversations of faith. Is the school, 50 years later, faithful to the vision of its founders? Is it still a safe, sane place for the transmission of faith? Has it remained, in the words of the founders, "the servant of God and the church in every respect?"[7] Does it remain "the key to the future of the church" as Mennonite leader Clarence Fretz had proposed in 1953?

Throughout the decades the school has faithfully served the church—seeking to transmit the heritage of faith. In this sense the vision endures. But over the years the church itself has changed, continually updating its vision. "The church has changed so much," said Noah Good in 1990, "that much of what we conscientiously and seriously promoted in the early years is now rejected or has become a joke. . . . One thing seems clear to me. The school did not lead the church away from its biblical simplicity; the church led the way and the school fell in line and did so easily."[8] Asking if the school remained faithful to its original vision is perhaps a moot question. Did the school faithfully serve a church whose own character and vision evolved over the years? That is the paramount question.

Dorm girls gather for a sewing party in 1959. By 1990 the decor of dorm rooms had changed.

A Well-Rounded Education

J. Paul Graybill spoke of a well-rounded education. The founders hoped "to give young people an appreciation of true values, expressed in loyalty to the church and a life of service to God and our fellow men."[9] Although committed to academic rigor, the early visionaries knew that a school is more than a school. They understood that schools embody and articulate, often in quiet ways, the values of their communities.

Students learn more than technical procedures and scientific facts. They learn to appreciate, to discriminate. They absorb the constellation of values esteemed by their communities. Teachers are more than disseminators of facts; they are models. Administrators are not mere decision-makers; they demonstrate understandings of power and community. The hidden curriculum of the school—the things learned beyond the classroom—impacts the world view of students perhaps as significantly as the formal concepts of the classroom. Moral commitments made in hallways and over lunch tables may, in the long run, parallel the significance of formal instruction.

This does not belittle the official curriculum. It does mean, however, that a well-rounded education encompasses the physical, spiritual, social and intellectual domains of life. The school's founders were committed to this understanding of education—one that is both holistic and value-laden—embedding values in both the hidden and formal curriculum; one that articulates the ideals of faith cherished by the Mennonite community at every turn. That commitment has endured. The ideals fluctuated and the convictions shifted over the years, but the motivating vision has persisted. Ideal as it sounds, this commitment to a well-rounded education has been fraught with risks. It has involved making moral judgments, sifting right from wrong, sorting good from evil—judgments which in the course of time may appear foolish. Such an education has meant scrutinizing not only the academic credentials of prospective teachers but their faith commitments and life styles as well. Such an education rejects the modern distinction between public and private life. It understands that faculty life styles communicate the values of faith more cogently than formal classroom proclamations.

This approach to education considers the value assumptions hidden in textbooks and other reading materials. A commitment to holistic education converts the surprises of life—a death, an accident, a fire, a flood—into teachable moments for reflection and growth. Such an education understands that the ethos of a school—its social and spiritual climate—communicates values, along with its teachers. Chapel services become the central arena for recalling and reminding the community of its common commitments. A

value-laden education views the process of decision-making in faculty meetings, student discipline and strategic planning as essential as the outcome
itself.[10]

Religious schools are not the only ones concerned with values. Public
schools sometimes ban books, bar plays and expel students because such schools
also embody the concerns of their constituents. Indeed, in public education it
has became fashionable to call for value commitments across the curriculum
and to develop programs to clarify them. All schools teach values of one sort
or another. Religious schools simply represent particular communities committed to a distinctive set of values. For example, in a recent survey, 96 percent
of LMH faculty said that "peace should be a major emphasis" in the school's
curriculum. The study concluded that a distinguishing feature of LMH is its
dedication to peace.[11]

Patrons of the '90s may chuckle at the moral discernment of former years—
forbidding public drama, banning music instruments and clipping off faculty
mustaches. But such policies were genuine attempts to inject value commitments into all dimensions of school life. Constituents over the years have
disagreed over particular expressions of values, but the story of Lancaster
Mennonite High School is indeed a story of value education. The moral
judgments of the trustees, the ever-changing boundaries of the appearance code
and the seven-fold covenant signed today by students and parents reflect an
enduring commitment to a well-rounded education. Such an education means
that the diplomas disbursed on breezy June days by the Mill Stream represent
more than academic achievement; they symbolize a cluster of cherished values.

How then, is a well-rounded education measured? What are the criteria of
a quality education? Should quality be defined by outside accrediting agencies,
the academic standards of the larger society, the values of a religious community, the actualization of a particular school's own vision, or the judgments of
its professional staff? Should religious schools seek to meet the standards of
excellence prescribed by outside agencies of accreditation or aim to conform
to the highest values arising from their own religious heritage, or some mix of
both? The answers to these questions perhaps betray a school's grasp of its own
identity, as well as its ability to articulate its mission in the context of its
heritage.

The Margin of Difference

What difference does such a commitment to values make? In the early days
the margin of difference between LMS and public schools was quite obvious.
The "pretty plain operation" by the Mill Stream was clearly distinguishable

The faculty of 1950-51. Principal J. Paul Graybill on the left. A larger and more diverse faculty gather by the Mill Stream in the fall of 1990.

The Faculty Quartet in 1960. Left: Arnold Moshier, Charles Longenecker, Edwin Keener and Elton Moshier. A faculty quartet performs barbershop-style at a dinner theater in April 1988. Left: Daniel Wenger, Clyde Hollinger, Charles Longenecker and Dennis Kauffman.

from public high schools, not only in the dress of students and staff, but in the curriculum, the attitude of teachers, and in its relationship to the church. The margin of difference is less obvious today. A recruitment poster invites students to "Discover the Difference" at LMH. What is that difference now?

In exit interviews with guidance counselors, seniors frequently mention Christian friendships, caring teachers and chapel services as distinctives of an LMH education. Faculty make a concerted attempt to weave Anabaptist values of Christian discipleship, peacemaking and service into the marrow of the curriculum. Required Bible courses are an obvious difference. The common experience of daily chapel cultivates a distinctive sense of community. What other differences set the school apart?

Careful attention to selecting teachers committed to transmitting a heritage of faith remains paramount. Although faculty are not dismissed capriciously, formal tenure, an organized union and labor strikes are missing. A jubilee fund for faculty and staff offers short-term loans in time of emergency. In addition to a biannual patron survey, the school seeks in a variety of ways to tap the mainstream of patron sentiment when formulating and interpreting policies. Constituency support—expressed in vigorous bidding at an auction, saying yes to a phonathon request, attending an alumni dinner theatre, participating at parent-teacher fellowships and in hundreds of hours of volunteer time—cultivates ownership and partnership.

Some visitors to the school are surprised to learn that student lockers remain unlocked. Other observers marvel that senior classes can take an overnight trip to Washington D. C. without serious misbehavior. Some of the typical trappings of public schools are missing at LMH—cheerleaders, marching bands, football, dances and a prom.[12] The American flag, of course, is gone, along with its salute and the sounds of the national anthem. At times a prayer, a moment of silence or a few words on sportsmanship preface the beginning of home games. In times of war students are reminded that God loves the whole world and calls the followers of Christ to love their enemies.

Mini-courses devoted to service projects, as well as gospel and drama teams performing in churches and retirement homes, highlight the ongoing tradition of service. An annual work day designed to support school and community projects reminds students of the value of serving others. A call for modesty and simplicity, as well as a taboo on military clothing and decorative jewelry, etch the lines of distinction in the student dress code.

These obvious differences, important as they may be, are overshadowed by subtle shades of mutual respect, partnership, friendship and care that circumscribe the character of the school. While its margin of difference may be less obvious at first glance, it remains substantial, however. What difference does that difference make in the long run?

The Margin of Outcome

Recent educational literature champions attempts to measure student outcomes. The long-term influence of a school, however, eludes easy measurement. The roster of variables that shape student lives involves a complex interaction between personal attitudes, parental interest, friendship ties, church relationships, faculty-student bonds, extracurricular experiences, as well as a multitude of other concrete events. Charting a school's impact requires tracing students into their adult lives and gathering careful data on their backgrounds and families. A fair analysis also necessitates comparable data on Mennonite students attending public schools. Such a long-term, comprehensive analysis of the impact of LMH and other Mennonite high schools does not exist.[13]

There are, however, some suggestive studies. LMH and public school graduates were compared in a study of nearly 1,700 Mennonites who graduated between 1970 and 1980 in the Lancaster area. On all the comparisons—Mennonite church affiliation, church attendance, church participation, leadership involvement and participation in service agencies—LMH graduates scored higher than their public school counterparts. This evidence speaks well for LMH but does not pinpoint the distinctive contribution of family, congregation and school.[14]

Softer, short-term indicators also point to the LMH difference. Principal Thomas noted that LMH graduates are six times more likely to volunteer for a service stint with the Eastern Mennonite Board of Missions than students from other schools.[15] "It's tremendously rewarding," reflected Noah Good, "to see the thousands of alumni who have gone through the school. Many found life companions here and then found their way into business or church work, partly at least through the influence of the school." By 1991 nearly 200 alumni were serving as ordained leaders across the Mennonite Church.[16] Many, of course, may have entered the ranks of church leadership despite the school. What is certain, however, is that the likelihood of graduates having active church involvement soars when family, church and school work in concert, mutually reinforcing one another.[17]

In many ways LMH has acted as an intersection—a meeting place of sorts. Students learn to know teachers whose influence trails them for many years. They encounter ideas that shape their convictions and steer their behavior for decades. They meet God in quiet moments, in the discipline of Bible study, in

Basketball in the old gym in the early 1970s. A new gym provided space for a growing sports program.

An early quartet and the Creative Worship Team of 1990-91 illustrate changes in dress styles and artistic expression. Advisor Dan Dietzel on left.

the comforting words of a friend and in the stirring sermon of a chapel service. Over the decades students have been introduced to leaders from across the church who visit the campus as chapel speakers. Many students discover and

Figure 9.2

Top Ten Alumni Surnames*

Surname	Frequency
1. Martin	217
2. Stoltzfus	211
3. Weaver	196
4. Miller	153
5. Hess	124
6. Landis	103
7. Groff	84
8. Hershey	81
9. King	78
10. Mast	73

* Based on graduation surnames, 1943-1990.

embrace their Anabaptist heritage for the first time by the Mill Stream.

"It was a good place to rebel," reflects alumna Ruth Detweiler Lesher. "You could test values and experiment with independence in a loving environment without getting into serious trouble." "LMH was a kind of leveler," recalls Edna Wenger. "Some students got more fancy and others more plain."

Friendships blossom at LMH and continue into adult life. Students from other states, different congregations and multi-racial backgrounds join hands in friendship by the Mill Stream. These social ties, often enduring over the years, are one of the less obvious but more significant contributions of the school. Some of the connections become significant indeed. Spouses find each other: of some 6,000 alumni, 1,128 married a graduate, yielding 564 Mill Stream marriages by the spring of 1991.[18] In all of these ways the school is an intersection—a meeting place that has made a difference.

This intersection of faith offers students a fresh view of the church. Their sometimes parochial experience in local congregations is often transformed. As they receive the heritage of faith, they encounter an international family. In a variety of ways, via classroom and chapel speakers, student exchanges and excursions overseas, students develop connections with other Mennonites around the world. They discover a heritage of faith that extends beyond their local congregation. Their experiences of faith stretch backwards into sixteenth century Anabaptist history and bond them across cultural lines into a larger Anabaptist family scattered around the globe.

This sense of membership in a larger family of faith is, in many ways, a more enduring legacy than training in specific academic skills. Exposure to the contemporary Anabaptist vision fuses students in new and significant ways into the Mennonite family of faith. Although present day students do not share a uniformity of practice like those of earlier years, LMH today provides a uniformity of experience that links newcomers into the larger community of faith. Former executive secretary of Mennonite World Conference and member of the first LMH graduating class, Paul Kraybill, described LMH alumni around the world in a wide range of vocations. "I've seen the quality of these people and the depth of their commitment. I've seen them put it together in the world and it really works. It's real. It's genuine."

Scores of Mennonites have grown into mature faith outside the walls of a church school. And some who attended LMH never subscribed to the faith of the founding fathers. Some of the Mill Stream marriages soured and ended in divorce. Some alumni, for a variety of reasons, carry painful memories of their days on campus and others have turned their backs on the community of faith. Although not a sure cure for all that ails the church, religious schools—along-

The cooks in 1958 and 1991. Changes in both menu and attire occurred between these years.

side family, congregation and community—do facilitate the transmission of
faith.

Parochial schools do not exist solely for the sake of students. They serve
other less obvious functions as well. A school like LMH assembles a reservoir
of intellectual talent as faculty from a variety of disciplines struggle to translate
the Anabaptist vision into contemporary practice. This rich resource benefits
the church not only through student contact, but in many other ways as well.
The Mennonite Church of the Lancaster area would surely be poorer without
the nearby pool of faculty talent.

Like other church-related institutions, church schools symbolize a group's
ability to articulate its vision and commitments in a tangible way. The bricks
and mortar, the gifts of dollars and time, and the energy and commitment of
staff and volunteers give visible expression to the soul of the community. LMH
in this sense embodies the marrow of community values. All who participate
in the life of the school—staff, friends, parents and donors—are reminded of
the things that are cherished, the things that matter, the things worthy of
sacrifice. In this sense the school educates the broader church community and
builds commitment to the common cause of Christian education.

The school continues to serve the church through public campus programs
and hundreds of student-led programs in congregations over the years. Campus
facilities frequently host churchwide gatherings, as well as weddings, special
meetings and informal reunions. In all of these ways and more, the school not
only exists for students, it waits on the larger church community as well.

The desire of alumni to have their children encounter what they experienced
a generation earlier is perhaps the most telling gauge of effectiveness. The real
significance of a Mill Stream education often swells in the hearts of alumni,
sometimes in direct relation to their distance from it. Difficult to measure,
impossible to quantify and hard to explain, the LMH experience for a multitude
of reasons shaped a cluster of warm memories that many alumni now hope to
pass on to their children. That testimony, perhaps more critical than the
approval of accrediting agencies or other measures of outcome, certifies the
enduring significance of the school's education.

The Membrane of Memories

Education is largely a process of constructing memories. Memories are
powerful: they shape conviction, motivate behavior and stir passion. These
images from the past shape our response to the future. The membrane of
memories encompassing the history of LMH is complex and varied. Memories
of significant teachers and classroom discussions galvanize convictions even

The school dining hall at two different times and locations: the ground floor of the old Yeates barn in 1947-48 and the basement of the chapel in 1990-91.

some 50 years later. Bygone moments of spiritual renewal remind many alumni of their pilgrimage of faith. They also warmly recall pleasant times and youthful pranks. Others still feel the pain and anger of discipline. For the most part, however, alumni support is strong today, energized by good memories and the integrity of the school. J.D. Stahl spoke for many when he said, "I remember many friends and teachers at LMH with fondness. It was a sheltered place that allowed me to question old certainties while becoming aware of my ties to past, to family and to church."

History has an uncanny way of flipping the sincerest convictions of one era into objects of folly later. It's easy to snicker today at tales of gospel tracts, stuffed in bottles, floating down the Mill Stream in search of unsaved souls. Stories of couples being allowed to hold hands while skating, only if they wore gloves, still evoke laughter in the '90s. Current students and alumni may scorn early administrators who painted strings on the veilings pictured in *Laurel Wreath* photos to make them comply with the dress code. Such antics were sometimes necessary to prevent a ruckus in the church or to mask the negligence of delinquent girls. "In the early years the school did what we felt was biblical and right in light of church teachings," said Noah Good. "We tried earnestly and hard to hold back and suppress some of the things that the school now promotes and glories in. . . . A very different church atmosphere prevailed in the 1940s. . . ."[19]

History, however, may have the last laugh. Sincere commitments of the '90s will surely bring some chuckles to later generations. The gift of historical humility offers grace to temper—but not eliminate—bold commitments of the present. It reminds us that each generation, despite its sincerity, is held captive to the impulses of its times. The gift of historical perspective frees us from undue anxiety in the present moment. For in the words of teacher A. Grace Wenger, "The mischievous students made some of the best church leaders."

What of all the efforts to pass on the faith by the Mill Stream? Were they worth it? Did the efforts nurture convictions strong enough to swim against the currents of the time? The hothouse plants were surely not wilting. The kernels of faith were firm despite the shedding of their outer husks. Noah Good summed up the 50-year journey: "Frankly, I feel the school has been good for the church. If the people closely related to it could speak today, I'm sure they'd say 'we'd do it again!'"

Worth doing again! That surely is a glorious memory—a testimony that the faith is being passed on with integrity. A cause for celebrating Jubilee!

Appendix A

Educational Staff
1942-1992

Achenbach, Miriam L.
  (Maust) 1964-67
Asbury, Edith M. 1979-82
Banks, Janet C. 1978-
Bauer, Roger E. 1969-70
Bauman, Harvey W.
  1947-60
Baumgartner, Jeffrey L.
  1990-
Beaman, Marian M.
  (Longenecker) 1963-66
Bender, Robert M. 1974-79
Birkness, Cindy L. 1989-90
Bogedian, Linda J. 1977-81
Bomberger, Doris (Good)
  1951-53, 1957-58
Bomberger, James R.
  1957-61
Bontrager, Edith S. 1983-87
Bontrager, Elizabeth R.
  1986-89
Borkholder, Michael L.
  1991-
Breneman, Janet M.
  1972-73, 1978-80
Brenneman, Harold H.
  1954-57
Brubaker, J. Allen 1961-62
Brubaker, J. Dean1987-90
Brubaker, J. Lester 1946-55,
  1970-83
Buckwalter, Kenneth B.
  1970-72
Buckwalter, Marlene W.
  1970-72
Burkholder, Christine G.
  (Landis)1973-76
Bueno, Daniel M.1971-74
Bueno, Jeanette R. 1971-73
Byler, Jesse T.1953-58
Carey, Cheryl J.
  (Kreider)1984-88
Carpenter, Sidney M.
  1948-50
Charles, Anna Lois 1962-71
Charles, H. Raymond
  1959-66
Charles, Jonathan E.
  1974-80

Charles, Rhoda
  (Reinford)1976-79
Clemmer, Fern E.1985-
Cloyd, P. Daniel 1985-87
Colliver, Verna M.
  (Mohler)1963-67,
  1968-70
Culp, Erla M.
  (Oberholtzer)1950-56
Culp, G. Richard 1952-57
Denlinger, Ruth E. 1956-57
Detweiler, Lowell M.
  1967-70
Dietz, Myron S.1957-
Dietzel, Daniel L.1974-
Dietzel, Joanne H. 1979-80
Diffenbach, Karen L.
  (Emery)1977-79,1981-
  82,1983-85
Drescher, James M. 1970-73
Eby, Joyce L.1963-66
Eby Omar E.1960-63
Eby, Wilmer M.1964-65
Erb, J. Henry 1962-64
Esh, Calvin E. 1984-
Eshleman, Ellen Keener
  1949-50
Evans, Duane M. 1990-
Frederick, Isaac L. 1972-
Fretz, Clarence Y. 1955-56
Frey, Nicholas B. 1987-90
Garber, J. Clarence 1955-63
Gehman, Carol R. 1966-69
Gehman, Janet N. 1965-86,
  1988-
George, Elias E. 1977-84
Glick, Charlotte J.
  (Holsopple)1973-78
Glick, Delmar J. 1974-78
Good, I. Merle 1972-74
Good, James M. 1960-62
Good, Leon W. 1987-
Good, Lois A. 1948-53
Good, Noah G. 1942-77
Good, Phyllis P. 1972-74
Graham, S. Kathryn 1956-57
Grasse, Carolyn J. 1976-80
Graybill, J. Paul 1942-53

Graybill, Rhoda Mae
  1963-66, 1967-70
Greenlee, Rhoda (Lapp)
  1971-72
Greenwald, Susan E. 1990-
Grier, Carolyn M. 1984-87
Grieser, Michael C.1985-88
Groff, Geoffrey C. 1988-
Groff, Marlin G. 1988-
Guntz, Harold B. 1979-85
Gyger, Karen S. 1981-
Haas, Melford R. 1971-74
Haines, Leland 1961-62
Hamilton, David L. 1976-78
Harnish, Roy W. 1951-54
Hayes, M. Arlene
  (Sensenig) 1970-72
Heatwole, Mary Ethel
  1957-59
Heisey, J. Wilmer 1989-
Heller, Joseph L. 1973-77
Helmus, Linda S. 1987-89
Helmuth, Phillip N. 1975-76
Hershey, Andrew M. 1991-
Hershey, Charles D. 1957-58
Hershey, Noah L. 1961-69
Hess, Ernest M.
  1968-69,1970-73,1975-
  1991
Hess, James R. 1960-61
Hess, Mahlon M. 1943-45
Hess, Miriam 1970-71
Hess, Myra E. 1943-51
Hofer, Galen J. 1984-85
Hoffer, Donald E. 1976-77
Hollinger, Aaron H. 1956-58
Hollinger, Clyde M. 1975-
Hollinger, Edward B. 1986-
Hollinger, J. Clair 1968-76
Hooley, Jane L.
  (Myers)1988-
Horst, Galen R.1976-77
Hostetter, Gwendolyn L.
  1985-86
Hostetter, Philip L. 1985-87
Houser, Mary Lou 1977-89,
  1990-
Hummel, Keith E. 1960-64

Shertzer, A. Willard
   1963-64
Shirk, Allan W. 1965-68,
   1984-
Short, Jane L. 1973-74
Showalter, Louise E.
   1972-79
Smeltz, Edmund 1964-65
Smucker, John D. 1986-87
Smucker, Myrna H. 1976-83
Stahl, Susan H. (Leaman)
   1960-62
Stauffer, Irene 1959-60
Stewart, Roseanne S.
   (Breneman)1973-76
Stichter, Connie L.
   (Weaver) 1974-76
Stoltzfus, James Lowell
   1969-71
Stoltzfus, Aden D. 1990-
Stoltzfus, Mary E. (Cox)
   1954-56
Stoltzfus, Miriam R.
   (Weaver) 1947-48
Stoner, Clyde B. 1942-45,
   1946-84
Suderman, June A. (Sauder)
   1965-66
Swartley, Kenton E. 1985-91

Taylor, A. Marie (Peifer)
   1964-66
Thomas, David N. 1964-72
Thomas, J. Richard 1973-
Thomas, J. Samuel 1986-88
VanPelt, Deborah G. 1985-
Wagaman, John W. 1968-69
Weaver, Amos W. 1946-72
Weaver, Anna Mary
   1950-52
Weaver, J. Irvin 1966-70
Weaver, John W. 1950-52
Weaver, Marilyn
   (Hollinger) 1971-73
Weber, Dorothy G. 1980-
Weber, John S. 1971-74,
   1975-81
Wenger, A. Grace 1956-66
Wenger, Carolyn L.
   (Charles) 1965-67,
   1968-69
Wenger, Chester L., II
   1974-79
Wenger, Daniel L. 1966-76,
   1979-
Wenger, Edna K. 1942-74
Wenger, John S. 1942-47
Weaver Wenger, Kathryn
   1986-88

Wenger, Lester Larry 1962-
Wenger, Rhoda H. 1965-72
Wenger, Sheri L. 1986-
Wert, Beverly Ann
   (Shreiner) 1962-63
Wert, Daniel D. 1959-60
Wert, Robert K. 1960-61,
   1963-66
Wise, David S. 1987-
Witmer, H. Howard
   1961-62, 1967-71
Yates, Helen M. (King)
   1962-63
Yoder, David W. 1976-89
Yoder, Elwood E. 1982-86
Yoder, Jason J. 1988-89
Yoder, Jeffrey T.1988-
Yoder, John O., II 1968-70
Yoder, Joy E. 1981-85
Yoder, Marvin 1958-59
Yoder, Miles E. 1979-
Yoder, Rhoda B. 1980-81
Yoder, Timothy L. 1989-
Yost, Sadie Mae 1951-58
Young, David S. 1982-83
Zeager, Alma M. 1980-85
Zimmerman, Kathryn
   (Reitz) 1985-88
Zook, Floyd I. 1965-74

Appendix B
Principals and Assistant Principals
1942-1992

Brubaker, J. Lester	Principal 1970-79, Superintendent 1979-83
Dietz, Myron	Faculty-Student Relations 1969-70, Assistant Principal 1970-71
Good, Noah G.	Dean 1942-70, Principal 1969-70
Graybill, J. Paul	Principal 1942-53
Groff, Marlin	Assistant Principal 1988-
Hess, Ernest	Assistant Principal 1971-73, 1975-7; Acting Principal 1978-79; Principal 1979-82
Keener, Clayton. L.	Principal 1963-67
Miller, J. B.	Assistant Principal 1973-74
Rice, Vernon	Assistant Principal 1974-75
Thomas, J. Richard	Assistant Principal 1978-83, Principal 1983-
Weaver, Amos W.	Principal 1953-63
Witmer, H. Howard	Principal 1967-69
Yoder, Miles	Assistant Principal 1983-

Appendix C

Lancaster Mennonite High School
Board of Trustees
1942-1991

Baer, Alvey S. 1971-77
Beiler, Harvey 1973-76
Book, G. Parke 1943-57
  Chair (1942-50)
Bowman, Richard L.
  1982-86
  Vice Chair (1983-86)
Brubaker, Jacob G. 1949-53
Brubaker, John S. 1950-53
Brubaker, Landis H.
  1942-71
  Treasurer (1950-63)
Brubaker, Roy M. 1954-62
Burkholder, Carl G. 1975-77
Carrasco, German 1990-
Chiles, Lawrence F. 1986-89
Clymer, Martin D. 1950-52
Detweiler, Willis F. 1960-62
Dich, Philip N. 1990-
Diffenbach, Beulah 1979-82
Eby, Clair B. 1954-58
Eby, Lloyd M. 1956-78 Vice
  Chair (1964-77)
  Chair (1977-78)
Eby, Sem 1942-47
Garber, Parke M. 1964-71
Gingrich, Mervin M.
  1985-91
Gochnauer, John H.
  1942-48
  Vice Chair (1942-48)
Good, Leon W. 1985-88
Good, Lewis C. 1958-61
Graybill, Carl E. 1983-85
Graybill, Ira T. 1942-48
Greider, Howard G. 1942-49
Groff, Clarence V. 1959-71
Harnish, John H. 1969-83
  Chair (1971-77)
Hershey, J. Eby 1972-83
Hershey, Kathy J. 1987-90
Hershey, Nelson H. 1983-
Hershey, Noah L. 1971-74
Hertzler, Truman 1983-
Hess, Daniel S. 1989-
Hess, James H. 1943-79

Vice Chair (1949-50)
  Chair (1951-71)
Hess, Joseph H. 1952-76
  Treasurer (1973-76)
Hess, Paul S. 1988-
Hollinger, Lloyd L. 1963-
  Vice Chair (1978-79)
Hoover, Carl L. 1987-
Horst, Otho 1988-
Horst, William S. 1956-66
Hostetter, James W. 1986-
Hurst, Luke A. 1942-55
  Vice Chair (1954-55)
Kauffman, Robert 1971-74
Kennel III, Christian
  1984-87
King, David 1988-
King, Naaman E. 1975-86
Kraybill, John R. 1942-63
  Secretary (1942-62)
Landis, Martin S. 1953-55
Landis, Raymond E.
  1964-79
  Secretary (1971-79)
Lapp, Alice W. 1988-91
Lauver, Raymond C.
  1964-83
Leaman, Elmer D. 1955-70
  Secretary (1964-65)
Leaman, James R. 1981-87
Lehman, Eunice C. 1979-85
Lehman, Maurice E. 1970-74
Long, Donald C. 1986-1989
Longenecker, Martin M.
  1973-85
Lopez, Samuel 1985-90
Lutz, Clarence E. 1942-53
  Treasurer (1942-50)
Martin, Erwin G. 1954-56
Martin, Esther H. 1987-
Martin, Gerald E. 1991-
Martin, Irvin S. 1967-88
Martin, Joseph B., Sr.
  1981-90
Martin, Richard B. 1967-70
Miller, Clair 1977-83

Miller, Larry D. 1986-
Mohler, J. Harold 1983-89
Myer, Amos W. 1942-43,
  1947-61
Nafziger, Nelson C. 1990-
Nauman, Jacob W. 1959-81
Newswanger, Larry W.
  1977-79
Nissley, Mervin 1971-73
Risser, Harold L. 1974-82
Robinson, Lindsey A.
  1989-90
Root, J. Clyde 1977-87
Rutt, Clarence H. 1956-69
  Secretary (1965-69)
Rutt, John M. 1973-
  Treasurer (1976-)
Samuel, Mary J. 1987-90
Shank, Aaron M. 1949-63
  Vice Chair (1956-63)
Shank, Lucille 1985-88
Shearer, Elmer L. 1950-58
Shellenberger, Shelly R.
  1963-77
Shelly, James C. 1979-85
Shenk, Henry G. 1990-
Shenk, Ray J. 1960-67
Siegrist, Joanne L. 1982-
Shertzer, Amos W. 1959-60
Smucker, Paul M. 1975-
Stahl, Jacob A. 1971-79
Stauffer, Connie F. 1986-
  Secretary (1986-)
Stauffer, Harold S. 1971-77
Steffy, Jason J. 1976-91
  Vice Chair (1977-78)
  Chair (1978-91)
Stoltzfus, Christian L.
  1976-83
Stoltzfus, George B. 1954-55
Stoltzfus, Isaac 1987-
Stoltzfus, LeRoy S. 1948-54
Stoltzfus, Stephen R.
  1960-61
Stoner, Elam S. 1942-63
Thomas, Vince 1991-

Warfel, Amos H. 1979-88
Weaver, A. Earl 1976-
Vice Chair (1986-90)
Chair (1991-)
Weaver, Alvin M. 1971-83
Vice Chair (1979-83)
Weaver, Amos W. 1942-53
Weaver, Cleo W. 1982-85
Weaver, Dale M. 1987-

Weaver, Melvin L. 1975-87
Weaver, Paul H. 1949-77
Weaver, Robert E. 1983-
Vice Chair (1990-)
Weaver, Victor R. 1971-78
Wenger, Benjamin H. 1989-
Wenger, Luke D. 1978-82
Secretary (1979-82)
Wert, Earl M. 1962-69

Witmer, Enos W. 1949-51
Witmer, Ray 1977-86
Secretary (1979-82)
Yost, Ray S. 1949-76
Treasurer (1964-73)
Youndt, Raymond E. 1991-
Zimmerman, G. Harold
1975-87

Appendix D

Yearbook Dedications
1946-1987

1947 Our Christian Faculty
1948 Brother Noah G. Good
1949 Brother J. Paul Graybill
1950 Our Parents
1951 Brother Clayton L. Keener, Sister Lois N. Garber and Sister Ellen K. Eshleman
1952 Our Home Pastors
1953 The Alumni
1954 Brother Donald Jacobs
1955 Christian Education
1956 Our Parents
1958 The Faculty
1959 Donors
1960 Our Parents, our School Teachers, our Pastors and Sunday-School Teachers
1961 Brother J. Irvin Lehman
1962 Edna K. Wenger, Noah G. Good and Clyde B. Stoner
1963 Brother Amos Weaver
1964 Brother Myron S. Dietz

1965 Brother H. Raymond Charles
1966 Sister A. Grace Wenger
1967 Noah G. Good
1968 Charles B. Longenecker
1969 Edna K. Wenger
1970 Arnold Moshier
1971 David N. Thomas
1973 The Original Building on campus
1974 Mr. Daniel Wenger
1975 Mr. Robert Miller
1976 Dr. J. Lester Brubaker
1977 The Student Body
1980 Miss Janet Gehman
1981 Mabel Bowman
1982 Coach Vernon Rice
1983 Mr. Clyde Hollinger
1984 Mr. Richard Thomas
1985 Mrs. Mary Lou Houser
1986 Mr. John Landis
1987 Aaron Martin

Appendix E

Commencement Speakers
1943-1991

1943	Noah H. Mack	1968	Paul T. Yoder, M. D.
1944	John H. Mosemann	1969	John R. Mumaw
1945	John E. Leatherman	1970	David Augsburger
1946	Nevin Bender	1971	Merle G. Stoltzfus
1947	Chester K. Lehman	1972	David W. Shenk
1948	Milton G. Brackbill	1973	M. Hershey Leaman
1949	Howard H. Charles	1974	Richard C. Detweiler
1950	John L. Stauffer	1975	Donald Jacobs
1951	George R. Brunk	1976	J. C. Wenger
1952	James M. Shank	1977	John M. Drescher
1953	Harold G. Eshleman	1978	Arthur G. McPhee
1954	Paul Lederach	1979	William D. Hooley
1955	J. C. Wenger	1980	Freeman J. Miller
1956	James R. Hess	1981	Myron S. Augsburger
1957	John L. Stauffer	1982	Joseph Shenk
1958	David Thomas	1983	Richard C. Detweiler
1959	John Hess	1984	Calvin Shenk
1960	Clarence Y. Fretz	1985	J. Lawrence Burkholder
1961	Richard C. Detweiler	1986	Paul M. Zehr
1962	Paul Miller	1987	Michael A. King
1963	John M. Drescher	1988	A. Grace Wenger
1964	Elmer G. Kolb	1989	Lindsey A. Robinson
1965	Myron S. Augsburger	1990	Victor E. Stoltzfus
1966	Donald Jacobs	1991	J. Samuel Thomas
1967	J. Lester Eshleman, M.D.		

Appendix F

Class Songs
1943-1991

1943	Onward and Upward With Christ	1956	Our Lives for Service
1944	Lead Us, Father	1957	Thy Will, Our Way
1945	Excelsior with Christ	1958	Forward Ever Faithful
1946	Embarking with Christ	1959	Forth in Our Master's Will
1947	Through Trials to Triumph	1960	Thy Path, Our Chosen Way
1948	Through Him We Conquer	1961	Our Talents for Thy Task
1949	Lead On, O King Eternal	1962	Our Hands in Thine, Lead On
1950	Onward, Ever Serving	1963	Our Hands for Thy Harvest
1951	Our All for Christ	1964	Ready Tools for the Master
1952	He Goeth Before	1965	Launching with a Living Christ
1953	Our Talents, Lord Are Thine	1966	Reflections of Thy Love (poem)
1954	Lead On, O Shepherd True	1967	Lamps Lit with Thy Love
1955	Forward in Faith	1968	Glowing Embers on Thy Altar

1969 A Ray of Thy Love
1970 An Answer for Peace
1971 We Live Loving
1972 Create Our Tomorrows, Lord
1973 Not Finished, Just Begun
1974 Loving & Giving
1975 Shower Us, O Father, with Your
      Wonderous Love
1976 All Our Lives We've Been Looking for
      the Future
1977 As We Turn and Reflect on Our
      Childhood
1978 Our Journey

1979 Trust Me, Follow Me
1980 A Living Brotherhood
1981 Living by Faith
1982 All We Can Be
1983 Movin' On
1984 Building on Every Dream
1985 Keep Our Eyes Focused on You
1986 The Time Has Come
1987 Well Done
1988 In His Love
1989 The Next Time
1990 Places in the Heart
1991 Chasing Our Dreams

Appendix G
Class Mottos
1943-1990

1943 Onward and Upward with Christ
1944 Lead Us, Father
1945 Excelsior with Christ
1946 Embarking with Christ
1947 Through Trials to Triumph
1948 Through Him We Conquer
1949 Lead On, O King Eternal
1950 Onward, Ever Serving
1951 Our All for Christ
1952 He Goeth Before
1953 Our Talents, Lord Are Thine
1954 Lead On, O Shepherd True
1955 Forward in Faith
1956 Our Lives for Service
1957 Thy Will, Our Way
1958 Forward, Ever Faithful
1959 Forth in Our Master's Will
1960 Thy Path, Our Chosen Way
1961 Our Talents for Thy Task
1962 Our Hands in Thine, Lead On
1963 Our Hands for Thy Harvest
1964 Ready Tools for the Master
1965 Launching with a Living Christ
1966 Reflections of Thy Love
1967 Lamps Lit with Thy Love
1968 Glowing Embers on Thy Altar
1969 Golden Rays in Thy Sunrise
1970 Demonstrators of Thy Peace
1971 We Live Loving
1972 Create Our Tomorrows, Lord
1973 Not Finished, Lord, Just Begun

1974 Loving and giving makes life worth
      living.
1975 All the flowers of all the tomorrows are
      in the seeds of today.
1976 It's not the lofty sails, but the unseen
      wind, that moves the ship.
1977 Something of ourselves remains
      wherever we have been.
1978 My step today leads to my tomorrow.
1979 Go where there is no path and leave a
      trail.
1980 I know not where my path may lead,
      but I know whom I will follow.
1981 God has not called us to be successful,
      but to be faithful.
1982 We ask for courage to be individuals,
      the strength to change our worlds.
1983 We cannot discover new oceans unless
      we have the courage to lose sight of the
      shore.
1984 The past is our heritage,
      The present our responsibility,
      The future our challenge.
1985 With anxiety we loosen our grip on
          the past;
      With enthusiasm we embrace
          the present;
      With faith we reach for the future.
1986 God's strength behind us, His deep
      concern for us, His love within us, and
      His arms beneath us are more than
      sufficient for the job ahead of us.
1987 Today well lived makes the past

meaningful and the future possible.
1988 Guided by the past, living in the present, we anticipate the future, confident that God's loving hand will lead us.

1989 Without a dream what can happen? Without God who can dream?
1990 We're determined to believe, to dream, and to believe in our dreams.

Appendix H
Class Gifts
1943-1991

1943 Bell-ringing clock
1944 Two trellises and roses
1945 Porch furniture
1946 Loudspeaker equipment
1947 Five indoor bulletin boards
1948 Speaker's stand for chapel
1949 Lamps and posts at girls' dormitory
1950 Pillars at end of driveway
1951 Two oil paintings
1952 Library books
1953 Lancaster Mennonite School sign at entrance
1954 Shrubbery and trees
1955 Clocks for classrooms
1956 Outdoor water fountain
1957 Public-address system
1958 Speaker's stand and chairs for auditorium
1959 Shrubbery for chapel
1960 Painting school motto in chapel
1961 Outdoor bulletin board
1962 Library books
1963 Public-address system equipment and library books
1964 Classroom building clock
1965 Intercommunication system
1966 Renovation of Campus Cove
1967 Drapes in chapel
1968 Landscaping around classroom building and gift for library expansion

1969 Gift for student center
1970 Gymnastic equipment
1971 Draperies and furnishings for offices
1972 Public Address system in chapel
1973 Equipment in home economics suite
1974 Folding chairs
1975 Stage curtain for auditorium/gym
1976 Building fund and stage curtain
1977 New public-address system in central office
1978 Maple trees and computer equipment
1979 New chapel curtains
1980 Outdoor bleachers and wooden benches
1981 Video tape recorder, camera and monitor
1982 New school sign
1983 Bleachers and team benches
1984 Band saw for wood shop
1985 Furniture for the new office lobby
1986 Wooden benches for lobby
1987 South African Student Exchange Fund
1988 Landscaping for front campus
1989 Public-address system for auditorium/fine arts center
1990 Public-address system for auditorium/fine arts center
1991 Art work in plaza of auditorium/fine arts center

Appendix I

Alumni
1943-1991

Class of 1943

David M. Ebersole
Robert D. Ebersole
J. Kenneth Fisher
Fannie M. Frankhouser
Ivan J. Glick
Anna Martha (Groff)
   Denlinger S
Lester D. Hershey
Ruth (Hess) Turman
Paul N. Kraybill +
John C. Kurtz V,M
C. Nevin Miller +,*
John K. Miller T
Elizabeth (Sauder) Eshleman
Mary (Stauffer) Todd
Jean (Wolgemuth) Breneman
J. Maynard Yoder P

Class of 1944

J. Elvin Denlinger
Miriam (Ebersole) Charles
Clyde K. Glick
Ruth N. Heiss
James R. Hess P
Naomi (Hess) Wenger
Illa Mae (Homsher) Shank
Martha (Kling) Augsburger
Rhoda (Krady) Lehman +
Rachel (Kraybill) Brubaker
Blanche (Kreider) Gingrich
Arlene (Landis) Hege T
J. Dale Landis V
Anna (Lefever) Hershey
Mary Elizabeth (Lutz) Good
Mae (Marks) Fothergill
Elvin L. Martin
H. Florence Miller
Ruth (Miller) Stauffer
M. Martha Myer
Ruth (Newcomer) Gehman
Mahlon Harold Palmer
Rebecca (Riehl) Ulrich *
Miriam (Sensenig) Gingerich
Mildred (Shirk) Fisher
Vera (Stauffer) Kauffman
Anne (Stoltzfus) Witmer
Luke G. Stoltzfus M
Alta B. Weaver
Miriam (Weaver) Stoltzfus S
Ruth (Zeiset) Rohrer
Ruth N. Zimmerman

Class of 1945

Miriam (Bair) Buckwalter T,+
Verna (Brubaker) Hess
Anna Ruth (Charles) Jacobs S
J. Delmar Ebersole
Ellen (Eby) Shearer +
Sylvia (Ernst) Grosh
Rhoda M. Graybill
Ruth (Graybill) Smith
Elsie (Hartz) Weaver
Lois (Kraybill) Stahl M,*
Martha (Landis) Hess

Erika (Lehnhoff) Malin
Eli L. Miller
Erma (Peifer) Schwebbach
Olive (Phenneger) Kennel
E. Warren Rohrer V
Earl W. Rohrer
Mildred (Rutt) Rohrer
Harold F. Shearer
Elizabeth (Shirk) Diffenderfer
Helen (Stauffer) Keiper
Anna Mary Weaver
Esther S. Weaver
Paul H. White
Earl W. Witmer P
Ruth (Zook) Rutt

Class of 1946

Jay M. Bechtold
Norman W. Brackbill
Verna (Breneman) Leaman
Ivan G. Charles V
Esther (Fisher) Leichty
Glenn E. Gehman
Katherine(Hertzler)HallmanT,*
   Martha (Horst) Kurtz
Frank A. Kennel
Naomi (Kennel) Yoder
Daniel M. Krady P,M,L
Ruth (Krall) Shellenberger
Janet H. Kreider
Alta M Landis
Lois (Landis) Miller
Kenneth V. Lehman +
Ruth (Longenecker) Bechtold
Marion (Marks) Doebler
Edna (Metzler) Brunk
Earl R. Mohler
Cora (Ober) Hess
Virginia (Poley) Brown
Dorothy (Reisinger) Singer
Anna Mae (Reist) Musser
Mary Lois (Rutt) Enck
Ruth (Shenk) Landis
Betty (Shirk) Byler
Mary (Shirk) Frederick
Ruth (Shue) Weber S
Arlene (Stauffer) Longenecker
Verna (Stauffer) Musser
Merle G. Stoltzfus
Sarah (Stoltzfus) Fisher
Naomi (Thomas) Ebersole
Rhoda (Thomas) Buchen
Ivan R. Troxel
Arthur D. Wenger

Class of 1947

Vivian M. Beachy
Lester A. Blank
Elizabeth (Brubaker) Zook
J. Robert Byler
Sidney M. Carpenter
Alma Eby
Anna M. Eby
Elizabeth A. Frank
Anna M. Frey M,*
Mildred (Graybill) Tillman

Orpha (Graybill) Harnish
Amy (Groff) Kreider
Henry W. Harnish
Melvin H. Hess
Abram M. Hostetter L
Robert E. Hostetter
Mary (Huber) Meisky
Arthur J. Kennel
Naaman E. King
Rhoda M. King
Daniel N. Kraybill
Paul S. Kurtz P
Levi Lantz +
Alma (Lefever) Weaver S
James C. Lutz
Roy M. Martin
Janet (Mellinger) Martin
A. Arlene Miller
Anna Miller
Lois (Miller) Hoffer
Helen (Mosteller) Teleskie
Lillian Mosteller
Arlene (Peifer) Walter T
Katherine (Phenneger) Weaver
Mary A. Riehl
Paula R. Seitz
Chester B. Sensenig +
Ralph G. Shank +
Lois (Shirk) Hollinger
Susan (Shreiner) Hess
Ada M. Smoker
Reba J. Smoker
Lloyd B. Stauffer
Edna (Stoltzfus) Ebersole
Jay H. Stoltzfus
Evelyn (Weaver) Good
Irvin D. Weaver
John W. Weaver V
Thelma B. Wolgemuth
Julia M. Yoder
Rosanna (Yoder) Hostetler

Class of 1948

Paul L. Bender V
Betty (Cox) Stoltzfus
Earl Denlinger
Ruth (Dick) Nolt
Henry Z. Eby
Rachel M. Fisher
Lois (Good) Stockheim
Edna (Groff) Martin
Mildred V. Groff
Mary (Hartman) Aument
Jacob Hartz
Mary Jean Heiss
Mary (Heistand) Herr
Dorothy (Herr) Stoltzfus
Susan (Herr) Burkholder S
Verna (Herr) Groff
Hiram R. Hershey
Albert E. Hornberger
Henry W. Horning
David C. Hostetter
Anne (Keener) Gingrich
Harlan L. King
Miriam (King) Graybill
Pluma (King) Hostetter
Ruth (Kling) Alger T

Lena (Kurtz) Carpenter
Ira B. Landis
Arlene (Lapp) Glick
Lois (Leaman) Garber
Albert H. Mast
Milford S. Mast
John H. Mellinger
Arlene (Miller) Weber
Pauline (Miller) Kreider
R. Herbert Minnich P
John L. Ruth M,L,*,+
Lydia (Sensenig) Kurtz
John B. Shenk
Norman Shertzer
Erma (Stauffer) Hunsberger
J. Marvin Stauffer
Lewis Swartzentruber
Ada Ruth (Umble) Lapp
Alice (Weaver) Beachy
Kenneth J. Weaver
Pauline (Weaver) Stockdale
Ruth (Wert) Swartz
David H. White
Bessie R. Yoder
Corena (Yoder) Stauffer
Dorcas (Yoder) Rolon
Henry W. Zehr

Class of 1949

Naomi (Brubaker) Rowe
Ruth (Brubaker) Yovanovich
Leota Brunk
Galen Buckwalter
Naomi (Burkholder) Frank
A. Martha (Denlinger) Stahl
Clara (Ebersole) Cutman
Nyla (Ebersole) Witmer
John L. Fisher
Donald H. Gehman +
Isaac N. Glick
Ray S. Glick
Doris (Good) Bomberger S
Miriam (Groff) Brubaker
David M. Harnish
Paul Hartz
Anna Ruth Hess
Lena (Histand) Hunsberger
Arlene (Hollinger) Martin
Mabel (Horst) Eshleman
Jeanette Hostetter
Shirley (Kauffman) Hartz *
Laurence S. King
John H. Kraybill
Esther (Kurtz) Stoltzfus
Martha (Kurtz) Stoltzfus
Janet (Leaman) Heistand
Marian (Leaman) Neff
Harry G. Lefever
Martha Jane Lutz L
Eunice (Martin) Keller
Donald C. Mast L
Oliver S. Mast
Norma (Metzler) Hostetter
Joyce (Miller) Hartz
Eugene W. Peifer
Ellen (Petre) Martin T,M,L
Ruth (Ranck) Bare
Dorothy (Reifsnyder) Huber

Harold E. Rohrer
Clarence H. Rutt
Glenn E. Rutt **P**
Esther Sanderson
Erma (Sensenig) Rohrer
Charles Shenk **V**
Helen (Shenk) Good
Romaine (Shenk) Miller
Warren G. Shenk
Alma K. Stoltzfus
Esther (Stoltzfus) Wilson
Irene (Stoltzfus) Weber
Gladys (Swartz) Keener
Carolyn (Swartzentruber) Mast
Mabel (Weaver) Hernley
Ralph E. Weaver
Victor R. Weaver
Ruth Westenberger
Robert O. Zehr

Class of 1950

Nevin A. Beachy
Allen R. Beiler
Hilda (Bender) Swartz
Joan (Bergey) Maggio
Betty (Blank) Martin
Alta (Bomberger) Noll
Mary Jane (Breneman) Eby
Anna Brubaker
Kenton K. Brubaker **P**
Mildred (Clymer) Martin
Miriam (Clymer) Stoltzfus
John Denlinger *
June (Denlinger) Leaman
Mary Alice (Denlinger) Kreider
Merill Derstine
Thelma (Eby) Landis
Arlene (Eshleman) Pierantoni
J. Olleck Forry
Milton S. Good **V**
Almeda (Groff) Landis
Vida Jean Grove
Helen (Herr) Shenk
J. Merle Herr
James W. Herr
Thelma (Hershey) Kreider
John C. Hostetter
Marian (Hostetter) Sangrey
Helen (Keener) Hess **T**
Ada Nancy King
Jean (Kraybill) Shenk
Erma (Kready) Wenger
James M. Krady
Edwin J. Landis
Jay B. Landis *,+
Paul G. Landis **L**
Roma (Lapp) Norris
Ivan B. Leaman **M**
Helen (Lehman) Ranck
Charles B. Longenecker
Benjamin F. Martin Jr.
Carol (Mast) Swartzentruber
D. Leon Mast
Carl Mellinger
Mildred B. Miller
Walter L. Miller
Richard L. Musser
M. Jean (Myers) Graham
Mildred (Myers) Forry
Christian G. Peifer
Ethel (Petre) Martin
Ruth (Ressler) Hoober
Doris (Risser) Martin
Lois (Ruth) Kennel **S**
Norman G. Shenk
Pearl (Stoltzfus) Lapp
Virgil D. Stoltzfus
Arlene (Weaver) Stauffer

Melvin R. Weaver
Ruth Weaver
Gladys (Wert) Yoder

Class of 1951

Earl R. Auker
Louella (Beiler) Mosteller
Titus Bender *,+
Dorothy (Boll) Witmer
John Buckwalter
Anna Mae Campbell
Wilbur M. Ebersole
Aaron Eby
Shirley (Gehman) Keller
James M. Gingrich
John C. Groff
Mary Ellen (Groff) Dula
Rachel (Harnish) Hershey
Rhoda (Hartz) Weaver
Sara Jane Hayworth
Benjamin D. Hershey
Ellen (Hershey) Neff
Mary (Hershey) Herr
Martha (Hertzler) Mullin **S**
Andrew B. Hess
I. Wilmer Hollinger **P**
Elvin M. Horst
Luke R. Hurst
John K. Kauffman
Grace L. (Kerr) Hall
Ernest N. Kraybill **V,M**
Miriam (Landis) Bauman
Rachel (Landis) Stahl
Alta (Leaman) Metzler
M. Hershey Leaman
Virginia (Mast) Hertzler
Selena (Mast) Horning
John J. Metzler **M**
J. Robert Miller
Thelma (Moyer) Jones
Edna (Musser) Stoltzfus
Dorothy (Mylin) Weidman
Evelyn (Nice) Godshall
Mabel Irene Pickel
Ethel (Ranck) Miller
Evan D. Riehl
Anne (Sauder) Siegrist
Miriam (Sauder) Landis
Ruth (Sauder) Hollinger **T**
Mary L. Sensenich
Dorothy (Shenk) Burkholder
Elma (Shenk) Delp
Lois (Stauffer) Nissley
Dorcas (Stoltzfus) Morrow
Joyce (Stoltzfus) Stapleton
Lois (Stoltzfus) Petersheim
Nathan Stoltzfus
Ellen (Weaver) Good
Gerald E. Weaver
J. Irvin Weaver
Esther (Weiser) Hamilton
Elizabeth A. Wenger
Clyde W. Witmer
Angeline (Zehr) Solway
Michael M. Zehr
Ruth (Zimmerman) Yoder

Class of 1952

Martha (Bair) Hershey
Willard Beachy
Galen N. Benner
Geraldine G. Bennington **S**
Velma (Bomberger) Weaver
Betty (Book) Kreider
Doris (Brubaker) Martin
James D. Brubaker **M,+**

Arlene (Byler) Gingerich
Edna (Denlinger) Weaver
Manford R. Embleton
Jesse T. Enck
Eunice (Graybill) Enck
Marjorie A. Ernst
Janet N. Gehman
Dorothy (Glick) Yoder
Eunice (Good) Miller
Abram B. Groff
E. Harold Herr
Roy D. Herr
Martha (Hershey) Yoder
James D. Hess
Herbert Histand
Dorothy (Hoober) Frey
Lena (Horning) Brown
Arlene (Huber) Minnich
Eunice (Hurst) Lehman *
Barbara (Keener) Reed
Marie (Keener) Riehl
Vernon C. Kennel
Elmer E. King
Susanne J. King
Chester I. Kurtz
Evelyn (Leaman) Quinn
Georgia (Lefever) Martin
Allen G. Martin
J. Robert Martin
Millard L. Martin
Leona (Mast) Peters
Maxine (Mast) Eash
Lloyd G. Metzler
N. Parke Miller
Rachel (Miller) Burkholder
Nadine (Ogburn) Hauck
Irene (Peifer) Miller
Harold E. Reed **L**
Barbara (Rutt) Longenecker
Anna (Shrock) Brenneman
Mabel (Sensenich) Gehman
Geraldine (Shenk) Heisey
Alma (Shenk) Albrecht **T**
Henry G. Shenk
Mary Louise (Shertzer) Grove
Emma (Shetler) Brubaker
Anna Mary (Smoker) Yoder
Lillian (Smoker) Yoder
Allen S. Weaver
Carolyn (Weaver) Zeiset
J. Clyde Weaver
Naomi Weaver
Richard L. Weaver **P**
Ann (Wenger) Miller
Esther (Westenberger) Zeiset
Barbara (White) Wicker
Robert L. Yoder **V**
Vernon Zehr
Harry B. Zimmerman
Rhoda (Zimmerman) Landis
Doris (Zook) Brubaker
Marvin E. Zook

Class of 1953

Naomi D. Bechtold
Betty (Becker) Steffy
Florence (Beiler) Groff
Gladys (Beiler) Shearer
Richard G. Blank
Barbara (Breneman) Hurd
Naomi Brubaker
Rhoda (Buckwalter) Salim
Marian (Carpenter) Heisey
Rhoda (Clymer) Sauder
Marian (Denlinger) Rabe
Anna (Eby) Hennelly
Omar Eby
Donald H. Frank

Jean (Frey) Weaver **S**
Janet (Fuss) Ihle
Ruth (Good) Denlinger
Sara Jane (Graybill) Swartz
C. Victor Groff
John M. Harnish
Helen (Heistand) Neuenschwander
John B. Herr
John L. Hershey **M,L**
Joann (Hess) Zimmerman
Mervin G. Hess
Edna (Hoover) Parr
Lewis Kauffman
Rhoda (Kauffman) Grove
Loretta (King) Lapp
Paul J. King
David L. Kniss **V**
Vernon H. Kratz **P**
James L. Kreider
Lloyd E. Kreider
Grace (Landis) Bailey
Mark G. Landis
Erma (Lapp) Myers
Elta M. Lauver
David M. Leaman
Elnora (Leaman) Frank
Esther (Leaman) Kniss
Paul A. Leatherman
Ella (Lefever) Peters
Mary Louise (Lefever) Metzler
Wilmer R. Lehman +
Esther L. Lutz
James E. Metzler
Lois Ruth (Mylin) Keller
Mabel (Ness) Baral
Elsie B. Nissley
Reba (Nissley) Hess **T**
Sara Risser
Mary (Rissler) Blacksmith
James Sauder
Carolyn (Swartz) Albrecht
Edna (Tyson) Brubaker
Almeda (Wadel) Martin
Joyce (Wagaman) Suders
Anna Mae (Weaver) Weber
Arlene L. Weaver
Evelyn (Weaver) Witmer *
Lillian M. Weber
Barbara (Weiser) Jones
L. Larry Wenger
Robert B. Wenger
Esther (Wert) King
Freda (Wert) Zehr
Arthur C. Wise
Lois (Witmer) Good
Lois B. Wolgemuth
Ruth (Yost) Kornmayer
Dorothy (Zook) King

Class of 1954

Kathy (Baer) Lehman
Grace (Beachy) Mast
Dorothy (Bauman) Heller
Elam W. Beiler
Beatrice E. Benner
Cornelia (Book) West
Edna (Brubaker) Mellinger
Lowell M. Detwiler
Miriam Eberly
Ethel (Ebersole) Metzler
Mariana (Ebersole) Longenecker
Mary Ellen (Eby) Leaman
Miriam (Eby) Tucker
Ruth Frank
Anna Ruth (Garber) Keener
John H. Gehman

Paul J. Gehman
Ellen May Gerlach
Aden K. Gingerich **P**
Esther (Graybill) Peachey
Charles L. Groff
Rhoda (Groff) Miller
G. Evan Harnish
Earl S. Herr
Pauline (Herr) Mast
Charles D. Hershey **+**
Grace (Hess) Wolfgang
Mabel (Histand) Detweiler
Harlan Hoover
Eugene H. Horst
Emma (Hurst) Hoover
Mary (Kauffman) Martin
Rhoda C. Kennel
Ruth (Kolb) Graybill
Maynard Y. Kurtz **L**
Thelma (Landes) Mack
Robert M. Landis
Elizabeth (Leaman) Lehman
Ethel (Leaman) Sell
Cora E. Lehman
Milton P. Lehman **V,***
Helen (Longenecker) Lapp **S**
Kenneth E. Martin
Erma (McCall) Blair
Arlene (Mellinger) Yager
Donald L. Mellinger
Erma (Mellinger) Shirk
Doris (Metzler) Burkhart
Marvin S. Moyer
Marvin S. Musser
Esther Ruth Neff
Clarence Nissley
Joanne (Peifer) Sweigart
Martin E. Peifer
Lois (Riehl) Dyck
Daniel G. Rohrer
Elsie (Rohrer) Lehman
Laverne (Sensenig) Martin
Calvin E. Shenk
Harry B. Shenk
Susan W. Snavely
Harold G. Stoltzfus
Richard G. Stoltzfus
Willard M. Swartley **M**
Lillian (Swartz) Knouse
Mary Ellen (Umble) Ness
Gloria (Weaver) Rissler
Miriam (Weaver) Nauman
Pauline (Weaver) Boll
Lloyd D. Wenger
Helen (Wert) Peachey
Nancy (Wert) Augsburger
Esther (White) Bhaquandas
Dorothy Ann Yoder
Mary (Yoder) Wanyoike
Helen Zehr
Phyllis (Zehr) Ezard
Gilbert S. Zook
Mary (Zook) Saner **T**

Class of 1955

Melvin H. Barge
Robert H. Bosley
Arlene (Brubaker) Gehman
Daniel C. Durborow
Joyce Findley
Paul W. Gehman
Alice (Good) Martin
Huldah (Graybill) Petersheim
Nancy (Graybill) Beiler
J. Lester Groff
Paul M. Harnish
Eileen (Hart) Landis
Connie (Heisey) Stauffer **T**

Donald L. Hershey
J. Daniel Hess **L**
Esther (Hess) Becker
Alice (Herr) Shenk
Verna (Hershey) Yost
Grace (Hostetter) Weaver
Mary Jane (Horning) Stoltzfus
D. Amos Horst
Joyce (Horst) Kreider
Lois (Hurst) Weaver *****
Lois (Krady) Hartzler **+**
Nevin M. Kraybill
Barbara (Lamp) Brubaker
John G. Landis **V**
William E. Leakey
Marie (Leaman) Shenk
Lois (Leatherman) Bomberger
Florence B. Lefever
Agnes Lehman
Geraldine (Martin) Kunkle
Marla A. Martin
J. Ross Mast
James L. Maust
Dorothy (Mellinger) Lantz
Eileen (Miller) Benner
Ethel (Mohler) Haas **S**
Jane (Mosemann) Swarr
Mary Ellen (Myer) Shertzer
Ethel (Myers) Shenk
John H. Neidig
Orpha Newswanger
Jane (Peachey) Lind
Mary Lois (Petre) Wilfong
Anna Mary Reed
Dorcas (Reed) Danner
Esther (Reed) Nelson
John M. Rutt
Janice W. Sensenig
David W. Shenk **P**
Elizabeth C. Shertzer
J. Daniel Shertzer
Marie L. Snavely
Jean (Stanley) Pfeiffer
Harold S. Stauffer **M,+**
Dale W. Stoltzfus
Elvin J. Stoltzfus
John K. Stoltzfus
Marian (Stoner) Winey
Betty (Strong) Zehr
Verna (Sweigart) Gockley
Marvin L. Weaver
Miriam (Weaver) Buckwalter
Romaine (Weaver) Huber
Ruth (Weaver) Stoltzfus
Luke D. Wenger
Roy E. Wert
Anna (Whissler) Houser
K. Grace (Witmer) Shenk
E. Ray Witmer
Edith (Yoder) Nissley
Earl B. Zimmerman
J. Harold Zook

Class of 1956

Erla (Becker) Smith
Naomi (Beiler) Keiper
Lois (Brubaker) Zimmerman
Nevin K. Brubaker
Eugene Buch
John R. Buckwalter
J. Roy Burkhart
Albert Chariton
Margaret (Denlinger) Hart
Dorothy (Ebersole) Boll
Ruth (Ebersole) Zimmerman
Susan Ebersole
Kenneth R. Eby
Leanne (Engle) Jamison

Anna Mae (Forrester) Weaver
Elsie Mae (Farrel) Martin
John D. Gerlach
Richard M. Glick
Ruth (Good) Yoder
John H. Groff
Mary Jane (Harnish) Gerlach
Sarah (Harnish) Alderfer
J. Stanford Herr
Carrie (Hershey) Strickler
Helen (Hershey) Kreider
James L. Hershey
Margaret (Hertzler) King
Anna Mary (Hess) Glazewski
Clyde W. Horst
Evelyn (Horst) Sauder
Marjorie (Hostetter)
    Swartzentruber **+**
Esther (Jones) Hackman **L,+**
Sara Marie (Kauffman) Shenk **S**
Harold G. King
Nathan G. King
Frances (Kreider) Martin
J. Edward Kurtz
Anna Lois Lehman
J. Donald Martin
Lois (Martin) Zimmerman
Mary Ann (Martin) Martin
Grace (Mast) Stoltzfus
Leroy Mast
Nelda (Mast) Graber
Vernon A. Mast
Doris (Mellinger) Sensenig
Lois E. Mellinger
Mary Ann (Mellinger) Martin
Wayne Miller
Marian (Rutt) Stoltzfus
Esther (Sauder) Wert
Donald M. Sensenig **P**
Ruth Ann (Sensenig) Kopp
Dorothy A. Shenk
Joseph C. Shenk **M**
Robert D. Shenk
Elam G. Stoltzfus
Hazel (Stoltzfus) Grove
Ruth Ann (Stoltzfus) Glick
Larry L. Strickler
A. Richard Weaver **V**
Dale M. Weaver
Edith (Weaver) Gehman
Irvin G. Weaver
Robert Weaver
Kenneth L. Weiderrecht
Daniel L. Wenger
Susan (Wenger) Smucker
Alma (Wert) Yoder **T**
Daniel D. Wert
J. Richard Winters
David M. Wyble *****
Alta (Zimmerman) Mellinger

Class of 1957

Doris (Allen) Perkins
Anne (Angstadt) Brubaker
Marie (Baer) Davis **T**
Melba (Beiler) King
Richard L. Benner **V**
Donald L. Brubaker
James C. Bucher
Elva (Buckwalter) Beach
Marian (Buckwalter)
Paul H. Buckwalter
M. Elvin Byler
Alta (Charles) Sensenig
Harold E. Chubb
Pauline (Chubb) Sumner
J. Paul Clymer
Lois (Denlinger) Boyer

Ruth (Eberly) Harnish
Dorothy A. Eichelberger
Ruth (Erb) Martin
Ann (Enck) Shertzer
Gerald B. Felpel
Dorothy (Fields) Nornhold
Janet (Fleagle) Yeager
Lois (Garber) Buchen
Ray M. Geigley
Lena (Glick) Steiner
Melvin R. Glick
R. Joy (Glick) Hess
Shirley (Glick) Wenger
Anna Lois (Good) Boll
C. Alton Good
Lois Graybill
Alma (Gochenaur) Shultz
Dorothy (Groff) Ranck
Lois (Groff) Landis
Madeline (Groff) Sollenberger
Eunice (Harbold) Luckenbaugh
R. Wilbur Herr
Erma (Hess) Brunk
James H. Hess
Nancy (Hess) Stoltzfus **S**
Glenn R. Horst
Nelson R. Horst
Grace (Hurst) Byler *****
Mabel (Hurst) Weaver
Laban Kauffman
Lillian (Kauffman) Beiler
Marian (Kauffman) Lapp
Betty Lois (Keener) Miller
David C. Kennel
Rosella (King) Schrock
Ruby (King) Dorsey
Caroline (Kurtz) Plank
Ruth (Lamp) Haupt
Faith M. Landis
Ruth (Landis) Lutz
Lena (Lapp) Deguire
Reta (Lapp) Esch
Susan (Leaman) Stahl
William C. Leatherman
John B. Leonard **P**
John A. Lutz **L**
Rhoda (Martin) Weaver
Michael M. Mast
Paul D. Mast
Doris L. Mellinger
Kenneth H. Mellinger
Richard E. Metzler
Andrew G. Miller
Jeanette (Miller) King
Lester Miller
Mary (Miller) Sweigart
James M. Mohler
Ernest E. Mummau
Alvin H. Musser
Miriam (Myer) Martin
R. Wesley Newswanger
John M. Nissley
Dorothy (Peifer) Metzler
John E. Reed
Verna (Rohrer) Beachy
Dorothy Mae Sensenich
Ruth Ann (Sharp)
    Himmelreich
James C. Shelly
Janet (Shertzer) Kebede
Kenneth Shirk
Martha (Shirk) Johnson
Dorothy (Shue) Geigley
Clair Smith
Alma (Smoker) Groff
Alfred J. Stauffer
Anna (Stauffer) Keller
Mildred (Stauffer) Gonzalez
Elvin R. Stoltzfus

Mary Ellen (Stoltzfus) Groteluschen
Ronald L. Stoltzfus
Velma (Strite) Horst
Lawrence H. Umble
Luke H. Wenger **M,+**
Esther (Wert) Clymer
Robert K. Wert
Glenn D. Wise
Dorothy (Wissler) Zehr
Jean (Witmer) Bender
Ella (Yoder) Stutzman

Class of 1958

Margaret L. Allen
Kenneth H. Barge
Joy (Beiler) Horst
Miriam (Boll) Metzler
Marian (Book) Groff
H. Wesley Boyer
Mary Lou Brubaker
Thelma (Brubaker) Diem
Samuel S. Burkholder
Abram H. Clymer
John M. Clymer
Martha (Charles) Pepper
Joyce (Chubb) Kisamore
Ruth Ann (Eberly) Gingrich
John W. Eby
J. Wilmer Eby
Anna Mary (Engle) Hess
Beryl Forrester
Barbara Ann (Gehman) Horst
Margaret A. Gehman
Lois (Glick) Hostetter
Fern (Graybill) Brunner **L**
David B. Groff
John H. Groff
Ruth (Harnish) Hertzler
Faye (Hershey) Mummau
Jean (Hershey) Buckwalter
Miriam G. Hess
Esther (Horning) Boll
Miriam (Horst) Engle
Daniel L. Kauffman
Edna (King) Hershberger **+**
M. Jane (King) Stoltzfus
Verna (King) Miller
John W. Kreider
Ruth (Kreider) Spangler
Christine (Kurtz) Troyer
Cora S. Kurtz **M**
J. David Lapp
Mary (Leaman) Zuniga *
Andrew Leatherman **V**
David R. Lefever
A. Larry Lehman
Evelyn (Lehman) Shaar
Mary Lois (Lehman) Martin
Emma (Longenecker) Frederick
Barbara (Martin) Weber
Elaine (Martin) Horning
Margaret (Martin) Hawbaker
Noah S. Martin **P**
Lydia (Miller) Yoder
Mary (Mosemann) Lichty
Beula (Moyer) Peele
Mervin H. Myer
Larry W. Newswanger
Leon H. Oberholtzer
Grace (Ogburn) Miller
Amy Marie (Peifer) Taylor
Erma (Sauder) Wenger
Arthur P. Sensenig
H. Mardene Sensenig
Ruth (Sensenig) Burkholder
Janet (Shank) Eberly **T**
Rosetta (Sheeler) Hoffman

Anna K. (Shenk) Eby
Gerald L. Shenk
Harold A. Shenk
L. Dale Shenk
Nancy Shirk
Jeanette (Smoker) Eby
Lois (Snavely) Frey
Elam K. Stauffer
Helen (Steffy) Eshleman
Karl D. Stoltzfus
Kenneth Stoltzfus
Miriam (Stoltzfus) Seigfried
Susanna M. Stoltzfus **S**
Fred A. Umble
M. Glen Umble
E. Miriam (Weaver) Nolt
H. Lorraine Weaver
Irvin C. Weaver
Janet (Weaver) Newswanger
Lois (Weaver) Bird
Annetta (Wenger) Miller
Ruth (Wyble) Bushong
Rhoda (Zeager) Hertzler
Faye (Zimmerman) Earhart
Leona (Zook) Oberholtzer

Class of 1959

Esther (Baer) Mast
Patsy (Baer) Groff
Chester Bauman
Barbara (Beiler) Stoltzfus **T**
Elaine (Beiler) Stoltzfus
Verna (Beiler) Miller **S**
John N. Benner
John Bomberger
Lorraine (Boll) Shirk
Martha (Boll) Nissley
Paul R. Breneman
Roy L. Brubaker
Trilda J. Bucher
Ruth (Buckwalter) Willis
Doris (Campbell) Deiter
Laura Mae (Carpenter) Kreider
Mahlon Charles
Erma (Clymer) Horning
Joan (Daniels) Rivera
Howard D. Detweiler
Naomi (Eberly) Gochenaur
Marlin S. Ebersole
Eleanor (Engle)Horst
Nancy (Farwell) Marshall
Lois (Fretz) Keener
Hazel (Garber) Charles
Catherine (Glick) Bryant
Kathryn (Good) Sensenig
Kenneth L. Good
Gladys (Graybill) Schofield **+**
Paul S. Groff
Dorothy M. Harnish
Dorcas (Harnly) Bomberger
Virginia (Hart) Saner
Twila (Herr) Rawlings
Rhoda (Hershey) Yost
Vera (Hershey) Todd
Patricia (Hess) Witmer
Pauline (High) Winters
Harvey W. Horning
Eunice (Horst) Banzhoff
Thelma (Horst) Groff
John Hostetter
Anne (Jones) Allen
Marlin Kauffman
J. Clyde Keener
James E. Keener
Kenneth N. Keener
Leavitt M. Keener **+**
Merle J. King
Donald L. Kreider

Calvin S. Kurtz
Ira A. Kurtz
Esther (Landis) Kurtz
Jay L. Lehman
Lola M. Lehman
Dale K. Longenecker
Edward M. Longenecker
Lucille (Mack) Stoltzfus
Benjamin L. Martin
Thelma (Martin) Riley
Ernest S. Mast **P**
Verda (Mast) Geib
Miriam (Maust) Achenbach
Ellene (Mellinger) Myer
Clair W. Metzler
Dorothy (Miller) Chupp
Lester R. Miller
Martha (Miller) High
Thomas J. Miller
Lucille (Moyer) Donovan
Ruth (Musser) Lapp
David H. Myer
J. Calvin Nafziger
George Narvell
Carl K. Newswanger
J. Marlin Nissley *
Gerald Ogburn
Betty Jane (Reed) Myer
Paul E. Reed **M**
Sue (Russell) Lehman
Joyce (Rutt) Eby
David L. Sauder
Lois Sauder
D. Milford Shank
Miriam (Shank) Wert
Beverly (Shreiner) Wert
Mary Elizabeth Siegrist
Ellen (Smoker) Hess
Carol (Stauffer) Busch
Andrew D. Stoltzfus **V**
Anna (Stoltzfus) Shank
Barbara (Stoltzfus) Benner
Carol (Stoltzfus) Dishman
Vera (Stoltzfus) Keener
M. Duane Swartzentruber
Martha (Sweigart) Bensinger
Elsie (Thomas) Hess
A. Ruth (Warfel) Groff
Joyce (Weaver) Mummau
Lillian (Weaver) Shaum
Lois (Weaver) Martin
Richard B. Wenger
J. Lloyd Wert **L**
Lois (Wert) Chamness
Melvin J. Wert
Donald Winters
M. Lonnie Wu
Catherine (Yost) Godshall
J. Allen Zendt
Lois (Zimmerman) Good
Mark B. Zimmerman

Class of 1960

Benuel S. Beiler
Melvin L. Beiler
Harold Blank
Mabel Jean (Boll) Baum
Ruth (Bucher) Torielli
Eileen (Buckwalter) Stone
Everett G. Buckwalter
Fannie (Buckwalter) Shell
Linda (Buckwalter) Breneman
A. Edith Charles
Paul L. Charles
Ruth (Clymer) Kolb
Grace (Delp) Jones **T**
Grace (Ebersole) Leaman
Dorothy Mae (Eby) Wert

H. Laverne Eby
Lois (Eby) Hollinger
Wilmer Esbenshade
Carl R. Frank
Doris (Frey) Diller
Paul L. Garber
Esther (Gehman) Martin
D. Marvin Glick
Doris (Glick) Stauffer
Robert H. Gochenaur
Conrad S. Graybill
Robert E. Graybill
Shelley W. Graybill
Anna Margaret Groff
Dorothy J. Groff
Miriam (Groff) Wenger
Ruth (Harnish) Shenk
Martha (Harnish) Glick
Mary (Harnish) Groff
Anna Mae Herr
Barbara (Herr) Ranck
Ellen (Herr) Longacre
Betty Louise Hershey
J. David Hertzler
Janet (Hertzler) Pobst
Ernest M. Hess
J. Harold Hess **V**
John H. Hess
Larry A. Hess
Paul S. Hess
John A. Hochstetler
Janice (Horst) Walsh *
Reba (Horst) Umble
Darlene (Hostetter) Byler
Reba (Kauffman) Ranck
Barbara (Keener) Kraybill
Ruth (Keener) Martin
Elmer E. Kennel
Frank R. King
Rose Marie King
Ruth (Kurtz) Landis
Wayne D. Kurtz
Richard K. Lantz
Barbara (Lapp) Kauffman
Eva (Leaman) Martin
J. Mervin Leaman
James H. Leaman
Peter R. Leaman
Carroll J. Leaman
Alton K. Longenecker
Carl E. Martin
Elmer R. Martin
Eugene R. Martin
Leo E. Martin
Rachael (Martin) Freed
Rhoda (Mast) Longenecker
A. Clair Mellinger **M**
Doris (Mellinger) Engle
Martha (Mellinger) Steager
Barbara (Miller) Brubaker
Galen G. Miller
J. Mervin Miller
John H. Miller
Kenneth Miller
Naomi (Miller) Sensenig
Jean (Moyer) Shonk
Miriam (Moyer) Shenk
Christian W. Mosemann
Lorraine (Murphy) Sheeler **+**
Lois (Myer) Hess
Nelson Nafziger
Aaron H. Newswanger
Rosemarie (Ney) Althouse
Mary Jane Nissley
Mabel (Nolt) Wendel
Jay Oberholtzer
Naomi (Oberholtzer) Gerrard
Rosanne (Peifer) Rohrer
Clayton C. Ranck

John R. Ranck
Bertha (Sauder) Metzler
R. Clair Sauder
Arlene (Sensenig) Hayes
Lamarr Sensenig
Alice Shank
Carolyn L. Shank
Gerald E. Shank
Donald P. Sheeler +
Roberta (Sheeler) Horning
Joanne (Shertzer) Sensenig
Allan W. Shirk **L**
Robert L. Shreiner
Mary (Smucker) Dowling
Sarah (Snader) Shearer
Freida (Stauffer) Nussbaum
Paul W. Stauffer
Clarence S. Stoltzfus
Elizabeth (Stoltzfus) Metzler
Ethel (Stoltzfus) Shank
Monroe Z. Stoltzfus
Alta Mae (Strite) Bussard
Marilyn (Strong) Leaman
David H. Thomas **P**
Dale L. Umble
Dorothy (Umble) Leatherman
Mary (Wagaman) Golden
Donna (Weaver) Bucove
Edward Glenn Webb
Ruth Ann (Wert) Shirk **S**
Harold E. Yeager
Esther (Zimmerman)
  Villaneuva
Veronica (Zimmerman) Ranck
Mervin R. Zendt

Class of 1961

Lois E. Angstadt
Janet (Barge) Hoover
Paul Beiler
Florence (Benner) Witmer
R. Leona (Bontrager) Slavin
Ethel (Brubaker) Reed
J. Roy Brubaker
Elaine (Buckwalter) Stoner **M**
Mary (Buckwalter) Brubaker
Kathleen (Burkhart)
  Fellenbaum
John D. Byler
Lois (Chubb) Shank
Sybil (Culhane) Bethard
Naomi (Dagen) Shenk
Fannie (Detweiler) Thomas
A. David Ebersole
Sarah H. Ebersole
Lloyd M. Eby
J. Henry Erb
Joyce (Erb) Brunk **L,+**
Geraldine (Esbenshade) Martin
Dorothy (Eshbach) Baltozer
Ruth (Fox) Fellabaum
Lydia (Gehman) Martin
Karl G. Glick
R. Victor Glick
Donald E. Good
Miriam (Good) Musser
Nancy (Good) Kimmet
Lois (Graybill) Lantz
William D. Graybill
Doris E. Groff
Mary Jane Groff
Daniel B. Harnish
Esther (Harnish) Breneman
Cleo R. Hershey
Doris (Hershey) Martin
J. Donald Hershey
J. Kenneth Hershey
Kathryn (Hershey) Yost

Mary Ann (Hershey) Shreiner
Miriam (Hershey) Ruhl
Jacob S. Hess
John W. Hess
Joseph M. Hess
William M. Hess
Carl L. Hoover
Dorothy (Horst) Wadel
Norlene (Horst) Hess
Anna (Hostetter) Glick
Doris (Hostetter) Graber
Ruth Anna (Kauffman) Smoker
Miriam (Keener) Eby
Virgil R. King
Titus S. Kurtz
Elizabeth (Landis) Nissley **S**
Martha (Landis) Zimmerman **T**
J. Mervin Lantz
Roy G. Lapp
Ruth Ann (Leaman) Stauffer
Stephen Leatherman
Carol (Lefever) Lewis
Dale H. Lefever
Galen H. Lehman
James L. Leonard
Rhoda (Longacre) Coffey
Reba (Longenecker) Crill
Dale R. Martin
Delbert E. Martin
John R. Martin
Henrietta (Martin) Shertzer
Joanne (Martin) Denlinger
Marie (Martin) Thomas
Mary Jane (Martin) Sauder
Rhoda (Martin) Kunkle
Susan (Martin) Weber
Wesley S. Mast
Lois (Mellinger) Glick *
Martha (Mellinger) Martin
P. Dale Mellinger
Harold W. Metzler
Betty (Miller) Miller
J. Glenn Miller
Janice (Miller) Hess
Ann (Mohler) Zimmerman
Ed Moshier +
Charmaine (Murphy) Thomas
J. Robert Musser
Dorothy (Myer) Strickler
Naomi (Myer) Davis
Twila (Nafziger) Ryan
Blanche (Newswanger)
  Renshaw
Kenneth M. Nissley
Nancy (Nissley) Hess
Nancy M. Nissley
Richard L. Nissley
Ruth Ann (Nolt) Yost
James R. Ranck
Ruth (Reed) Wentzel
H. Richard Sauder
Naomi (Sauder) Burkholder
Ruth (Seigrist) Breneman
Miriam (Sensenig) Myer
Joyce (Shaub) Musser
Rachel (Shank) Wadel
Dorothy (Shenk) Keener
John W. Shertzer
Ida (Shirk) Weaver
Faye (Stauffer) Landis
Margaret (Stauffer) Leonard
Martine (Stauffer) Shelly
Mary (Steffy) Reem
Anna M. (Stoltzfus) Groff
Lois (Stoltzfus) Graybill
Loretta (Stoltzfus) Martin
Gerald L. Stoner **P**
Donald H. Strickler
Marlin E. Swartzentruber

Barbara (Thomas) Landis
Donald R. Thomas **V**
Melvin H. Thomas
Dennis R. Umble
Susan (Umble) Eby
John Clair Weaver
Norma (Weaver) Herr
Reba (Weaver) Wissler
Susan (Weaver) Godshall
Anna W. Wenger
Wilmer R. Wenger
Jean (Whisler) Koser
Darlene (Wissler) Reighard
Robert R. Wyble
Constance (Yoder) Heatwole
Edna (Yoder) Mast
Leon C. Yost
Eileen (Zimmerman) Weaver
Ethel (Zimmerman) Clugston
Levi B. Zimmermen
Ruth (Zimmerman) Horst

Class of 1962

Lois Barge
Mary (Boll) Metzler
Vida K. Beiler
Esther (Binkley) Mayer
Rhoda (Book) Mast
Effielow (Boyden) Fleagle
Robert Buckwalter
Joanne (Cambell) Hershey
Ruth (Clugston) Miller
Joseph Dhansis
Mary (Eberly) Matthews
Donna (Ebersole) Miller
Mark E. Eby
David A. Erb
Mary (Erb) Champ
Becky (Forwood) Nicholson
Rachel (Fretz) Yoder
Darlene (Frey) Martin
Arlene (Garber) Leaman **S**
Joyce (Garber) Shultz
John M. Gehman
Carolyn (Glick) Peterson
Ruth Ann (Good) Martin **T**
Alan W. Graybill
Thelma J. Graybill
Harold M. Groff
Miriam (Groff) Harnish
Norma (Groff) Gehman
Sarah Jane (Groff) Landis
Robert E. Harnish
Dervin Hart
Theo (Hayes) Perkins
Miriam (Herr) Kreider
Carol (Hershey) Miller
Doris (Hertzler) Moyer
Janet Hess
Rhoda (Hess) Stoner
Dwane L. Hostetter
Anna Ruth (Hostetter)
  Breckbill
Mary (Huber) Hadaway
Paul R. Hurst
Chester W. Kauffman
Eva (Kauffman) Schrock
Regina (Kauffman) Chaney
Eugene N. Keener
Evelyn N. Keener
Velma (Keener) Scholl
Evelyn (Keeport) Bomberger
Joy (King) Yoder
Mary Jane (Kreider) Hoober
Clyde E. Kuhns
Arlene (Kurtz) Kreider
Rodella (Kurtz) Weaver
Salome (Kurtz) Leinbach

Frederick J. Lamp
Lois (Landis) Shenk *
Darlene (Lapp) Sweigart
Glenn M. Leaman
E. Lewis Leaman **P**
Harold E. Lefever
C. Ronald Lehman
Gerald R. Lehman
Glenn M. Lehman **M,+**
Sharon (Lehman) Witmer
Vera (Lefever) Kurtz
Anna (Mast) Bishop
Elsie (Mack) Mast
Arlene L. Martin
Arvid L. Martin
Esther (Martin) Bucher
Lucille (Martin) Groff
Nadine (Martin) Martin
Phoebe (Martin) Good
Evelyn (Mellinger) Souders
Phebe M. Mellinger
Anna Lois (Metzler) Hess
Fred H. Miller
Judith (Miller) Houser
L. Glenn Miller
Marian (Miller) Lefever
Ruth Anna (Miller) Reitz
Sanford Miller
Dale S. Moyer
J. Emmett Murphy
Dale E. Myer
Kenneth Reed
Melvin N. Reitz
Cletus E. Ressler
Charles T. Rexroad
Carl N. Rutt **L**
Anna Elizabeth (Sauder) Helfer
Marian J. (Sauder) Bauman
Mary E. Sensenig
John B. Shenk **V**
Nancy (Shenk) Stauffer
Julia (Stauffer) Witmer
Harold L. Shirk
Lorraine (Showalter) Martin
John L. Shreiner
Betty (Siegrist) Keperling
Barbara (Stauffer) Cantey
Lawrence C. Stevens
Charity (Stoltfus) Tourney
R. Irene (Stoltzfus) Byers
Minnie (Stover) Weaver
Betty Lou (Umble) Buckwalter
Ella Mae (Weaver) McElwee
Elizabeth (Weaver) Bonnar
Jay Nelson Weaver
Marlene (Weaver) Buckwalter
Elaine (Wenger) Good
Paul W. Wenger
Gerald M. Whisler
James S. White
Galen Yeager
Ilva (Yoder) Hertzler
Velma (Yoder) Magill
Nancy (Zimmerman) Garber
Glenn W. Zendt
Verna (Zook) Stoltzfus

Class of 1963

Helena (Bade) Lutz
Arlene (Beiler) Gipe
Barbara Ella Beiler
Mary Anne (Beiler) Leaman
Stanley Benner
Lois (Boll) Stauffer
Ruth Ann (Breneman) Heisey
A. Lloyd Brubaker
Eleanor (Brubaker) Peifer
J. Dale Brubaker

Henry L. Buckwalter
Judith Buckwalter
Anna Mary Charles
Lois Ruth (Charles) Zeiset
Robert C. Charles
David H. Clymer
James W. Clymer
Marian (Ebersole) Clapper
M. Richard Eby
Joan (Edwards) Hostetter
Janet Erb +
Ruth Ann (Eshbach) Mann
John Henry Fox
Donald L. Frey
Miriam (Frey) Lentz
Carol R. Gehman
Wilma (Gerhart) Zimmerman
Willard Gingerich
J. Kenneth Gochnauer
Barbara (Good) Beamer
Jane (Good) Hess
Joyce (Good) McFadden
Miriam (Graybill) Thomas
Patricia (Graybill) Brubaker
Earl S. Groff
Glenn Herr
Joyce (Herr) Bomberger
Sharon (Hershey) Hershey
David S. Hess
E. Anne (Hess) Stoltzfus M
Sue Ellen (Hess) Youmans
Marilyn (Hollinger) Weaver
Janet (Horning) Hartzler
J. Linford Horst
John H. Hottenstein
Elva Jane (Huber) Ebersole
Paul C. Kennel
John J. Kling
Donald B. Kraybill +
J. Lloyd Kreider
Norma Jean (Kreider) Weaver
J. Richard Landis
Alta Mae (Lapp) Shultz
Twila (Lauver) Finkbiner
Lois (Lefever) Gascho
Jean (Lefever) Miller
Pauline (Lefever) Zook
Rosene (Lefever) Hornberger
Rachel(Lehman) Brubacker
Elaine (Longenecker) Clymer
William Longenecker
Carolyn (Martin) Mellinger
Eldon J. Martin
Irvin S. Martin Jr.
Jerry E. Martin
Leon H. Martin
Nancy Jane (Martin) Hienbach
Nelson E. Martin
Nelson W. Martin P
Wilmer R. Martin
Dorcas (Metzler) Martzall
Mae (Mast) Stoltzfus
Glenn E. Metzler
Janet (Miller) Dombach
John M. Miller
Ruthanne (Miller) Lowe
Luke B. Mosemann
Nancy (Moyer) Musser
Julia (Mull) Rohrer
Nancy (Myer) Witmer
Rhoda (Myer) Smoker
Mary Jane Myers
Rachel (Myers) Sullivan
Donald O. Nauman
Lois (Nolt) Kime
Carolyn (Oberholtzer) Martin
Elvin H. Peifer
Loren O. Petersheim
Anna (Ranck) Petersheim

Janet (Ranck) Martin
Norma (Rohrer) Neff
Nora (Russell) Dehart
Marian R. Sauder
Blair Seitz L
Helen (Sensenig) Zimmerman
Lois (Shank) Davidson
Wayne L. Shank
Kathryn (Shelly) Leatherman
Margaret (Shelly) Jones
Doris (Shenk) Mohler
A. Mary (Shertzer) Martin
Elvin N. Shertzer
Ellen (Showalter) Hartzler
J. Donald Siegrist
Ray H. Siegrist
Julie (Shreiner) Heller
Alta (Stauffer) Yoder
Sanford Stauffer
Doris (Stoltzfus) Sullivan
George B. Stoltzfus V
John W. Stoltzfus
Mary Jane (Stoltzfus) Eby
Rachel (Stover) Weaver
Kenneth Strite
Lucille E. Strite
Linford L. Swartzentruber
Anna Mary (Thomas) Risser
Marian L. Umble
J. Donald Warfel
Eunice (Weaver) Warfel
Melvin R. Weaver
Betty (Wenger) Good S,*
Dortha (Wise) Neil
Dawn (Wissler) Van Horn
Janet (Witmer) Peifer
Ferne (Yoder) Gochnauer
Melanie (Yoder) Ressler
Raymond E. Youndt
Mary (Zeager) Sweikert
Erla (Zimmerman) Nauman
Laban G. Zimmerman

Class of 1964

Melvin S. Ash
Elmeta (Augsburger) Shelly
Conrad Baer
Elsie (Beiler) Beiler
Mildred J. Beiler
Sherrill (Beiler) Martin
Doris (Blank) Lefever
Vera (Bollinger) Wadel
Fannie Mae (Borntreger)
  Kramer
Joseph E. Bontrager
Clemmie (Boyden) Richards
Marianne (Breneman)
  Oberholtzer
Ruth (Brubaker) Zimmerman S
Marilyn (Bucher) Shaub
Rachel (Burkholder) Martin
Kenneth E. Campbell
Stanley E. Champ
James R. Charles
Jeffrey Crawford
Melvin R. Eby
Miriam Enck
Harry M. Erb
Phoebe (Erb) Gallagher
Paul C. Fretz L
J. Richard Frey V
Linda (Frey) Frey
Martha (Forrester) Rowland
Jean (Forwood) Greer
Faye (Garber) Yoder
Lois (Garman) Knauff
Isaac W. Gehman
John H. Gehman

Robert L. Gerlach
Ann (Ginder) Simonetti
James Glick
Karl Gochnauer
Glenn L. Good
Leon E. Good
I. Merle Good *
Rhoda (Good) Sensenig
Hubert P. Graybill
Leonard L. Groff
John Henry Harnish
Lorraine (Hershey) Graybill
Darlene (Hertzler) Snader
Joanne (Hess) Siegrist
Rosalie (Hess) Roland
Clyde M. Hollinger +
Eileen (Horning) Byler
Melba (Horst) Eshleman
Naomi (Horst) Weaver +
Donna (Hostetter) Moseman
Robert D. Hostetter
Helen (Howard) Beck
Elva Jean (Huber) Kreider
Anna Ruth (Hurst) Martin
David G. Kauffman
Nedra (Kauffman) Denlinger
Samuel A. Kauffman
Audrey (Keener) Hilsher
Joseph B. Keener
Mary Lois (Keener) Kreider
Larry J. Kennel
Carolyn (King) Runyon
Elizabeth (Kling) Leaman
Leona (Kraybill) Myer M
Charles H. Kreider
Frederick M. Kreider
Martha (Kreider) Zimmerman L
Ruth L. Kreider
Ray E. Kuhns
Dorothy (Kurtz) Martin
Lois (Kurtz) Miller
Paul J. Kurtz
Pat (Lackey) Eby
Elaine (Landis) Hollinger
H. Lester Landis
Ruth (Landis) Evans
Nevin D. Lantz
Jean (Lapp) Battig
Virginia (Lapp) Eby
Judy (Lauver) Martin
James R. Leaman
Allon H. Lefever
Ernest W. Lefever
Mary (Lefever) Reed
Ava Lee (Longenecker) Martin
Darlene (Longenecker) Landis
Betty Lou Martin
J. Melvin Martin
Yvonne (Martin) Martin
Harry R. Mast
Linda (Mast) Semke
Martha Ann (Mast) Eby
Theodore L. Mast
Betty Jane (Meck) Heisey
Kenneth E. Miller
Samuel L. Miller
Donald S. Moyer
Elsie (Moyer) Stauffer
Lee E. Mummau
H. Everett Myer
Joyce (Nafziger) McCarty
Ralph L. Nafziger
C. Melvin Neff
Marian (Newswanger) Bedford
Jay L. Nissley
Louise (Nolt) Kreider
Lorraine (Peters) Burkholder
Irene (Reed) Zimmerman
Sylvan G. Ressler

J. Nelson Sangrey
Emory F. Scholl
Ruthella (Schrock) Smith
Mary (Sensenig) Zimmerman
James M. Shank
Ruth (Shank) Burkholder
Jay M. Shaub
Richard Shellenberger
Lois (Shreiner) Brubaker
Don Showalter
David Siegrist
Harold Siegrist
Joyce (Snader) Sauder
Elvin K. Stauffer
Ada (Stoltzfus) Longenecker
M. Clyde Stoltzfus
Martha (Stoltzfus) Thomas
Ruth Ann (Stoltzfus) Mininger
Janet M. Stoner
John H. Stover
E. Carole (Strong) Smith
James H. Thomas P
James R. Thomas
Gerald R. Umble
Nancy (Umble) Walker
Eunice (Wadel) Lehman
Kenneth L. Walter
Dale L. Weaver
Ellen M. Weaver
Faye (Weaver) Good
Gladys (Weaver) Zeiset
Sara (Weaver) Zeiset
Edith (Weber) Leaman
James R. Wert
J. Richard Witmer Sr.
Barbara (Yoder) Epley
Donald E. Yoder
Judith (Yoder) Nafziger
Henry Youndt
Ethel (Zendt) Latta
Nancy (Zimmerman) Martin
Paul M. Zimmerman

Class of 1965

Josephine (Bade) Peters
Jay Harvey Beiler
Sadie (Beiler) High
H. Charles Benner
Orpha (Beyer) Weaver
Alta (Boll) Metzler
J. Nevin Boll
Phyllis (Bomberger) Groff
Esther (Bontrager) Leese
James L. Bowman
Mary Louise (Breneman)
  Landis
Nancy (Breneman) Yoder
Paul Eugene Breneman
Rachel (Brubaker) Horst
Robert L. Brubaker
Darlene (Buckwalter) Sharp
J. Clair Buckwalter P
Larry Champ
Kenneth E. Charles
Levi H. Charles
James N. Clymer
Jeanette (Clymer) Bueno
Joanne (Detweiler)
  Swartzentruber
Naomi (Ebersole) Brubaker
Carl I. Eby
John E. Eby
Miriam (Eby) Jones
Helen (Eckman) Zimmerman
Joan (Esbenshade) Swope
Wilmer Esbenshade
Gerald W. Eshleman
Robert M. Eshleman

Carolyn (Fly) Schantz
Priscilla (Forry) Garrett
Esther Fox
David E. Frey
Anna Lois (Gehman) Groff
Janet (Gehman) Henry
Mary (Gehman) Miller
Rosene (Gerlach) Garman
Rebecca (Glick) Benner
Delmar W. Glick
Carol (Good) Groff
Harold B. Good
Lorraine (Good) Cutrer
Ruth (Good) Todd
W. Richard Good
Emma E. Graybill
L. Jean (Graybill) Martin
Mildred (Graybill) Gerlach
Galen G. Groff
Miriam (Groff) Long
Shirley A. Groff
Brenda Harbold
Elizabeth (Harnish) Siegrist
Lorraine Harnish
Arlene (Herr) Stambaugh
Glenn C. Hershey
Irvin Hershey
Martha (Hershey) Wittmer
Alice (Hess) Shirk
C. Richard Hess
Esther H. Hess
Gloria (Hess) Bender
Martha (Hess) Clymer
Susan (Hess) Guengerich
Jane (High) Sangrey
Dorothy (Hilsher) Frey
Wayne C. Hochstetler
Janet (Hoover) Habecker
Ellen (Horning) Sensenig
Lucy (Horning) Nolt
Gerald R. Horst
Helen (Hostetter) Hershey
James W. Hostetter
Norma (Howe) Zook
Joyce A. Huber
Mary (Hurst) Frey
Mary Louise (Hurst) Hostetter
Mary Kathryn (Hurst) Landis **M**
Darlene (Kauffman) Miller
James D. Kauffman
Judith (Kauffman) Beiler
Kenneth R. Kauffman **V**
J. David Keener
Ruby (Keener) Gochnauer
Ruth (Kennel) Zale
Alvin L. King
Rhoda (Kolb) Nolt
Joyce E. Kuhns
Wayne L. Kuhns
John David Landis **L**
Joyce (Landis) Eby
J. Ray Landis
Mary Ellen (Landis) Groff
Rhoda (Landis) Cicero
Lois (Lantz) Sauder
Dale Lapp
Clair H. Leaman
Edith (Leaman) Groff
W. James Leatherman
A. Ronald Lefever
Mary (Lefever) Beitzel
Louise (Lehman) Ervin
Carol (Martin) Hottenstein
Dale E. Martin
Donna (Martin) Dombach
Doris (Martin) Claborne **T**
Larry L. Martin
Larry L. Martin
Lois (Martin) Martin

Harold R. Mast
Irma (Mast) Linacre
Ruth Ann (Martin) Longacre
Phyllis (Martin) Strickland
Sandra (Martin) Rissler
Clifford G. Miller
Marian (Miller) Torkelson
Paul F. Miller
R. Elaine (Miller) Thomas
Barbara Mosemann
Anna (Myer) Shertzer
Eldon Nafziger
Lois A. Nafziger
Anna Ruth (Neff) Eshleman
Galen Newswanger
Lois Nissley
Nancy (Nolt) Ressler
Theresa (Ramer) Brubaker
Carol Ann (Rice) Spratt
Betty (Risser) Hoover
Marilyn (Rohrer) Campbell
Susan (Rohrer) Kershner
Dennis H. Ruth
Lauretta (Rutt) Eshleman
Delmar L. Sauder
Esther (Sauder) Sensenig
Glenn E. Sauder
Janice (Sauder) Esbenshade
Raymond W. Sauder
Robert L. Sauder
Warren R. Sauder
Wilmer Sauder
Mary (Seitz) Melhorn
Velma (Sensenig) Campbell
Virginia (Shearer) Pickell
Maynard Shirk
Susan Darlene Shirk
Rhoda (Smoker) Harnish
Pearl (Snader) Lantz
Jean (Stauffer) Eby
Lowel M. Stauffer
Carolyn (Steffy) Horst
David R. Stoltzfus
Donald J. Stoltzfus
Etta (Stoltzfus) Esch
Jean (Stoltzfus) Groff
Verna R. (Stoltzfus) Adams
Janet (Stoner) Wenger
Richard D. Strite
Goldie (Swartzentruber) Fretz
Mary Ann (Umble) Hess
Ruth (Ulrich) Walsh
Dale E. Weaver
Darlene (Weaver) Boll
Eileen (Weaver) Charles
Grace (Weaver) Kauffman
Janet (Weaver) Kreider
Leon Weber
Lois (Weber) McPherson *
Benjamin H. Wenger
Daniel Wenger
David A. Wenger
Irvin Wenger
Jewel (Wenger) Showalter +
Margaret (Wenger) Johnson **S,+**
Mary Ellen Witmer
David R. Wolgemuth
Glenn Wyble
Audrey (Yoder) Seigrist
G. Lorene (Yoder) Horst
Samuel Yoder
Stephen K. Yoder
Clair Zimmerman
Loren L. Zimmerman
Ruth (Zimmerman) Martin
Miriam (Zook) Stoltzfus

Class of 1966

Ruth (Angstadt) Mast
Shirley (Baer) Kurtz
Norma (Barge) Horst
Moses M. Beiler
Dawn (Benner) Sterling
Paul W. Bentzel
Doris (Bieber) Brownsberger
Sylvia (Bomberger) Snader
Miriam F. Book
Gerald Lee Bowman
Richard L. Bowman
Forrest D. Boyden
J. Paul Bucher **V**
Melvin E. Buckwalter
Rhoda G. Burkholder
Anne Carpenter
David E. Charles
H. Dwayne Charles
Twila Jean Charles
Esther R. Christophel
Donald R. Clymer **P**
Kendra (Crist) Cross
Robert L. Eberly
Sarah (Eby) Kurtz
R. Elvin Engle
Paul S. Erb
J. Marlin Eshbach
Leon C. Eshleman
Mildred (Fox) Kilmer
Donna (Frey) Myers
W. Kenneth Frey
Fred M. Garber
James R. Garman
Sara (Gehman) Martin
Anne Louise (Glick) Derrick
Charles L. Good
Janice (Graybill) Alspaugh
Joyce (Graybill) Miller
Marie (Graybill) Hoover
Jean (Groff) Krause
Mary Kathryn (Groff) Gehman
Robert D. Harnish
Sanford L. Hege
J. Robert Herr
Carl E. Hershey
Miriam (Hershey) Martin
J. Allen Hershey
Daniel S. Hess **L**
Gerald B. Hess
Luke C. Hess
M. Christina (Hess) Glanzer
Maris R. Hess
Ruth Ann (Horining)
  Bruckhart
Esther (Horst) Martin
Judith (Horst) Kauffman
Clifford D. Hoover
Esther (Hoover) Bucher
J. Nelson Horst
Lester S. Horst
M. Glenn Horst
Paul M. Hostetler
Naomi (Hostetter) Sensenig
J. Elvin Huber
Lois Jean (Huber) Breneman
C. Glenn Hurst
Elsie Mae (Kauffman) Beachy
Iva (Kauffman) Lapp **S**
Linda (Keener) Tyson
Lois E. Keener
John R. Kennel
Donna (Kraybill) Godfrey
J. Elvin Kraybill **M**
Leon D. Kurtz
Lorraine (Landis) Wenger
Merle E. Lantz
Etta (Lapp) King

Louise (Lauver) Glick
Sara (Leaman) Keener
Martha (Lefever) Weaver
Alta (Lehman) Landis
Galen R. Lehman
J. Marlin Lehman *,+
Nancy (Lehman) Kuhns
Rachel (Lehman) Keeler
Rachel (Lehman) Stoltzfus
Alvin G. Longenecker
Gloria (Longenecker) Lehman
Lynn (Marshall) Billett
Betty Martin
Betty (Martin) McGee
Ernest W. Martin
Ethel (Martin) Campbell
Gerald E. Martin
Jane (Martin) Hoover
Lyle K. Martin
Mary K. (Martin) Ramos
Clair I. Mast
Dale J. Mast
Emily Grace (Mast) Yantzi
Nathanael Mast
Stuart A. Mast
Janet (Meck) Sensenig
Miriam (Metzler) Hess
Orpha M. Metzler
Carolyn (Miller) Miller
Daniel G. Miller
David E. Miller
Dorothy (Miller) Torkelson
J. Lowell Miller
Richard Eugene Miller
James L. Miller
Rosemary (Miller) Stratton
Virginia (Mummau) Siegrist
David Glen Musser
Miriam Arlene Musser
Earl E. Myer
Barbara (Nafziger) Miller
Ruth Ann (Nissley) Kritzer
Leonard E. Nolt
Lois (Peifer) Myer
Phyllis (Pellman) Good
A. Kenneth Ranck
Karen (Ranck) Rush
Joseph D. Reed
Larry Reed
Lois (Reitz) Miller
Marian (Ressler) Yoder
Marlin G. Ressler
Donald L. Sauder
James N. Sauder
Nelson Sauder
Aileen (Schlabach) Warfel
Barbara (Shellenberger) Huber
Donald Shellenberger
Irene (Shelley) Eshbach
Donald Showalter
J. Marvin Siegrist
Miriam (Siegrist) Hershey
Wanda (Smoker) Creeger
Charlotte (Stauffer) Shaffer
Nancy (Stauffer) Wenger
Annie (Stoltzfus) Donaldson
Eldon R. Stoltzfus
Mary (Stoltzfus) Boll
Rhoda (Stoltzfus) Longenecker
Rosanne (Stoltzfus) Graber
James C. Stoner
Kenneth L. Stoner Sr.
Linda (Stoner) Garber
Ruth E. Stover
Larry D. Temple
Evanna (Umble) Hess **T**
J. Richard Umble
Willis P. Umble
Albert S. Weaver

Donald M. Weaver
Doris (Weaver) Hershey
Galen L. Weaver
Irene M. Weaver
Elaine (Weber) Kurtz
Ben Wenger
Jane (Wenger) Showalter
Martha (Wenger) Harnish
L. Ann (Wert) Shellenberger
Stanley Wine
Doretta (Wissler) Hall
Mary Louise Wolgemuth
Inez J. Yoder
Marcella (Yoder) Kerstetter
Martha (Yoder) Stoltzfus
M. Jane (Yoder) Yutzy
Sanford K. Yoder
Ernest L. Youndt
Patricia (Yunginger) Leaman
Marie (Zimmerman) Miller
Mark Zimmerman
Martha Zook

Class of 1967

E. Sue (Beiler) Fisher
Mary Joan (Beiler) Smoker
Louise (Benner) Baerg
James Blank
Esther (Boll) Wine
Doris (Breneman) Meehan
Erma (Breneman) Miller
Janet Breneman
J. Richard Breneman
Carolene (Brubaker) Highfield
Susan (Buchen) Bollinger
Orpha G. Burkholder
David P. Buckwalter
Esther (Byler) Bontrager
Rudy Byler
Anita (Charles) Ranck
Linda (Charles) Byler
Jeffrey D. Crist
Lester K. Denlinger
Lois (Denlinger) Clymer
Linda (Detweiler) Derstine
Jane (Deiter) Wenger
Mildred (Ebersole) Martin
Beth (Eby) Weber
Caroline (Eby) Huber
J. Lorraine (Eby) Breneman
Lois (Eby) White
Marian (Fox) Gaffney
J. Nelson Frey
Nancy Frey S
Glenn D. Garman
Ann (Gingrich) Martin
Donald E. Gingrich
Lois (Gingrich) Garman
Margaret (Gingrich) Varner
Paul H. Glick
Doris (Gochnauer) Bange
Daniel F. Good
Marlin W. Good
Jay M. Groff
Martha (Groff) Mellinger
Richard P. Groff
Dianna (Haldwell) Hart
Ellen (Harnish) Beachy
Carlene (Hart) Schaeffer
Jay Harlin Hege
James R. Hershey P
Jeanette (Hershey) Sauers
Lois B. Hershey
Marlin R. Hershey
Rebecca (Hershey) High
Duane Hertzler
Kate (Hess) Kooker
Rachel (Hess) Gordon

Judy (High) Smoker
Frances (Hilsher) Nissley
L. Dennis Hochstetler
Ellen (Horst) Helmuth
Joyce (Horst) Leaman
Mildred (Horst) Ranck
Carolyn (Hostetter) Martin
Joseph S. Hottenstein
Norma (Huber) Strite
Sharon (Hurst) Stoltzfus
Sharon (Kanagy) Heatwole
Amos L. Kauffman
Anita (Kauffman) High
Glenford D. Kauffman V
J. Marvin Kauffman
Marilyn (Keener) Zeager
Kathleen (Kennel) Fox
Marie (Kennel) Stoltzfus
Wilmer Keperling
Eugene Kraybill
Robert M. Kreider
Kenneth Kurtz
James G. Landis
Marian (Landis) Harnish
Naomi (Landis) Byler
Wendell J. Lantz
Edith (Lapp) Crist
Gladys (Lapp) Martin
Tobias G. Leaman
Shirley (Lefever) Sites
Melvin L. Lehman L
Rebecca (Lehman) Monserrate
Dianne (Longenecker) Stover
Rhoda (Longenecker) Stoltzfus
Betty (Martin) Hurst
Doris (Martin) Haarer
Janice L. Martin
Kenneth E. Martin
Larry L. Martin M
Linda (Martin) Fasnacht
Louann E. Martin
Richard L. Martin
Rosene (Martin) Hollinger
Jay E. Mellinger
Marian (Mellinger) Denlinger
Carolyn E. Metzler
Daniel E. Miller
Dennis G. Miller
Gene C. Miller
Mildred (Miller) Holderread
Patricia (Miller) Bender
David W. Moyer
Sharon (Moyer) Strite
Marianne (Musser) Charles
Richard H. Musser
Ruth (Myer) Brubaker
Judith (Nafziger) Chaldu
Lucille (Nafziger) Ositko
Barbara S. Nissley
Lois (Oberholtzer) Weaver
Janet (Ogburn)Sensenig
Jane (Peifer) Moyer T,*
Jean (Ranck) Cann
John S. Redcay
Anna Ruth (Risser)
    Zimmerman
Donald R. Risser
Sharon (Ruth) Kuhns
Marianne (Rutt) Zimmerman
Gordon L. Sangrey
Anna Mary Sauder
David K. Sauder
Larry R. Sauder
Nathan Schlabach
Delores (Schrock) Mast
Judith (Shank) Martin
Louise (Shank) Mast
Elaine (Shaub) Todd
Daniel E. Shenk

Luke N. Shertzer
James E. Shreiner
Naomi H. Siegrist
Mervin Smucker
Fannie (Snader) Gochnauer
Alvin L. Stoltzfus
Elmer Stoltzfus
Gerald A. Stoltzfus
Janice (Stoltzfus) Carper
Julie (Stoltzfus) Mumma
J. Lowell Stoltzfus
Lee Stoltzfus
Linda (Stoltzfus) Reed
Naaman W. Stoltzfus
Ruth (Stoltzfus) Jost
Susie (Stoltzfus) Horst
Wilma (Stoltzfus) Eby
Marvin Stoner
Eleanor (Strite) Martin
Anna (Sweigart) Shirk
Lloyd S. Swisher
Barbara (Thomas) Landis
David L. Umble
Mary Ellen (Van Ormer)
    Kennedy
Elaine (Warfel) Stauffer
Clyde L. Weaver
J. Lester Wagner
Barbarba (Weaver) Hershey +
Clair H. Weaver
David L. Weaver
Esther (Weaver) Shorter
Larry L. Weaver
Levi Y. Weaver
Yvonne L. Weaver
Esther (Wenger) Gingrich
Ivan S. Wenger
Ray Mark Wenger
Janice (Wert) Miller
James L. Wolgemuth
Amy (Yoder) Herr
Doris A. Yoder
Linda (Yoder) Grove
Ken Yoder
Max B. Yoder
Rosanna (Yoder) Deitrick
Janet Zeager
Joyce Zimmerman
Fern (Zimmerman) Zook

Class of 1968

Kenneth O. Beam
J. Nelson Bechtold
Miriam A. Beiler
Omar J. Beiler
Vernon L. Beiler
Elwood C. Bollinger
James M. Bontrager
Melvin R. Breneman
Donald B. Bucher
Kenneth Bucher
Kathryn (Burkhart)
    Mauersberger
Lester M. Burkholder
Yvonne (Carter) Jones
Esther (Charles) Wenrich
Rachel L. (Charles) Kreider
Arlene (Clymer) Smith
John D. Crist
Naaman L. Eberly
Janet (Ebersole) Martin
Elizabeth Esbenshade
Linda (Esbenshade) Geissinger
Esther L. Fretz
Anthony L. Frey
Leslie R. Frey
David A. Gehman
Joyce (Gehman) Quackenbos

Nancy (Gehman) Leaman
Martha (Gerlach) Charles
John M. Gingrich
Rosene (Gingrich) Sugden
Elmer D. Glick
Daniel D. Good
Elaine (Good) Riley
Luke W. Good
Marlin W. Good
Mary (Good) Lapp
Rhonda (Good) Kalend
Ruth J. Good
Jean (Graybill) Lehman
Orval C. Graybill
Faye (Greenawalt) Hess
Carolyn E. Groff
Ruth (Groff) Zimmerman
Cheryl (Harbold) Eshbach
Ruth (Harnish) Mast
Larry E. Herr
Rachel (Herr) Frey
Everett Lee Hershey
Glenn D. Hershey
Jane (Hershey) Mininger
J. Wilson Hershey
Jerry L. Hershey
Miriam (Hershey) Gieg
David L. Hess
Deborah (Hess) Kipfer
Elma (Hess) Burkholder
Henry M. Hess M
H. Laverne Hess
Pauline B. Hess
Sue (Hess) Yoder
V. Jean (Hess) Horst
Rhoda (High) Yost
L. Kenneth Hollinger
Evelyn (Horst) Duncan
Lois (Horst) Kennedy
G. Marlin Horst
Margaret (Horst) Frost
Martha Horst
Mervin D. Horst
J. Maynard Hostetler
Miriam (Huber) Cornish
M. Carol (Kauffman) Stoltzfus
Herbert S. Keener
Martha J. Keener
Robert E. Keener
Lois C. Kennel
Deryl G. Kennel
Richard L. Kennel
Susan (Kennel) Watkins
Daniel L. King V
Fred M. King
Glenn A. King
James L. King
Linford D. King
Margie (Kreider) Martin
Patricia (Kreider) Johnson
Ronald E. Kreider
Anne (Landis) Kilheffer
Carolyn (Landis) Esbenshade
Marian (Landis) Funk
Velma (Landis) Hershey
Donna (Lapp) Rempel
Galen A. Lapp
Barbara (Lauver) Brubaker
James G. Leaman
Kenneth G. Leaman
Susan (Leaman) Showalter
L. Joanne Lefever
Arlin D. Lehman
Kathleen (Lehman) Lehman
Linda (Longenecker) Kropf
Arlene (Martin) Hollinger
Barbara (Martin) Riehl
Elaine (Martin) Nissley
J. Nevin Martin

Miriam (Martin) Nichols
Carol Ann (Mast) Swailes
David W. Mast
Fanny (Mast) Geig
Harlan L. Mast
Herbert L. Mast
Shirley A. Mast
Eunice I. Metzler **T,+**
Ernest L. Miller
Gerald E. Miller
Janet (Miller) Harnish
Joseph E. Miller
Joyce (Miller) Good
Lloyd D. Miller
Louise (Miller) Beachy
Paul E. Miller
Fern (Mishler) Miller **S**
Ann (Mosemann) Overly
Lolita (Mumma) Haverstick
Grace I. Musser
Carol (Nafziger) Good
J. Kenneth Nafziger
Naomi (Nafziger) King
Helen (Neff) Lehman
Thelma (Nissley) Kreider
Gladys (Nolt) Boettcher
Faye (Peifer) Gehman
Wilmer W. Reed
Kenneth D. Reinford
Lorraine (Reitz) Allen
Grace A. Ressler
Diane (Rheinheimer) Durell
H. Brian Risser
James R. Rohrer
Marilyn (Rohrer) Barnett
Joan L. Ruth
Ruth Ann (Rutt) Stoltzfus
Evelyn M. Sauder
Jean (Sauder) Horst
Paul D. Sauder
Phoebe (Sauder) Nafziger
Dale N. Seibel
Nancy R. Seitz
David L. Shank
Flo (Shank) Lehman
Eileen (Shellenberger)
  Detweiler
Susan (Shellenberger) Smoker
Norma (Shenk) Watterman
Susan (Showalter) Halterman
Raymond P. Siegrist
Lillian L. Smith
Jay M. Smoker
Kenneth L. Smoker
Lena (Smoker) Stoltzfus
Rose (Smoker) Olsen
Barbara (Smucker) Kanagy
Samuel L. Smucker
Esther M. Snader
David B. Stauffer
Philip E. Stauffer **P**
Shirley (Stauffer) Burris
Audrey (Stoltzfus) McClune
Ben B. Stoltzfus
Glenn L. Stoltzfus
Lydia (Stoltzfus) Stoltzfus
Ruth (Stoltzfus) Stoltzfus
Ruth Ann (Stoltzfus) Stoltzfus
Constance (Stutzman)
  Breneman
Sheryl (Summers) Jantzi
Fern (Swartzentruber) Baker
Glenda (Swartentruber) Byler
Judith (Swartzentruber) Hess
Susanne (Temple) Kumar
A. Daniel Thomas
J. Samuel Thomas
Mary Jane (Todd) Gerlach
Ronald N. Umble

Elaine (Weaver) Hart
Ronald L. Weaver
Ruth (Weaver) Moyer
Rhoda (Weber) Mack **L,***
Barbara (Yoder) Davison
Carol (Yoder) Stutzman
Carolyn (Yoder) Yoder
Clinton E. Yoder
Joann (Yoder) Hursh
J. Wesley Yoder
R. Aurthur Yost
Thelma (Zink) McEvoy
Kathryn (Zook) Gingerich

Class of 1969

Melba (Augsburger) Ebersole
Patricia (Baer) Stoltzfus
Barbara (Beam) Wingfield
June (Bechtold) Rose
Rose (Beidler) Yoder
Marlene (Beiler) Eckman
Stephen E. Beiler
Lucy (Bontrager) Yoder
Elvin R. Bowman
Kenneth R. Brackbill
Betty (Brubaker) Martin
Dale L. Brubaker
Glenn S. Brubaker
Robert L. Bruckhart
K. Thomas Buchen
Margaret (Buckwalter) Miller
Alta Jo (Byler) Nisly
Mervin L. Charles
Paul M. Charles
Teresa (Clemmer) Alderfer
Dolores (Clymer) Beiler
Andrew L. Creamer
Rhoda (Denlinger) Blank
Anna Louise Detweiler
Abram W. Diffenbach **V,***
Doris (Dise) Brubaker
John D. Ebersole
L. Marlin Eby
Merle (Erb) Mast
Betty (Eshleman) Zimmerman
Carol (Fox) Evans
Mervin E. Frey
Susan (Furtak) Heimbach
Lowell D. Gehman
Virginia (Glick) Graybill
Howard Good **M**
Linford L. Good
Deborah Green
Jere M. Groff
Joyce (Groff) Martin
Miriam (Groff) Miller
Dennis A. Harnish
Mary (Harnish) Ginder
James R. Hershey
Dale Hertzler
Glenn A. Hertzler
Dorothy J. Hess
Elaine (Hess) Linder
Mary (Hess) Bell
Raymond H. Hess
Mary Ann (Hollinger) Bowman
Rosanne (Hollinger) Gingrich
Faith R. Hoover
Nelson C. Hoover **P**
Lois (Horning) Good
Julia (Horst) Redcay
Ida Mae (Hostetler) Overholt
Joyce (Hostetter) Thomas
J. Larry Huber
J. Norene Huber
Almeda (Kauffman) Yoder
B. Edwin Kauffman
Carolyn (Keener) Hoover

Fred A. Keener
Gerald H. Keener
Judith (Keener) Bomberger
R. Gerald Keener
Barbara A. Keller
Ellen (Kennel) Shank
Esther (Kennel) Lamartine
Tom Kennel
David Kraybill **L**
James E. Kreider
James E. Kurtz
Karen (Kurtz) Gross
Leonard S. Kurtz
Mary (Kurtz) Hostetler
Abram N. Landis
Clair D. Landis
Helen Mae (Landis) Imhoff
Lois (Landis) Miller
Ruth Ann (Landis) Benfield
Thelma (Lantz) Penman
Ann (Lapp) Ranck **S**
Daniel Ray Lapp
Rhoda (Lapp) Nissley
Gerald Leaman
Marian (Leaman) Mininger
Theodore G. Leaman
Vera (Lefever) Jones
Daniel R. Lehman
Daryl R. Lehman
Mary Ann (Lehman) Sauder
Ronald E. Lehman
Daniel Lind
Joyce (Lentz) Hess
Audrey (Longenecker) Bender
Elsie (Longenecker) Shank
J. William Longenecker
Esther (Martin) Kline
Janet (Martin) Weaver
Judy (Martin) Rasmussen
Naomi (Martin) Diffenbach **T**
Philip E. Martin
Stephen L. Martin
Carol (Mast) Stoltzfus
James G. Mast
James H. Mast
Linda (Metzler) Sauder
Carolyn (Miller) Brubaker
James E. Miller
J. Martin Miller
Karen (Moshier) Shenk
Betty (Moyer) Risser
Joanne (Musser) Ginder
Mabel (Neff) Bitts
Ella Newswanger
Jay W. Nissley
Ruth (Ogburn) Brougher
Linda (Petersheim) Mosemann
Joseph Ranck
Mary Ann (Redcay) Ruth
Herbert E. Reed
Martha (Reitz) Nauman
Jane (Risser) Nolt
Nancy (Rohrer) Sauder
Peggy (Rowell) Miller
Kenneth E. Sands
Clair H. Sauder
Jay W. Sauder
Raymond M. Sensenig
Duane Shank
Barry L. Shirk
Carl M. Shirk
Ruby (Showalter) Denlinger
Theda (Siegrist) Klemm
Carol (Smoker) Ebersole
Lloyd E. Smoker
Ronald L. Smoker
Stephen E. Smoker
Martha (Snader) Stoltzfus
John Daniel Stahl

Ellen (Stauffer) Gunning
Jay M. Stauffer
Kenneth Stauffer
Miriam (Stauffer) Szelistowski
Ruth (Steinhauer)Reinford
Ann (Stoltzfus) Brendle
Carl Stoltzfus
Dale K. Stoltzfus
Dwight L. Stoltzfus
Katie (Stoltzfus) Mast
Kenneth L. Stoltzfus
Linda (Stoltzfus) Lambert
Mervin W. Stoltzfus
Rose (Stoltzfus) Huyard
Verna (Stoltzfus) Acker
David E. Stoner
Donald E. Stoner
Larry L. Stoner
Rose (Stutzman) Graber
Doris (Swartzentruber) Ebersole
Mary (Sweigart) Weiler
Allen R. Umble
Cheryl (Weaver) Zimmerman
David W. Weaver
Doris Weaver
Harlan L. Weaver
Janet L. Weaver
Jesse L. Weaver
Larry R. Weaver
Lorraine (Weaver) Sauder
Annie Wenger- Keller
Chester L. Wenger
Doris (Wenger) Wissler
H. Thomas Wert
Marian (Whisler) Brubaker
Delbert Wissler
Jean (Witmer) Stauffer
Lois (Witmer) Gehman
Bonnie (Yoder) Hofstetter
Glenn Yoder
Lynn E. Yoder
John Thomas Yoder-Lehman
Linda (Youndt) Keens
Audrey (Yunginger) Rohrer
Linda Zimmerman
Ruth Ann (Zimmerman)
  Graybill
Lois Ann (Zook) Mast

Class of 1970

P. Maynard Baker
Marian (Bechtold) Kanode
Thelma (Blank) Delong
JoAnn (Bontrager) Zehr
M. Ray Bowman
Ruth Ann (Bowman) Martin
Arlene (Breneman)
  Oberholtzer
Lois (Breneman) Hege
Dorothy (Brubaker) Landis
Harlan E. Brubaker
Ruth (Brubaker) Troyer
Ruth (Bucher) Mellinger
Raymond G. Buckwalter
Carolyn (Byler) Hobbs
Jay S. Carpenter
Doris (Charles) Weaver
Grace (Charles) Sensenig
Jonathan E. Charles
Lois (Charles) Blake
Mary E. (Charles) Heisey
Galen J. Clemmer
Roy N. Clymer
James R. Deiter
Rosalee (Diffenbach) Schneck
Fern (Dise) Miller
Daniel G. Eberly
Jay D. Ebersole

Nyla (Ebersole) Wenger **S**
Dennis L. Eby
Julia (Eby) Swartz
Elma (Engle) Zehr
Charlotte (Eshleman) Verherne
L
Marianne (Fisher) Weaver
Mark L. Fly
J. Ray Frederick
Dennis L. Frey
Dale M. Garber **P**
Eunice (Gehman) Heisey
Darlene (Gerlach) Noll
Eileen (Gerlach) Hoover
John W. Gerlach
Lois J. Gerlach
J. Andrew Glick
Samuel L. Glick
Judith (Gochnauer) Herr
Dennis B. Good
Eunice W. (Good) Clemmer
Marian (Groff) Keener
James M. Harnish
Marvin E. Harnish
Marian E. Harnish
Lois (Harnly) Keller
Laverne (Heller) Kreider
Elaine (Herr) Hoover
Doris (Hershey) Neff
Glenn R. Hershey
Jay M. Hershey
Nancy (Hershey) Carbaugh
Sue (Hershey) Martin
Carl A. Hess
Daniel R. Hess
Edna (Hess) Kilheffer
James D. Hess
Lois (Hess) Nafziger
Margie (Hilsher) Frey
Walter E. Hochstetler
David L. Hollinger
Evan E. Hoover
M. Eugene Horst
Nancy (Horst) Perkins
Sue (Horst) Vanderford
Marcia (Hunsecker) Frye
Ray N. Hurst
Wilmer M. Hurst
Clair E. Kauffman
Ellen (Kauffman) Eby
Dennis D. Keener
Doris (Keener) Lefever
Joyce (Keener) Weaver
Paul D. Keener
J. Edwin Keens
Christian D. Kennel
Mark B. Kraybill
John A. Kurtz
Paul N. Kurtz
Benjamin L. Landis
Dean E. Landis
Josephine (Landis)
  Swartzentruber
Joyce (Landis) Herr
Mary (Landis) Martin
Shirley (Landis) Hackman
Vida J. Landis
Judy (Lantz) Hershey
Rachel (Lauver) Erb
Elta (Leaman) Nissley
Sue (Leaman) Smoker
Carol (Lefever) Hershey
Nancy (Lefever) Reitz
Raymond H. Lefever
Ellen (Lehman) White
Jason L. Lehman
Loretta (Lehman) Collins
Patricia (Lehman) McFarlane
Nancy (Longenecker) Pellegrini

Ronald E. Lutz
Richard Malloy
Daniel L. Martin
Glen D. Martin
Joy (Martin) Weaver
Norma (Martin) Stauffer
Rhoda (Martin) Mast
Ruth Ann (Martin)
  Zimmerman
Ada (Mast) Kauffman
David L. Mast
Susan (Mast) Dick
Lillian (Metzler) Yoder
Judy (Miller) Kolb
Leon E. Miller
Mary Ellen (Miller) Smith
Sandra (Miller) Layton
Harold M. Moyer
Carolyn (Mummau) Beachy *
Jane (Musser) Chisebwe
Janet (Musser) Heller
John D. Nafziger
Donald M. Neff
Sharon (Nissley) Harnish
Kenneth R. Pellman
Beverly (Ramer) Zimmerman
Sally (Reed) Miller
Esther (Reitz) Eshleman
Raymond E. Reitz **M**
Linda (Rohrer) Landis
Richard B. Sauder
Janice (Schrock) Root
Lena M. Sensenig
Jeanette (Shank) Yoder
Henry M. Shellenberger
Sharon (Shenk) Risser
Daniel H. Siegrist
Terry L. Smoker
Mary Ann (Smucker) Miller
Sara Jane (Snader) Weaver
Rhoda (Sollenberger) Lehman
Deborah (Stauffer) Hoover
Carol Marie Stoltzfus
Daniel B. Stoltzfus
G. Eileen (Stoltzfus) Hall **T**
Isaac H. Stoltzfus
Warren L. Stoltzfus
Daniel Swartzentruber
Ivan M. Umble
Linda J. Umble
Loretta (Umble) Sharp
Cheryl (Weaver) Landis
Julia A. Weaver
Nelson J. Weaver
Priscilla (Weaver) Jutzi
Sharon (Weaver) Kilheffer
David E. Weber +
Robert E. Wenger
Judy (Yoder) Morgan
Ruth Ann (Ziegler) Fly
Eunice (Zimmerman) Martin
Jay M. Zimmerman
Roy W. Zimmerman
Duane E. Zook **V**

Class of 1971

Ruth (Ash) Christner
Allan L. Asper
Ronald J. Baer
Thomas A. Bashore
Marlin E. Bechtold
Jewel (Beidler) Byler
Ruth (Beiler) Hollinger
Vena M. Beiler
Timothy E. Benner
E. Eugene Beyer
Janet (Bowman) Elbalghiti
Joanne (Breneman) Showalter

Rebecca Buchen
Mary (Buckwalter) Hess
Esther M. Burkhart
E. Merle Burkholder **P**
Mary Ann (Byler) Christophel
James R. Carpenter
Eugene R. Denlinger
Steven L. Denlinger
Ruth (Detweiler) Lesher *
Linda (Dise) Beyer
Kenneth B. Eberly
Linda (Ebersole) Berry
Sylvan R. Esh
Stephen M. Freed
Sandra L. Gehman
David L. Gingrich
David R. Gingrich
Mary Ann (Glick) Graber
Betty (Gochenaur) Rohrer
James E. Gochnauer
Nancy (Gochnauer) Hoover
Karen (Good) Chasez
Rebecca (Graybill) Landis
David N. Groff
Linda (Groff) Martin
Joel H. Hackman +
Joanne (Harnish) Forry
Rhoda (Herr) Martin
Charles E. Hershey
Linda (Hershey) Ebersole
Dean M. Hertzler
Susan A. Hertzler
Gloria (Hess) Frey
Joseph D. Hess
Sara (Hess) Zeager
Jeryl L. Hollinger
Marian (Hollinger) Rutt
Nancy (Hoover) Bagge
Phyllis (Hoover) Stoltzfus
Sharon (Horning) Cody
Janet (Horst) Lichty
Alma C. Hostetter
David J. Hostetter
Mary Ann (Hostetter) Shisler
Milton G. Howe
Robert L. Huber
Evelyn (Hunsecker) Jensen
Linda (Kauffman) Yost
Rosene S. Kauffman
Susie (Kauffman) Beiler
William C. Kauffman
Lamar H. Keener
J. Robert Keller
John D. Kennel
Philip N. Kennel
Glenda M. King
Hilda (King) Stoltzfus
Rosa King
Sanford L. King
Ann King-Grosh
Charles M. Kline
A. Ruby (Koerner) Miller
Nathan J. Kolb
Ronald S. Kraybill
Ray M. Kreider
Samuel H. Kurtz
Jean (Landis) Yordy
Brenda (Lapp) Tomassetti
Judy (Lapp) Kauffman
Ronald H. Leaman
Steven L. Leaman
Rhoda (Lehman) Stoesz
Sondra (Lehman) Funck
Faye (Lentz) Stauffer
Ray A. Long
Joyce (Longacre) Brubaker
David G. Longenecker
Ferne (Longenecker) Miller
Randall L. Longenecker

Donna (Mack) Shenk
Susan (Martin) Giershick
Anthony L. Mast
Robert E. Mast
Rowena (Mast) Stoltzfus
Joseph A. Mayberry
Arlene (Metzler) Carpenter
Jay E. Mogel
Kay (Moshier) McDivitt
Robert E. Nafziger
Margaret (Nauman) Thomsen
Carol (Neff) Horst
Sharon (Newcomer) Cleek
Barbara (Nissley) Good **L**
Betty (Nissley) Livengood
Joyce (Nissley) Smoker
Sheryl (Petersheim) Ehst
Joanne (Ranck) Dirks
Donna (Reinford) Clemmer
Janet (Rheinheimer) Bechtold
Keith N. Rohrer
Philip M. Rutt **V**
Faye (Sangrey) Clark
M. Yvonne (Sangrey) Zeiset
Dorothy E. Shank **S**
Glenda (Shank) Martin
Susan (Sheeler) Martin
James W. Shenk
N. Gerald Shenk
Helen (Showalter) Hertzler
Paul D. Smoker
Jerald L. Smucker
Marlin L. Smucker
Hannah (Souder) Hunter
H. Wilmer Stauffer
Jere M. Stauffer
Amos K. Stoltzfus
Cheryl (Stoltzfus) Lapp
Don M. Stoltzfus **M**
Edith (Stoltzfus) Burkholder
N. Craig Stoltzfus
Stephen Stoltzfus
Jean (Stoner) Hackman
Linda (Stoner) Dueck
Rosalene (Strickler) Maul **T**
J. Marlin Stutzman
Karen (Stutzman) Stoltzfus
Ivan R. Troxel Jr.
Aldine (Weaver) Musser
Donna L. Weaver
Kathleen (Weaver) Burger
Marian (Weaver) Gingrich
Ronald R. Weaver
Sheryl (Weaver) Stutzman
Janice (Weber) Tutt
Deborah (Wenger) Landis
Ronald Wenger
Sara (Wenger) Shenk
Rachel (Wolgemuth) Denlinger
Gloria (Yoder) Diener
Karen (Yoder) Miller
Rachel Fern Yoder
Shirley (Yoder) Miller
Timothy J. Yoder
Dale T. Youndt
Dorothy (Zeager) King
Hilda J. Zook

Class of 1972

Gerald R. Baer
Frances (Beam) Gunzenhauser
E. Kenneth Beiler
Orpha Joy Beiler
Warren E. Beiler
Brenda (Blank) Buckwalter
Philip E. Bontrager
John A. Brubaker +
Kenneth B. Bucher

Nancy (Bucher) Wright
Neta (Buckwalter) Kimel
Sharon (Burkholder) Anders
Carol (Charles) Peachey
Paul E. Charles
Rosene (Clymer) Hess
John S. Dietz
J. Clarence Ebersole
Luanne (Ebersole) Horst
Lloyd C. Eby
Susan (Engle) Freed
Richard D. Esh
Beulah (Fox) Mall
Karen (Frank) Rutt
Philip M. Freed
Anita K. Frey
Ruth Ann (Frey) Linberg
C. Eugene Gerlach
Susan (Gingrich) Martin
David D. Glick
Fredrick L. Good
Linford W. Good **P**
Mary Ann (Good) Hoover
Clayton S. Graybill
Doris J. Harnish
Erma (Harnish) Shultz
Patricia (Hernley) Martin
Ira C. Herr
John R. Herr
Andrew M. Hershey
Rosanne(Hershey) Swartzentruber
Sarah (Hershey) Nafziger
C. Rachel (Hess) Maust
Dale E. Hess
Naomi (Hess) Weber
P. Bruce Hess
Rachel (Hess) Webster
Richard B. Hess
Richard H. Hess
Lorraine (High) Stoltzfus
Jane (Hollinger) Good
Bernice Hoover
Karen (Hoover) Copenhaver
Betty Lou (Horning) Eberly *
Joyce (Horst) Sheeler
Thomas A. Horst
Carol S. Jones **L**
Betty (Kauffman) Esh
Harold R. Kauffman
Louella (Kauffman) Gray
Richard W. Kauffman
Steven G. Kauffman
Twila (Keener) Mast
Barry King
Clair I. King
Patricia (King) Schrock
Sharon (Koerner) Johnson
David Koppel
J. Nelson Kraybill
James A. Kurtz
Elaine Landis
Jacqueline (Landis) Sands
Jean L. (Landis) Sensenig
Melvin C. Landis
Shirley A. Landis
Regina (Lapp) Stiles
Charlene (Lehman) Harnish
D. Jean (Lehman) Showalter
Miriam (Lind) Messersmith
Carolyn (Martin) Kopp
Delmar Martin
Don L. Martin **V**
Doris E. (Martin) Hinze
E. Gary Martin
Karen (Martin) Ours
Kenneth L. Martin
Miriam (Martin) Frey
Naomi (Martin) Miller

Twila (Martin) Nations
Loretta (Metzler) Horst
Grace (Miller) Siegrist
Judith (Miller) Bomberger
Marian (Miller) Nissley
Lois (Musser) Esch
James Musser
Sara (Nafziger) Shelly
Phyllis J. Nissley
Pamela (Parks) Woods
Ruth (Ramer) Toribio
Anna Mary (Redcay) Smoker
Nathan L. Redcay
Henry Redmond
Jeanette (Reed) Weaver
Rhoda (Reinford) Charles
Marilyn (Ressler) Kreider
Julya (Rigby) Frederick
Miriam (Risser) Zehr
Esther L. Rohrer
Carl D. Sands
L. Karl Sangrey
Nancy (Sauder) Manring
Donald R. Sell
Charlotte (Shaub) Ortiz
Carolyn F. Showalter
Lloyd Smoker
Marlin R. Smoker
Ada Darlene (Snader) Hostetter
Carol Joyce Stauffer
Grace (Stauffer) DeWald
Randall L. Steffy
Betty Lou Stoltzfus
Darlene (Stoltzfus) Smoker
Larry J. Stoltzfus
Lee J. Stoltzfus **M**
Linda (Stoltzfus) Richardson
Lorraine C. Stoltzfus
Lynetta (Stoltzfus) Snyder
Muriel (Stoltzfus) King
Nathan A. Stoltzfus
Eugene R. Strite
Rebecca (Thomas) Noll **T**
J. Mark Wagner
Deborah (Weaver) Weaver
Esther (Weaver) Seibel
Jean (Weaver) Minnich
Julia (Weaver) Sensenig
Karen (Weaver) Sensenig **S**
Miriam (Weaver) Huckeba
Stephen K. Weaver
Gerald L. Wenger
Hans Wenger
Larry L. Wenger
Ruth A. (Witmer) Kulp
John David Wolgemuth
Mary (Wolgemuth) Bixler
Nancy (Yunginger) Keefer
Joanne (Zimmerman) Martin

Class of 1973

Paul Angstadt
Edith (Augsburger) Weaver
David Baer
Charlene (Beam) Frank
Wayne L. Becktold **P**
Kae (Beiler) Groshong
Luke Beiler
Martha (Beiler) Miller
Curtis Book
Gerald S. Breneman
David W. Brubaker
Doris (Brubaker) Wenger
Sheryl (Buckwalter) Eberly
Wendy (Burchfield) Doherty
Donna (Burkhart) Shank
Kevin N. Burkholder

Phyllis (Byler) Maust
Faith (Charles) Stauffer
Joseph I. Charles
Sylvia (Clymer) Helmuth **S**
Alan Diffenbach
Arlene (Eberly) Kennell
Linda (Eberly) Miller
Lois (Eberly) Stoltzfus
Marian Eberly
Mary (Ebersole) Engel
Doris (Eby) Metzler
Lynn L. Eshleman
Cindy (Forry) Herr
Carl Fredrick
Grace (Garber) Hollinger
Judith (Garber) Zook
Robert M. Gehman
Nelson R. Gingrich
Karen Glass-Hess
C. Jane (Gochnauer) Brubaker
Robert W. Good
David H. Graybill
James L. Groff
Jean (Harnish) Hoover
Karen (Heller) Ruiz
Bernell J. Hernley
Edward W. Herr
Joyce (Hershey) King
Rosemary (Hershey) Miller
Carol (Hess) Martin
Jane (Hess) Nicholas
J. Richard Hess
J. Robert Hess
Mary Lois (Hess) Clay
John Hollinger
Donald L. Hoover
Eileen (Horning) Weaver
Rodney Horning
Margaret (Horst) Smith
Sue (Horst) Kanagy
Dale R. Hostetter
Rosene (Hostetter) Burkholder
Leanna (Hottenstein) Metzler
Kenneth L. Hurst
Barbara (Kauffman) Freeman
Judy (Kauffman) Holleger
Twila (Kauffman) Yoder
Sharon (Keener) Yeager
William S. Keens
Janet (Keller) Blosser
James Kennel **M**
Lowell King
Marvin King
Dorcas Kraybill-Hutton
Connie (Kreider) Bender
Floyd W. Kurtz
Phillip D. Kurtz **V**
Donna (Landis) Brubaker
Jay Landis
Ruth Ann (Landis) Miller
Steven Landis
Reba (Lantz) King **L**
N. Carol (Lapp) Stoltzfus
Ronald M. Leaman
Audrey (Lehman) Swartzentruber
Ruby (Lehman) Wright
David I. Lennon
Jean (Lentz) Martin
Terry D. Longenecker
Glenda (Mack) Childs
Brenda (Martin) Sauder
D. David Martin
Dale G. Martin
Gilbert N. Martin
Glen R. Martin
Linda (Martin) Martin
Ray L. Martin
Revenda (Martin) Nolt

Susan A. (Martin) Eby
Larry D. Mast
Frederick D. Miller
Merle G. Miller
Phyllis (Miller) Swartz
Lynn (Moore) Leaman
Leslie (Murphy) Book
Ruth (Musser) Good
Marlin Nafziger
Doris (Neff) Sell
Paul N. Newcomer
Mary Ellen Nissley **T**
Milford M. Nissley
Carolyn (Nolt) Kuhns
Charlotte (Nolt) Smoker
Frank L. Nolt
Arnold L. Petersheim
Robert Petersheim
Waneta (Petersheim) Freeman
Alta (Raifsnider) Shank
Elizabeth (Reitz) Carlson
Marlene (Ressler) Martin
Cheryl (Rohrer) Hess
Russell Rohrer
Mary Beth (Rutt) Kautz
J. Dennis Sangrey
John E. Sauder
Ray Sauder
Ellene (Siegrist) Gerow
Melvin Sensenig
Marilyn (Shenk) Charles
Jean (Shearer) Stoltzfus
Kathryn (Smoker) Miller
V. Daniel Smoker
Ada (Snader) Martin
Naomi (Snader) Hannay
Mary Ella Stauffer
Joseph A. Stahl
John D. Stauffer
Sharon (Stauffer) Graybill
Linford Stoltzfus
Joyce Stoner
William Street
Beverly (Strickler) Hess
Darlene (Strickler) Solari
Joyce (Strite) Lehman
Ruth Ann Swartzentruber
Rachel (Thomas) Pellman
Kenneth M. Umble
Marlin R. Umble
Shirley (Umble) Lambert
Beth (Weaver) Gingrich
D. Lamar Weaver
Donald E. Weaver
Janice (Weaver) Long
Karen J. Weaver
Pauline (Weaver) Webb
S. Marlene (Weaver) Ulrich
Jay Nelson Weaver
Joyce (Weaver) Hess
Carol L. Weber
Sharon (Weber) Lauzus
Mark R. Wenger
Dwight Wissler
Arlene (Witmer) Yoder +
Barbara (Witmer) Brubaker
Donna (Witmer) Charles
Doris (Witmer) Fahnestock
Veryl Witmer
Joan (Yoder) Mills
Rhoda (Yoder) Fisher
Janice (Zeiset) Weaver
Keith L. Zimmerman

Class of 1974

Lindell (Albin) Asper **T**
Anna (Allgyer) Weaver
Betty (Bechtel) Yoder

Marlin R. Beiler
Rachel (Beiler) Blanck
Yvonne (Beiler) Groff
Judith (Benner) Frei
Beverly (Blank) Gray
Lynne (Bomberger) Williams L
Christopher S. Book
Rodney M. Breckbill
Debra (Brenneman) Kohl
Joanne (Brubaker) Wenger
Nancy (Brubaker) Gochnauer
Lois (Buchen) Kennel
Linda (Burkholder) Weaver
Cynthia Carter
Stephanie Carter
Ellen (Charles) Aronson
Stephen G. Charles
Marilyn (Clemens) Hostetler
Sharon (Clymer) Landis
Karen (Deiter) Harnish
Glen M. Denlinger
Rebecca M. Dietz
Gerald L. Engel
Keith H. Eshleman
Lois (Forry) Landis
Lois (Forwood) King
Dean L. Frank
Mariann (Frederick) Martin
Joe C. Garber
Lester W. Gehman
Norman G. Gerhart
Dale R. Gingrich
James N. Glick
Susan (Glick) Ruth
Verna (Glick) Beiler
Patricia (Gochnauer) Lee
Delores (Good) Shirk
Dorcas (Good) Breckbill
John H. Graybill
Anita (Groff) Lowry
John Harvey Groff
Marlin G. Groff
Ruth (Harnish) Yoder
Nancy (Herr) Charles
Rose A. Herr
Connie (Hershey) Knight
Eileen (Hershey) Newcomer
James E. Hershey
Janice (Hershey) Kreider
Kathleen Hershey
Randall J. Hershey
Steven R. Hershey
Julia M. (Herzler) Quickel
Merle E. Hertzler
Philip R. Hertzler
Andrew B. Hess
Gerald D. Hess
Joesph S. Hess
Joyce (Hess) Shertzer
L. Sue (Hess) Kawase S
Brenda J. (Hollinger) Grimes
Sharon (Hoover) Whitely
Doris (Horst) Toll
J. Elvin Hostetter
David T. Kauffman
Galen R. Kauffman
James M. Kauffman
Arlin J. Kennel V
Fred R. Kennel
Kenneth D. King
William S. King
Fred L. Kniss
Daniel W. Kurtz
Kenneth D. Kurtz
Betty (Landis) Peifer
Nancy (Landis) Abreu
Tim N. Landis
Bonita (Lapp) Rohrer
Glenda (Lapp) Derstler

James R. Lapp
Miriam K. Lauver
David H. Lefever
James B. Lefever
Donna (Lehman) Gerhart
Joyce J. Lind
Duane B. Longenecker +
Brenda (Martin) Hurst
Jay L. Martin
Joanne (Martin) Miller
Robin D. Martin
Sharon (Martin) Kurtz
Sharon (Martin) Lefever
Thomas A. Martin
Julia (Mast) Horst
Naomi (Mast) Moyer
Lois (Miller) Zook
Michael L. Miller
Shirley (Miller) Hershey
Sylvia (Musser) Eberly
Kenneth L. Nafziger P
Shirley (Nafziger) Lyne
Dale E. Nissley
Susan (Patterson) Martin
Ann (Raifsnider) Howard
Joyce (Ranck) Reed
Darrell J. Redcay
Loretta (Redcay) Gehman
Randall L. Redcay
Marian (Reitz) Harnish
Richard E. Reitz
Marilyn (Rheinheimer) Umble
Patricia Rohrer
Vera A. Rohrer
Carol (Rutt) Landis
Twila (Sauder) Smoker
Evelyn (Singer) Givens
Marjorie S. Shenk
Ann (Smoker) Crawford
Reba (Smoker) Beeson M
Timothy J. Smoker
Carolyn (Smucker) Bauer
Ruthie (Smucker) Smoker
David L. Snader
Lou Ann (Snyder) Gehman
Rachel K. Stahl
Grace (Stoltzfus) Miller
Jay M. Stoltzfus
Jolene (Stoltzfus) Shippy
Nolan L. Stoltzfus
Barry D. Stoner
Darlene R. Stoner
Larry G. Stoner
Janet (Troxel) Morrison
Jay M. Umble
Sandra (Umble) Lusby
Bonnie (Weaver) Tincher
Leonard M. Weaver
Patricia (Weaver) Smith
Sharon L. Weaver
Diane (Weber) Reitz
Nelson E. Weber
Ann (Weinhold) Balmer
Stephen L. Wert
D. Lamar Witmer
J. Robert Witmer
Sheryl (Witmer) Benzinger
Ruth (Wolf) Wagner
Elizabeth (Wolgemuth) Johns
Andrew B. Wright
Hope E. Yoder
Joanna (Yovanovich) Dohner
Rebecca (Zeager) Ebersole
Cynthia (Zimmerman) Musselman
Cynthia (Zimmerman) Rouvre
Regina (Zook) Yoder
Ronald E. Zook

Class of 1975

Philip M. Baker-Shenk
Erma Diane Bechtel
Harold L. Bechtold
Clair E. Beiler
Philip B. Beiler
Carol (Blank) Longenecker
Myron V. Bontrager
Dale E. Bowman
Beth (Breneman) Yoder
Anne (Brubaker) Roth
Rachel (Brubaker) Witmer
Shirley B. Bucher
Sandra (Burkhart) Smoker S
Jay M. Burkholder
Samuel G. Charles
Sharon (Charles) Weaver
Sharyn (Charles) Tieszen
Clair L. Dise
Allen W. Dzugan
J. Lamar Eberly
Willard L. Eberly
Calvin E. Esh
Marilyn (Fisher) Hollinger
Gerald L. Frey
John D. Frey
Marion (Gehman) Good
Nelson D. Gehman
Sally (Gehman) Martin
Rhonda (Gibson) Cochrane
Trula N. Gingrich
Twila N. Gingrich
Thelma E. Gochnauer
C. Bernell Good P
Marge (Good) Balsbaugh
S. Jeanne (Good) Horst
Stephen J. Good
James L. Groff
Galen J. Guengerich
Carol (Haller) Hurst
Philip N. Hargrow
Clifford L. Harnly L
Lynn G. Heller
Rosene (Hernley) Rohrer +
Cindy (Herr) Shellenberger
Eugene H. Herr
Heidi N. Hershey
Karen (Hershey) Roes
Sylvia (Hershey) Martin
Fred Hertzler
James E. Hess
Jeanne (Hess) Martin
Richard H. Hess
Susan (Hess) Chupp
Susan (Hess) Rittenhouse
Darla (High) Berg
J. Daniel Hollinger
Jeffery Hoover
Shirley M. Hoover
Kathleen (Horning) Brubaker
Arnold R. Horst
Joyce (Horst) Rusin
Sharon (Hurst) Harnish
David C. Jacobs
J. Kenneth Kauffman
J. Robert Kauffman
Marlin D. Kauffman
Mary Jane (Kauffman) Miller
Norman R. Kauffman
Daniel W. Keener
John H. Kilby
Willliam L. Kilby
Amos J. King V
Donna (King) Mosebach
Jeffrey L. King
Rodney D. King
Beverly (Kreider) Jacoby
Diane (Kreider) Keller

Joan (Kreider) Buckwalter
Karen (Kreider) Stoltzfus
Sharon (Kunkle) Stauffer
Edward L. Landis
Marie (Landis) Burkholder
Timothy D. Landis
Ivan D. Lantz
Donna (Lapp) Stoltzfus
Glenn A. Lapp
Wayne E. Lapp
Lois (Leaman) Jantzi
Nelson E. Longenecker
Philip A. Lutz
Daryl Mack
Calvin J. Martin
Darrell R. Martin
Dawn (Martin) Hollinger
Eileen (Martin) Stahl
Harold K. Mast
Wanda (Matthews) Kilby
Brenda (Metzler) Reist
Angela (Miller) Petersheim
Eric Miller
Fred A. Miller
Marilyn (Miller) Denlinger T
Paul D. Miller
Jon E. Moore
Bert A. Nestlerode
Philip N. Newcomer
Kathy (Newswanger) Martin
J. Melvin Nissley
Marilyn (Nissley) Swartz *
Audrey M. Patterson M
Audrey (Petersheim) Mast
Lynn A. Petersheim
Richard L. Petersheim
Naomi S. Ranck
Velma (Redcay) Landis
Michael R. Rheinheimer
Gerald E. Risser
Judy (Rohrer) Diller
Norvel C. Rohrer
Marilyn F. Ruth
Karen (Sands) Lytle
Janice (Sangrey) Bucher
Regina (Sensenig) Siegrist
Harold M. Shellenberger
Ann Marie Shenk
Cyndi (Shenk) Dawson
Donald L. Shenk
Henry L. Shenk
Lowell R. Showalter
Susan (Siegrist) Zimmerman
Pearl (Singer) Schwartz
Allen G. Smoker
Velma (Smoker) Sensenig
Ada (Smucker) Groff
Julie (Snyder) Zimmerman
Joy (Stahl) Weaver
Loretta (Stauffer) Esh
J. Scott Steffy
Cynthia (Stoltzfus) Beiler
Mary Beth (Stoltzfus) Jones
Miriam (Stoltzfus) Beiler
Ruth Ann Stoltzfus
Sara (Stoltzfus) Bushong
Vernon L. Stoltzfus
Dennis L. Stoner
Doris (Umble) McCreary
Sue (Umble) Verdegem
Doris J. (Weaver) Kling
Edgar A. Weaver
E. Eugene Weaver
Fred L. Weaver
Jerle B. Weaver
Joy (Weaver) Hershey
Marlin D. Weaver
Rachel (Weaver) Tann
R. Dennis Weaver

Roland R. Weaver
Vernon W. Weaver
Karen (Weinhold) Weiler
Philip R. Wenger
Sharon (Wert) Kauffman
Betty Witmer
David M. Witmer
Ellen (Wolgemuth) Rinier
John J. Yoder
Joy (Yoder) Maust
Lisa L. Yoder
Richard C. Yunginger
John C. Zimmerman
Judith (Zimmerman) Walter
Abraham Zuniga

Class of 1976

Lorraine (Albin) Williams
Franklin D. Albrecht **P**
Andrew F. Augsburger
James W. Baer
Rosene (Beachy) Eby
Dan H. Becker
Dale L. Beiler
Floyd D. Beiler
Karen J. Beiler
Loretta (Beiler) Smucker
Paul E. Beiler
Miriam (Breneman)
  Brenneman
J. Richard Brenneman
Sharon (Buckwalter)
  Seldomridge
Vincent L. Buckwalter
Rosemary R. Burkholder
Laverne (Clymer) Lindner
Brenda (Dagen) Beiler
Deryl L. Denlinger
Ronald K. Denlinger
Annette (Diffenbach) Hertzler
Naomi (Dutcher) Leaman
Donna (Eby) Buckwalter
Elaine (Eckman) Stoltzfus
Jay R. Embleton **V,+**
Carol Jean (Engel) Lantz
Leslie E. Erb
Susanna Jane (Esh) Fisher
Joseph A. Forry
Audrey (Frank) Rohrer
Mary Elizabeth Frankhouser
Susan (Frey) Howard
Susan (Frey) Steffy
Twila J. Frey **T**
Jo Anne K. Funk
Fred R. Garber
Lyle J. Gascho
Diane E. Gehman
Florence (Gehman) Weber
Judith (Gerlach) Beltz
Marie (Ginder) Miller
Barbara L. Gingrich
Lynn (Gish) Walker
Erika (Good) Norton
Joyce (Good) Doberstein
Marcia (Good) Maust **L**
Jeffrey D. Harnish
Rosene (Harnish) High
Shirley (Harnish) Redcay
Susan (Herr) Neff
Cynthia P. Hess
Lucille (Hess) Witmer
Nancy (High) Engel
Julia (Hollinger) Wray
J. Ronald Horning
Rachel (Horst) McLaughlin
Sharon (Horst) Bollinger
Cindy (Hostetter) Talbott **S**
Sylvia (Hostetter) Weaver

G. Robert Hostetter
Kathy (Hostetter) Mast
Margaret M. Huth
Thelma (Kauffman) Olinger
Joanna (Keener) Colby
J. Willard Keener
Grace (Kennel) Zimmerman
Suzanne (Kepiro) Yoder
Galen E. King
Kevin Paul King
Michael L. King
Barry R. Kreider
Brenda (Kreider) Pascotti
Debbie L. Kreider
Dottie (Kreider) Toronchuk
Cheryl J. Landis
Janice (Landis) Martin
Richard E. Landis
Sarah (Landis) Stoltzfus
Sharon (Landis) Embleton
Maria (Landrau) Zayas
Sanford D. Lapp
Frances (Leaman) Shenk
Timothy J. Lease
Yvonne (Lefever) Hershey
Doris (Lehman) Kauffman
Doris A. Lehman
Robin (Lehman) Snyder
John D. Lehman
Crystal Lehman-King
Rosanne (Longenecker) Shenk **M**
C. Conrad Martin
Fredrick L. Martin
Irvin R. Martin
Judith (Martin) Weaver
Linford L. Martin
Patricia (Martin) Henderson
Regina M. Martin
Amanda (Mast) Graybill
Freda (Mast) Petersheim
Steve G. Mast
Rosene (Metzler) Gehman
Barbara (Miller) Keener
Glenn E. Miller
Cynthia (Nafziger) Detweiler
Joyce (Neff) Slabaugh
Steven C. Neff
Ann (Newswanger) Weaver
Carolyn (Nissley) Stoltzfus
Elaine (Nolt) Patterson
I. Wesley Nolt
Hilda Rosa Oyola
James L. Ranck
Ronald L. Ressler
Robert L. Rohrer
S. Darlene Rohrer-Meck
Sue (Rutt) Glick
Joyce (Sauder) Davenport
Rhonda (Sauder) Weber **L**
Cynthia (Sell) Redcay
Christine (Sensenig) Hertzler
Wanda C. Shipe
Chris R. Slabaugh
Barb (Smoker) Dolinger
Karen (Smoker) Brooks
Betty (Smucker) Lull
Eugene Z. Smucker
John D. Stahl-Wert
Clair Stauffer
Esther (Stauffer) Wenger
James Stauffer
Jeffrey M. Stauffer
Joyce (Stauffer) Enck
Joan (Steffy) Ranck
Aden D. Stoltzfus
Brenda (Stoltzfus) Kauffman
Calvin D. Stoltzfus
Clayton E. Stoltzfus
Dorothea (Stoltzfus) Hostetter

J. Myron Stoltzfus
Kevin J. Stoltzfus
Linda (Stoltzfus) Wingard
Melody (Stoltzfus) Stoltzfus
Suellen M. Stoltzfus
David R. Stutzman
Dorothy (Stutzman) Yesilonis
Brenda (Sweigart) Neff
Carl E. Thomas
Art K. Umble
Judith F. Weaver
Linford A. Weaver
Sylvia (Weaver) Yoder
Valerie (Weaver) Derk
Wilma (Weaver) Horst
Cheryl J. Weber
Linford R. Weber
Shirley (Weber) Migliazza
Ann L. White
Dennis L. Witmer
Jon K. Witmer
Jesse Wolgemuth
William M. Wood
Charity (Yoder) Lapp
Dean E. Youndt
Lester A. Zeager
M. Craig Zimmerman
June E. (Zimmerman) Kreider
Reynold L. Zimmerman
Sharon (Zimmerman) Good

Class of 1977

Audrey (Augsburger) Groff
Joanne Marie Beachy
Daniel G. Beiler
Lorraine (Bender) Brown
Lamar M. Benner
Marcia J. Benner
Ivan J. Blank
J. Michael Bontrager
Leon M. Bowman
Mary (Bowman) Brown
J. Larry Breneman
Dennis Brubaker
Richard L. Buckwalter
William R. Buckwalter
Carol (Burkhart) Spicher **S**
Virgie G. (Burkholder) Hurst
Leonard J. Clymer
Philip J. Dietz
William Dimitris
Nancy E. Downs
Cynthia (Ebersole) Blank
Jane (Eby) Meck
Linda (Eby) Ringer
Brenda (Esch) Epp
Leanne (Eshleman) Benner
Marty (Fisher) Smucker
Debra (Frederick) Groff
Sandra (Frey) Thomas
Jane (Gehman) Wiens
Carolyn (Geib) Stauffer
Tammi (Gibson) Nash
Robin (Gleim) White
David L. Gochnauer
Lauren R. Good
Marcus A. Good
Daryl C. Groff
Devon Eugene Groff
E. Lois (Groff) Hershey
Millard Hahn
Cheryl (Harnish) Burkholder
Randal G. Harris
Joanne (Herr) Good
Verna Mae (Hershey) Kerns
Jeanette (Hertzler) Martin
Joe David Hertzler
Carol Y. Hess **T**

Dean F. Hess
Esther (Hess) Jackson
Kathleen (Hess) Shuman
Louann (Hollinger) Weaver
Shirley (Hollinger) Plank
Jay Hoover
Larry L. Horning
Shirley A. Horst
Rhonda (Hostetter) Lapp
Ina Sue (Housman) Fox **P**
Jay Huber
Steven D. Jarvis
Cindi (Kanagy) Reeser
Janet (Kauffman) Stauffer
Jeanette (Kauffman) Brooks
Ruth Ann (Keens) Martin
Susan (Kennel) Lincoln
Timothy L. Kennel
David R. King
Leon S. Kraybill **L**
Cheryl (Kreider) Shank
Joni C. (Kreider) Alzate
Marian (Kreider) Groff
Susan (Kreider) Smith
Gary L. Kunkle
Dale L. Landis
Kenneth H. Landis
Bertha C. Lantz
Doug E. Lapp
Joyce (Lapp) Schmidt
Randall L. Lapp
Timothy J. Lapp
Lillian (Lauver) Weaver
Marilyn (Lehman) Miller
Nancy (Lehman) Allgyer
Gregory L. Lehr
Jo Ann Longenecker
Carol A. Martin
Cheryl (Martin) Martin
Dean Edward Martin **V**
Gerald K. Martin
Lauren R. Martin
Alvin E. Mast
Daniel D. Mast
David L. Mast
Audrey D. Metzler
Dennis E. Metzler
Lawrence D. Metzler
Donald B. Miller
Krista (Miller) Petersheim
Lois (Miller) Glick
Miriam (Miller) Frey
Ron Eugene Miller
Linda (Nafziger) Beiler
Yvonne (Nafziger) Miller
Christine (Newswanger) Reiste
Hong T. Nguyen
Maurice Nissley
Gregory S. Oberholtzer
Judith (Peifer) Bowman
David L. Peters
Greg Petersheim
Debra (Pierantoni) Gibson
Lloyd M. Raifsnider III
Patsy (Ranck) Rhodes
Twila (Redcay) Stoltzfoos
Grace Reed
Philip Reinford
Linda (Ressler) Hunt
Carmelo M. Rodriquez
Anna (Rohrer) Ressler
Linda Kay (Rohrer)
  Longenecker
Nancy L. Ruth
Ann L. Rutt
Mervin S. Rutt
D. Jeanette (Sangrey) Barber
Joanne L. Sauder
Kathleen (Schnupp)

Buffenmyer
Beth E. Sensenig
Carolyn (Sensenig) Hoffman
Sharon (Sensenig)
  Swartzentruber
Margaret L. Shenk
Ronald L. Shenk
Dale E. Shirk
Linden A. Showalter
Brenda (Simpson) Brackbill
Thomas C. Smith
Charity (Smoker) Stoltzfus
Mary Lou Smoker
Darlene K. Snader
David L. Snader
Rhoda (Snavely) Eberly
Eunice (Stahl) Zeager
Audrey (Stoltzfus) Fetters
Brenda J. Stoltzfus
Chester L. Stoltzfus
Duane C. Stoltzfus **M**
Eric W. Stoltzfus
Mervin L. Stoltzfus
Nathan L. Stoltzfus
Randy J. Stoltzfus
Vernon S. Stoltzfus
Wilma J. Stoltzfus
Judy M. Stoner
Brian L. Thomas
Julie Tran
Joanne (Umble) Weaver
William L. Umble
Carmen (Weaver) Horst
J. Marlin Weaver
Lamar Conrad Weaver
Lucinda (Weaver)
  Swartzentruber+
Mark A. Weaver
John F. Weber
Phyllis (Weaver) Weiler
Sharon (Weaver) Nolt
Susan (Weaver) Martin
Sandra (Wert) Groff
Harold Wharton-Hege
Cynthia B. Witmer
Gina (Witmer) Plain
J. Leonard Wolf
Jay Michael Yoder
Nathan D. Yoder
Nancy (Yoder) Harnish
Mary (Yunginger) Rittenhouse
Ranee C. Zimmerman

Class of 1978

Judy (Albrecht) Bunting
Melanie A. Baer
Julia (Bare) Horst
Laurie (Bartlett) Abel
William Beam
Deborah L. Becker
Marian E. Becker
John Wayne Beiler
Nelson R. Blank
Judy (Brower) Groff
Jan A. Brubaker
Lois J. Brubaker
Nathan W. Brunk
Alice (Buckwalter) Schmidt
Brenda (Burkhart) Blank
Anna (Burkhart) Martin
Brenda G. Burkholder
Daniel E. Charles **M**
Phyllis (Charles) Beachy
Steve Charles
Lois Ann Deiter
Cynthia (Denlinger) Mast
Dwayne L. Denlinger
Mary Ann (Denlinger) Lehman

Anna Lois Dietz
Donna (Eberly) Horst
Judy (Eberly) Ricca **+**
Barbara (Esh) Lapp **T**
Louise (Eshleman) Yoder **L**
Kevin R. Espenshade **L**
Edythe (Finney) Roggie
Kathy June Frey
James P. Gamber
David A. Garber
Dawn (Garber) Meck
Nancy R. Garman
Daryl L. Gehman
Ronald L. Geib
Nelson R. Geigley
Beverly (Ginder) Hurst
Kenneth L. Gingrich
Paul R. Gingrich
Dennis L. Glick
Carol (Good) Yoder
Don M. Good
Deborah (Gotshall) Kauffman
Sandra (Graber) Bauman
Geoffrey C. Groff
Herbert E. Groff
J. Randall Groff
Norman L. Hahn
Nevin L. Herr
Clifford N. Hershey
Nathan R. Hershey
J. Randall Hertzler
Sharon (Hess) Hostetter
John A. Hiestand
Linda (High) Stoltzfus
Brenda (Hollinger) Augsburger
Edwin R. Hollinger
Ellen R. Hollinger **S**
Joseph L. Hollinger
Joyce (Hollinger) Haller
Linda (Hornberger) Hildebrand
Mervin E. Horst
N. Timothy Horst
Arthur N. Hostetter
Chris Nelson Hostetter
Galen H. Hostetter
Sandra (Huber) Lutz
Alan R. Jacobs
Lamar E. Kanagy
Michele (Kann) Anderson
R. Faye Keener
Deborah (King) Bowman
Dorothy (King) Burkhart
Earl D. King
Sharon (King) Wilbers
Rosemary Knapp
Jeanette (Knechtel) Moser
Linda (Kreider) Metzler
Elvin Kurtz
Debra (Landis) Herr
Karl R. Landis **P**
Santa Landrau
Paul E. Lantz
Lois M. Lapp
Richie D. Lapp
Anne (Leaman) Klassen
Naomi (Leaman) Weaver
Yvonne (Leaman) Garber
Joy C. Lehman
Stephen R. Lehman
Rebecca (Lease) Brasch
Anne L. Martin
Anne (Martin) Weaver
Audrey (Martin) Snader
Cathleen (Martin) Long
Cheryl (Martin) Horst
Daniel L. Martin
Janet (Martin) Yoder
J. Donald Martin
Maietta (Martin) Ludwig

Raedella (Martin) Martin
Rose Ann (Martin) Gonzales
Sylvia (Martin) Swartzentruber **+**
Harvey E. Mast
Titus McCrone
Naomi (Metzler) Martin
Barbara L. Miller
Jane Y. Miller
Jay B. Miller **V**
Susan E. (Miller) Auker
June (Nafziger) Eberly
R. Bruce Newswanger
Wanda (Nolt) Musser
Kathleen (Oberholtzer) Sauder
Carmen (Oyola) Rivera
Luis E. Oyola
Richard E. Patterson
John H. Pogue
Carol (Raifsnider) Gehman
Faye (Ramer) Ting
Eileen J. Ranck
James Ranck
Peggy (Ranck) Nolt
Glenda (Redcay) Martin
Betty (Reiff) Buch
Joyce (Reinford) Hunsberger
Kathy (Rheinheimer) Embleton
Wanda J. Rohrer-Heyerly
Janice (Sangrey) Mitchell
Gary L. Sauder
J. Anthony Sauder
James L. Sauder
Laura A. Schmucker
Cheryl (Sell) Hollinger
Anne R. Sensenig
Robert Dale Shearer
Kathleen (Shelley) Gerig
J. David Shenk
Nancy (Slabaugh) Spicher
Glenn R. Smoker
Sheryl (Smoker) King
Jay W. Smucker
Marcus A. Sollenberger
Joann (Stauffer) Mellinger
M. David Stauffer
Ruth (Stauffer) Martin
Sherry (Starr) Steiner
Cindy (Stoltzfus) Fyffee
Gerald S. Stoltzfus
J. Dale Stoltzfus
Joyce (Stoltzfus) Blank
Karen (Stoltzfus) Horning
Mahlon J. Stoltzfus
Mary Beth (Stoltzfus) Martin
Rhoda (Stoltzfus) Kroeker
Ralph E. Swartzentruber
D. Richard Thomas
Pamela Tucker
Richard T. Walter
Kevin D. Warfel
Carol (Weaver) Collins
Kenneth L. Weaver
Lorraine (Weaver) Leininger
Martha J. Weaver
Timothy J. Weaver
Gerald L. Weinhold
J. Darryl Wenger
J. Richard Wenger
Jsmes N. Wenger
O. Martin Wenger
Tom M. Wenger
Richard L. Winey
Jeffrey G. Witmer
R. Lamar Witmer
Ruth M. Wolgemuth
Susan (Yocum) Simonson
Karl D. Yoder
Leon D. Yoder
Daniel Youngquist

Class of 1979

Anita (Augsburger) Hostetter
Michael C. Beachy
Diane (Beam) Alvarez
Douglas J. Beam
Ann (Beiler) Lapp
Fanny (Beiler) Smucker **S**
Larry L. Beiler
Rosalind Beiler
V. Kevin Beiler
C. Grant Bitterman
Charlotte (Blank) Martin
Kathleen (Boll) Keener
Elizabeth A. Brandt
Kay (Breneman) Haldman
Cathy (Brubaker) Keener
Edward D. Brubaker
E. Rosene (Bruckhart) Weaver
Barbara L. Burkhart
Janet (Burkhart) Groff
Donna M. Carper
Teresa (Dagen) Graybill
Rebecca (Dorwart) Weis
Lee Eugene Ebersole
Jerry L. Embleton
Joyce Elaine Erb
Fred L. Esbenshade
Linda (Esh) Hershey
Dale R. Frank
Kere J. Frey
Elaine (Garber) Ostrum
Dale L. Gehman
Douglas M. Gerlach
John D. Gerlach Jr.
Karen (Glick) Beckler
Herbert H. Graybill
Dean L. Groff
Kathleen (Groff) Nissley
Sherry (Groff) Snader
Jean E. Herr
Dale L. Hershey
Ronald L. Hershey
Paul J. Hertzler
Bertha M. Hess
Park E. Hess
Randall L. Hollinger
Suzanne (Horning) Baker
Judy (Horst) Peterson
Lester D. Horst
Stanley R. Horst
Jerry D. Hostetter
Kathy (Hostetter) Faber
Karen (Hostetter) Miller
Wendy D. Huber
Rosa Huyard
Jay G. Keener
Sue Ellen (Keener) Bender
Elvin N. Kennel **P**
Robert L. Kilby
Dorothy (King) Bontrager
Cheryl (Kreider) Carey
Jeffrey C. Kreider
Brad L. Kunkle
Marianne (Kurtz) Yoder
Charlene M. Landis
Herbert E. Landis
Ira Jay Landis
Stuart L. Landis **V**
Diane (Lantz) Umble
Janelee (Lapp) Strain
Philip R. Lapp
Samuel J. Lapp
Deborah J. Leaman
Larry L. Leaman
Laurie (Leaman) Lundquist
Grace (Lefever) Stoltzfus **T**
Kate (Lehr) Quinn
Michael L. Longenecker

Sharon Lopez
Anne (Martin) Dienner
Kathy (Martin) Frey
J. Darryl Martin
Randall S. Martin
A. Rebecca (Mast) Martin
Bruce J. Mast
Dale J. Mast
Regena (Mast) Burkhart
Sharon L. Mast
Cathy (Matthews) Bausman
Edwin B. Miller
J. Mark Miller
Marcella (Miller) Reynolds
M. Lamar Miller
Valerie (Miller) Baer
W. Edwin Miller
Ronald L. Mummau **M**
Gerald R. Mylin
Earl L. Neff
James L. Nissley
Nancy (Nolt) Burkholder
Edward B. Nyce
Dean R. Peters
John Petersheim
Ralph L. Petersheim
William K. Poole
Eileen (Raifsnider) Wheeler
Esther (Ramer) Zoss
Merle L. Ranck
Beth (Ritz) Meder
Heather Rodenberger **+**
Brenda (Rohrer) Landis
Dawn (Root) Zook
John David Sauder
Leon M. Sell
Gary Sensenig
Geoffrey L. Sensenig
Pearl Sensenig
Phyllis (Sensenig) Weaver
Nelson E. Shaiebly
Anita (Shelly) Maneval
J. Edward Shenk
Kevin R. Shenk
Steve L. Shenk **L**
J. Jacob Shirk
Karen (Shultz) Baynard
John W. Smoker
Karen (Smoker) Hillyard
James E. Smucker
Nathan G. Snyder
J. Merle Sollenberger
Marjorie (Stauffer)
   Montgomery
Cynthia (Steffy) Stayrook **+**
Arthur R. Stoltzfus
Clair Eugene Stoltzfus
Dale Eugene Stoltzfus
Dwight L. Stoltzfus
Ernest L. Stoltzfus
Grant H. Stoltzfus
Henry Stoltzfus
Joy (Stoltzfus) Snader
Keith N. Stoltzfus
Marilyn (Stoltzfus) White
Marlin L. Stoltzfus
Pearl (Stoltzfus) Beiler
Randy Lee Stoltzfus
Susan (Stoltzfus) Smoker
Tina (Stoltzfus) Frey
Wayne L. Stoltzfus
Barbara (Stoner) Carper
Beverly K. (Stutzman) Smeltzer
Lenardo Torres
Joanne (Troxel) Skaggs
Cheryl R. Weaver
Clarence M. Weaver
Jeffrey L. Weaver
Kathy (Weaver) Hertzler

Linda (Weaver) Snader
Miriam (Weaver) Agnew
Jean (Weber) Good
Jeff K. Weber
Clifford R. Wenger
Karen (Wenger) Meyers
Brenda (Wert) Berthold
Susan (Wise) Deputy
Duane L. Witmer
Naomi Yovanovich
Deborah (Zeager) Musselman
Diane (Zimmerman) Brunk
Philip K. Zimmerman

Class of 1980

Todd L. Andre
Paul D. Bechtold
David Becker
Marlin E. Becker
Robert L. Beiler
Steven J. Beiler
Dean M. Benner
Glenda (Beyer) Frey
Chris L. Bitterman
Keith W. Blank
Kathy (Breneman) Funk
Marlane (Breneman) Martin
Nancy (Brisbin) Hunt
Linda G. (Brubaker) Beiler
Seth Brubaker
Romaine (Bruckhart) Hollinger
Timothy L. Buckwalter
Glenn M. Burkhart
Ronald L. Burkhart
Rebecca (Burkholder) Shade
Eunice G. Charles
Ruth (Charles) Martin
Miriam (Clymer) Hurst
Rachel (Dorwart) Anderson
Linda (Eberly) Lauver
Marilyn (Eberly) Siegrist
Roger L. Esbenshade
Keith L. Espenshade
Christine E. Esch
Randall E. Esch
Rodney H. Eshleman
J. Kenneth Fisher
Raymond J. Fisher
Karl H. Frey
D. Frederic Gehman
Karen (Geigley) Anderson
Daria (Gillin) Huber
Cheryl (Gingrich) Martin
Ali Golabchi
Cheryl (Good) Munson
Kendra (Good) Rittenhouse
Patricia (Good) Russell
Dwight L. Groff
Larry K. Groff
Marcia L. (Groff) Smith
Merle E. Groff
Gregory J. Harnish
Janet (Harnish) Stauffer
Donna (Harris) Ponessa
Karen (Hess) Brown
Kathy (Hess) Dagen
R. Keller Hopkins
Beverly (Hostetter) Landis
Loretta (Hoover) Eby
Barbara (Huber) Lapp
John David Huber
Deryl M. Hurst
Dave B. Kachel
Glenn R. Kauffman
Nancy F. Kauffman
Kathleen (Keener) Shantz
Donna (Keller) Keener
J. Michael Keller

Phoebe (Kennel) Haupert
Curtis G. King
Kristal (King) Graber **S**
Timothy L. King
Beverly J. Kurtz
Carol L. Landis
Darryl L. Landis **P**
Jeffrey Mark Landis
Randy L. Lantz
Reuben Lapp
M. Pauline (Leaman) Godfrey
J. Paul Lefever
Diane (Lehman) Poole
J. Conrad Lehman
Raymond D. Lehman
David E. Lentz
Fred Longenecker
Deeter S. Lutz
Darrell L. Martin
Jeanette Martin
Karen (Martin) Forsyth
Linda J. (Martin) Espenshade
Linda (Martin) Hertzler
Philip L. Martin **V**
Robert Charles Martin
Ruth (Martin) Martin
Sue A. Martin-Senter
Susan J. Mast
Carl A. Mellinger
Cathy A. Mellinger
Michael P. Metzler
Celia (Miller) Torres
Dwight V. Miller
Joann (Miller) Hopkins
Nanette (Miller) Lamb
Beatrice N. Muganda
Judith (Mylin) Bowman
Lisa (Neil) Gilbert
Cheryl A. Nissley
Lois Ann (Nolt) Hess
Dawn (Oberholtzer) Winey
Diana (Patterson) Jacobs
Janet (Petersheim) Caley
Naomi (Petersheim) Glick
Benson W. Prigg
Cathy (Quinn) Mahorney
Dale E. Ranck
Parke H. Ranck
Charlene (Rohrer) Ranck
William G. Rohrer
Dale Root
Patricia (Sangrey) Dence
Janet (Sauder) Mellinger
Jay Richard Sauder
Philip Sauder
Bonita (Schnupp) Vlastaras
Loretta A. Seigle
Cynthia R. Shenk
J. Elvin Shenk
Dawn (Smith) Dalbow
Timothy L. Smoker
Darrell R. Snader
Donald P. Snader
Mary Lois (Stahl) Shenk
Korina A. Stauffer **T**
Julia (Steffy) Horst
Brent Stoltzfus
Donna (Stoltzfus) Neufeld
Esther (Stoltzfus) Deiter
Harold S. Stoltzfus
Jeanette (Stoltzfus) Blank
Juanita (Stoltzfus) Shenk
J. Durrell Stoltzfus
Leonard J. Stoltzfus
Pearl (Stoltzfus) Koenig
Vernon D. Stoltzfus
Lowell G. Stutzman
Rebecca K. Sweigart
Ardel (Tharp) Breon

Karel (Umble) Fisher
John C. Walter
Scott A. Walter
Steve L. Warfel
Donald J. Weaver
J. Brian Weaver
J. Michael Weaver
Lorraine (Weaver) Martin
Wendy Weaver
Monroe L. Weber-Shirk
Juanita Weber-Shirk
Joy (Wenger) Martin
D. Eugene Winters
Lois (Wise) Ndlovu
Debra S. Witmer
Sharon (Witmer) Yoder **L**
Randall L. Witmer
Diane (Yoder) Smucker
Evan M. Yoder
Jeff D. Zehr
Bonnie (Zimmerman) Hoover
Kristina (Zimmerman) Wagner
Larry J. Zook

Class of 1981

E. Scott Augsburger
Melanie (Barge) Stoltzfus
Linford D. Beachy
Sharon (Beachy) Pase
Chester O. Beiler
Christine (Beiler) King
Betty (Blank) Bauder
Joann (Bomberger) Philbin
Janice (Breneman) Weaver
Joann Brenneman
J. Calvin Bucher
Larry A. Burkart
Mary Ann (Buckwalter) Kilgore
Cindy (Carper) Hummer
Randall L. Denlinger
David B. Diffenbach
Jay L. Dombach
Gerald C. Eberly
Kendra (Eberly) Meyers
Daryl L. Ebersole
Steven Ray Eby
Joy A. Esbenshade
Wilmer S. Esh
Naomi (Frederick) Ruth
Jill (Frey) Wagner
Stacey Lynne Folk
Geraldine (Gehman) Reimer
Joanna (Gehman) Horning
Jonelle N. Gingrich
Joel S. Gish
Carol (Good) Burns
Judith A. Good
Steven Kent Graybill
Garry L. Griffin
Beth L. Harnish
Jay Harnish
Martha (Harnish) Rineer
Tonia (Harnish) Shultz
Julia Ann Herr
Carl E. Hershey **P**
Dale R. Hershey
Lawrence E. Hershey
Virginia (Hershey) Kreider
D. Donald Hess **V**
Daniel R. Hess
Darlene (Hess) Gehman
H. Joy (Hess) Stutzman
Marlene K. Hess
Linda A. High
Steven L. High
Colleen (Hollinger) Keller
Darryl R. Horst
Paul W. Horst

Timothy L. Hostetler
Suzanna (Howe) Snader
Diane (Hurst) Vincent
Anita (Kanagy) Burkholder
William E. Kanode
Charles Kauffman
Jeffrey B. Keefer
Joy (Keener) Martin T
Jolene M. Kennedy
Joy (Kennel) Hershey
Bruce E. King
Janet King
Jay Allen Kreider
Renee (Kreider) Leap
Eileen M. Kurtz
Karla (Landis) Sensenig
Kaye (Landis) Martin
Scott E. Landis
Shelby (Landis) Swartley
Shirley (Landis) Hershey
Kevin L. Lapp
Susan (Lapp) Esh
David E. Leaman
Philip B. Leaman
David M. Lefever
Emmett R. Lehman, Jr.
Gerald M. Lehman
Joann K. Lehman
Betsy (Leininger) Rudy
Phillip E. Longenecker
Dale L. Martin
Daniel W. Martin
Nancy M. Martin
Eldon R. Mast
Darrel L. McMichael
John D. Meck
B. Elaine (Mellinger) Brubaker
Bonita (Miller) Sauder
Cynthia (Miller) Schwartz
Eileen M. Miller
Karla S. (Miller) Esh
Samuel I. Miller
Terri (Miller) Michael
Twila (Miller) Sauder
Valerie (Miller) Weaver
Stephen L. Minnich
Gregory L. Myer
Sharon (Nissley) Kurtz
Brian D. Nolt
Joyce (Nyce) Longenecker
Steven S. Oberholtzer
Michelle J. Peifer
Kenton G. Peters
Nathaniel P. Pierantoni
Gary M. Pittman
Gwendolyn K. Reed
Twila (Reinford) Detweiler
Kathryn (Reitz) Zimmerman
Daniel E. Ressler
Marjorie (Rheinheimer) Silver
Sandra K. Ritz
Jane (Rutt) Weaver
J. Steven Rutt M
Rebecca Sue Rutt
Dianne (Sauder) Sensenig
Donna (Sauder) Gockley
Glenn Q. Sauder +
J. Donald Sauder
Diane Scarlota
William F. Schall
Duane L. Sell
Kevin J. Sensenig
L. Marie (Sensenig) Brenner
Lynne (Sensenig) Brubaker
Melvin L. Sensenig
Eric G. Shank
Beverly A. Shenk
Doris A. Shenk
Mary Anne (Shenk)

Sommerfeld
Mervin D. Shenk
P. Nelson Shertzer
Kathy (Shultz) Hess
R. Grace (Smoker) Petersen
Lloyd K. Smucker
Gayle (Sollenberger) Smoker
Becky (Stauffer) Wand
James R. Stauffer
Colleen J. Stoltzfus
Cynthia J. Stoltzfus
Jane (Stoltzfus) Clevenstine
Kendra (Stoltzfus) Siemers
Leanna (Stoltzfus) Weaver
Nancy (Stoltzfus) Craul
Theda (Stoltzfus) Jones S
David L. Stoner
Lowell E. Strickler
Marianne B. Stutzman
Steven A. Umble
Carol A. Weaver
J. Robert Weaver
Jenelle (Weaver) Miller
Philip M. Weaver
Richard L. Weaver
Carol Ann (Wenger) Gehman
Cynthia (Wenger) Birkness
Dawn (Wenger) Moore
Dawn (Wenger) Weaver
Gordon L. Wenger
J. Michael Winey
Kristine (Yoder) Duncan L
Mary (Yovanovich) Berguson
Mervin E. Zeager
Duane E. Zimmerman

Class of 1982

Barry Lee Adams
Charles H. Albrecht P
Carlton P. Baer
Gregory L. Barge
Michael Becker
Jennifer (Beiler) Carl
Leon M. Beiler
Lynette (Beiler) Garber
Rosalyn F. (Beiler) Dienner
Miriam E. Blank
Jewel (Boll) Garber
Paul Mark Boronow
Elaine (Brunk) Frey T
Erika L. Buchen
Herbert W. Burkhart
Linda L. Burkhart
Jesse D. Charles
Nancy (Charles) Rexroad
Brenda (Delp) Keller
Elaine (Engle) Zimmerman
Samuel M. Esh
Joanne L. Freed
Jewel (Gehman) Martin
Douglas L. Geib
Alicia J. Gingrich
Karen Jean Gingrich
Calvin W. Glick
Sarah (Glick) Andrews
Robert H. Gochenaur
Gary E. Groff
Joanne K. Groff
Susan (Groff) Sollenberger
Betty (Hampton) Weaver
Janet L. Herr
Donna (Hershey) Lehman
Betty (Hertzler) Eberly
Valerie (Hertzler) Rheinheimer
C. Edward Hess
Janice L. Hess
Twila J. Hess
Barbara (High) Martin

Marylee (Hill) Swisher
Charles A. Hoober
Elizabeth E. Hoober
Margery Ann Hostetler
Mary Jane (Horst) Leaman
Heidi (Housman) Oberholtzer
Kevin L. Hurst
Joyce R. Kauffman
Eileen (Kennel) Krabill
Mary Ellen Kennel
Kenton R. King
Kyle D. King
Lisa M. King S
Loretta (King) Buser
Sandra (King) Harnish
Terry (Kraybill) Rice
Gerald A. Kreider
John E. Kreider
Karen (Kreider) Peifer
B. Scott Kunkle
Mervin E. Kurtz +
Nathan J. Lapp
James M. Leaman
Jonathan G. Leaman L
Paul G. Leaman
Daniel C. Lehman
P. Mark Lopez
Beth (Lutz) Schock
Jane E. Manning
James L. Martin
Mary (Martin) Kennel
Patty (Martin) Metzler
Rachel (Mast) Deeds
Ralph A. Mast
Sandra R. Mast
Dale L. McMichael
Fred D. Metzler
Barbara L. Miller
Carmen E. Miller
Rebecca (Miller) Valazquez
John H. Minsek
Kenneth L. Neff
John L. Nissley
Vernon S. Nolt
Audrey (Oberholtzer) Kreider
Connie (Peifer) Becker
Stephen R. Petersheim
Harry J. Philpot
Allison (Pierantoni) Wilson
Keith Ranck
Nancy L. Ranck
Pamela (Ranck) Nolt
Linford R. Reed
Melvin W. Ressler
Lori (Scheid) Caldwell
Sharon (Seitz) Doll
Patricia A. Shelly
Audrey J. Shenk
Bonnie (Shenk) Martin
Doug L. Shenk
Harold K. Shenk
R. Daryl Shenk
Jeanne (Shirk) Sahawneh
Kristina (Shultz) Lehman V
Patrick J. Smith
Sharon (Stauffer) Reeser
Albert J. Stoltzfus
Emilie S. Stoltzfus
Glenn D. Stoltzfus
Lois (Stoltzfus) Smucker M
Marilyn (Stoltzfus) Hershey
Sherilyn (Stoltzfus) Lapp
Tracy Sue Thomas
Roxanne (Trimble) Dowlin
Ricardo C. Walters
Debra J. Warfel
Curtis B. Weaver
Daryl Weaver
Donna K. Weaver

Linda (Weaver) Good
Paula R. Weaver
Rose (Weaver) Burkhart
Cynthia A. Weber
N. Jean (Weinhold) Olivo
Heidi A. Wenger
Sherri (Wenger) Hartshaw
Brenda L. Wise
Keith D. Witmer
Rosalie (Witmer) Wichterman
Nathan Lamar Yoder
C. Randall Zimmerman
Robert G. Zook

Class of 1983

David A. Beachy
Brenda Beiler
Loren Beiler
Sam Jay Beiler
Sam R. Beiler
Sharilynn (Beiler) Wolgemuth
Bryan D. Blank
Paul D. Blank
Charles Bowen
Carol J. Brubaker
Marlene F. Brubaker
Suzanne(Buckwalter)
    McEllhenney
J. Steven Burkhart
Paula F. (Burkholder) Smoker
M. Scott Clemmer
Joyce E. Cramer
John R. Curtiss
Susan M. Detwiler
Julie M. Esh
Martha A. Fisher
Heather D. Forry
Linda S. Garber
Roger C. Garber
J. Dwane Gehman
Debra (Geib) Smith
Marie A. Gingrich
Sandra (Gochnauer) Shaiebly
Carl R. Good
Jeanette (Good) Christophel
Rosene (Good) Martin
Brian L. Groff
David E. Groff
Lisa (Groff) Nyguist
Yvonne (Groff) Nyce
David F. Harnish
April Henderson
James M. Hertzler
Elizabeth A. Hess
Karen (Hess) Groff
Larene (Hess) Miller
Mark Hickson
Lori L. High
C. Eaton Hopkins
Elaine (Horst) Shenk
Ray A. Huber
Janice (Hurst) Burkholder
J. Michael Hurst
Kevin Keener
Audrey J. King
Gerald R. King
Marilyn (King) Martin V
Carl D. Kniss
Charlene M. Kraybill
Valerie R. Kreider
Jewel H. Kurtz
Dwane L. Landis
Michael P. Landis M
Seth R. Landis
J. Ernest Lapp
Rhonda M. Lapp
Janita (Leaman) Forney
Doug P. Lehman

Barb (Leininger) Martin **L**
Kenton L. Longenecker
J. David Lutz
Bryan L. Martin
Dawn E. Martin
Douglas P. Martin
Frederick D. Martin
Gary N. Martin
Gregory S. Martin
Jay E. Martin
Kathy Sue (Martin) Smucker
Steve J. Martin
Janet Eileen Mast
Valerie A. Mast
Carla (Metzler) Kulp
Cynthia (Miller) Burkhart
Jean L. Miller
Karen R. Miller
David E. Minnich
Michael Moran
Yvonne (Nauman) Boxleitner
I. Dwane Newswanger
Lynda J. Newswanger
Michael A. Nolt
Kenneth W. Nyce **P**
Jon David Petersheim
Jeanine M. Pfeiffer **M**
J. Robert Ranck
Donald L. Reiff
Karen (Rheinheimer)
    Gochenaur
Nora Riehl
Dwight L. Root
Carl E. Sauder
H. Alan Sensenig
Trudy (Sensenig) Smith
Teresa (Shertzer) Groff
G. Dean Smith
H. Dwayne Smoker **+**
Mervin L. Smucker
Robert C. Stauffer
Kristine E. Stoesz
Brenda J. Stoltzfus
Judy M. Stoltzfus
Larry L. Stoltzfus
Scott M. Stoner
Lamar A. Strickler
Sheryl A. Thomas
Linda S. Umble
Lori Ann Umble
Dawn (Weaver) Isley
Dawn E. Weaver
Diane (Weaver) Lutz
Elizabeth Anne Weaver
Mardelle (Weaver) Root
Rebecca L. Weaver
R. Todd Weaver
Timothy L. Weaver
Jodi (Wenger) Adams
Byron C. Wert
Phillip A. Winey
Kenneth L. Winters
Sandra (Winters) Heisey
Judy (Witmer) Horst
Randall S. Wolgemuth
Ben Yao
Edith E. Yoder **T**
Gwendolyn (Yoder) Snader **S**
Nelson R. Zimmerman
Rochelle (Zimmerman) Kniss
Dwayne L. Zook

Class of 1984

Lynda S. Albin
Elizabeth J. Anderson
Kenneth D. Becker
J. Derrell Beiler
Lisa (Beiler) Nafziger

Timothy J. Boronow
Daniel J. Boyer
Sharon (Buckwalter) Martin
Robert J. Carboy
Beth Ann Carpenter
Lynette D. (Charles) Huber
Glenda F. Deiter
Nathan M. Dietz
Rodney Eberly
Denise R. Eby
LeAnn (Eby) Groff
Mary Beth Eby
J. Marvin Fisher
Marlene Fisher
Darryl B. Frey
Jay A. Garber
Anthony K. Gehman
Sharon (Gingrich) Umble
Boni (Gochenaur) Landis
Nelson Jay Good
Vickie R. Griffin
Donna E. Groff **P**
Anne E. Harnish
Leon D. Harnly
Robb E. Helsel
Cheryl (Hess) Leaman **T**
Krystal Hershberger
Douglas C. Hertzler
Christopher G. High
Pamela High
Cynthia K. Hollinger
Clair Hoover
Anne (Horning) Becker
Patricia (Hostetler) Kratz
Susan K. Hostetter
Kathy L. Hurst
Dwight D. Huyard
Rosanne (Kampen) Gingerich
Bryan Keener
James M. Kepiro
Jana L. King
Kirby D. King
Neal B. King
Vanessa G. King
Linda K. Knouse
Rosella A. Kraybill
Philip E. Kreider
Christine L. Landis **M**
David B. Landis
Scott D. Landis
Steve V. Lantz
Gary L. Lapp
Gerald V. Lapp
Michael O. Lapp
Jeffrey B. Leaman
Rodney A. Lefever
Jean Lehman
Rhoda Lehman
Kimberly D. Linderman
Douglas E. Longenecker **V,+**
Regina A. Lutz
Barbara Martin
Cheryl Lynn Martin
Cyndi J. Martin
Cynthia L. (Martin) Roth
Dan L. Martin
Eugene R. Martin
Gwenda (Martin) Snader
Randall L. Martin
Roberta (Martin) Maynard
Steven R. Martin
E. Dale Mast
E. Dean Mast
Donald L. Mellinger
Lois Jean Mellinger
Dean R. Miller
Michael Miller
Ronald J. Miller
Lucille (Mohler) Hollinger

Judy (Nissley) Rohrer
Gary M. Nolt
Gloria J. Petersheim
Ruth Anna Petersheim
Suzanne (Quick) Beiler
James M. Raifsnider
Dawn J. Ranck
Rondi (Reed) Hoover
Sandra (Regier) Unruh
Anthony Resto
Ester Riehl **L**
Gerald W. Rohrer
Michael Rohrer
Jean L. Sensenig
Jonathan C. Shenk
Jacalyn F. Shirk
Leona Ann Shirk
C. Deron Smith
Jeffery P. Smucker
Reba (Smucker) Esh
Donna (Snyder) Brubaker
Kristine K. Snyder
Doris A. Stauffer
Beverly (Stoltzfus) Kreider
Brenda S. Stoltzfus
Carolyn (Stoltzfus) Biggs
Linford R. Stoltzfus
Myron D. Stoltzfus
Joan (Stutzman) Morales
Bettina (Thomas) Landis
Thomas S. Tursack
Linda (Weaver) Renno
Kristin (Weaver) Woods
Sharon Weaver
Virgil R. Weaver
Mary Ann Weber
Daniel R. Wenger
Scott N. Wenger
Denise (Witmer) Hess
Rhonda R. Witmer **S**
Dwight W. Yoder
Elaine (Yousey) Zehr
Karen S. Zehr

Class of 1985

Janet E. Alger
Yvonne C. Bachman
B. Anthony Beiler
Thomas D. Beiler
Audrey (Blank) Landis
Marilyn Blank **T**
Sharyn D. Blank
Donna (Boll) Brubaker
Tina S. Book **S**
Beth Ann Brubaker
Ranita N. Buchen
Robert L. Buckwalter
Daniel S. Burkhart
Anita (Denlinger) Yoder
David Detwiler
Richard Detwiler
Benjamin Dorsey
Dawn M. Drumheller
Dawn Marie Eberly
David R. Eby
Edwin D. Engle
Sheila R. Esch
Ruth Ann Fisher
Wilma Faye Fisher
Steven T. Fox
Joy R. Frey
Dawn M. Garber
Wendell I. Gehman
Sharon (Geigley) King
Jonathan S. Gish
Sam M. Glick
Lori (Good) Rohrer
Gary L. Groff

J. Marlin Groff
Darrel E. Harnish
Kay (Herr) Book
Brian W. Hershey
Regina S. Hershey
Anne E. Hertzler
Chris A. Hess
David W. Hess
Merrill G. Hill
Carla Sue Hollinger
Jerry Hollinger
Scott E. Hoober
Donna (Horst) Kurtz
Lenora F. Hostetler
Martin W. Kampen
Bryan L. Kauffman
Sharon R. Kauffman
June (King) Kauffman
Leon King
Nolan L. King
Eugene D. Kraybill
Cheryl L. Kreider
Donna (Kunkel) Harnly
Douglas D. Kurtz
Eric A. Kurtz
Lois E. Kurtz **V**
Lori L. Landis
Marilyn (Landis) Martin
Sharon (Landis) Hess
Irene E. Lapp
Jean Y. Leaman
Marcella J. Leaman
Galen L. Lehman
Rebekah (Lehr) Sinners
David E. Martin **M,+**
Janae M. Martin
Kent M. Martin
Tonja L. Martin
Weldon J. Mast
William R. Mast
Gerald R. McDowell
Glenda F. Metzler
Denise (Miller) Martin
Donna (Miller) Sauder
Duane A. Miller
J. Robert Miller
Jeffrey D. Mohler
D. Scott Montague
Wilda E. Moreno
Jeffrey L. Myer
Eric N. Nafziger
Teresa (Nauman) Nolt
Loretta (Newswanger) Kuepfer
Karen (Nolt) Beiler
Barb (Nyce) Reesor **V**
David A. Oakes
Fred Oberholtzer
Craig A. Peifer
Duane A. Petersheim
Rodney L. Petersheim
Thomas M. Pierantoni
Carl E. Ranck
Rhonda K. Ranck
Gary L. Reiff
P. Brian Repine
Eugenia Romero
Ruth Romero
Kristina K. Roth
Kathy J. Rutt
Martha A. Salim
Jean L. Sauder
Roger E. Sauder
Joanne M. Shelly
Alica B. Shenk
Roger L. Shenk
Cynthia (Shirk) Horning
Ron M. Shultz
Lorinda B. Siegrist **L**
Randall Sinners

Joy F. Smucker
Mikelle Annette Stauffer
Jan (Steffy) Mast **P**
Cheryl (Stoltzfus) Landis
Debra R. Stoltzfus
Glenn L. Stoltzfus
Gloria (Stoltzfus) Shirk
Rosie (Stoltzfus) Lapp
Jon E. Stutzman
Melody A. Swartz
Yegoyant Thermilus
Amy L. Weaver
Deborah R. Weaver
Dwain C. Weaver
Elizabeth Ann Weaver Kreider
T. Kay Weaver
Keith H. Weber
Heidi (Wenger) Deacon
Jerold L. Wenger
L. David Wenger
Rhonda (Witmer) Good
Rodney K. Witmer
Robert D. Wood
Marcia J. Zehr
Janet (Zimmerman)
    Zimmerman

Class of 1986

Michelle Y. Achenbach
Linda S. Albrecht
Tammy L. Arment
Corlene (Beachy) Landis
Brad D. Beiler
Kristine K. Beiler
Linda S. Beiler
Rose A. Berkheimer
Daniel G. Brown
Angela F. Brubaker
Lois (Burkhart) Beiler **T**
Jodi E. Byers
Alicia Byler
Kendra Y. Campbell
Jack Carey
Kenneth Carper
Kim Carper
Jennifer Craighead
Duane R. Dagen
Vernon L. Denlinger
Bitual Desta
Gregory K. Dillman
Luis Duenas
Joanne K. Eberly
Brian D. Ebersole
Clair D. Eby
Theresa A. Eby
Lynette M. Engle
Marvin Lee Fisher
Matthew Fisher
Barrett E. Freed
Robin (Frey) Setlock
Kristina L. Garrett
Dwayne L. Geib
Bruce E. Gingrich
Michelle L. Glick
Vonda (Gochenaur) Smoker
Michelle D. Good
Trudy L. Good **M**
Charmaine Gray
Kimberly Gray
Tony N. Graybill
Scott Greiner
Eric S. Groff
Marvin R. Groff
Kevin R. Haller
Chris Hampton
Jan D. Harnish
Kim (Harnish) Gehman
J. Alex Hartzler

Suzanne (Herr) Weischedel
Jennifer Hershey
Dan W. Hess
Melissa A. Hess
Rosene Hess
Judy (Horning) Weaver
Ruth (Hoover) Moyer
Cindy Ann Horst
H. Steven Horst
Megan A. Howry
Earl R. Hurst
Leslie A. Hurst
Barbara (Kauffman) Harvey
Ben M. Kauffman
Levi S. Kauffman
G. David Keener
Kendall D. King
Wanda (King) Fisher
Marcella Kraybill **S**
Darrell Kreider
Jennifer Kreider
Pearl L. Kreider
Dwayne J. Landis
Dwight E. Landis **P**
Sheila (Landis) Hoffman
Dwight N. Leaman
Rhonda S. Leaman
Gerald S. Leatherman
Dirksen Lehman
Amy E. Levengood
Marta Longacre
Sherri (Longenecker) Fisher
    V,+
Carissa K. Martin
Donna (Martin) Shenk
Doug B. Martin
Lori (Martin) Weaver *
Philip D. Martin
Roger D. Martin
Sherry L. Martin
Teresa D. Martin
Timothy R. Martin
John J. Mast
Michelle R. McDivitt
Lynette M. Mellinger
Duane L. Metzler
Richard K. Miller
Janelle K. Mohler
Sandra Moreno
Denyce Nafziger
Ryan W. Newswanger **M**
Jill M. Nissley
Dean E. Oberholtzer
Gina (Oberholtzer) Burkhart **L**
Dawn C. Patrick
M. Dean Peifer
Marilyn (Petersheim) Eberly
Sam M. Petersheim
Samuel C. Petersheim
Kimberly A. Phipps
Lynare (Pipitone) Black
Diane L. Reed
Gennifer E. Reed
Stephen Reed
Jennifer K. Reese
Jay E. Reiff
Jamie R. Risser
Coleen B. Rohrer **V,+**
Jay E. Rohrer
Haggeo Romero
Tripet Rutanarugsa
Kevin A. Sensenig
Starla (Sensenig) Hess
Lisa (Shearer) Lindenmuth
Jill P. Sheeler
Carol (Shenk) Bornman
Steven E. Shirk
Lynndell R. Showalter
Douglas R. Smoker

Charlene F. Stoltzfus
Phillip D. Stoltzfus
Melissa Stoner
Brian L. Todd
Jeffrey E. Weaver
Rosemary G. Weaver
Sue Ann Weaver
William R. Weaver
Jalisa (Weber) Gingrich
Michael S. Wert
J. Richard Witmer
K. Sue Witmer
Brian S. Yoder
James E. Yoder
Amy L. Zimmerman
Jerry L. Zimmerman

Class of 1987

Lurleen G. Beiler
Courtney J. Bender **L**
Ronald M. Blackstone
Robert E. Bomberger Jr. **P**
Andrea D. Bontrager
Marvin L. Brubaker
Duval L. Denlinger
Sosena Desta
Daniel S. Detwiler
Tim R. Detwiler
Andy Dula
Janelle K. Eby
Philip Eby
Christopher S. Ferrari
Marlene Fisher
Wilma Fern Fisher
Shawn L. Garman
Philip N. Garrett
Rodney L. Gerlach
Todd L. Gingrich
Donna M. Glick
J. Stephen Good
Jean (Groff) Good
LaVonne S. Good
Lucinda D. Harnish
John G. Harnly
Deana R. Hein
Carolyn J. Herr
David L. Herr
Jevon M. Herr
John R. Hertzler
Michael O Hertzler
Dwayne A. Hess
Lisa M. Hess **+**
Philip A. Hess
M. Sean High
Christopher Hoover
Janelle R. Hoover
Joy Hoover
Amy J. Horst
Michael A. Horst
Steven R. Horst
Theresa L. Horst
Jeffrey A. Hostetler
Kimberly Hostetter
Ruth (Huete) Rios
Janelle M. Hurst
Linford R. Hurst
Caroline S. Kauffman
Mary Ann(Kauffman)Stoltzfus **M**
Denise R. Keener
Emma Jean Kennel
Beverly Ann King
Kathy (King) Zook
Sonya M. Kniss
Krista (Kurtz) Myer
Sandra E. Lacerda
Debra (Landis) Landis
Karen L. Landis
Pamela J. Landis

Stephanie Lantz
Glen D. Lapp
Gregory L. Lapp
Kerry Lapp
Jeremy K. Leaman
Conrad B. Lehman
Joy (Lehman) Ritter
Bruce A. Leininger
Kevin D. Longenecker
Fernando Lora
Benjamin C. Lustig
Renny S. Magill
Gary E. Martin
Krissy K. Martin
Kristen (Martin) Wiley
Linford D. Martin **S**
Loren J. Martin
Michael L. Martin
Sandra D. Martin
Timothy D. Martin
Duane D. Mellinger
Quentin L. Miller
Rebecca A. Miller *
Rod E. Miller
Kenneth R. Mohler
Randall C. Montague **+**
Darla (Musser) Martin
Gwen E. Musser
Carol L. Ness
Regina M. Newswanger
Darin L. Nissley
Steven P. Nissley
Jay L. Nolt
Lisa M. Nolt
Katrina Oberholtzer
Terry L. Petersheim
Laurie A. Quick
Charles Rechtsteiner
Craig Reed
Dawn M. Regener
Jane L. Rice
Rhea L. Roggie
Gerald E. Rohrer
Kevin J. Rutt
Lorri (Sapp) Beck
Randall L. Sauder
Rhonda L. Sauder
Richard L. Sauder
Vernon L. Sauder
Diane (Schnupp) Oberholtzer **T**
Valerie L. Shank
Tina N. Sharp
Douglas J. Shenk
Kathy J. Shenk
Philip J. Shenk
Jennifer L. Shultz
Diane J. Smith
Melissa Smith
John R. Smucker
Dina M. Snader
Ronald J. Snyder
Sheila R. Snyder
Brian Stauffer
Chad M. Stoltzfus
Lamar K. Stoltzfus
Charlynn Thomas **M**
Diane L. Thomas
Sharlene Walters
Amy Warnick
Peter M. Weaver
Marianne (Weidman)
    Hernandez
Andrea L. Wenger
Charles L. Wenger
Jeffrey L. Wenger
Douglas L. Wert
Abby (Wirth) Brevick
Todd M. Witmer
Kris (Wolgemuth) Kauffman

Randy D. Yoder
Timothy P. Zehr
Brenda (Zimmerman) Reed
Lisa C. Zimmerman
Lynda C. Zimmerman
Marcella J. Zimmerman

Class of 1988

Alicia M. Anderson
Pamela (Ayers) Newcomer
Andrea J. Beck
Karen (Becker) Newswanger
Nancy (Beckett) Mellot
Beverly R. Blank
Geraldine M. Boll
Brent J. Brubaker
Karen L. Brubaker **P**
Lisa R. Brubaker
Roy D. Brubaker
Amy L. Brunk
Denise M. Buchanan
J. Kenneth Bucher
Chad D. Byler
Stephen R. Byler *
Yvonne A. Chisenhall
James Cloyd
Merecis Diaz
J. Eric Dombach +
Peter Dula **M**
Andrew L. Eby
Sheldon G. Esch
Daryl E. Eshleman
Jennifer L. Ferrari **M,***
Rosa L. Fisher
Derek E. Frey
Melissa S. Garber
Carolyn J. Gerlach
Glenda J. Gingrich
Steve E. Godshall
Lee A. Good
Caprice Gray
Donna J. Groff
Rodney L. Groff
Heidi L. Haselhorst
Sheryl A. Hawbaker
Charles B. Haws
Daryl F. Heller
Matthew W. Helm
Michelle L. Helm
Darin L. Herr
Carol M. Hershey
Corinne L. Hershey
Dawn L. Hess
Doris J. Hess
N. Eugene Hess
Laurie L. Hoober
Daryl L. Hoover
Joyce Y. Hoover
Lamar M. Hoover
Randy L. Hoover
Maureen H. Horlacher
Susan R. Horst
Amy C. Houser
Aura D. Huete
Audrey K. Hurst
Darwin L. Hurst
Dorlee R. Hurst
Julie Ann Hurst
Lori M. Hurst
Wendel L. King
Sharon R. Koch
Keita Kogoma
Cindy L. Kreider
Donna L. Kreider
Kurt W. Kreider
Lulama Kunene
Randy L. Kunkel
David D. Kurtz

Eugene A. Kurtz
Brenda M. Landis
Maria E. Lao
Brian M. Leaman
Patrick D. Leaman **S**
Judy L. Leatherman
Karin W. Levengood
Amy S. Martin
Chris J. Martin
Craig E. Martin
Devon W. Martin
Juanita Martin
Tana L. Martzall
Joy A. McIlvaine
Brian S. Miller
Ilisa M. Miller
Karen S. Miller
Krista L. Miller
Kristel L. Miller
Kristin L. Miller
Mark M. Miller
Roger K. Miller
John Mokonyama
Denise (Musser) Martin
Gerald K. Musser
Shawn H. Musser
Aimee M. Myers
Karen L. Myers
Patrick J. Myers
Brian D. Nauman
Denise (Newswanger) Horning
Roger L. Newswanger
David J. Nieczyporuk
Hiroko Nishiyama
K. Mark Nissley
Janell M. Nolt
Janet L. Nolt
June L. Nolt
Jennifer L. Peifer **L**
Maggie Perez
Joy Lynn Pfeiffer
Veronica Lynn Putnam
R. Marvin Ramos
Darrell L. Ranck
Pamela R. Ranck
Douglas R. Redcay
Jeffrey L. Reiff
Eric G. Replogle
Jesse Romero
John A. Salim
Jason K. Samuel
J. Robert Sangrey
Adam P. Sapp
David E. Sapp
Laurie S. Sauder
Renita (Sauder) Martin
William Schultz
Kathy A. Sensenig
Kent A. Sensenig
J. Kenneth Shaiebly
Tonya J. Sharp
G. Todd Sheeler
Janelle R. Shenk
Timothy D. Shenk
Darla J. Shertzer
Melissa D. Shirk +
Bethany A. Shull
Marlon Lonnie Smoker
Robert L. Snyder **V**
Lynelle Sollenberger
Ronald E. Stark
Johann O. Stauffer
Bryan D. Stoltzfus
Duane A. Stoltzfus
Dwight D. Stoltzfus
Eileen R. Stoltzfus
Lawrence Stoltzfus
Philip D. Stoltzfus
Kenneth L. Stoner

Karen J. Stutzman
Julie I. Surotchak
Marcella Swartzendruber
Craig M. Thomas
Loren K. Todd
Radella S. Todd
Michelle L. Umble
Jay L. Weaver
Julia E. Weaver
Mark W. Weaver
Neil L. Weaver
Roger L. Weaver
Steve C. Weaver
Stephen S. Wehibe **T**
Philip T. Wert
Andre Williams
Patricia Winters
Melinda S. Wise
Clair L. Zeager
Andrea J. Zehr
Ted G. Zeiset
Steven A. Zook

Class of 1989

Tsedale Addisu
Jacqueline M. Anderson
Jonathan Matthew Beck
Mariamawit Bekele
Madeline L. Bender
Mariame Berhanemeskal
Yerufael Berhanemeskal
Kimberly A. Boll
Joyce R. Boyer
Lori A. Brechbill
Daryl E. Breneman
Robert L. Brubaker
Donna R. Burkholder
Janelle R. Byler
David A. Chmielowiec
Lisa M. Conrad
Jeanine S. Denlinger
Rachelle E. Denlinger
James C. Diener
David T. Dietz
Bradley J. Dillman
Richard John Donnelly
Timothy E. Duvall
Dana N. Dymond
Andrew C. Erts
Wendell S. Esbenshade
Jeffrey S. Fair
Darrell M. Fisher
Raymond L. Fisher
Beth A. Frank
Daniel L. Fry
Ronald K. Gardiner
Stephen M. Garrett
Carolyn J. Geigley
Beverly J. Gingrich
Vicki A. Gingrich
Valerie Ann Glick
Tonia R. Graybill
Carolyn R. Groff **V**
Cindy J. Groff **T**
Julie (Hampton) Philpot
Donna J. Harnish
Duane E. Harnly
Andrea J. Haverstick
Maren F. Heinemann
Joel R. Heisey
Brenda J. Herhei
Jonel M. Herr
Dwayne M. Hershey
Roman A. Hess
Bryan R. High
Scott A. High
Susan M. Hoffer
Allison G. Hoober

Clifford L. Horst
Nevin L. Horst
Sheldon L. Horst
Tina N. Horst
Sharon B. Hostetter
Brian L. Hurst
Krista L. Hurst
Stephen A. Judd
Loren R. Kampen
Darvis E. King **S**
Lorne E. King
Nedra L. King **P**
Randy L. King
Steve R. Kratz
James E. Kraybill
Gerald D. Kreider
Robert B. Kreider
Kornel J. Kurtz
Paula D. Kurtz
Darvin B. Landis
Edie A. Lantz
Herman D. Lapp
Kim L. Lapp
J. Welby Leaman
Shawn Glenn Leaman
Jeffrey A. Lefever
Angela G. Lehman
Anne L. Lehman
Jerry N. Lehman
Jennifer M. Leister **M**
Lori A. Leonard
Kymberly L. Liese
Faith R. Loftis
D. Stephen Long
Jennifer L. Longenecker
Jon M. Lustig
Blain Mamo
Henock Mamo
Jewel D. Martin
Mike I. Martin
Steven R. Martin
Rhonda (Meck) Miller
Binyam Melekot
Sharon M. Mellinger
Erika S. Metzler
J. Patrick Miller
Julia L. Miller
Timothy A. Mohler
P. Dwain Moyer
R. Diane Moyer
Richard Eugene Musselman
Sheryl L. Myer
Christina M. Neill
Steve L. Ness
Timothy J. Neufeld
Daryl S. Newswanger **M**
Sheri L. Nissley
Tanya Lee Nissley
Beth A. Noll
Andrea R. Oberholtzer
Myron L. Otto
Tricia M. Peifer
Kim S. Petersheim
Karen E. Poe
Fred L. Ranck
Rodney L. Redcay
Jeff S. Reiff
Wanda L. Reinford
Beth M. Risser
Barbara A. Rohrer
Lugene R. Rosenberry
Sofia Samatar
G. Scott Sangrey
Christopher D. Sauder
Marla B. Sauder
Matthew R. Sauder
Teresa J. Sauder
Elaine M. Shenk
David A. Sholes

Timothy K. Shreiner
Wesley D. Siegrist
Allyson Christine Siviglia
Carol A. Smith
Kim (Snader) Stark
Matthew J. Snavely
L. Todd Stauffer
Monique D. Stauffer
Thomas H. Stauffer
Darvin L. Stoner
Jeffrey D. Stutzman
Bryon J. Temple
Matthew D. Warfel
Paula M. Weaver
Timothy L. Weaver
Corey L. Wenger
Randy L. Wenger
Daniel Allen Wise
Douglas S. Witmer
Steven L. Witmer
Mehari Woldamlak
Christine L. Wright
Sharon J. Youndt
Vincent C. Youndt
Dan A. Zehr
Karen (Zeiset) Sauder
Sarah Zeleke
Angela R. Zimmerman *
Dana Lynelle Zimmerman
Diana R. Zimmerman +

Class of 1990

Cynthia Sue Anderson
Titile Asfaw
Daniel Assefa
Nannette J. Atwater
Kelly A. Baker
Stephen R. Beachy
Philomena M. Behmer
Brent E. Beiler
Mary Jo Beiler
Yvonne M. Beiler
Fasika Berhane
John N. Boll
Jonathan M. Bollinger
Ted R. Book
Sherri L. Bowman
Phebe Breneman
Lowell M. Brown
Keith A. Brubacher
Margaret Grace Brubaker
Michael A. Brubaker
R. Anothony Brubaker
Steven T. Brubaker
Katrina J. Cann
Valerie L. Clemmer L
Jennifer Lynn Cline
Cynthia D. Clymer
Kenesa Debela
Duane M. Denlinger
Sheri K. Denlinger
K. Joelle Detwiler
Grace A. Dich
Jennifer D. Diener
Danielle K. Diller
Kathy L. Doll
Scott R. Dombach
Steven K. Douple
Cynthia A. Ebersole
Dawn L. Eby
J. Michael Eby
Nicole L. Eby
Charlene Faye Engle
Vanessa K. Enns
Erica E. Erb
Andrew C. Erts
Keturah J. Esh
Laurie J. Eshleman

Darin T. Espigh
Gennet Fantu
Todd Michael Fike
Deborah M. Furman
Johanna Rebekah Gardiner
Milena Gebremeskel
Erica S. Godshall
Jan M. Good P
Jolyn K. Good
Kenton J. Good
Bryan L. Groff
Kimberly D. Groff
Joel Haile
Bernie L. Harnish
Melanie K. Hawbaker
Dione K. Hege
Carla L. Heisey
Lisa J. Heller
Amy L. Herr
Jill M. Herr
Julie R. Herr
Keith G. Hershberger +
Heather N. Hershey
Krista Joy Hershey
Audrey C. Hess
Dean R. Hess
Dwight A. Hess
Marlin J. Hess
Rita E. Hess
Wing T. Heung
DeLynn N. Hoover
Douglas H. Hoover
Karen M. Hoover
Sharon E. Horning
Carol A. Horst
Heather Lynn Horst
Karen R. Horst
Adam C. Hostetter
Kimberly A. Hurd-Breneman
Nathan A. Kauffman
Brent L. Keener
Sheri J. Knutsen
P. Rodney Kraybill
Wanda R. Kraybill
Gary D. Kreider
Mardel J. Kreider
Doreen K. Landis
Vicki M. Landis
Matthew J. Leaman
J. Andrew Lehman V
Scott A. Leik
Rosa M. Linares
Gabrielle B. Liss
Lynn E. Longenecker
Teyent LouLou
Ryan P. Magill
Greta L. Martin
Karen (Martin) Erts
Patrick L. Martin
Sonja D. Martin
Austin R. Mast
Renee C. Meck S
Beth Ann Miller
Greg L. Miller
Keith L. Miller
Lori M. Miller
Melanie A. Miller
Michelle T. Miller
Renee E. Miller
Brenda M. Moalusi
C. Adam Morris
Lori Lynn Mumma
Daniel R. Murray
Charity D. Musser
Dwayne K. Musser
Judy S. Musser
Yvonne Myer
Herman I. Nafziger
Shawn L. Nafziger

Andrew J. Nissley
Monica D. Nissley
W. Anthony Parks
Darlene Pena
Greg L. Petersheim T
Orpha R. Petersheim
William R. Phipps
Ryan D. Ranck
Heidi Rechtsteiner
Scott E. Regener
Glenda K. Reiff
Kathleen A. Rhodes
Aurelio Romero
Edwin A. Romero
Ismail A. Salim
Sheryl A. Sensenig
Troy A. Sensenig
Elaine Janette Shank
Gregory B. Shaub
Keith J. Shaubach
Pam J. Shenk
Todd D. Shertzer
Christy D. Shull
Glenda J. Shultz
Brett E. Shumaker
Brian D. Smoker
Brian C. Snyder
Randall J. Snyder
Andrew L. Steckbeck
Charlene F. Stoltzfus
David A. Stoltzfus
Heidi A. Stoltzfus
James L. Stoltzfus
Ladina J. Stoltzfus *
Lori F. Swartzendruber
Seneshaw Tamirat
R. Alex Tellado
Anita S. Thomas
Kurtis D. Thomas
Steven L. Thomas
Bonita A. Todd
LaGina M. Tomaino
C. Douglas Umble
Keith L. Umble
Korey L. Umble
Dennis F. Vroman
Chad L. Warfel
Krista S. Weaver
Valerie S. Weaver M
Jennifer L. Wenger
Melani M. Wenger
Robin A. Wenger
Tabiso Williams
Fredrick K. Winey
Jennifer H. Wright
Amy Anne Yoder
Fred J. Zeiset
Crystal J. Zimmerman
Wanda L. Zimmerman M
Connie M. Zook

Class of 1991

Befekadu Aberra
Amanda May Amaral
Werner C. Ammann
Jarra Asfaw
Nathan D. Ayers
Amy Dawn Baker
Melissa Ann Behmer
Heidi E. Beiler
Valonda M. Bender
Gary Blank
Ella M. Blessing
Joann Bollinger
Steven Paul Braun
Kendra Joy Breneman
Derick Scott Brubaker
Kathryn Bucher

Gregg A. Buckwalter
Kenneth Charles Jr.
Sherri Lynn Coleman
Kristin Michelle Daveler
Darryl DePasquale
Surane Debela
Denbele Dula
Frederick Lee Eberly
Michael Eby
Stephen M. Eisenberger
Cathy L. Eshleman
Thomas L. Eshleman
Larry Alan Fahnestock
Tenaye Fantu
Jennifer L. Fasnacht
Jeremy Fisher
Twila Jean Fisher
Kenneth Matthew Forrey
Melanie Joy Forshey
Kristopher L. Frey
Stephanie Lorraine Fuller
Melanie Lynn Garber
Joseph A. Gascho
Wakgari Gemechisa
Yodit Getachew
Pamela Gingrich
Beletshachew Girma
Debra K. Good
Juanita J. Good
Kurtis P. Good
Peter Alan Good
Thomas D. Grassell Jr.
Amy Genevieve Greene
Melissa Christine Groff
Rosalyn Faye Groff
Tina Joy Groff
Heidi Noelle Habecker
Crystal Joy Haller
Sarah Hallman
Jacob A. Harnish
Matthew B. Hartzler
Jannah Rochelle Heisey
Lynnea Jean Heisey
Denise Ann Hershey
Rebekah Jane Hershey
Karen E. Hertzler
Julia Marie Hess
Julie Renee Hess
Elizabeth Nichole High
Dorcas L. Hofstetter
Lorena Joy Horning
Sally Jo Horning
Jeffrey N. Horst T
Melissa J. Hostetter
Shirley Faye Hostetter
Chad Gregory Hurst
Jay Nevin Hurst
M. Dalena Hurst
Lily Blen Kassahoun
Heidi Kautz
N. Norene King
Christina Lynette Kolb
Joy Louise Kraybill
Brent Ryan Kreider
Kirby L. Kreider
Ryan Lloyd Kreider
Sylvia Melinda Kreider
Brian D. Kurtz
Donavin Lamar Landis
Jonathan M. Landis
Kevin E. Landis
John H. Leaman III
Justin D. Leaman
Cheryl Y. Lehman
Charles R. Maines
Cynthia A. Martin
Delayne Martin
Jennifer L. Martin
Laurel Martin

Lisa Kay Martin
Lori Ann Martin
Shawn Martin
Timothy L. Martin
Daniel Lamar Mast
Loretta Lynn Mellinger
Helen Mesfin
Jonathan A. Metzler
Bryan P. Milich
J. Melissa Miller
Janelle Lynn Miller
Josie Marie Miller
Keith Edwin Miller
R. Christianne Murphy
Janelle J. Musser
Nevin Lloyd Musser
Carmen Joy Myers
Brent Douglas Nauman
Ryan Eugene Newswanger

Bradford T. Nicarry
Rebecca J. Nissley
Brendon Robert Nolt
Trace L. Oberholtzer
Flor Azucena Palacios
Kendra Jo Peifer
Michael Peifer
Krista Eileen Poe
Steven Neil Prichard
Steven Loren Reiff
Tisha L. Reitnauer
Mark Elliot Roberts
Julia Rose Rohrer
Richard D. Rohrer Jr.
Michelle Louise Rose
Roger Rudy
Darin L. Rutt
Jude Zachary Samuel
Kristen Lee Sangrey

Jan Alene Sauder
Katrina Jane Sauder
Kurt Edward Schlenbaker
Corinne Marie Seymour
Donald Brent Siegrist
Lynette J. Siegrist
Cauleen M. Smith
Ty Douglas Smucker
Arlisa Snavely
Rachel Snavely
Bruck Tesfaye
Adam Tessera
Jennifer Ann Thomas *
M. Janelle Thomas **L**
Kristin R. Umble **M**
Matthew John Van Hekken
Derek Warnick
Kurt Rydell Weaver **P +**
Timothy Scott Weaver

Tina L. Weaver
Natoshia Jolynn Wenger
Rachel Dawn Wenger
Rebecca L. Wenrich
Cynthia J. Wert
Katrina Ann Wert
D. Loren White
Debra Kay Wolgemuth
Alisa Marie Wolgemuth
Jeffrey Worley
Misiker Yilma
Michael Yohannes
Emmalie Ellen Zak **S**
Wendell D. Zeiset
Lara Ziegler
Amy Janelle Zimmerman
Jonathan Paul Zimmerman **VP**
Malcolm Brett Zwally

Notes

Chapter 1
Charting a Different Course, Pre-1940

1. The cleanup is described by Kautz (1942:251) and Good (1943b:270).

2. *Intelligencer Journal*, September 5, 1940.

3. Some early Anabaptists were willing to use the sword but most rejected the use of violent force and advocated nonresistant love. An introduction to Mennonite history is provided by Dyck (1981), Klaassen (1973) and Weaver (1987).

4. Clare (1892), Klein (1924) and Wickersham (1885) report that the Mennonites established the first school in Lancaster County in the Willow Street area in 1712. Other Mennonite schools, as well as Lutheran, Reformed, Presbyterian, Moravian and Quaker schools, were also organized by early settlers.

5. Wickersham (1885:166-167).

6. For a history of education in Pennsylvania, see One (1934) and Wickersham (1885). The development of schools in Lancaster County is traced by Clare (1892), Ellis and Evans (1883) and Klein (1924).

7. Garber (1934).

8. Wickersham (1885:290-338) describes in detail the development of the 1834 Free School Law and the widespread opposition to it. Ellis and Evans (1883: 677-685) describe a bitter revolt in Lancaster County's Brecknock Township.

9. Good (1980).

10. Good (1980).

11. *Herald of Truth* (1895:135), see also Bucher (1908).

12. Brubaker (1966:37-42).

13. Bishop Minutes, October 7, 1927.

14. Wenger (1930:75-80). "Who Should Educate Our Children?" was also the title of a widely circulated tract by Shem Peachey distributed by the Mennonite Parochial School Association of Smoketown, PA.

15. Garber (1934).

16. Glick (1945:6).

17. For a brief history of this incident see Kraybill (1989:122-124).

18. For a history of the development of Locust Grove Mennonite School see Brubaker (1966) and *Locust Grove Mennonite School 1939-1989* (1990).

19. Brubaker (1966) provides an excellent history of the Mennonite elementary school movement.

20. *Mennonite Yearbook* (1990-91) reports a listing of Mennonite schools across the nation. This roster likely underestimates the number of schools and it does not include one-room Old Order Mennonite schools. Mennonite-related schools in the Lancaster area are listed in *Directory of Schools* (1990-91).

21. Juhnke (1989:162-177) provides an overview of the development of Mennonite schools and colleges at the turn of the century. Although the (Old) Mennonite Church had established three academies by 1917, two other Mennonite denominations (the General Conference Mennonite Church and the Mennonite Brethren) had established other schools prior to 1894.

22. For a history of Eastern Mennonite School see Pellman (1967).

23. Six high-school level academies established by various Mennonite denominations between 1893 and 1917 eventually evolved into colleges. Some of these colleges continued to offer a high school curriculum on their campuses. The new wave of building freestanding high schools began with Lancaster Mennonite School. For a history of

Mennonite secondary schools consult *The Mennonite Encyclopedia V*, (1990:803-806).

24. Ruth (ND:1033).

25. Discussion of the proposed school in the Lancaster area is recorded in the diary of Weaverland bishop Ben Weaver, reported by Ruth (ND: 1033), and discussed in the *Lancaster Mennonite School Bulletin* (1942-43:11).

26. Bishop Minutes, October 18, 1933.

27. The exact number of bishops varied from time to time because a younger bishop would sometimes be selected to assist one in failing health.

28. The *Mennonite Yearbook* (1940) records the number of bishop districts, congregations and ordained leaders.

29. A tribute to Henry Garber (1888-1968) and a summary of his contributions are reported in the *Missionary Messenger*, April (1969:8-17).

30. Documentary evidence that Garber wrote the petition is lacking; however, several of the signers believe that he was the author. Signers of the petition included Elmer G. Martin, Clayton L. Keener, Jacob T. Harnish, John H. Gochnauer, Henry F. Garber, G. Parke Book, Floyd S. Graybill, Sem Eby, John R. Kraybill, Ira D. Landis, Clarence E. Lutz, John H. Mellinger, Milton Brackbill, James H. Hess and B. Charles Hostetter.

31. *Intelligencer Journal*, September 5, 1940.

32. Gochnauer (1942a). Although the broadside referred to girls wearing slacks for gym classes, Edna and Grace Wenger report that the more typical practice of the late '30s and early '40s was a one-piece suit with elastic bloomer legs and no sleeves.

33. Weaver (1946:245).

34. Good (1943a:14).

35. Lancaster Mennonite Church Membership Survey, 1940. Amos Horst collection. The survey lists a total of 5,505 Lancaster Mennonite Conference wage earners.

36. Lehman (1945:4).

37. Conant (1965) and Sher (1977) discuss the transformation of public high schools.

38. *Report* (1908:ix).

39. *Schools* (1947:48).

40. The Mill Creek meandered through the campus property. The campus community gradually called the creek the Mill Stream, especially after the school newspaper was called the *Millstream* in January 1943. Reflecting common usage, Mill Stream is used throughout the text when referring to the creek.

Chapter 2
Staking Out a Middle Ground, 1940-1942

1. The debate on high school attendance continued for several years. Noah Good (1946) discussed it in a *Millstream* article at the end of the school's fourth year.

2. Graybill (1945b:99-109). Although this promotional manual was published after the school began, it thoroughly summarizes objections from the outstart and Graybill's refutations.

3. Begun in 1708 as an amalgamation of Anabaptism and Radical Pietism, the Brethren were known as German Baptist Brethren and more popularly as "Dunkers" until 1908 when they began using the name Church of the Brethren.

4. Bishop Minutes, March 11 and 14, 1940.

5. *Intelligencer Journal*, March 15, 1940.

6. *New Era*, September 4, 1940.

7. *Intelligencer Journal*, September 7, 1940.

8. *New Era*, September 7, 1940.

9. Horst (1940:1-3).

10. The 1967 *Laurel Wreath* (1967:18) reports that the favorable vote carried by 51 to 49 percent. I have been unable to find documentation of the vote. Bishop David Thomas said that a two-thirds majority was required for conference actions at that time, thus making it unlikely that the vote was 51 to 49 percent. Several informants do not remember an actual percentage vote, but all report that it "was very close," passing by only one vote or one percentage point.

11. Bishop Minutes, April 3,4, 1941.

12. A copy of the questionnaire is in Horst's files. Neither completed questionnaires nor tabulated results are available in his files.

13. Bishop Minutes, June 19, 1941. Emphasis added.

14. The Constitution was formulated by a group of three bishops—Simon Bucher, Amos Horst and Henry Lutz—appointed on June 19, 1941. The Constitution was approved by the bishops on September 8, 1941, and ratified by the Conference on October 3, 1941. The Bishop Minutes from the October 3, 1941 conference do not report the action to approve the Constitution. The Bishop Minutes immediately before (September 8, 1941) and after (October 14, 1941) clearly indicate the Conference approved the Constitution on October 3. This is further corroborated by Graybill (1967:1).

15. The twelve trustees included Parke Book (chairman), John Gochnauer (vice chairman), John Kraybill, Clarence Lutz, Sem Eby, Elam Stoner, Howard Greider, Landis Brubaker, Amos Weaver, Amos Myer, Luke Hurst and Ira Graybill.

16. *Pastoral Messenger*, January 1942:3-4.

17. The search for a site is recorded in the minutes of the trustees as well as in Kraybill (1962).

18. Trustee Minutes, February 26, 1942.

19. *Intelligencer Journal*, April 30, 1942.

20. Biographical profiles of Noah Good can be found in Lehman (1991:9-10) and in *New Era*, April 20, 1991.

21. The original responses are held in the Lancaster Mennonite School Collection at the Lancaster Mennonite Historical Society.

22. The best history of the property was written by Weaver (1951:395,405). Mellinger (1943:19-21), Bennett (1952) and Good (1950) also provide historical glimpses of the property. On the history of the Yeates school consult Klein and Diller (1944:274-277), Miller (1909:733-745), Minnich (1947) and Klein (1924:1018-1019).

23. *Yeates* (1919). A charming description of life at the Yeates Boarding School is provided by philosopher Charles Hartshorne (1990), a student there between 1911-1915.

24. For a description of this tragedy, consult Mellinger (1943:19-21).

Chapter 3
Safeguarding the Church, 1942-1943

1. U.S. Census of 1940 and Lancaster Mennonite Conference Church Membership Survey of 1940 in Amos Horst Collection.

2. The *Rules and Discipline* of Lancaster Mennonite Conference were revised in 1942-43 and approved by the Conference body in September 1943.

3. Bishop Minutes, 1912-1933. See also Mack (1930).

4. The *Constitution* (1941) spells out the safeguards rather explicitly.

5. Gochnauer (1942b:5-6).

6. Lichty (1984) has written an unpublished biography of Graybill. A biographical profile of Graybill can also be found in Landis (1976).

7. Graybill (1948) proposed ten ways that church schools would promote missions. He described the role of the Bible in a Christian high school in Graybill (1946).

8. Graybill (1945c:55-56).

9. Good (1943c).

10. Graybill (1958:3-4). Emphasis in text added.

11. Graybill (1950:3).

12. Graybill (1945d:97-98). Emphasis in text added.

13. Student regulations are described in the *Constitution* (1941), the minutes of the Supervising Committee, the *Bulletin* (1942-43), and in an October 12, 1942, letter to parents.

14. Good (1975).

15. Good (1943d).

16. *Intelligencer Journal*, September 11, 1942.

17. *New Era*, August 29, 1942.

18. First year activities are reported by Good (1943b) and in the *Millstream* (1943).

19. Opening activities are described in the *Bulletin*, October (1942).

20. Graybill (1943) and the *Bulletin*, October (1943).

21. The academic program is outlined in the 1942-43 catalog of Lancaster Mennonite School.

22. The dedication service is described in the *Millstream*, March 1943:21-23.

23. Supervising Committee Minutes, November 23, 1942 and December 1, 1942.

24. From 1943 through the 1960s the paper was titled *The Mill Stream*. In the early '70s it became *Mill Stream*. From the late '70s through 1991 it was called *Millstream*, the variant used throughout the text.

25. Supervising Committee Minutes, November 24, 1942 and J. Paul Graybill letter to C. C. Cressman, March 8, 1949.

26. *Mennonite Yearbook* (1990-91:123-124). Earlier Mennonite academies which evolved into high schools were affiliated with Mennonite colleges. LMS was the first free-standing high school with its own campus and administration.

27. Report of the Principal, 1942-43.

Chapter 4
Drawing the Lines of Faithfulness, 1943-1953

1. *Students' Handbook of Information* (1949).

2. *Students' Handbook of Information* (1949).

3. Weaver (1946).

4. Moses Gehman letter to Henry Lutz, December 8, 1945.

5. A promotional flier with a hand-drawn diagram of the proposed building was distributed in January of 1946.

6. Edna Wenger reports that chapel in the first year of school was held in room D of the classroom building. Later, rooms B and C were opened into room D to accommodate more students. In the fall of 1947 chapel shifted to the auditorium.

7. Bishop Minutes, September 15, 1947.

8. Good(1949:28-29) describes the design and utilization of the new girls' dormitory.

9. Trustee Minutes, September 5, 1949 and October 3, 1949.

10. The story was told in the following sources: *Millstream*, May 1952, *Laurel Wreath*, 1952, Trustee Minutes, May 5, 1952 and *Intelligencer Journal*, April 29, 1952.

11. Trustee Minutes, November 1, 1948.

12. Bishop Minutes, November 3, 1949.

13. Trustee Minutes, July 1, 1950 and November 6, 1950.

14. Supervising Committee Minutes, March 26, 1952.

15. Trustee Minutes, April 4, 1949.

16. Supervising Committee Minutes, May 5, 1952.

17. Trustee Minutes, July 4, 1949.

18. Clayton Keener letter to the Religious Welfare Committee, April 12, 1949.

19. Supervising Committee Minutes, March 25, 1952.

20. Trustee Minutes, February 6, 1950.

21. Harvey Bauman letter to Noah Good, March 27, 1952.

22. Discipline Committee Minutes, April 21, 1952, May 19, 1952, May 21, 1952.

23. Graybill (1951).

24. Radios were banned for ministers and frowned upon for lay members. The use of radio for broadcasting in Gospel ministries was forbidden and the cause of some dissension.

25. The 1954 *Rules and Discipline* only "encouraged" the use of "ties" on the head covering whereas the 1943 *Rules and Discipline* required ties. The 1943 *Rules and Discipline* did not mention singing but the 1954 document "required that only congregational singing be engaged in the worship services." Singing in small groups was permitted for special outreach services in jails and hospitals, etc.

26. Graybill (1951).

27. Graybill (1951).

28. Some observers describe his health failure as a nervous breakdown which may have been linked to a sense of failure in not being able to uphold high church standards at LMS.

29. Amos Weaver remembered Graybill saying these words as Weaver assumed the new role. Amos Weaver was elected principal by the Bishop Board on January 22, 1953. There were no other nominees for the office.

30. Graybill (1953).

Chapter 5
Expanding the Vision, 1953-1967

1. The bishops appointed a Nonconformity Committee that functioned from 1955 to 1971. The committee held special conferences and published a variety of pamphlets. J. Paul Graybill (1949) wrote a series of lessons on "Biblical and Practical Nonconformity."

2. Good (1990) provides a biographical account of Weaver's life.

3. Weaver (1957b:27).

4. Weaver (1965). Apparently some faculty members were critical of Weaver's condemnation of the Beatles. Three days later, on November 15, 1965, he sent a letter to all the faculty explaining the reasons for his "shock treatment" in the chapel talk.

5. Emphasis in text added.

6. Two issues of *The Report Card* (March 1955 and November 1956) are devoted to discussions of the need for new facilities.

7. The January, 1956 issue of *The Report Card* contains several essays on agriculture and the church as well as plans for the proposed agriculture building.

8. Lehman (1956:8).

9. Hess (1955:4-5).

10. Weaver (1957a:11).

11. The Study Committee was composed of representatives from several conference organizations. Leadership came primarily from the Mission Board, which needed a facility to accommodate the annual missionary conference.

12. The trustees acted in March 1, 1965 to change the constitution of the school so that other high schools and junior high schools could fall under their jurisdiction.

13. Trustee Minutes, May 4, 1964.

14. Trustee Minutes, November 7, 1960 and February 13, 1961.

15. Trustee Minutes, May 7, 1962.

16. Trustee Minutes, April 4, 1960.

17. Good (1975:150).

18. Amos Weaver letter to Amos Horst, February 2, 1956.

19. Harvey Bauman letter to Charles Longenecker, May 22, 1958.

20. The May 1989 issue of *Missionary Messenger* includes a major section in tribute to H. Raymond Charles.

21. *Millstream*, May (1955:3).

22. Trustee Minutes, August 2, 1965.

23. Anthropologist Gertrude Huntington made these observations in a 1972-74 study of the school reported in Hostetler, Huntington and Kraybill (1974:71).

24. The request is reported in the Trustee Minutes of February 5 and 12, 1962.

25. Trustee Minutes, May 3, 1965, May 31, 1965 and May 2, 1966.

26. Trustee Minutes, May 3, 1965.

27. *Millstream*, December 1955: 8-9.

28. Weaver (1960:1000).

29. Bishop Minutes, September 20, 1962.

30. Trustee Minutes, October 3, 1966.

31. The *Rules and Discipline*, Lancaster Mennonite Conference, 1954. Emphasis in text added.

32. Good (1955:4-5).

33. The change in the school constitution permitting radios, record players and tape recorders was approved by Lancaster Conference in the spring of 1962.

34. "Objectives For Music Instruction for Lancaster Conference Schools," undated mimeograph report. The committee was formed in July of 1965.

35. Although television was not commonplace until the mid 1950s, it was already anticipated and prohibited in the 1943 *Rules and Discipline* of Lancaster Conference.

36. Noah Good letter to John Kraybill, December 6, 1955.

37. Bishop Minutes, October 18, 1956.

38. Longenecker and Shank letter to the trustees dated March 29, 1960.

39. Trustee Minutes, July 4, 1960.

40. Bishop Minutes, April 19, 1962.

41. Annual Report of the Dean, 1966.

Chapter 6
Setting a New Direction, 1967-1972

1. The two-page, single-spaced statement was signed by faculty members Luke Shank, Charles Longenecker, Myron Dietz, Wilbur Lentz, Edna Wenger and Alta Hoover. It was sent in March of 1967 to the trustees as well as to the Religious Welfare Committee, the moderator, and the secretary of Lancaster Conference.

2. Other members of the five-person committee included Paul Bender, principal of Belleville Mennonite School, and Roy Lowrie, Jr., principal of the Delaware Valley Christian School. Paul Kraybill served as secretary of the committee. The related correspondence and documents suggest that he was a major force in shaping the committee's work.

3. Both actions were taken in the October 19,1967, Bishop Board Meeting.

4. Principal's Annual Report 1969-70, p. 3.

5. James Hess letter to Clarence Lutz dated August 15, 1968.

6. Handwritten draft of memo dated December 3, 1968, to the Supervising Committee and trustees from Charles Longenecker.

7. This division, resulting in the formation of the Eastern

Pennsylvania Mennonite Church, is described by Garber (1979).

8. Handwritten notes of comments given to the trustees by James Hess on February 3, 1969.

9. Memo to the trustees from the faculty Publicity and Public Relations Committee, February 11, 1969. A three-page summary of the discussion with the trustees appears with the Trustee Minutes of February 11, 1969.

10. A cover letter to the survey, dated April 16, 1969, indicated that two congregations from each bishop district were selected to participate in the survey. Although the survey was apparently conducted, the results are not accessible in historical files.

11. Letter from Larry Newswanger, president of the Alumni Association, to James Hess, chair of the trustees, March 14, 1969. A three-page accompanying document details many of the suggestions of the alumni group.

12. Minutes of a Special Advisory Committee, meeting on June 23, 1969, Stanley Kreider secretary.

13. The idea of leasing land for a motel east of the Mill Stream along Route 30 was first proposed by the trustees in a September 1, 1969 meeting. After numerous meetings with real estate agents, attorneys and representatives from a prospective motel, the trustees took action on January 11, 1971, to enter into a lease agreement with representatives of the Willow Valley Motel. After receiving "objections from a large number of our church constituency and faculty members of the school and public relations in general . . ." the board requested a release from the agreement in their November 8, 1971, board meeting, ending some two years of debate over the "motel project."

14. Richard Hess and Allen Stoltzfus presented this proposal to the trustees on August 6, 1970. The trustees, however, did not see fit to rent the rooms in the girls' dorm "at this time."

15. Faculty Meeting Minutes of April 24, 1969, with representatives from the trustees.

16. Letter from faculty member Larry Wenger to the trustees, May 5, 1969.

17. This Administrative Advisory Committee (James Hess, Clarence Lutz, H. Raymond Charles, Paul Kraybill and J. Lester Brubaker) had been appointed by the trustees on August 8, 1967, to continue the work of the earlier outside evaluation committee. They continued to advise the trustees throughout the '69-'70 school year.

18. *Millstream* editorial, April 1970.

19. As a member of the Administrative Advisory Committee, Paul Kraybill also served on the Philosophy Study Committee and the Constitutional Revision Committee until January of 1970, when he resigned to become the executive secretary of a churchwide Commission on Church Organization. The correspondence surrounding the organizational changes at LMS suggest that he played an important role in the new directions.

20. The 1970 constitution made it possible for Lancaster Conference to operate several schools. It called for a superintendent responsible for the coordination of all schools and a principal within each school. The superintendent, approved by the bishops, could recommend the appointment of principals to the respective boards of trustees, although the title of superintendent was not used for the new principal of the high school. Brubaker was appointed principal by the bishops.

21. Ernest Hess, in personal conversations, noted that the shift away from Bishop Board control was happening in relationship to other Lancaster Conference institutions as well during this era.

22. Emphasis added to quotation.

23. Emphases in the text of this section are added.

24. Hostetler, Huntington and Kraybill (1974:95). These observations were made by Anthropologist Gertrude Huntington.

25. Emphasis added to quotation.

26. J. Paul Graybill letter of May 18, 1970, to David Thomas.

27. The invitation to Brubaker came in a December 10, 1968, letter from James Hess, chairman of the trustees. On December 15, an ordination at the Willow Street Mennonite Church marked the first time an ordained leader in the Lancaster area was not required to wear a plain suit to preach.

28. J. Lester Brubaker letter of February 24, 1969, to James Hess.

29. A meeting on December 17,1969, at the high school clarified the transition to the new principal in a two-page memo of understanding. Brubaker would be employed as principal on a two-fifths basis beginning June 1, 1970. He would be administratively responsible for the '70-'71 school term, including the recruitment of the faculty. He would assume full-time responsibilities as principal in the summer of 1971.

30. J. Lester Brubaker letter to James Hess and copy to David Thomas on March 4, 1970. The news release appeared in the Lancaster papers on March 2, 1970.

31. The dissertation was written by Brubaker (1966) in the mid '60's.

32. Principal's Report, 1969-70:3.

33. J. Paul Graybill letter of April 30, 1968, to David Wenger.

34. 1967 *Laurel Wreath* Dedication.

35. Noah Good memo to Myron Dietz on October 13, 1969.

36. These comments were included with the results of the survey conducted by the Sports and Physical Education Committee in the fall of 1968.

37. *Millstream*, February 1969.

38. Larry Newswanger letter to James Hess, February 12, 1969.

39. Memos exchanged between Lowell Stoltzfus and Noah Good on November 7, 1969.

40. Noah Good letter to the trustees on November 12, 1969.

41. Letter to trustees from Faculty Recreation Committee, December 15, 1969.

42. Everett Newswanger in Public Relations Committee minutes, September 27, 1971.

43. *Millstream*, April 1970.

44. The Student Affairs Committee minutes of October 5, 1970, chart the changes which the trustees approved on October 12, 1970. The trustees on March 13, 1972, gave their blessing to scrimmage games with public schools.

45. *Millstream*, April 1971.

46. New trustee Jacob Stahl, for example, wrote a three-page letter to the board chair on October 14, 1970, following the trustee action to permit interscholastic athletics. Stahl cited seven concerns about the decision which he thought was moving the school in the wrong direction.

47. *Intelligencer Journal* editorial of February 17, 1971, was devoted to the student work day. The letter from President Richard Nixon was dated March 30, 1971.

48. Principal's report to the trustees, March 2, 1970.

49. Trustee action on August 9, 1971.

50. Trustee Minutes, October 11, 1971.

51. Trustee Minutes of January 11, 1971 and February 14, 1972, respectively.

52. A contract was first developed in the last years of the Good administration at the suggestion of the outside evaluating committee. It was further refined and employment conditions stipulated more specifically in legal language for

the '70-'71 year.

53. Annual Report of the Principal, July 12, 1971.

54. Annual Report of the Principal, July 10, 1972.

Chapter 7
Professionalizing the Program, 1972-1983

1. Hostetler, Huntington and Kraybill (1974: 110).

2. The reference to the cape dress and plain suit in the Bishop Minutes, October 18, 1973, was deleted at the next meeting of the bishops on November 20, 1973.

3. Bishop Minutes, November 20, 1975.

4. The decision was made by Lancaster Conference on March 19, 1981. Congregations were also expected to follow the Conference constitution approved on September 12, 1977. The March 1981 decision marked 100 years since the first written *Rules and Discipline* of 1881.

5. Faith Mennonite High School and Terre Hill Mennonite High School began in 1975 and 1985 respectively. Sensenig (1991) describes the formation and culture of the Terre Hill school.

6. Annual Report of the Principal, July 1977.

7. Ernest Hess diary, March 23, 1973.

8. *Laurel Wreath* (1981:85).

9. Student Forum Minutes, October 29, 1968, and Supervising Committee Minutes, November 11, 1968, November 20, 1968. A *Laurel Wreath* (1969:102) photo confirms the flag's return to a "quiet corner of the library." See the *Laurel Wreath* (1973:40) for a view of the flag in the lobby.

10. Jane Short letter of May 12, 1974, to a Mrs. Herr.

11. To trace the 1973-74 flag discussions consult the Social Studies Department "Statement of Concern on the Presence of an American Flag at LMHS" dated December 3, 1973; Principal's Notes, January 14, 1974, April 8, 1974; Faculty Minutes, May 6, 1974; *Millstream*, April 1974; and Trustee Minutes, January 21, 1974, April 8, 1974 and April 15, 1974.

12. LMH joined MACSA in 1971-72 and MSEC in 1972-73. In 1974 it joined the National Christian Schools Educational Association which later became the Association of Christian Schools International (ACSI), Trustee Minutes, January 21,1974. Membership in ACSI terminated after the 1983-84 term.

13. For a chronology of the controversy of this debate, consult the Trustee Minutes, October 22, 1979, May 19, 1980, April 26, 1982 and July 26, 1982.

14. *Millstream*, May 1975.

15. *Millstream*, December 1977.

16. Principal's Notes, March 1981.

17. *Laurel Wreath* (1982:98).

18. Principal's Notes, November 14, 1977.

19. *Laurel Wreath* (1983:97).

20. The former Student Forum became Student Council in 1971.

21. Kauffman (1983:12-13).

22. J. Lester Brubaker letter to parents, June 15, 1977.

23. Principal's Report, May 1982.

24. Hostetler, Huntington and Kraybill (1974).

25. This program was called Diversified Occupations (DO) after 1983.

26. *Millstream*, January 1973.

27. Trustee Minutes, January 23, 1978.

28. Principal's Notes, June 6, 1975, Trustee Minutes, December 17, 1979.

29. *Millstream*, May 1975.

30. Student comments were summarized in a May 20, 1977, letter from Myron Dietz to Dale Stoltzfus in New York City.

31. Education Committee Minutes, May 15, 1979.

32. Trustee Minutes, March 10, 1975 and June 16, 1980. The 1970 Statement of Philosophy had been slightly revised in 1976 as noted in the Trustee Minutes of April 12, 1976. The revision in 1980 was more significant.

33. Trustee Minutes, July 19, 1982.

34. Student Affairs Committee Minutes, April 16, 1973 and Trustee Minutes, May 7, 1973.

35. Charles Longenecker memo to J. Lester Brubaker, January 30, 1974 and Trustee Minutes, February 11, 1974.

36. Student Affairs Committee Minutes, March 18, 1974, Trustee Minutes, April 8, 1974 and April 15, 1974.

37. Student Affairs Committee Minutes, October 11, 1973 and Trustee Minutes, May 13, 1974. *Wandering* was only published two years. Later, in 1981-82, *Silhouette* was published.

38. Trustee Minutes, April 8, 1974 and *Millstream*, March 1974.

39. Trustees on October 20, 1975, approved holding an annual festival.

40. Trustee Minutes, December 8, 1975.

41. Trustee Minutes, March 8, 1976. The results of the poll of 167 respondents were reported in an eight-page document, Summary of Drama and Movie Questionnaire, dated December, 1976.

42. Trustee Minutes, April 25, 1977.

43. Revised drama guidelines and the new instrumental music policy were approved by the trustees on March 21, 1977. Permission to participate in District Orchestra was given on June 20, 1977.

44. Trustee Minutes, April 23, 1979.

45. Trustee Minutes, June 18, 1979 and October 15, 1979.

46. Trustee Minutes, July 23, 1980. An instrumental recital was planned for the spring of 1980.

47. Students entered the chorus five years after they participated in district band and orchestra because LMH already had many opportunities for choral expression. Clyde Hollinger letter to Donald Kraybill, March 13, 1991.

48. Trustee Minutes, November 12, 1973.

49. Bishop Minutes, September 18, 1972, Trustee Minutes, January 21, 1974 and April 15, 1974.

50. *Millstream*, October 1973.

51. Trustee Minutes, March 8, 1976 and July 23, 1979.

52. Student Affairs Committee Minutes, February 26, 1974.

53. Student Affairs Committee Minutes, March 2, 1976.

54. Trustee Minutes, December 19, 1977.

55. *Millstream*, May 1978.

56. Trustee Minutes, July 17, 1978.

57. Trustee Minutes, January 15, 1979. The survey was hurriedly sent out on January 17, 1979. The results appear in handwritten notes in a copy of the Trustee Minutes of January 15, 1979.

58. Trustee Minutes, January 15, 1979, January 22, 1979 and Glen Sell letter read to the trustees on January 22, 1979.

59. This tally of the vote is not recorded in the Trustee Minutes. It is the recollection of one faculty member. Another faculty member remembered the vote as nearly unanimous.

60. Annual Report of the Principal, 1979-'80.

61. Trustee Minutes, April 28, 1980.

62. Principal's Notes, October 1982.

63. *Laurel Wreath* (1982:12).

64. *Millstream*, November 1973.

65. Principal's Notes, June 7, 1977.

66. Trustee Minutes, March 10, 1975.

67. Trustee Minutes, April 25, 1977.

68. *Millstream*, February 1978.

69. Trustee Minutes, February 12, 1973 and September 20, 1976.

70. Decisions related to the beard and mustache are recorded in the Principal's Notes, March 8, 1976 and April 12, 1976, as well as in the Trustee Minutes, March 8, 1976, April 12, 1976, April 24, 1978 and January 15, 1979.

71. Trustee Minutes, April 24, 1978.

72. Kraybill (1987:318-319).

73. Principal's Notes, November 20, 1978.

74. Principal's Notes, November 20, 1978.

75. Marge Stauffer letter to the trustees in the fall of 1978.

76. *Laurel Wreath* (1978:13).

77. The revision that led to dropping the veiling requirement is recorded in Trustee Minutes, April 23, 1979, June 18, 1979, July 23, 1979 and in the minutes of the Appearance Code Review Committee, May 24, 1979, June 5, 1979 and June 18, 1979.

78. Nineteen out of a total of 87 senior women wore a visible veiling. Many of those without a veiling in their senior photo likely still wore it for worship services.

79. See Scott (1986:44-51) for a history of the changes of headgear and other dress practices at LMH. Some discrepancies between his chronology and this one occur because the school year spans two calendar years.

80. Bishop Minutes, August 23, 1979 and Trustee Minutes, October 15, 1979.

81. Landis (1976:1).

82. *Laurel Wreath* (1978:138-139), *Millstream*, February 1978.

83. Trustee Minutes, April 9, 1973.

84. A great deal of time and resources were devoted to the development of the junior high project in the mid-1970s. An extensive record of this activity can be found in the Trustee Minutes as well as in the minutes of a special Junior High School Planning Committee.

85. Trustee Minutes, April 18, 1977 and Bishop Minutes, April 21, 1977.

86. Brubaker actually served three-fourths of the time as superintendent of LMH and one-fourth of the time as superintendent of the Lancaster Conference Board of Education.

87. Principal's Notes, May 1984, Trustee Minutes, May 21, 1984. Hess was given an honorary high school diploma at commencement in 1984 to celebrate the 50th anniversary of his ordination to the ministry.

88. Lancaster Christian School added a senior high program which pulled some non-Mennonite students away from LMH. The two Mennonite high schools that likely enrolled some LMH prospects were Faith Mennonite, 20 miles east of Lancaster, established in 1975, and Shalom Christian Academy, which opened in 1976 near Chambersburg, PA.

89. Principal's Notes, November 10, 1975.

90. Summary results of an evaluation of the principal by faculty, 1977-78.

Chapter 8
Partnering Together, 1983-1991

1. The Principal's Notes of February 1987 estimated that with a revised formula, 44 percent of high school age students in the Lancaster and Atlantic Coast conferences attended LMH. When students living in the immediate Lancaster area were considered, those attending LMH rose to 66 percent.

2. The 75 percent of students classified Mennonite/Anabaptist in 1991 came from the Lancaster Mennonite Conference (51 percent), the Atlantic Coast conference (16

percent), other conferences of the Mennonite Church and related Anabaptist denominations such as the Brethren in Christ and the Church of the Brethren.

3. Ethiopian students began coming in 1985 when Bitul and Sosena Desta arrived. Later an Ethiopian Mennonite pilot sent his children to LMH. The family recommended LMH to friends and gradually more and more Ethiopian students came, not only for a quality education, but also to bypass social turmoil and the military draft of their country. Many of the Ethiopian students were not Mennonites.

4. Summary of 1991 LMH graduates, collected by the LMH guidance office in the fall of 1991.

5. Annual Report to Lancaster Mennonite Conference, December 1985.

6. Trustee Minutes, October 9, 1985.

7. The *New Era*, April 25, 1988, carried a front page headline on the mall purchase, as well as an editorial the next day. See also *Intelligencer Journal* editorial and accompanying story on April 26, 1988.

8. The ground breaking is reported in *Bridges*, November 1990. Other articles charting the planning of the auditorium/fine arts center are reported in *Bridges*, November 1989, February 1990 and February 1991.

9. The average tuition in 1990-91 for the Association of Christian Schools International in northeastern U.S. was $3,334. Tuition at many private Christian schools exceeds $4,000.

10. Calculations are based on the Consumer Price Index of 16.3 in 1942 and 129.9 in 1990, yielding an adjustment factor of 7.9693. Thus the $135 tuition of 1942 yields an adjusted rate of $1076 when multiplied by 7.9693. I appreciate the assistance of Professor Randy Trostle in obtaining the CPI figures.

11. Trustee Minutes throughout the '80s are replete with references to this issue. For several key discussions, consult the Trustee Minutes on January 18, 1982, April 25, 1983, July 25, 1983, April 16, 1984, September 10, 1984, October 8, 1984, October 28, 1985, September 14, 1988 and October 24, 1988.

12. For significant minutes leading to the adoption of the new bylaws consult Trustee Minutes, October 22, 1990, January 2, 1991, January 28, 1991 and Bishop Minutes, November 15, 1990.

13. The new bylaws adopted in January of 1991 actually list a dozen duties of the Quarterly Board. Only the major responsibilities are identified in the text.

14. The Religious Welfare Committee is composed of two bishops from Lancaster Conference and an overseer appointed by the Atlantic Coast Conference.

15. New Articles of Incorporation were approved by the trustees on January 28, 1991.

16. Article I of the bylaws approved January 28, 1991.

17. Summarized in the Principal's Report of December 1986, emphasis added.

18. 1991-92 Course Catalog of Lancaster Mennonite High School. Transfer students without previous Bible courses are required to take one Bible course each year they attend LMH.

19. *Bridges*, November 1988 and February 1989.

20. The program for gifted students is described in *Bridges*, May 1989, as well as in the school's policy manual.

21. Letter from four parents to the trustees dated May 10, 1988, and Trustee Minutes, May 11, 1988 and June 8, 1988.

22. *Laurel Wreath* (1985:101).

23. Annual Report to Lancaster Mennonite Conference Annual Meeting, March 1987.

24. Comparisons of SAT scores between schools is precarious because the percentage of students taking the

voluntary test varies widely from school to school.

25. Campus Chorale also sang at an earlier Pennsylvania Music Educators Convention in the mid-'80s.

26. Hostetler, Huntington and Kraybill (1974:224-229).

27. Principal's Report, May 1986.

28. Trustee Minutes, April 23, 1984.

29. Principal's Report, May 1984.

30. Trustee Minutes, February 20, 1984.

31. Appearance code policy 1990-91 and 1991-92.

32. 1990 parent survey on appearance code.

33. 1990 parent survey on appearance code.

34. Trustee Executive Committee Minutes, May 9, 1990.

35. Veiling Committee Minutes, March 6 and March 20, 1984, as well as the Trustee Minutes of January 23, 1984 and April 23, 1984.

36. Principal's Report, February 1989, Trustee Minutes, March 8, 1989 and the 1990-91 appearance code.

37. 1990-91 student appearance code.

38. Principal's Report to Lancaster Mennonite Conference, September 1985.

39. Internal memo to homeroom teachers on March 23, 1987.

40. A brief overview of the project is presented in *Bridges*, February 1991. The trustees approved the working model on May 8, 1991.

Chapter 9
Celebrating Jubilee

1. Trustee Minutes, April 16, 1984.

2. 1990 U.S. Census reported in *New Era* , January 24, 1991.

3. Graybill (1967:13).

4. The objectives also appear in Article III of the Constitution and bylaws for Lancaster Mennonite Conference Schools, October 3, 1941.

5. Faculty Manual, 1990-91, Educational Objectives.

6. Lancaster Mennonite School Philosophy of Education.

7. Lancaster Mennonite School *Bulletin*, 1942-43:14.

8. Noah Good letter to Donald Kraybill, December 25, 1990.

9. Lancaster Mennonite School *Bulletin*, 1942-43:15.

10. Sensenig (1991) in an ethnographic study describes the socio-political values held by faculty and students at LMH.

11. Sensenig (1991:100).

12. The junior/senior spring banquet held at public restaurants, although not called a prom, has increasingly looked like one. In the late '80s and early '90s pressure for dancing increased. The issue was raised in the Principal's Report of May 1990, June 1990, August 1990 and February 1991.

13. A discussion of evaluation issues and an assessment of the short-term impact of several Mennonite high schools is reported in Kraybill (1977a and 1978). Hess (1975) and Kraybill (1975 and 1977b) provide an evaluation of the short-term impact of Lancaster Mennonite High School. The following studies and research projects have all focused on Lancaster Mennonite High School: Hess (1975, 1977), Hostetler, Huntington and Kraybill (1974), Kraybill (1975, 1977a, 1977b, 1977c, 1978, 1987), Kraybill, Charles and Espenshade (1979) and Sensenig (1991).

14. The study was conducted by students at Eastern Mennonite College under the supervision of John Eby (1986). The percentage differences between LMH and public school graduates on six dimensions of church involvement ranged from 7 to 14 percent—all favoring LMH graduates. These descriptive comparisons favor LMH but do not provide causal evidence that the differences are directly attributable to the school.

15. Principal's Report to Lancaster Conference, September 1984. This figure referred specifically to participation in the Discipleship Ministries Program.

16. This estimate is based on a comparison of the current alumni list with the roster of ordained leaders in the *Mennonite Yearbook, 1990-91*. It does not include LMH alumni who were ordained in other denominations.

17. Coleman and Hoffer (1987:230-232), in a study of public and private high schools, conclude that a school's supporting community constitutes an important source of "social capital" that enhances the long-term impact of the school.

18. This was the total in the spring of 1991. The number, of course, increases over time. Some of these partners may have become acquainted with each other after graduation.

19. Noah Good letter to Donald Kraybill, December 25, 1990.

Primary Sources

Annual Reports, Dean and Principal of Lancaster Mennonite School, 1943-1990

Brochures, pamphlets and handbooks of Lancaster Mennonite School, 1941-1991

Constitution and By-laws of Lancaster Mennonite Conference Schools, 1941, 1966, 1970, 1991

Lancaster Mennonite School Collection, Lancaster Mennonite Historical Society Archives

Minutes, Lancaster Mennonite School Board of Trustees, 1941-1991

Minutes, Supervising Committee of Lancaster Mennonite School, 1942-1957

Minutes, Lancaster Mennonite Conference Bishop Board, 1912-1990

Minutes, Faculty of Lancaster Mennonite School, 1942-1990

Minutes, various committees of Lancaster Mennonite School, 1942-1991

Monthly Principal's Report, 1971-1991

Bridges, Lancaster Mennonite School, 1974-1991

Bulletin, Lancaster Mennonite School, 1942-1971

Directory of Schools, 1990-1991, Board of Education, Lancaster Mennonite Conference

Gospel Herald, Mennonite Publishing House

Herald of Truth, Mennonite Publishing House

Intelligencer Journal, Lancaster Newspapers, Inc.

Laurel Wreath, 1946-1991

Millstream, 1943-1991

Missionary Messenger, Eastern Mennonite Board of Missions and Charities

New Era, Lancaster Newspapers, Inc.

Pastoral Messenger, Lancaster Mennonite Conference 1941-1950

REPORT, Lancaster Mennonite School, 1975-1991

Report Card, Lancaster Mennonite School, 1955-56

Rules and Discipline, Lancaster Mennonite Conference, 1943, 1954, 1968

Interview Sources

J. Lester Brubaker, 1990, 1991
Landis Brubaker, 1972
H. Raymond Charles, 1986**
Myron S. Dietz, 1990
Omar Eby, 1990
Mary Shirk Frederick, 1990
Harry Gerlach, 1990
Ivan Glick, 1990, 1991
Paul Glick, 1991
Noah G. Good, 1972, 1990, 1991
J. Paul Graybill, 1972
Ernest M. Hess, 1972, 1990
James H. Hess, 1972

Myra Hess, 1990
B. Charles Hostetter, 1990
Lois Garber Kauffman, 1990
Clayton L. Keener, 1972
John R. Kraybill, 1972, 1990+, 1991
Paul N. Kraybill, 1990+
Stanley M. Kreider, 1990
Paul G. Landis, 1990
Charles B. Longenecker, 1990
Clarence E. Lutz, 1972
Eli L. Miller, 1991
Arnold J. Moshier, 1991
Jean Kraybill Shenk, 1990

Clyde B. Stoner, 1972
David N. Thomas, 1972, 1990
J. Richard Thomas, 1990, 1991
Amos W. Weaver, 1972
Daniel Weaver, Jr., 1988*
Ella Weaver, 1991
Harvey Weaver, 1991
Ralph Weaver, 1991
Edna K. Wenger, 1972, 1991
A. Grace Wenger, 1991
John S. Wenger, 1990
Samuel S. Wenger, 1972
H. Howard Witmer, 1972

Conducted by Donald B. Kraybill unless otherwise noted. Brief interviews were conducted by telephone with dozens of other unnamed persons. Extended interviews were taped and transcribed.

* Conducted by Charles Longenecker
+ Conducted by Fern Clemmer
** Conducted by John Ruth

Files of Correspondence
(Lancaster Mennonite Historical Society Archives)

J. Lester Brubaker
Henry F. Garber
John Gochnauer
Noah G. Good
J. Paul Graybill

Amos S. Horst
Clarence E. Lutz
Henry E. Lutz
Noah H. Mack
Clyde B. Stoner

Bibliography

Bennett, Paul Horatius
    1952   "A Brief History of the Lancaster Mennonite School Property." Unpublished MA dissertation. Bucknell University.

Brubaker, J. Lester
    1966   "A History of the Mennonite Elementary School Movement." Unpublished Ed.D. dissertation. University of Virginia.

Bucher, George
    1908   *The Garb Law*. Quarryville, PA: by the author.

Clare, Israel Smith
    1892   *A Brief History of Lancaster County*. Lancaster, PA: Argus Publishing Co.

Coleman, James S. and Thomas Hoffer
    1987   *Public and Private High Schools: The Impact of Communities*. New York: Basic Books, Inc.

Conant, James Bryant
    1965   *The Child, The Parent and the State*. New York: McGraw Hill Book Company.

Cressman, George R.
    1947   *A Digest of Pennsylvania School Laws*. Fourth Edition. New York: Prentice-Hall.

Dyck, Cornelius J.
    1981   *An Introduction to Mennonite History*. 2nd ed. Scottdale, PA: Herald Press.

Eby, John W.
    1986   "Study of Lancaster High School Graduates Between 1970-1980." Unpublished manuscript. Department of Business, Eastern Mennonite College.

Ellis, Franklin and Samuel Evans
    1883   *History of Lancaster County Pennsylvania*. 2 vols. Philadelphia: Everts and Peck.

Garber, Henry F.
    1934   "Contributions of a Loyal Church School." *Gospel Herald* October: 4.

Garber, Robert Bates
    1979   "The Sociocultural Differentiation of a Religious Sect: Schisms Among the Pennsylvania German Mennonites." Unpublished Ph.D. dissertation, University of Wisconsin-Milwaukee.

Glick, Daniel M.
    1945   "Report on Present Day Mennonite Elementary Schools in *Collected Papers* of the Fifth Annual Parochial School Meeting." Unpublished.
    1946   *The Historical Background of Christian Day Schools in the Mennonite Church*. Lancaster, PA: Lancaster Conference Schools.

Gochnauer, John
    1942a   "Lancaster Mennonite School." Broadside issued May 18.
    1942b   "Report of the Board of Trustees of the Lancaster Conference Schools." *Pastoral Messenger* April: 5-6.

Good, Ellen Weaver
    1990   "Handpicked by God for a Life of Service." *Christian Living* June: 13-15.

Good, Noah G.
    1943a   "Offsetting the Evil Influences of the Modern High School." In *Our Church Schools:* 14-15. A manual distributed by the Mennonite Board of Education.
    1943b   "One Year at Lancaster Mennonite School." *Gospel Herald* September: 270.
    1943c   "The Yielded Life." *Pastoral Messenger* January: 3-4.
    1943d   "The Place of Athletics in Education." *Millstream* April: 20-23.
    1946   "Who Should Go to High School?" *Millstream* June: 13-16.
    1949   "The New Girls' Dormitory." *Millstream* October: 28-29.
    1950   "Things Have Changed." *Millstream* December: 27-29.
    1955   "Report of the Dean." *The Report Card*, September: 4-5.
    1975   "The Beginning of Lancaster Mennonite High School." Unpublished manuscript.
    1980   "History of Mennonite Education in the Eastern Pennsylvania Area: 1710-1900." Unpublished manuscript.

Graybill, J. Paul
    1943   "Objectives of a Christian High School Education." *Millstream* March: 2-4.
    1945a   Ed. *Christian Day Schools for Mennonite Youth: A Promotional Manual*. Lancaster, PA: Lancaster Conference Schools.
    1945b   "Answering Objections Concerning Christian Schools." In *Christian Day Schools for Mennonite Youth: A Promotional Manual.*.
    1945c   "Popular Education and Mennonite View Points." In *Christian Day Schools for Mennonite Youth: A Promotional Manual*.
    1945d   "Regulations Safeguarding Our Schools." In *Christian Day Schools for Mennonite Youth: A Promotional Manual*.
    1946   "The Bible in a Christian High School." *Millstream* IV (June): 12-13.
    1948   "Church Schools in the Program of Missions." *Missionary Messenger* March: 4-5.

1949   *Biblical and Practical Nonconformity*. Lancaster, PA: Lancaster Mennonite Conference Bible School Board. Reprinted in 1951.

1950   "Encouraging The Pupil's Response to Christian Teaching and Environment." Unpublished presentation at Hess Mennonite Church ,February 25, 1950.

1951   "Chapel Address." Presented November 16, 1951. Unpublished manuscript.

1953   "Resumé of Eleven Years at Lancaster Mennonite School 1942-53." Unpublished paper.

1958   "Shall Our Church Schools Demand a Fuller Compliance To Church Standards than the Local Congregations Carry out in Practice?" *Pastoral* Messenger July: 3.

1967   "Lancaster Mennonite School: Past, Present, Future." Unpublished paper prepared for the 25th anniversary.

Hartshorne, Charles

1990   "A Boarding School in the Country: Religion, Nature, Becoming a Writer, 1911-1915." In *The Darkness and the Light*. Albany: State University of New York Press.

Hess, Ernest M.

1975   "A Study of the Influence of Mennonite Schools on Their Students in the Lancaster (PA) Conference of the Mennonite Church." Unpublished Ph.D. dissertation. Ohio State University.

1977   "A Comparison of Graduates from Lancaster Mennonite High School and Public High Schools." In *Ethnic Education: The Impact of Mennonite Schooling*. Donald B. Kraybill, ed. San Francisco: R and E Research Associates.

Hess, James H.

1955   "Shall We Enlarge Our Agriculture Course?" In *The Report Card* March: 4-5.

Horst, Amos S.

1940   "Providing High School Privileges Under the Auspices of the Lancaster Conference." Unpublished manuscript.

Hostetler, John A., Gertrude Huntington and Donald B. Kraybill

1974   *Cultural Transmission and Instrumental Adaptation to Social Change: Lancaster Mennonite High School in Transition*. Monograph, Final Report to U.S. Department of Health, Education and Welfare.

Juhnke, James C.

1989   *Vision, Doctrine, War: Mennonite Identity and Organization in America 1890-1930*. Scottdale, PA: Herald Press.

Kauffman, Dennis

1983   "Prayer in the Christian School." *Missionary Messenger* February: 12-13.

Kautz, Bernard B.

1942   "Lancaster Mennonite School." *Gospel Herald* June: 251.

Klaassen, Walter

1973   *Anabaptism: Neither Catholic nor Protestant*. Waterloo,Ont.: Conrad Press.

Klein, H. M. J. (ed)

1924   *Lancaster County Pennsylvania History*. 2 vols. New York: Lewis Historical Publishing Co., Inc.

Klein, H. M. J. and William F. Diller

1944   *The History of St. James Church, 1744-1944*. Lancaster, PA: St. James Vestry.

Kraybill, Donald B.

1975   "Ethnic Socialization in a Mennonite High School." Unpublished Ph.D. dissertation. Temple University.

1977a   *Ethnic Education: The Impact of Mennonite Schooling*. San Francisco: R and E Research Associates.

1977b   "Religious and Ethnic Socialization in a Mennonite High School." *The Mennonite Quarterly Review* 51 (October): 329-351.

1977c   "A Content and Structural Analysis of Mennonite High School Songs." *The Mennonite Quarterly Review* 51 (January): 52-66.

1978   *Mennonite Education: Issues, Facts and Changes*. Scottdale, PA: Herald Press.

1987   "The Mennonite Woman's Veiling: The Rise and Fall of a Sacred Symbol."*The Mennonite Quarterly Review* 61 (July): 298-320.

1989   *The Riddle of Amish Culture*. Baltimore: The Johns Hopkins University Press.

Kraybill, Donald B., Daniel Charles and Kevin Espenshade

1979   "Changes in Mennonite Youth Attitudes: 1974-1978." *Pennsylvania Mennonite Heritage* 2 (October): 20-25.

Kraybill, John R.

1962   "Retrospect After Twenty Years." Unpublished manuscript.

Landis, Ira D.

1946   "A Side Room in the Mennonite Way of Life." *Christian Monitor* September: 277-278.

1976   "J. Paul Graybill Ascends Higher." In *Mennonite Research Journal*. January: 1,5.

Lehman, Glenn

1991   "Noah G. Good: History Rooted in Family and Church." In *Mennonite Historical Bulletin* January: 9-10.

Lehman, J. Irvin

1956   "Conservation of Soils and Souls." *The Report Card* January: 8.

1990   *Spots on My Trousers: The Life and Loves of a Mennonite Minister*. Ed. by Martin W. Lehman, State Line, PA: Mennonite Historical Association of Cumberland Valley.

Lehman, John A.

1945   "To the Teacher." In *Collected Papers* of the Fifth Annual Mennonite Parochial School Meeting.

Lichty, Richard J.

1984   *Keeping House as the Lord Gives Grace: The Story of a Bishop and His Church (J. Paul Graybill 1900-1975)*. Unpublished Manuscript.

Locust Grove Mennonite School: 1939-1989
    1990   Smoketown PA: Locust Grove Mennonite School.
Mack, Noah
    1930   "The Situation in American Mennonitism: A Loud and Bitter Cry." *Gospel Herald* December: 818, 826-28.
Mellinger, John H.
    1943   "Before It Was L.M.S." *The Millstream* March: 19-21.
Mennonite Encyclopedia, The
    1956, 1990   5 vols. Scottdale, PA: Herald Press.
Miller, Jonathan W.
    1909   *History of The Diocese of Central Pennsylvania: 1871-1909.* Volume II. Frackville, PA: By the author.
Minnich, Herbert
    1947   "The School That Was Here." *Millstream* December: 14-15.
One Hundred (100) Years of Free Public Schools in Pennsylvania 1834-1934.
    1934   Harrisburg, PA: Department of Public Instruction.
Pellman, Hubert R.
    1967   *Eastern Mennonite College, 1917-1967.* Harrisonburg, VA: Eastern Mennonite College.
Public School Manual of Lancaster County, PA 1939-40.
    1940   Lancaster, PA: Lancaster County Public Schools.
Report of the Superintendent of Public Instruction.
    1908   Commonwealth of Pennsylvania. Harrisburg, PA: State Printer.
Schools for a New World.
    1947   Twenty-fifth Yearbook. Washington, DC: American Association of School Administrators.
Ruth, John
    N.D.   "Maintaining the Distinctive Principles: (1940-1945)." In *The Earth is the Lord's: A Narrative History* of
                  Lancaster Mennonite Conference. A forthcoming history of Lancaster Mennonite Conference. Manuscript.
Scott, Stephen
    1986   *Why Do They Dress That Way?* Intercourse, PA: Good Books.
Sensenig, Kenneth L.
    1991   "An Ethnographic Approach to the Study of Sociopolitical Views in Two Mennonite High Schools."
                  Unpublished D.Ed. dissertation. College of Education, Temple University.
Sher, Jonathan P.
    1977   *Education In Rural America.* Boulder, CO: Westview Press.
Weaver, Amos
    1946   "The Lancaster Mennonite School." In *Christian Monitor* August: 245-46.
    1957a   "From the Principal's Desk." *Millstream* January: 11.
    1957b   "From the Principal's Desk." *Millstream* May: 27-28.
    1960   "LMS." *Gospel Herald* November 15: 1000.
    1965   "Chapel Talk on the Beatles." Unpublished manuscript.
Weaver, J. Denny
    1987   *Becoming Anabaptist: the Origin and Significance of Sixteenth Century Anabaptism.* Scottdale, PA: Herald Press.
Weaver, Ralph E.
    1951   "History of the Lancaster Mennonite School Property." *Gospel Herald* April 24: 395, 405.
    1955   "History of the Lancaster Mennonite School Property." *Report* January: 2-3.
Wenger, A. D.
    1930   "The School Problem." *Gospel Herald* April: 75-80.
Wickersham, James Pyle
    1885   *A History of Education in Pennsylvania.* Lancaster, PA: Inquirer Publishing Co.
Yeates School, The
    1919   Bulletin 1919-1920, Lancaster, PA: Yeates School.

Index

About the Author

Donald B. Kraybill directs the Young Center for the Study of Anabaptist and Pietist Groups at Elizabethtown (PA) College where he is also Professor of Sociology.

He is the author of a variety of books, among them *The Upside-Down Kingdom*, *The Riddle of Amish Culture* and *The Puzzles of Amish Life*.

Kraybill has been active in research related to Mennonite education for many years.